Creatives Resources

INTERMEDIATE

2011–2012 YEARBOOK

The Education Center, Inc.
Greensboro, North Carolina

The Mailbox® 2011–2012 Intermediate Yearbook

Managing Editor, *The Mailbox* Magazine: Sherry McGregor

Editorial Team: Becky S. Andrews, Diane Badden, Kimberley Bruck, Karen A. Brudnak, Pam Crane, Chris Curry, David Drews, Tazmen Hansen, Marsha Heim, Lori Z. Henry, Troy Lawrence, Kitty Lowrance, Tina Petersen, Gary Phillips (COVER ARTIST), Mark Rainey, Greg D. Rieves, Hope Rodgers-Medina, Rebecca Saunders, Donna K. Teal, Sharon M. Tresino, Zane Williard

ISBN 978-1-61276-245-6
ISSN 1088-5552

Printed in the United States of America.

The Mailbox® Yearbook
PO Box 6189
Harlan, IA 51593-1689

HPS242163

Contents

www.themailbox.com

Reading and Language Arts

READING & LANGUAGE ARTS TIPS & TOOLS

Pantomimed Practice

Irregular verbs

For this whole-class activity, write irregular verbs on a class supply of paper strips. Then have each student make a two-column chart labeled as shown. Next, have a volunteer draw a strip and silently act out the verb so her classmates can name it. When a student correctly names the verb, have everyone, including the pantomiming student, record the verb. Then have each child look up the word in a dictionary to find its past tense form. **To extend the activity,** have each child make a three-column chart and find both the verb's past tense form and its past participle. ***Jackie Beaudry, Getzville, NY***

Irregular Verbs

bite	grow
blow	hide
break	pay
catch	read
choose	ride
cut	see
draw	stand
drink	swim
fly	throw
freeze	wear
give	write

Sophia

Irregular Verbs

Present Tense	Past Tense
give	gave
choose	chose

choose

Ringing In Reading Success

Main idea

Give your students practice identifying main ideas with this fun challenge! Provide access to picture books, loose leaf rings, index cards, and a hole puncher. Then set a due date and challenge each child to read 50 different picture books. After reading a book, the student lists its title and author's name on an index card and then records the book's main idea. Next, he punches a hole in the card and slides it onto his looseleaf ring. When the deadline arrives, celebrate students' reading with a popcorn party and fun certi-ficates (one for those who took on the challenge and one for those who met or exceeded it). Then have students share and compare their rings of reading success!

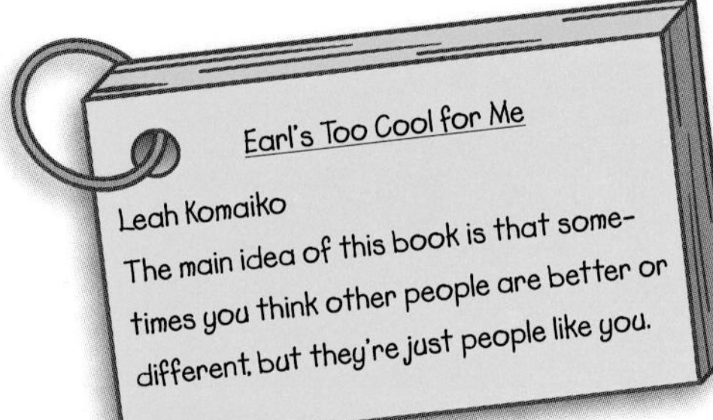

Have each student keep his ring of cards as a great resource for making text-to-text connections!

Make It Big!

Fiction comprehension

Wrap up your next novel study by having students create a big book about it. In advance, program index cards with tasks such as those shown. When you finish reading, give each small group of students a sheet of poster board and have the students draw a card. Then guide the group to complete the card's task. Punch four holes along the left edge of each completed poster and bind students' work with looseleaf rings. Have students who finish early work together to create the book's front and back covers and table of contents. Then present the finished book to the class and have each group, in turn, share its work. ***Nancy Welch, Abigail Adams Intermediate, Weymouth, MA***

Big Book Comprehension Tasks

- Describe and illustrate the story's most important setting.
- Show the main character at the beginning of the story and describe five of his or her most important traits.
- Describe and illustrate the story's main problem.
- Write and illustrate five important quotations from the story. List the page numbers where the quotes are found.
- Describe and illustrate the story's climax.
- Describe and illustrate the story's resolution.
- Show the main character at the end of the story and tell how he or she changes.
- Describe and illustrate the author's main message.

"A-sorted" Practice

Hyphenated compound words

Help students explore the rules for using hyphens in compound words with this easy-to-prepare center. Cut apart the rule and word cards from a copy of page 8. Fold a large sheet of construction paper in half and then in thirds to make six boxes. Then glue a rule card to each box. A student sorts the word cards onto the appropriate sections. When the child finishes, he folds a sheet of paper to make six boxes, labels them, and records his work. ***Jackie Beaudry, Getzville, NY***

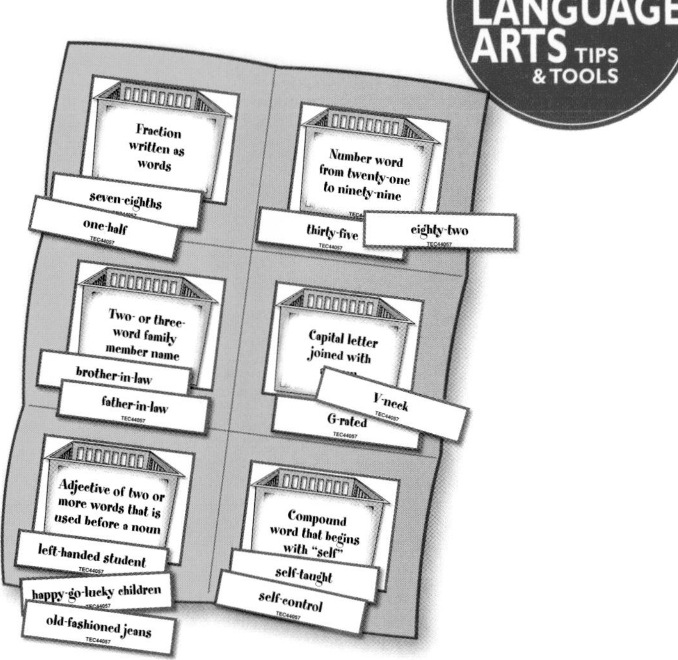

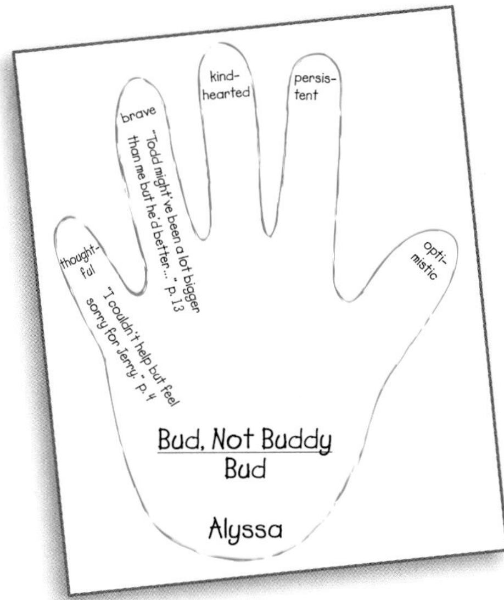

Hands-on Evaluation

Character analysis

For this activity, have each student trace her hand on a sheet of paper. Next, have her write the title of a current reading and a main character's name on the palm. Then guide the student to name five traits that describe the character, write each trait on a fingertip, and find an example of character dialogue, thoughts, or actions that show the trait. Have the student quote the first five to ten words of the supporting text on the appropriate finger and list the quote's page number at the base. Then have students use their notes to discuss or describe the character. ***Tracy Arnett, Indianapolis Junior Academy, Indianapolis, IN***

Finding Facts

Research, using websites

Use the organizer on page 9 to help students focus on extracting information when they visit websites. In advance, make a two-sided copy of the page for each student. Then display a sample website and guide students to fill out the organizer on one side. Next, have each student study a different website and complete the organizer on the flip side. Finally, have the student write a paragraph to summarize his research. ***Marciava Stovall, West Hoke Middle School, Raeford, NC***

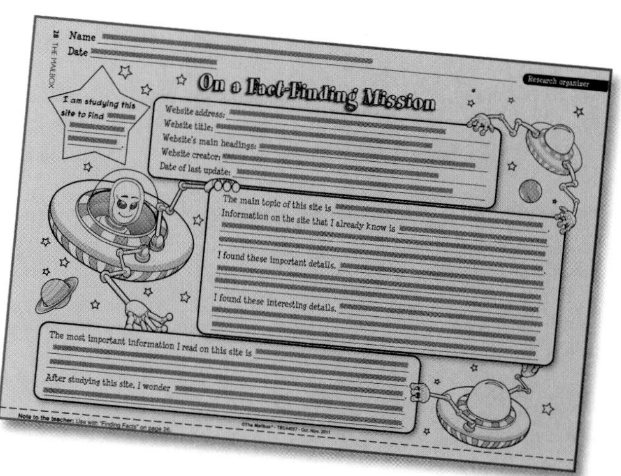

Hyphenated Compound Words Rule and Word Cards

Use with "'A-sorted' Practice" on page 7.

Fraction written as words TEC44057	Number word from twenty-one to ninety-nine TEC44057	Compound word that begins with "self" TEC44057
Two- or three-word family member name TEC44057	Capital letter joined with a noun TEC44057	Adjective of two or more words that is used before a noun TEC44057
T-shirt TEC44057	forty-seven TEC44057	happy-go-lucky children TEC44057
father-in-law TEC44057	two-thirds TEC44057	self-esteem TEC44057
left-handed student TEC44057	one-half TEC44057	brother-in-law TEC44057
thirty-five TEC44057	U-turn TEC44057	sister-in-law TEC44057
eighty-two TEC44057	self-employed TEC44057	V-neck TEC44057
one-way street TEC44057	seven-eighths TEC44057	mother-in-law TEC44057
one-fourth TEC44057	self-taught TEC44057	great-aunt TEC44057
old-fashioned jeans TEC44057	G-rated TEC44057	fifty-nine TEC44057
self-respect TEC44057	bottom-feeding fish TEC44057	self-control TEC44057
three-fourths TEC44057	U-boat TEC44057	sixty-three TEC44057

Name ______________________________

Date ______________________________

On a Fact-Finding Mission

I am studying this site to find ______________________________.

Website address: ______________________________

Website title: ______________________________

Website's main headings: ______________________________

Website creator: ______________________________

Date of last update: ______________________________

The main topic of this site is ______________________________.

Information on the site that I already know is ______________________________.

I found these important details. ______________________________

I found these interesting details. ______________________________

The most important information I read on this site is ______________________________.

After studying this site, I wonder ______________________________.

Note to the teacher: Use with "Finding Facts" on page 7.

READING & LANGUAGE ARTS TIPS & TOOLS

Wacky Word Antics

Plural possessives

For this hands-on practice, have each pair of students cut apart the noun cards on a copy of page 11. Then have the partners take turns drawing two cards. Each student writes the plural form of each word and then rewrites one word as a plural possessive, adding an apostrophe or an apostrophe s as necessary. Next, the child writes the second word to make a phrase—the wackier the better. When all the strips have been drawn, have each student write five fun sentences using her favorite phrases. As time allows, have each child write her wackiest sentence on the board and then read it aloud. ***Carol Lawrence, Madera, CA***

orange

tooth

The oranges' teeth really needed to be brushed!

A Resourceful Idea

Identifying and using appropriate resources

Give students practice choosing the best information source with this whole-class activity. Before beginning, have each child label five index cards as shown below and place the cards on her desk. Discuss each source and whether it has an online equal. Next, ask students to show you the best source for a state map. Guide students to hold up their "atlas" cards and quickly check their responses. Then ask another question. Discuss and repeat as time allows.

Show me the best source for a state map.

dictionary

encyclopedia

atlas

almanac

current newspaper

Show me the best source for finding

- the countries that are members of the United Nations *(encyclopedia)*
- a city's average temperature in January *(almanac)*
- the results of a city council meeting *(newspaper)*
- a state map *(atlas)*
- the number of syllables in a word *(dictionary)*
- Mexico's major exports *(encyclopedia)*
- current population information *(almanac)*

The Big Picture

Identifying theme, supporting ideas

Want to build students' confidence in naming a selection's theme? Try this. Display common themes in children's literature, such as those shown. Then name a popular children's movie and have each student record the title. Guide the child to choose a big idea or theme that fits the movie, write it under the title, and then explain why he chose it. Repeat with other children's movies and then have each student share his work with a small group. **To extend the activity,** collect an assortment of picture books. Then have the students in each small group choose a book, read it together, identify the book's big idea or theme, and explain their choice. ***Carol Lawrence***

Common Themes in Children's Literature

- Growing up can be hard, but you can overcome your fears and problems.
- Accept yourself.
- Accept others.
- It's good to have a family that supports you.
- Respect authority.
- You can learn to handle your problems.
- It's easier to solve some problems if you work with others.
- Friendship is important.
- Sometimes it takes more courage not to fight than to fight.
- Prejudice is harmful.

Despicable Me

It's good to have a family that supports you.

In the movie Despicable Me, one of the big ideas is that it's good to have a family that supports you. The main character is pretty miserable, and nothing he does goes well. Then he adopts three little girls. He learns to love and care about them, and his life gets better too.

Noun Cards

Use with "Wacky Word Antics" on page 10.

child TEC44058	frog TEC44058	tooth TEC44058
baby TEC44058	sheep TEC44058	orange TEC44058
monster TEC44058	pirate TEC44058	robot TEC44058
pickle TEC44058	shark TEC44058	goose TEC44058
mouse TEC44058	spider TEC44058	monkey TEC44058
castle TEC44058	laptop TEC44058	dragon TEC44058
dinosaur TEC44058	deer TEC44058	person TEC44058
bug TEC44058	foot TEC44058	pizza TEC44058
cactus TEC44058	die TEC44058	elf TEC44058
hippopotamus TEC44058	man TEC44058	woman TEC44058
fly TEC44058	gnome TEC44058	song TEC44058
movie TEC44058	singer TEC44058	bicycle TEC44058

READING & LANGUAGE ARTS TIPS & TOOLS

A Reader's Blog

Writing in response to reading

Want to hold students accountable for their independent reading? Try this! If you have a class blog, have each student use a copy of page 14 to plan a well-thought-out entry about his reading. If you don't have a class blog, guide each student to use a copy of page 14 to plan and write a pretend blog entry. Then have each student edit his work before posting it on the class blog or on a board titled "ReadandWrite.class—Here's What We Think." ***Carol Lawrence, Madera CA***

No More Spelling Demons

Spelling

Here's a fun-to-create center sure to keep students on their spelling toes! Have each pair of students decorate a clean fast-food container with construction paper and craft scraps to create a spelling demon. Glue a list of ten misspelled words students commonly misspell inside each container, and glue an answer key on the bottom. A student takes a spelling demon, opens the lid, reads each word, and spells it correctly on her paper. Then she flips the carton to check her work.

abowt
agin
allright
allmost
allways

about
again
all right
almost
always
another
answer
any
are

Are You a Fan?

Writing, presenting a persuasive speech

For this idea, have each student think about her favorite food, game, book, or movie. Then challenge the child to write a speech that will convince her classmates to become fans of the same thing. Guide each student to write an attention-getting description of her favorite item. Next, have the child write three reasons classmates should also like the item. Have the student close her speech with a convincing plea and then practice reading her work in her most persuasive voice.
Carol Lawrence

Have you read *The Mysterious Benedict Society?* This exciting book kept me interested on every single page.

tip To help students practice their speeches, ask a parent volunteer to videotape each child giving her speech. Then have the child watch her recorded speech and identify what she's doing right as well as what she needs to improve.

Just Browsing

Functional reading

For this reading center, round up surplus sales catalogs. Then post the directions and questions shown and have students rotate through the center. Patricia Twohey, Smithfield, RI

Directions:

1. Choose a catalog.
2. Imagine that you can buy one item from the catalog. Spend five minutes looking through the catalog. Then choose the item you would buy.
3. Read the item's description and study the catalog's order form. Then answer the following questions.

   A. What is the name of the catalog you chose?
   B. Why did you choose this catalog?
   C. Which item in this catalog would you most like to buy?
   D. Why did you choose this item?
   E. On which page is the item listed?
   F. What is the item's name and catalog number?
   G. Does the item come in different sizes or colors? If so, what would you choose?
   H. How much does the item weigh?
   I. Find the catalog's order form. Then find the shipping charges. How much would it cost to have this item shipped to you?

It's a Word Mash-Up!

Building vocabulary

Ramp up students' interest in words with this idea. Compare portmanteau words to musical mash-ups! (A portmanteau word is two words blended together to make a new word. In a musical mash-up, elements of two songs are combined to create a new song.) To begin, read aloud one of the portmanteau words shown and challenge students to guess which words were mashed up to make the new word. Repeat with four more portmanteau words. Next, announce two words and have students guess the mashed-up word they make. Repeat with the remaining words. Then give each pair of students a copy of page 15 and have them play a round of "Word Mash-Up!" to explore other portmanteau words.

Portmanteau Word	Words That Were Mashed Together
animatronics	animation + electronics
moped	motor + pedal
clump	chunk + lump
fortnight	fourteen + nights
guesstimate	guess + estimate
Internet	international + network
outpatient	outside + patient
waddle	wade + toddle
pang	pain + sting
meld	melt + weld

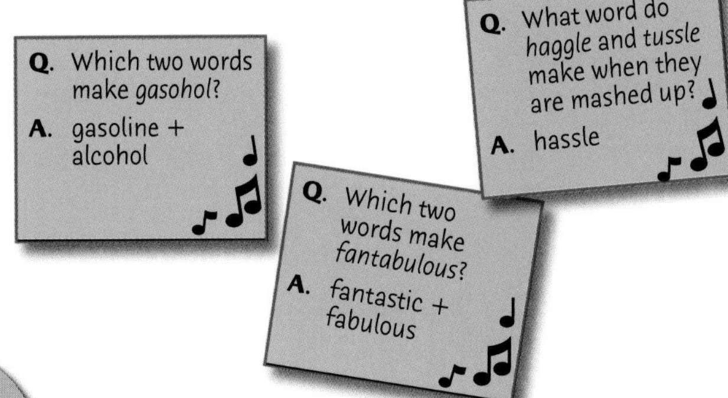

Speed Reading

Skimming text

Help your students learn to skim with these simple-to-follow steps! Carol Lawrence, Madera, CA

Seven Simple Steps to Skimming

1. Read the title.
2. Read the first paragraph.
3. Read the first sentence of the other paragraphs.
4. Read the headings and subheadings.
5. Notice pictures, charts, or graphs and read their captions.
6. Read each boldfaced word. If you don't know what the word means, read its sentence.
7. Read the last paragraph and then think about the main idea of these parts.

Reading organizer

ReadandWrite.class

A Reader's Blog

Search Go

Home About Contact Me

An Important Object From My Reading

My opinion about what I read and an example that shows what I mean

____

____

____

____

My Rating

☆☆☆☆☆

My hook (how I'll start my post and grab my readers' attention)

____

____

What I read

____

Why I read this

____

____

The most important event or idea

____

____

My conclusion (how I'll wrap up my post)

____

____

Archives

Search Go

Important Words

____

____

____

____

____

____

____

____

____

____

____

____

Posted by ______________________ on ______________________

Note to the teacher: Use with "A Reader's Blog" on page 12.

WORD MASH-UP!

Directions:

1. Cut apart the cards and stack them facedown.
2. Draw a card and read the question aloud to your partner. Check your partner's answer. If he or she is correct, your partner keeps the card. If not, return the card to the bottom of the pile.
3. Continue taking turns until all the cards have been correctly answered. The player with more cards wins.

TEC44059

Q. Which two words make *scrunch*?
A. squeeze + crunch
TEC44059

Q. Which two words make *docudrama*?
A. documentary + drama
TEC44059

Q. Which two words make *blog*?
A. Web + log
TEC44059

Q. Which two words make *e-zine*?
A. electronic + magazine
TEC44059

Q. Which two words make *brunch*?
A. breakfast + lunch
TEC44059

Q. Which two words make *edutainment*?
A. education + entertainment
TEC44059

Q. Which two words make *hazmat*?
A. hazardous + materials
TEC44059

Q. Which two words make *splatter*?
A. splash + spatter
TEC44059

Q. Which two words make *humongous*?
A. huge + monstrous
TEC44059

Q. Which two words make *gasohol*?
A. gasoline + alcohol
TEC44059

Q. Which two words make *fantabulous*?
A. fantastic + fabulous
TEC44059

Q. Which two words make *flop*?
A. flap + drop
TEC44059

Q. Which two words make *infomercial*?
A. information + commercial
TEC44059

Q. Which two words make *smog*?
A. smoke + fog
TEC44059

Q. What word do *chuckle* and *snort* make when they are mashed up?
A. chortle
TEC44059

Q. What word do *flutter* and *hurry* make when they are mashed up?
A. flurry
TEC44059

Q. What word do *globe* and *blob* make when they are mashed up?
A. glob
TEC44059

Q. What word do *squirm* and *wiggle* make when they are mashed up?
A. squiggle
TEC44059

Q. What word do *flame* and *glare* make when they are mashed up?
A. flare
TEC44059

Q. What word do *blot* and *botch* make when they are mashed up?
A. blotch
TEC44059

Q. What word do *gleam* and *shimmer* make when they are mashed up?
A. glimmer
TEC44059

Q. What word do *internal* and *communication* make when they are mashed up?
A. intercom
TEC44059

Q. What word do *emotion* and *icon* make when they are mashed up?
A. emoticon
TEC44059

Q. What word do *glamour* and *ritz* make when they are mashed up?
A. glitz
TEC44059

Q. What word do *bungle* and *stumble* make when they are mashed up?
A. bumble
TEC44059

Q. What word do *haggle* and *tussle* make when they are mashed up?
A. hassle
TEC44059

Q. What word do *parachute* and *troops* make when they are mashed up?
A. paratroops
TEC44059

Q. What word do *twist* and *whirl* make when they are mashed up?
A. twirl
TEC44059

Q. What word do *squeeze* and *crash* make when they are mashed up?
A. squash
TEC44059

Q. Which two words make *multiplex*?
A. multiple + complex
TEC44059

Note to the teacher: Use with "It's a Word Mash-Up!" on page 13.

Words from Characters in Greek Myths and Legends
cyclone (Cyclops) • chronological (Cronus) • synchrony (Cronus) • oceanic (Oceanus) • lunar (Luna) • hypnotic (Hypnos) • nocturnal (Nox) • pandemonium (Pan) • iridescence (Iris) • mnemonic (Mnemosyne) • hygienic (Hygeia) • tantalize (Tantalus) • narcissism (Narcissus) • hydraulics (Hydra) • odyssey (Odysseus)

Words That Came From Names (Eponyms)
Hamburger (Hamburg, Germany) • sandwich (John Montagu, Earl of Sandwich) • Frisbee (pie company owner William Frisbie) • diesel (auto engineer Rudolf Diesel) • braille (teacher Louis Braille) • America (explorer Amerigo Vespucci) • leotard (acrobat Jules Leotard) • fudge (seaman Captain Fudge) • saxophone (instrument maker Anton Sax) • vandal (Germanic tribe known as Vandals) • maverick (rancher Samuel Maverick) • sequoia (Cherokee chief Sequoia) • sideburns (Civil War general Ambrose Burnside) • boycott (army officer Charles Boycott) • pasteurize (bacteriologist Louis Pasteur)

Words From Roman Myths and Legends
jovial (Jupiter) • terrain (Terra) • terrace (Terra) • territory (Terra) • volcano (Vulcan) • solar (Sol) • solarium (Sol) • immortal (Morta) • mortal (Morta) • insomnia (Somnus) • furious (the Furies) • venerable (Venus) • martial (Mars) • fauna (Faunus) • salutation (Salus)

Words, Words, Words!

Building vocabulary

Want to encourage your students to learn lots of words? Try this! First, have each small group of students choose a list of vocabulary-building words from page 18. Next, give the duo a sheet of poster board and a dictionary. Then challenge the pair to create an eye-catching display that illustrates the words' meanings and gives hints for correctly spelling the words and remembering what they mean. When students complete their projects, have each pair present its work. Then post the displays in the hall with the title "A Wall of Wonderful Words." ***Isobel Livingstone, Rahway, NJ***

READING & LANGUAGE ARTS TIPS & TOOLS

Another Voice

Fiction analysis, point of view

For this critical-thinking activity, have each student choose a fairy tale or classic children's story. Have the student write a detailed retelling of the story. Next, have the child choose one of the story's lesser characters and imagine how different the events of the story might have seemed for that character. Then guide the student to create a detailed version of the story written from that character's point of view. Have the child divide each retelling into six parts and then follow the directions below to publish her work. Finally, have each student share her work with a partner.

Directions:

1. Fold a 14-inch-wide strip of bulletin board paper in half lengthwise. Then fold the paper in half in the opposite direction three times to create eight sections.
2. Open the paper. In the bottom left section, write the story's title. In the next section to the right, illustrate the story's most important event. Then write one section of your original retelling on each of the next five flaps to the right.
3. Fold down the top layer. Then cut along each folded line, stopping at the horizontal fold to create eight flaps.
4. On the first flap, write the story's title and your name. On the next flap, illustrate the character from whose point of view you wrote the second retelling. Then write one section of your story on each of the remaining flaps.
5. Using the fold lines as a guide, accordion-fold your paper to make a flip booklet.

Stick to the Facts!

Summarizing

Want students' summaries of informational text to get to the point and include only the supporting details? Try this small-group activity! After students read a nonfiction selection, guide them to name its main ideas, recording each one on an index card. Next, have each student list details from the reading that helped him understand it. Write each detail on a sticky note. Then guide students to identify the details that support the selection's main ideas and put those sticky notes on the appropriate cards. Set aside the details that don't support the main ideas, explaining that a summary includes only the details that support the main ideas. Finally, lead the group to summarize the selection using the notes. Follow up by having students practice the process with partners. ***Kim Minafo, Apex, NC***

A Bagful of Learning

Abbreviations, using a dictionary

To set up this engaging center, save the boxes from pasta, cereal, cake mixes, and other food items until you have five or more. Put the empty boxes in a grocery bag at a center along with a dictionary that has a section on common abbreviations. A child chooses a box and studies each of its faces. She jots down the product's name, makes a two-column chart as shown, and lists the abbreviations from the box. Then she looks up each abbreviation and records its meaning. She repeats the process with each box. After her work is checked, have the student tuck the page in her journal for a handy abbreviation reference. ***Carol Smallwood, Mt. Pleasant, MI***

Award-Winning Reading

Literary response

Here's a book report idea that has students honoring the books they read. Have each child read a fiction book and then decide which feature is the most prizeworthy: the theme, author's tone, author's style, characters, climax, or resolution. Next, have the child create a three-dimensional trophy that pays tribute to that aspect of the book. Then, on a copy of the certificate on page 19, have the student explain why the book earned the trophy. When the projects are due, hold a class awards ceremony and have each child introduce the book, read the certificate, and display the trophy. ***Ana L. Wilson, Riverside, IL***

Word Lists

Use with "Words, Words, Words!" on page 16.

Words From Characters in Greek Myths and Legends

cyclone (Cyclops) • chronological (Cronus) • synchrony (Cronus) • oceanic (Oceanus) • lunar (Luna) • hypnotic (Hypnos) • nocturnal (Nox) • pandemonium (Pan) • iridescence (Iris) • mnemonic (Mnemosyne) • hygienic (Hygeia) • tantalize (Tantalus) • narcissism (Narcissus) • hydraulics (Hydra) • odyssey (Odysseus)

Words From Roman Myths and Legends

jovial (Jupiter) • terrain (Terra) • terrace (Terra) • territory (Terra) • volcano (Vulcan) • solar (Sol) • solarium (Sol) • immortal (Morta) • mortal (Morta) • insomnia (Somnus) • furious (the Furies) • venerable (Venus) • martial (Mars) • fauna (Faunus) • salutation (Salus)

Hyphenated Compound Words

one-half • two-thirds • three-fourths • twenty-one • ninety-nine • jack-in-the-box • air-conditioning • all-purpose • drive-in • full-length • left-handed • right-handed • play-by-play • self-control • self-centered

English Words That Came From French Words

expose • traitor • attorney • religion • bizarre • charity • government • justice • authority • progress • brochure • debris • ticket • viola • pastor

Words With Tricky Vowel Patterns

police • attention • tension • reply • noisy • enjoy • about • power • booster • remove • tuna • looking • football • woodpile • grateful

Past Participle Forms of Irregular Verbs

begun • chosen • driven • fallen • flown • lain • ridden • risen • rung • shaken • shrunk • sprung • sung • sworn • swum

Words That Are Contractions and Multiple Contractions

you've • who's • it's • they're • wasn't • let's • you'll • it'll • we'll • we're • they've • there's • shouldn't've • mustn't've • wouldn't've

Words That Came From Names (Eponyms)

Hamburger (Hamburg, Germany) • sandwich (John Montagu, Earl of Sandwich) • Frisbee (pie company owner William Frisbie) • diesel (auto engineer Rudolf Diesel) • braille (teacher Louis Braille) • America (explorer Amerigo Vespucci) • leotard (acrobat Jules Leotard) • fudge (seaman Captain Fudge) • saxophone (instrument maker Anton Sax) • vandal (Germanic tribe known as Vandals) • maverick (rancher Samuel Maverick) • sequoia (Cherokee chief Sequoia) • sideburns (Civil War general Ambrose Burnside) • boycott (army officer Charles Boycott) • pasteurize (bacteriologist Louis Pasteur)

Really Long (Sesquipedalian) Words

interscholastic • superfluous • biodegradability • humanitarianism • absentminded • phosphorescence • discontinuation • authoritarianism • verbalization • transcontinental • acknowledgement • reminiscence • mispronunciation • sportsmanship • trustworthiness

Words With Suffixes *-ible* and *-able*

dependable • breakable • predictable • acceptable • audible • visible • compatible • legible • pleasurable • usable • comparable • deplorable • noticeable • manageable • changeable

Words With Suffixes *-ion*, *-sion*, and *-tion*

extinction • impression • congratulation • imitation • introduction • transmission • omission • collision • persuasion • erosion • determination • examination • perspiration • opposition • decomposition

Collective Nouns

clutch (chicks) • colony (ants) • covey (doves) • hive (bees) • gaggle (geese) • horde (gnats) • litter (kittens) • nest (snakes) • murder (crows) • herd (buffalo) • flock (sheep) • pack (wolves) • rookery (penguins) • plague (locusts) • parliament (owls)

This is to certify that the book

____,

written by _______________________________, *is hereby awarded the*

because ______________________________________

____

____

____

____

____

____

____

____

____

____

Signed ______________________________

____
date

TEC44060

In Other Words

Synonyms, antonyms

For this vocabulary-building challenge, program an index card with a different adjective for each student. (See the list.) Then give each child a card and have her list three synonyms for the adjective under it and then flip the card and write an antonym. Next, have the child use all five words in a creative sentence, making sure that each adjective is used to describe a different noun. Finally, have the child write her sentence on a paper strip, writing the five adjectives in a different color. Then post students' work on a display titled "In Other Words: Using Synonyms and Antonyms." ***Leigh Anne Newsom, Cedar Road Elementary, Chesapeake, VA***

Adjectives

beautiful	busy	light
happy	late	crowded
tired	studious	hot
interested	simple	cloudy
loud	difficult	small

Suzy's **small** kitten knocked over the **puny** fishbowl, which left the **petite** guppy flopping in an **undersize** pool of water and made a **huge** mess.

Read It Out Loud

Narrative poetry

To introduce students to longer narrative poetry, choose a poem that tells a good story, such as one of those shown. Next, explain the poem's challenging vocabulary ahead of time. Then read the poem aloud, reading with expression and enthusiasm. After that, point out that the poem is a story by guiding them to identify the main character or characters, the elements of its plot, and the story's theme. Then have each small group of students choose a narrative poem, decipher its challenging vocabulary, analyze the story, and then practice reading the poem aloud. Finally, have each group of students take turns reading its poem aloud and discussing the story with classmates.

"Paul Revere's Ride" by Henry Wadsworth Longfellow
"The Slave's Dream" by Henry Wadsworth Longfellow
"The Duel" by Eugene Field
"Adventures of Isabel" by Ogden Nash
"The Song of Hiawatha" by Henry Wadsworth Longfellow
"Casey at the Bat" by Ernest Thayer
"Casey—Twenty Years Later" by Clarence P. McDonald
"Casey's Revenge" by Grantland Rice
"A Visit From St. Nicholas" by Clement Clarke Moore
"The Raven" by Edgar Allen Poe

Picking up Speed

Scanning

Teach students how to scan a reading selection for specific information with these simple steps. Then have each child create a bookmark that summarizes the steps and encourage him to keep it handy when he's answering questions on any reading material. ***Carol Lawrence, Madera, CA***

How to Scan

1. Identify the information you need to find.
2. Let your eyes run over several lines at once.
3. Always keep the information you're looking for in mind.
4. Each time you see a heading or subheading, read it. Will the text under it include the information you're looking for? If so, scan the text under it. If not, skip the text under it.
5. Each time you see a date, number, name, or something in boldfaced print, glance at the surrounding words. Do they have the information you need? If so, start reading. If not, keep scanning.

Show Me!

Idioms

to blow off steam
to do or say something that helps you get rid of strong feelings such as anger or stress

to let the cat out of the bag
to accidentally say something that is a secret

Here's a whole-class game that helps students learn and remember what idioms mean. Copy and cut apart the idiom strips on page 22. Then have each small group of students draw a strip. Give each team a few minutes to read its idiom's definition and then plan a two-part charade. For part one, the group acts out the idiom's meaning. The team that guesses the idiom's meaning earns a point. For part two, the group acts out the idiom. The team that guesses the idiom earns a point. The team with the most points after all groups have performed wins. Follow up by reading aloud the idioms and having each student explain their actual meanings. ***Teri Nielsen, Tracey's Elementary, Tracy's Landing, MD***

One to One

Biography comprehension

After students read biographies, have them share what they learned with this simple project. First, a child cuts a copy of the pattern from page 23 on the thick outer lines. Next he folds and cuts out the pattern, as shown. Then the student unfolds his paper and decorates one end so that it looks like the subject of his biography when he or she was a child. Next, he answers the questions on the interior shapes. Then the child decorates the opposite end of his paper so that it looks like the subject as an adult. As time allows, have each student share his work with a partner.

Idiom Strips

Use with "Show Me!" on page 21.

to blow off steam to do or say something that helps you get rid of strong feelings such as anger or stress TEC44061	**to let the cat out of the bag** to accidentally say something that is a secret TEC44061
to play a game of cat and mouse to keep trying to find someone that is hiding from you TEC44061	**to catch somebody off guard** to surprise someone TEC44061
to burn the candle at both ends to be so busy that you stay awake too late and get up too early TEC44061	**to hang on to someone's every word** to listen very carefully to what someone says TEC44061
to eat your words to admit that what you said was wrong TEC44061	**to go through the roof or to hit the ceiling** to get very angry all of a sudden TEC44061
to rule the roost to be the person who makes all the rules TEC44061	**to keep your nose out of things** to not become involved in something TEC44061
to keep your nose to the grindstone to keep working without stopping TEC44061	**to look down your nose at somebody or something** to consider someone or something not important, or not as important as you are TEC44061
to have your nose out of joint to feel like you have been mistreated TEC44061	**to pay through the nose** to pay too much for something TEC44061
to thumb your nose at someone or something to show that you don't respect someone or something TEC44061	**to twist somebody's arm** to strongly encourage someone to do something he or she does not want to do TEC44061
to take up arms to fight with weapons against an enemy TEC44061	**to err on the side of caution** to choose an action that may not be the best choice but seems to be the safest choice TEC44061

Biography Pattern

Use with "One to One" on page 21.

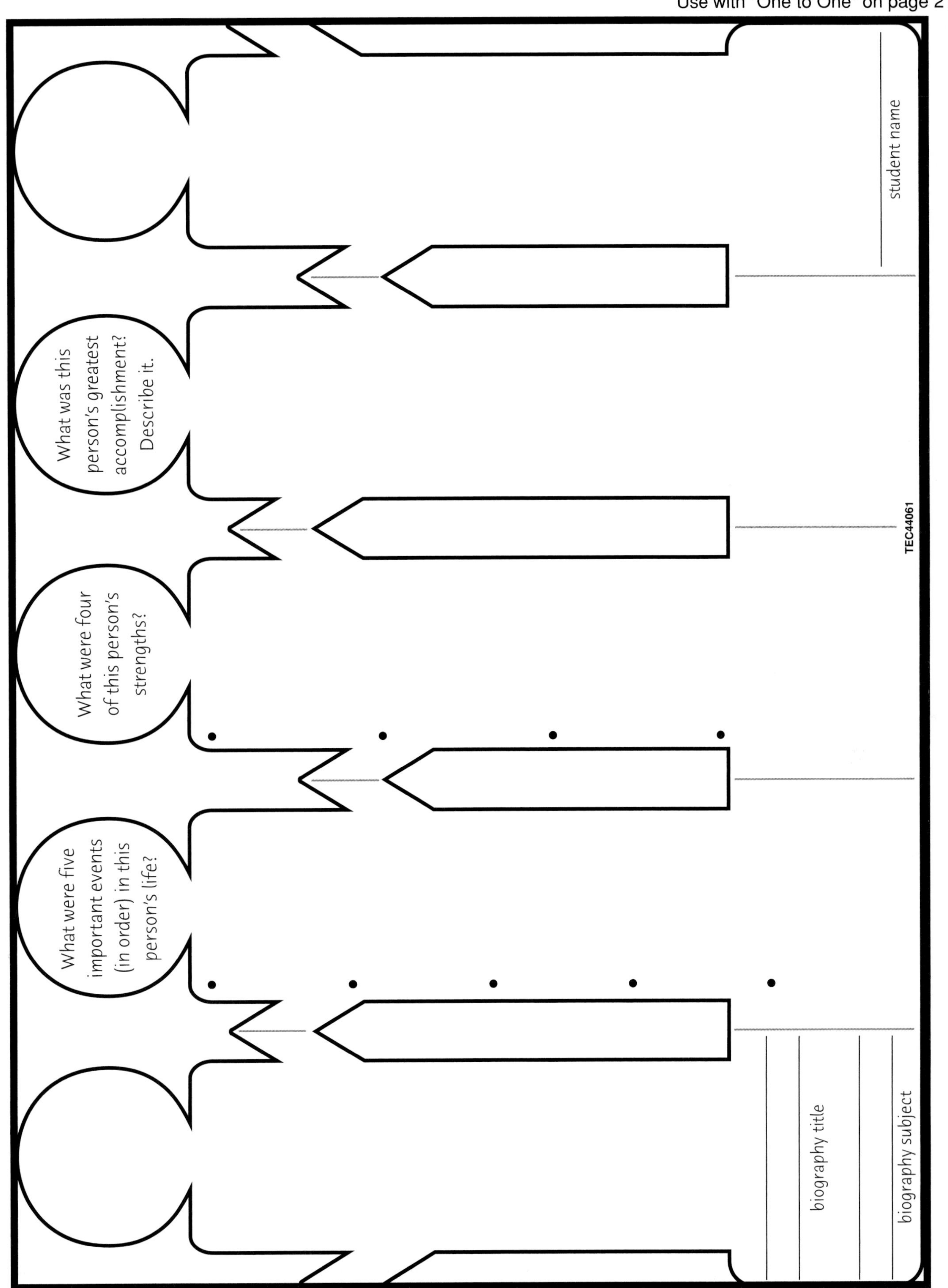

Cookie Caper

Sort each card according to the rules on the cookie jars.
When you finish, record each rule on your paper. Then record your sorting.

World's Best Dad

The suffix begins with a vowel, so the final *e* was dropped.

The suffix begins with a consonant, so the final *e* was not dropped.

Dear kids,
Stay out of the cookies!
Mom

Word Cards and Answer Key

Use with "Cookie Caper" on page 24. Students will need paper to record their work.

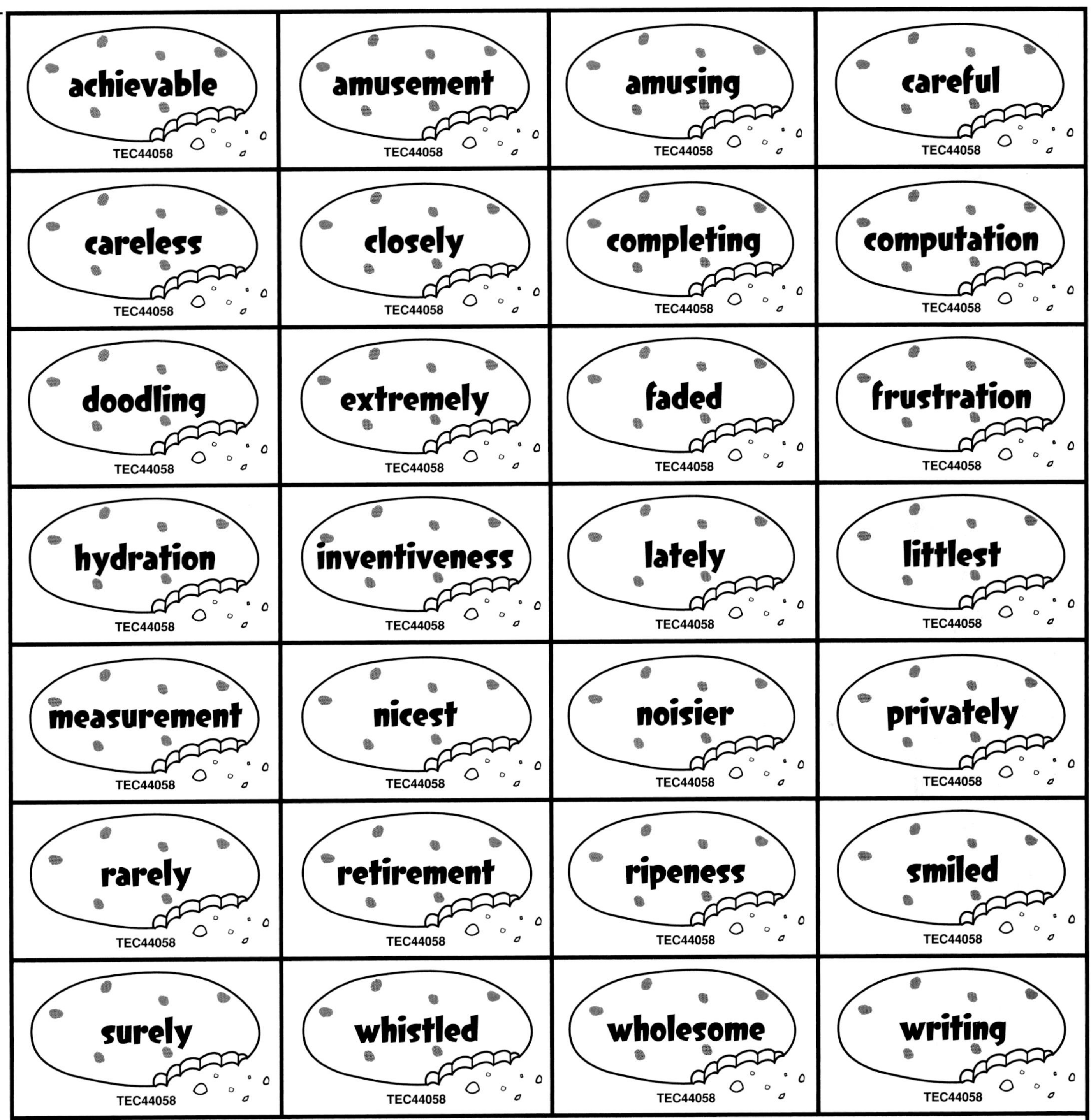

Answer Key for "Cookie Caper"

The suffix begins with a vowel, so the final e was dropped.

achievable, amusing, completing, computation, doodling, faded, frustration, hydration, littlest, nicest, noisier, smiled, whistled, writing

The suffix begins with a consonant, so the final e was not dropped.

amusement, careful, careless, closely, extremely, inventiveness, lately, measurement, privately, rarely, retirement, ripeness, surely, wholesome

TEC44058

And the crowd goes wild!

PRACTICE MAKES PERFECT!

Directions for two students:

1. Stack the cards facedown.
2. When it's your turn, take the top card and read the statement.
3. Choose the prefix from the mat that best corrects the boldface word.
4. Have your partner check the answer key. If you are correct, keep the card. If you're not correct, return the card to the bottom of the stack.
5. The player with more cards wins.

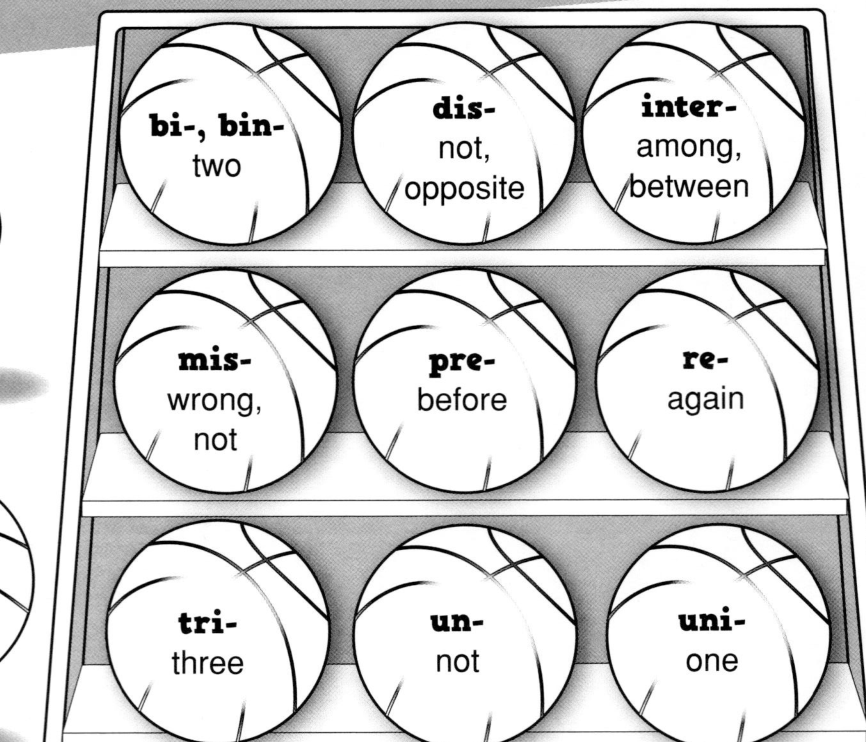

Center Cards and Answer Key

Use with "Practice Makes Perfect!" on page 26. Copy page 28 for your files. Then cut apart the cards and answer key on this page.

1 Bea T. Ball runs so fast she seems to **unappear** on the court. TEC44060	**2** By mistake, my mom thought halftime was called "**remission**." TEC44060	**3** Bea rarely fouls and never makes a **distake**. TEC44060
4 Before she went pro, I got a **triview** of Bea's skills at Hoops State University. TEC44060	**5** When Bea joined the team, the coach **preassured** the other players that Bea is not a ball hog. TEC44060	**6** I bet Bea could ride a **tricycle**. She's such a good athlete that she only needs one wheel! TEC44060
7 Bea's a **biathlete**; she runs, bikes, and swims to train. TEC44060	**8** One of the two wheels on her **intercycle** is flat. TEC44060	**9** Not everyone can dunk like Bea. She has **unicommon** skills. TEC44060
10 I **preagree** with the ref's call. Bea did not charge. TEC44060	**11** When she was in college, Bea set 20 **trischolastic** records. TEC44060	**12** Bea's fans rarely **disbehave** at one of her games. TEC44060
13 On game day, Bea shoots 100 free throws to **mispare** for the game. TEC44060	**14** I can't **precall** a game when Bea scored less than 40 points. TEC44060	**15** Bea wears a purple and gold **interform**. TEC44060
16 Did you know Bea speaks English and Spanish? She's **unilingual**. TEC44060	**17** When Bea was a kid, do you think she rode a **recycle**? TEC44060	**18** The other team is **misable** to block her. TEC44060
19 Bea's never **bihonest** with reporters; she always tells the truth. TEC44060	**20** As a professional athlete, Bea makes a lot of **disstate** trips. TEC44060	**21** Which team has the **unfortune** of playing against Bea tonight? TEC44060
22 If Bea didn't play pro basketball, she would be a **trischool** teacher for three-year-olds. TEC44060	**23** The coach had to **unithink** the game plan when Bea sprained her ankle. TEC44060	**24** Bea sponsors the **reannual** B-Ball Fantasy Camp twice a year. TEC44060
25 Missing a game because she's in a bad mood is **interacceptable** to Bea. TEC44060	**26** Bea's teammates played a joke on her and **uninformed** her about today's lineup. TEC44060	**27** The **disgame** practice was held 30 minutes before the tip-off. TEC44060
28 If Bea misses a shot, she tries to get her own **misbound**. TEC44060	**29** Bea just dyed her hair purple, gold, and black, so now it's **uncolored**! TEC44060	**30** After a long game, Bea **reties** her shoes and steps into fuzzy slippers. TEC44060

Answer Key for "Practice Makes Perfect!"

1. disappear
2. intermission
3. mistake
4. preview
5. reassured
6. unicycle
7. triathlete
8. bicycle
9. uncommon
10. disagree
11. interscholastic
12. misbehave
13. prepare
14. recall
15. uniform
16. bilingual
17. tricycle
18. unable
19. dishonest
20. interstate
21. misfortune
22. preschool
23. rethink
24. biannual
25. unacceptable
26. misinformed
27. pregame
28. rebound
29. tricolored
30. unties

TEC44060

Names ______________________________

Date ______________

The Midas Touch

A Game for Two Players

Directions:

1. Fold the answer key behind the page.
2. When it's your turn, choose a sentence. Circle the pronoun that correctly completes the sentence.
3. Have your partner check the key. If you are correct, write your initials in the box. If you are incorrect, erase your circle and do not initial the box.
4. When all the sentences have been completed, the partner who initialed the most boxes wins.

1. Midas was a mythological character; (he, she) was a very greedy king.	**2.** King Midas loved gold and believed (he, it) was the best thing in the world.	**3.** A god gave Midas the power to turn things to gold by touching (they, them).	**4.** The king loved (his, him) new power.
5. When the king turned flowers into gold, (it, they) shone.	**6.** The king was very pleased by all the gold that surrounded (it, him).	**7.** Eventually, King Midas's golden touch became a power (it, he) regretted.	**8.** When King Midas touched food, (it, they) turned to gold.
9. King Midas went to bed hungry, but (him, his) pillow turned to gold.	**10.** King Midas couldn't sleep; (he, it) couldn't eat.	**11.** Without thinking, the king hugged (her, his) daughter.	**12.** As soon as Midas touched the girl, (she, her) turned to gold.
13. The king's daughter could not sing or talk to (him, her) father anymore.	**14.** King Midas begged the gods to help (him, her).	**15.** One of the gods cared; (they, he) felt bad for Midas.	**16.** The god told King Midas to wash (it, his) golden touch away in a river.
17. The river's waters were magic; (they, it) washed away the king's golden touch.	**18.** The king washed everything (they, he) had touched in the river too.	**19.** King Midas realized (his, he) greediness had caused big problems.	**20.** Thankfully, the king did not notice that when the sand of the river was hit by the magic water, (they, it) turned gold.

Answer Key for "The Midas Touch"

1. he **2.** it **3.** them **4.** his **5.** they **6.** him **7.** he **8.** it **9.** his **10.** he **11.** his **12.** she **13.** her **14.** him **15.** he **16.** his **17.** they **18.** he **19.** his **20.** it

 How to use: Each pair needs a copy of the page. To increase the challenge, have students circle each pronoun's antecedent.

Here, Fishy, Fishy!

Directions for two players:

1. Cut apart the sentence cards and stack them facedown. Fold the key behind the directions.
2. When it's your turn, take the top card and read the sentence aloud. Record the card number and the word that correctly completes the sentence.
3. Then have your partner check the key. If you are correct, keep the card. If you are not correct, return the card to the stack.
4. The first player to correctly complete ten cards wins!

TEC44061

Answer Key for "Here, Fishy, Fishy!"

1. already	9. than	17. past
2. allowed	10. accept	18. right
3. they're	11. have	19. lose
4. choose	12. their	20. have
5. take	13. weather	21. farther
6. desert	14. well	22. Between
7. sight	15. too	23. they're
8. it's	16. are	24. already

TEC44061

1. Catfish Collins can hardly believe it's (already, all ready) time for the big fishing tournament. TEC44061

2. Each angler is (allowed, aloud) to use only one fishing pole. TEC44061

3. Many anglers take weeks to decide which fishing poles (their, there, they're) going to use. TEC44061

4. It took Catfish five weeks to (chose, choose) a fishing pole. TEC44061

5. Catfish is going to (bring, take) her top-secret bait. TEC44061

6. Even though she grew up in the (dessert, desert), Catfish is a champion angler. TEC44061

7. Watching the contestants preparing their gear is quite a (site, cite, sight). TEC44061

8. Catfish hopes to win first prize because (its, it's) a custom-made rod and reel. TEC44061

9. The first-place trophy is also bigger (then, than) her cat, Goliath. TEC44061

10. Catfish would gladly (accept, except) a cash prize too! TEC44061

11. Catfish wishes she would (of, have) brought more of her top-secret bait. TEC44061

12. Catfish and most anglers protect (there, their) secret techniques. TEC44061

13. Harry Herring thinks the (weather, whether) is perfect for a fishing contest! TEC44061

14. He had a cold last week, so he hopes he feels (well, good) enough to compete. TEC44061

15. This contest is (to, too, two) exciting to miss! TEC44061

16. Harry and his buddy (are, our) chatting about bait. TEC44061

17. In the (past, passed), Harry always used worms. TEC44061

18. It's important for Harry to choose the (write, right) bait. TEC44061

19. Harry's fishing buddy tells him there's no way he will (lose, loose). TEC44061

20. Harry says he could (of, have) been a professional angler. TEC44061

21. Harry doesn't know anyone who can cast a line (further, farther) than he can. TEC44061

22. (Between, Among) you and me, Harry will be hard to beat! TEC44061

23. Harry's parents called to say (their, there, they're) coming to the tournament. TEC44061

24. Harry caught a huge fish, and he's (already, all ready) headed to the judges' table. TEC44061

How to Use Copy this page for each pair of students. Students will need scissors, paper, and pencils.

Name ______________________________

Date ______________________________

Riding the Comprehension Trail

____
title

____
author

Beginning: ______________________________

Conflict: ______________________________

Rising action: ______________________________

Climax: ______________________________

Falling action: ______________________________

Resolution: ______________________________

CAUTION

Bonus: Read another book by the same author. Then analyze and compare its plot with this story's.

 How to use: Have each student use a copy of the page to analyze a story's plot.

Name ____________________

Date ____________________

Side by Side

Title: ____________________

Author: ____________________

The Selection's Three Most Important Points

2

3

What I Liked About This Selection

What I Didn't Like About This Selection

topic

Title: ____________________

Author: ____________________

The Selection's Three Most Important Points

2

3

What I Liked About This Selection

What I Didn't Like About This Selection

How to use: Have each student use a copy of the page to compare and contrast two nonfiction selections.

Name ______________________

Date ______________________

Reading organizer

Plot, cause and effect

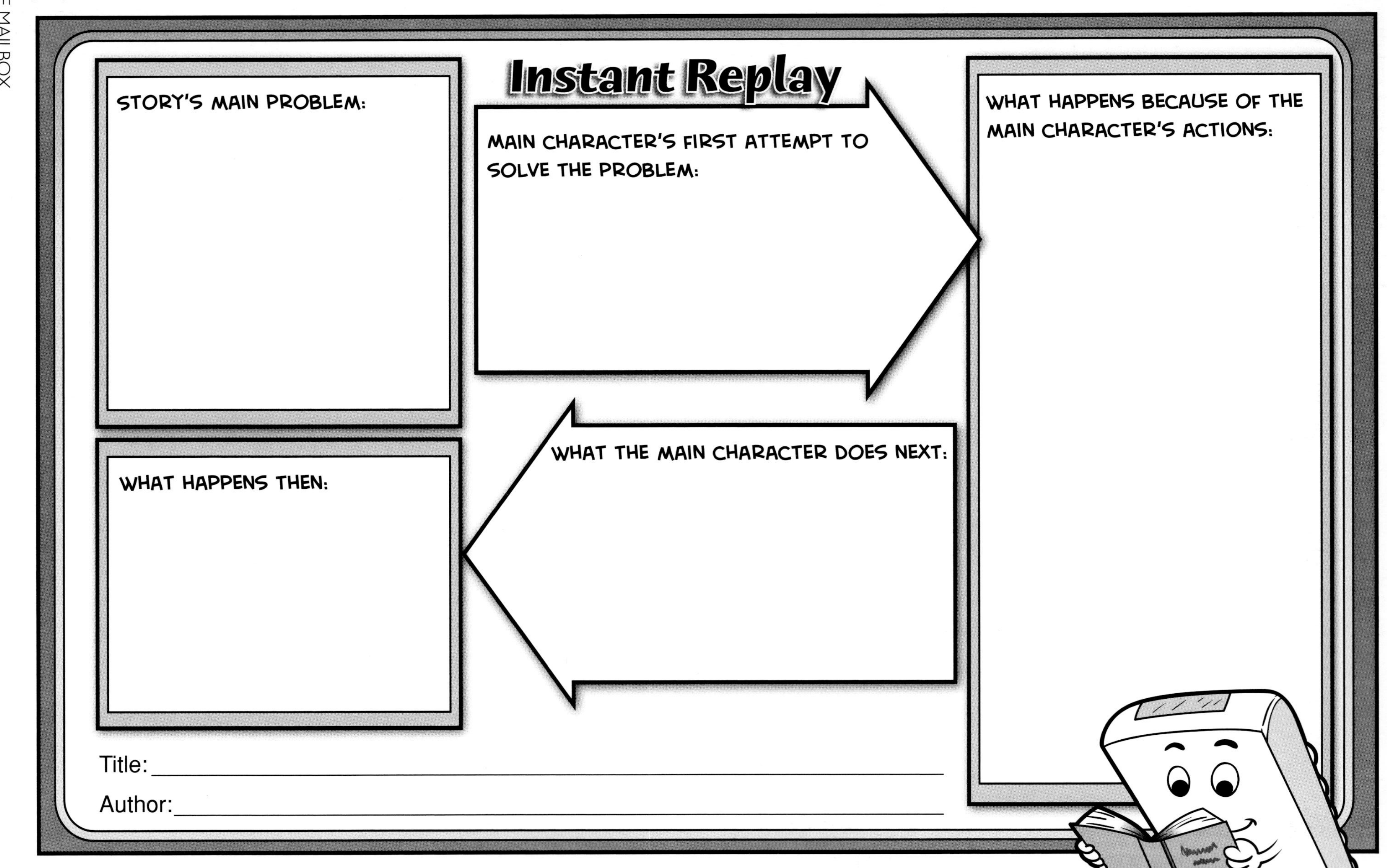

How to use: Have each child complete a copy of the organizer to analyze a story's plot through cause-and-effect relationships.

Name ______________________________

Date ____________________

Test Time

Write each verb in the past and present tenses, using *-ed* and *-ing*.

1. worry

worried

worrying

2. stir

3. delay

4. guard

5. gain

6. trap

7. squeal

8. question

9. quote

10. study

11. try

12. cram

13. sprawl

14. merge

15. learn

16. skate

Bonus: List the verbs you changed before adding *-ed* or *-ing*.

Name ______________________

Date ______________

In Other Words

I. Write the synonym or antonym that best replaces the *italicized* word or words. Use the thesaurus entries to help you.

______ **1.** Rex was restless yesterday, and then he had a *restless* night's sleep.

______ **2.** However, Rita got a good, *not restless* night's sleep.

______ **3.** Rita woke up early and got ready for the hike. She likes to be *ready*.

______ **4.** Rex is so sleepy today, he may seem *not reliable*.

______ **5.** Rex and Rita were required to take first aid classes, so they took the *required* class together.

______ **6.** Then Rita and Rex took the *not required,* advanced class.

______ **7.** Rita remembers their first hike, and when she *remembers* it, she always laughs.

______ **8.** Rita's *not realistic* goal was to hike ten miles in new boots.

______ **9.** Rita ignored her mom's *realistic* advice to wear old boots.

______ **10.** Rita thought her new boots were real leather, but she soon knew the leather was *not real.*

______ **11.** Rita was sorry she had *resisted* her mother's advice.

______ **12.** Now she was on a *remote* trail, and she had blisters on her toes.

______ **13.** When they stopped to rest, Rex was relaxed; Rita was *not relaxed.*

______ **14.** Rita took off her boots to *release* her blistered toes.

Bonus: Make a list of synonyms for *good* and *bad.* Underline four synonyms you can use in your writing.

ready • restless

ready *adj*
syn prepared, set
ant unready

real *adj*
syn genuine, true
ant bogus

realistic *adj*
syn down-to-earth, practical
ant unrealistic

relaxed *adj*
syn easygoing, casual, informal
ant tense

release *verb*
syn free, emancipate, loosen
ant detain

reliable *adj*
syn dependable, trustworthy
ant unreliable

remember *verb*
syn recall, reminisce, retain
ant forget

remote *adj*
syn distant, faraway, outlying
ant close, adjacent

required *adj*
syn compulsory, mandatory
ant optional

resist *verb*
syn dispute, oppose, repel
ant submit, yield

restless *adj*
syn uneasy, unsettled
ant restful

II. Using a thesaurus, find synonyms for each italicized word in the sentence below. Then rewrite the sentence.

Rita *knows* she *needs good* hiking boots, so she *finds* her *old*, *reliable* boots.

____

____

____

 • Key p. 307

Name ______________________________

Date ____________________

Stronger or Strongest?

Underline the comparative or superlative adjective in each sentence. If the adjective is correct, shade the matching circle. If the adjective is incorrect, write the correct form on the line.

An adjective's comparative (*-er*) form compares two things.

An adjective's superlative (*-est*) form compares three or more things.

1. Marc claims he is tougher than his brother Mike.
2. Marc says he has the biggest muscles in his family.
3. Mac is the younger of the three brothers.
4. Mac wants to know who is strongest—Marc or Mike.
5. Mike is shorter than Marc.
6. Mike is tallest than Mac.
7. Marc is the tallest one of all.
8. The family goes to a Test Your Strength game to find out which brother is the stronger.
9. The brother who wins will get the bigger prize.
10. The oldest brother goes first.
11. Marc is older than both of his brothers.
12. Marc picks up the bigger of all the mallets.
13. The mallet is heaviest than Marc expects it to be.
14. Mike uses the lightest mallet.
15. Mac chooses a mallet that is smaller than Mike's.
16. Marc doesn't ring the bell, but he is strongest than Mike.
17. Mike doesn't ring the bell either, but his swing is the wildest.
18. The littlest sibling in the family, Mikayla, walks up to the game.
19. She looks at Marc's mallet and asks for a largest one.
20. When Mikayla swings, she hits the bell, which proves she is strongest than all her brothers!

① ____________
② ____________
③ ____________
④ ____________
⑤ ____________
⑥ ____________
⑦ ____________
⑧ ____________
⑨ ____________
⑩ ____________
⑪ ____________
⑫ ____________
⑬ ____________
⑭ ____________
⑮ ____________
⑯ ____________
⑰ ____________
⑱ ____________
⑲ ____________
⑳ ____________

Test Your Strength!

Bonus: Write *C* next to each sentence that has or should have a comparative adjective. Write *S* next to each sentence that has or should have a superlative adjective.

Name ______________________________________

Date ______________________

A Confident Cultivator

Part 1: Add a suffix to each verb as guided. If the new word is a noun, shade the pumpkin. If the new word is an adjective, shade the gourd. If the new word can be used as a noun or an adjective, shade both foods.

Word Parts	Word	Noun	Adjective
1. solve – e + ent =			
2. defend + ant =			
3. study – y + ent =			
4. hesitate – ate + ant =			
5. defy – y + i + ant =			
6. insist + ent =			
7. serve – e + ant =			
8. contest + ant =			
9. propel + l + ant =			
10. superintend + ent =			
11. lubricate – ate + ant =			
12. please – e + ant =			
13. repel + l + ent =			
14. observe – e + ant =			
15. radiate – ate + ant =			

Part 2: Circle words from above in these sentences. Above each circled word, write *A* if the word's an adjective or *N* if it's a noun.

16. The superintendent was hesitant to correct the observant student.

17. The game show contestant was insistent that the words happy and content were similar but not the same.

18. In court, the defendant was defiant.

19. Jane's pleasant face was radiant when she was told she would no longer be a servant.

20. Joe reported that water is a solvent and oil is a lubricant.

Bonus: Write a rule that explains the directions for changing the words in items 1, 7, 12, and 14.

Name ____________________________

Date ____________________

To Catch a Lobster

Part 1

In each sentence below, circle each pronoun. Then underline the noun or nouns the pronoun replaces.

1. When Ben spent the day on a lobster boat, he learned a lot.
2. The boat's owners, Lola and Lou, have been working on boats since they were young.
3. Lola sets out lobster traps, or pots, one day, and she comes back in a day or two.
4. Each trap is connected to a colorful buoy so it will be easy to find.
5. Ben helps Lola and Lou look for and then pull up their pots.
6. Ben realizes the traps were baited with dead fish, and they are smelly!
7. Wearing gloves helps Ben keep the stinky smell off his hands.
8. If there are two or more lobsters in a trap, they might fight.
9. The first thing Lola does after she pulls a lobster out of a pot, is put a strong rubber band around both of its claws.
10. "How do you keep from getting pinched?" Ben asks Lola.

Part 2

Write the missing pronoun. (Use the word bank to help you.) Then draw an arrow to the noun or nouns each pronoun replaces.

11. Lola laughs as ____________ pulls a small lobster out of a trap.
12. As Lola tosses the lobster back, ____________ says, " ____________ get a lot of practice, and ____________ always wear gloves!"
13. Ben watches Lou pull up the next trap, and ____________ is amazed by the size of the lobster inside.
14. Lou pulls the enormous lobster out of the pot; ____________ is madly waving ____________ claws.
15. Even though Lola helps Lou, ____________ struggle to get bands around the lobster's giant claws.
16. Lola and Lou put fresh bait in ____________ traps and set ____________ out before ____________ head back to shore.

Bonus: Imagine that you take Ben's place. Rewrite sentences 1, 7, and 13 from your point of view.

Name ___________________________

Date ______________

Paws and Pals

Directions:

1. In each short, short story, draw an arrow or arrows to the main character or characters.
2. Circle the details that tell you where each story takes place.
3. Draw squiggly lines under each story's problem.
4. Draw a box around the event in each story that is the climax.
5. Answer the questions on another sheet of paper.

Home for Howie

My family and I went to the shelter to pick the perfect family pet. The first critter we saw was a beautiful collie, but it was too big for our apartment. Next, we spotted a cute calico cat. She walked back and forth in her cage, mewing softly. We thought she might be just right for our family. Then I started sneezing and sneezing. I guess I'm allergic to cats. We were just about to give up hope of finding a pet when we heard a pitiful howl. My brothers tore around the corner where they found an adorable little beagle named Howie. By the time we caught up with the boys, we could see they had found the perfect pet.

Not Just Another Saturday

I work at the animal shelter once a week. I got a call last Saturday about a stray kitten that had been spotted at a construction site. Grabbing a cat carrier and some cat treats, I headed to my car. I drove to the site and hopped out. There was no one at the site, and I couldn't see the kitten anywhere. I walked around and around the site. Finally, I heard something moving around under a truck. I peeked under the truck and spotted a tiny, cold, and scared kitten. I shook out a few treats. Then I got down on my knees and held out my hand. The cat began meowing and wobbling toward me. Soon the crying kitten crawled out from under the truck and right into my arms. I petted her, and she began to purr like a little motor boat. After I tucked the kitten into the carrier, we headed back to the shelter where we found her a loving home—mine!

1. Who is telling the story "Home for Howie"? How do you know?
2. Where does the story "Home for Howie" take place?
3. Why doesn't the family in "Home for Howie" adopt the collie or the calico cat?
4. Using what you know and what you read, tell why you think the beagle might have been perfect for the family.
5. Would "Finding the Perfect Pet" be a better title than "Home for Howie"? Why or why not?
6. Who is telling the story "Not Just Another Saturday"? How do you know?
7. Where does "Not Just Another Saturday" take place?
8. What is the main setting of "Not Just Another Saturday"?
9. What is the main problem in the story?
10. In the story's resolution, the author tries to surprise her readers. Were you surprised the narrator keeps the kitten? Why or why not?
11. Would "Finding the Perfect Pet" be a better title than "Not Just Another Saturday"? Why or why not?
12. Which story do you like better? Explain.

Bonus: Choose one of the short, short stories above. Write a paragraph that tells what happens next.

Name ____

Date ______________________

A Picture-Perfect Day

Use ‸ to add commas where they are needed. Then color each number by the code to tell why you added a comma or commas.

Color Code

separate items in a series = yellow

set off the name of a person being spoken to = blue

set off dialogue = purple

put before the conjunction in a compound sentence = green

separate an introductory word or words = red

1 It was a windy Saturday and my dad was planning to work most of the day.

2 Consequently it was my job to keep my little sister, Lillie, and myself busy all day.

3 We had two movies a new video game and lots of microwave popcorn.

4 There was plenty to do so I wasn't worried about staying out of Dad's hair.

5 All of a sudden we heard an ear-splitting crash.

6 Lillie screamed and we both ran to the window.

7 As we watched the gigantic oak tree in our yard crashed to the ground.

8 The mailbox our fence and a power line collapsed under the fallen tree.

9 As the TV screen faded to black, Lillie squealed "What are we going to do now?"

10 I realized we couldn't play video games watch TV or even pop any microwave popcorn!

11 I moaned, "This could turn into a long day Lillie."

12 Just then Dad came into the room carrying a big box.

13 He set the box down and announced "This box is the answer to your problems!"

14 "What is it Dad?" we asked.

15 "These are old family photos" he replied.

16 For the rest of the day Lillie and I went through the box of pictures.

17 As we looked at pictures, we got curious about our aunts uncles grandparents and great-grandparents.

18 When the power came on we made microwave popcorn and ate it while Dad took a break and told stories to go with the pictures.

Bonus: Draw a star next to the comma rule above that is the easiest for you to remember. Next, circle the rule that is the hardest to remember. Then write a sentence example for each rule.

Name ______________________________

Date ____________________

Who Wants to Know?

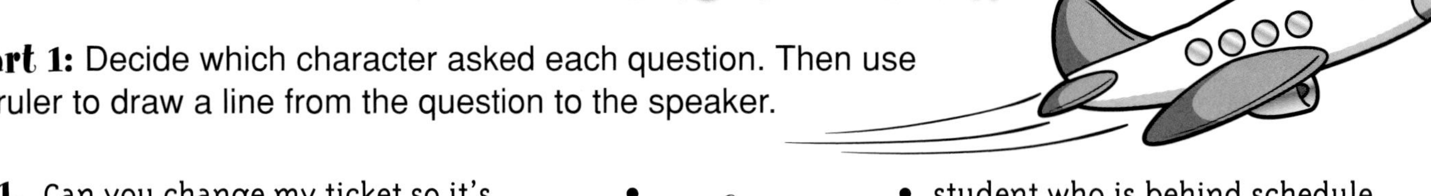

Part 1: Decide which character asked each question. Then use a ruler to draw a line from the question to the speaker.

1. Can you change my ticket so it's for a later flight?
2. How long have you had a fever?
3. Do you really think I need four new tires?
4. How many more stops are there before we get to school?
5. Do I have to wear a party hat?
6. What will happen if I turn mine in late?
7. Can you hold Spot still while I check his teeth?
8. How should I hold the steering wheel?
9. May I have a burger without any onions?
10. Why are you running in the hall?
11. Why did you stand up before I stopped the bus?
12. When are you going to clean your room?
13. Which of my little students is not sitting crisscross, applesauce?
14. How could I have kept her from kicking that goal?

C T O L B O P R S A J N Q D E O M G W

- student who is behind schedule on his science fair project
- teenager driving for the first time
- school principal
- student on a school bus
- veterinarian talking to her assistant
- airline passenger
- parent talking to a child
- school bus driver
- customer talking to an auto mechanic
- doctor examining a patient
- soccer player after losing a game
- kindergarten teacher
- teenager at a birthday party
- customer ordering fast food

Part 2: Name a person who might ask each question and then tell why he or she might ask it.

15. What is the best way to get there from here? ______________________________

____

16. Where should I sign my name? ______________________________

____

Where do crayons and markers go on vacation?

To answer the question, circle each letter above that doesn't have a line drawn through it. Then write the circled letters in order from top to bottom on the blanks.

"___ ___ ___ ___ ___ - ___ ___ ___"

Bonus: List five or more people who might ask the following question: Who is next in line?

Name ______________________________

Date ______________

CURTAIN CALL

A. Use the symbols shown to edit the story.

It was the friday morning, the day of the schoolplay. Emma said she couldnt eat breakfast because she was too nervus about being on stage. Emmas Mother told her over and over that she'd be fine

"But, mom," Emma whined "I'm really nervous. What if I for get my lines?" "I think You'll be fine, Emma" her mom said. "You're al ways making me laugh with your silly jokes, and riddles. You'll probly get on stage and absolutely love it."

The school day whized by, until it was time for the Play. Ms. Ellaneous, the school Principal, welcomd the audience, and thanked everyone for comeing. Then the lights dimmed and Ms. Ellaneous steped off the stage.

Every one waited for the curtains to open but they stayed shut. Ms Pelling, the music teacher, pulled hard on the ropes. nothing happened. So she pulled harder. All of a sudden, lost her balance and lurched forward, falling through the velvet Curtain onto the stage. Ms. Pelling stepped back, groan groaned, and brushed her self off. Then he quickly smiled, bowed and dashed backstage.

"Emma" she called, Would you please go out their and tell a few of your best jokes? While you do that, I'll figure out how to get these certains open!

Did you find 40 errors?

Editing Symbols

- ◯ Correct spelling.
- ℘ Delete or remove.
- ⁀‿ Close the gap.
- ^ Add a letter or word.
- # Make a space.
- ^, Insert a comma.
- ⊙ Insert a period.
- ' Insert an apostrophe.
- " Insert quotation marks.
- ≡ Make the letter a capital.
- / Make the letter lowercase.
- ¶ Start a new paragraph.

B. Write an ending to this story on another sheet of paper. Then use the symbols shown to edit your work.

Bonus: Write the whole story, making the corrections you've marked.

Name ______________________________

Date ______________________

A Royal Visit

Write the abbreviation for each term. Use a dictionary to help you.

Open wide, your highness!

1. automated teller machine _________
2. Ohio _________
3. manufacturing _________
4. temperature _________
5. *et cetera* (and so forth) _________
6. miles per hour _________
7. Central Intelligence Agency _________
8. senior _________
9. Tennessee _________
10. department _________
11. *exempli gratia* (for example) _________
12. tablespoon _________
13. hour _________
14. intensive care unit _________
15. *répondez s'il vous plaît* (respond, please) _________
16. ounce _________
17. Veterans of Foreign Wars _________
18. National Aeronautics and Space Administration _________
19. chief executive officer _________
20. building _________

Bonus: Tell what each abbreviation below stands for.

FDA govt. EPA
PIN natl.

Why did King Karl go to the dentist?

Write the letters from above in the puzzle to answer the riddle.

1 2 3 4 5 6 7 8 9 10 11 12 13 14 15 16 17 18 19 20

Name ______________________________

Date ____________________

An Eye on the Sky

If the sentence is a run-on, shade the feather.
Then correct the sentence in the space below it.

1 Bill and Bridget are excited about their bird-watching adventure.	2 They have studied all kinds of bird calls some calls sound the same.
3 Bridget is fascinated by the birds that are small, are delicate, and chirp softly.	4 Bill looks for big birds and he is often the first person to spot one.
5 Bill watches several birds fly by he thinks one is a bald eagle.	6 The birds with the brightly colored feathers are the easiest ones to spot.
7 Bridget is hoping to spot the smallest bird of all, the bee hummingbird.	8 This tiny bird only weighs about one-tenth of an ounce it's about as big as a walnut shell.
9 Bill dreams of spotting the world's biggest bird he wants to see an African ostrich in the wild.	10 This ostrich can weigh 345 pounds that's gigantic compared to a bee hummingbird.
11 Bridget spots two robins and a swallow and the bird Bill thought was an eagle is a crow.	12 By the end of the day, Bridget and Bill haven't seen many different types of birds.

Bonus: Choose three run-on sentences from above. Correct each one in a different way than you corrected it above.

Name ______________________

Date ______________________

Lots of Left Turns

Part 1: If the colon or set of parentheses is used correctly in each sentence, shade the number.

1	Zelda (the youngest racer at the track) believes she can win today's race.
2	At 60:0 AM, Zelda and her crew start getting ready.
3	Zelda makes sure she has everything on her list: a helmet, gloves, and boots.
4	Zelda's car built for speed (is gassed up and ready to go).
5	Seven racers line up at the start line: Zelda, Flash, Speedy, Quinton, Swifty, Hasty, and Dizzy.
6	The race (500 laps) will take a long time.
7	Max (the race's grand marshal waves the green flag to start the race.
8	It's exactly 9:42 when Zelda punches the gas and takes off!
9	At the first pit stop, three crew members: do everything on their lists fill the fuel tank, check the tire pressures, and clean the windshields.
10	Zelda (tired after 428 laps moves too far right and scrapes the wall.

Part 2: Add a colon, parenthesis, or set of parentheses to make each sentence correct.

1	Flash (known for his clever racing tactics is ready for the race.
2	Flash's crew follows its prerace checklist checking the fuel tank, checking each tire's pressure, and checking the engine's status.
3	By 800, Flash's car is set to race.
4	Flash (a speedy starter gets a quick lead.
5	Flash figures he has just three things to think about his car's speed, track conditions, and the other racers.
6	Zelda a daring young driver) passes Flash to take the lead.
7	Flash's pit crew one of the best in racing completes the last pit stop in record time.
8	Flash (confident he can win has already won four races this season!
9	Flash's car the number two is running well.
10	Flash closes in on Zelda the leader for 12 laps.

Hint: Use parentheses to set off information that is helpful or interesting but not extremely important.

Zelda (the fourth racer in her family) learned to drive when she was 12.

Hint: Use a colon to introduce a list or to show the time.

Flash has three good luck charms: a bobble head doll, a silver quarter, and a picture of his mom.

Bonus: Rewrite each incorrect sentence from Part 1, correcting the colon or parentheses mistakes.

Name ______________________________

Date ______________________

Time for a Bath!

If a word is spelled incorrectly, circle it.

1. beleive	**2.** nieghborhood	**3.** compound	**4.** preschol	**5.** annowncement
6. crouded	**7.** achieve	**8.** niether	**9.** handkercheif	**10.** frouning
11. allouance	**12.** kangaro	**13.** however	**14.** cauliflouer	**15.** masterpiece
16. balloon	**17.** mowntain	**18.** pouder	**19.** discount	**20.** crackdoun
21. niece	**22.** cieling	**23.** cowardly	**24.** drowght	**25.** hieght
26. grownd	**27.** shook	**28.** overloke	**29.** retreive	**30.** prowling

Then write the word's number and spell the word correctly.

(1) believe

( ) ______________________

( ) ______________________

( ) ______________________

( ) ______________________

( ) ______________________

( ) ______________________

( ) ______________________

( ) ______________________

( ) ______________________

( ) ______________________

( ) ______________________

( ) ______________________

( ) ______________________

( ) ______________________

( ) ______________________

( ) ______________________

( ) ______________________

( ) ______________________

( ) ______________________

Bonus: Sort the words into five groups according to their vowel patterns: *ei, ie, oo, ou,* and *ow.*

Name ______________________________

Date ____________________

Pick and Practice

CAUSE AND EFFECT!

Pick _____ activities to do.
When you finish an activity, color its number.

1 What might happen because of the event shown? Describe two different results.

Helen finished her homework early.

2 What might have caused the event shown? Describe two different causes.

Daniel dropped his lunch on his way to the table.

3 Look in one of your textbooks for examples of cause-and-effect statements. Look for key words or phrases. Record three examples and circle the key words.

as a result
because
consequently
this led to
since
due to

4 Cut out an interesting picture from an old magazine. Imagine that the photo shows the effect. Write a short story about the cause.

5 Choose a fairy tale such as *Cinderella*, *The Three Little Pigs*, or *Jack and the Bean Stalk*. Write six cause-and-effect statements about story events.

6 Decide whether each statement is a cause or an effect. If it is a cause, write the effect. If it is an effect, write the cause.

A. I had to cut a blob of bubble gum out of my hair.
B. I stood shivering outside the classroom door.
C. By the time I got to school, I forgot I was wearing a hat.
D. I found a hundred dollar bill!

7 What might have caused the action shown? What might the action shown cause?

8 Write four sets of cause-and-effect statements. Use the key words and phrases shown.

for this reason
if...then
since
therefore
then...so

9 Draw the diagram shown. Read the statement in the first box. Then complete the diagram.

If I found a dragon's egg... → then → [ ]
then → [ ] → then → [ ]
finally → [ ]

Independent practice grid: Program the student directions on a copy of this page with the number of activities to be completed. Then copy the page for each student.

Name ______________________________

Date ____________________

Pick and Practice

Pick _____ activities to do.
When you finish an activity, color its number.

1 Cut out an action picture from an old magazine or newspaper. Then fold a large sheet of construction paper in half. Glue the picture on one half of the paper. On the other half, write an action-packed story about what is happening in the picture. Use ten or more strong verbs in your story and circle each one.

2 Choose a picture book. List every verb used in the book. Then make a chart like the one shown and sort the words from your list into the appropriate columns.

Action Verb	Linking Verb	Helping Verb

3 Choose a favorite summertime sport. Write ten strong action verbs related to this sport, each on a different index card. Then illustrate each verb on the card.

swing

4 A *portmanteau* is a word that blends two or more words, such as *twist* + *whirl* = *twirl*. Invent five of your own action-word blends. Then write an equation to show how you made each one.

smack + mash = smash

5 Create a poster that will help classmates remember the linking verbs that are forms of *to be*—*am*, *is*, *are*, *was*, *were*, *be*, *being*, and *been*.

6 Cut out a newspaper or magazine article. Use red, green, and blue colored pencils to circle the verbs in the article. Circle the past-tense verbs in red. Circle the present-tense verbs in green. Circle the future-tense verbs in blue.

7 List eight words that can be used as either a noun or a verb, such as *plant*. For each word, draw a sketch that shows the word as a noun and a sketch that shows the word as a verb.

8 Write the past-tense forms for each of the irregular verbs shown. Then choose six of the past-tense verbs and use them in sentences.

freeze	**drink**
break	**raise**
bring	**set**
begin	**speak**
catch	**swim**

9 Write ten sentences using verb phrases that include one or more of the helping verbs shown.

shall	could	has	was
should	may	do	were
will	must	did	am
would	have	is	being
can	had	are	been

We have been standing in line for one hour!

Independent practice grid: Program the student directions on a copy of this page with the number of activities to be completed. Then copy the page for each student.

BRAIN BOOSTERS

LANGUAGE ARTS

Brain Booster 1

List ten or more words that begin with *z.* Which ones would be listed after *zebra* in the dictionary?

Brain Booster 2

If O = S and X = T in this sentence, what is the entire quotation?

"XAJ LBMOX OXJQ BO XAJ AYMTJOX."

Marie de Vichy-Chamrond, 1697–1780

TEC44056

Brain Booster 3

Write a noun, a verb, and an adjective that begin with each of your initials. Then create a wacky sentence using all nine words. (Add more words if you need to.)

verb adjective
noun noun
adjective verb
verb noun adjective

TEC44056

Brain Booster 4

Can you spell more three-letter words using the letters in *special* or the letters in *delivery*? Make two lists.

special
delivery

TEC44056

Brain Booster 5

A sentence that uses every letter of the alphabet at least once is called a *pangram.* Write a pangram.

a b c d e f g h i
j k l m n o p q
r s t u v w x y z

TEC44056

Brain Booster 6

The words *lamb* and *comb* both end with silent *b*s. List six or more other words that end with silent *b*s. Then name two or more words with silent *b*s that are not at the words' ends.

TEC44056

Brain Booster 7

Which of these words would be included on a dictionary page with the guide words *mint* and *miser*? List eight more words that would be on the page.

misdeed
miracle
mitten
minor
minute
mist
mirror

TEC44056

Brain Booster 8

Draw and then name five or more nouns that are always plural.

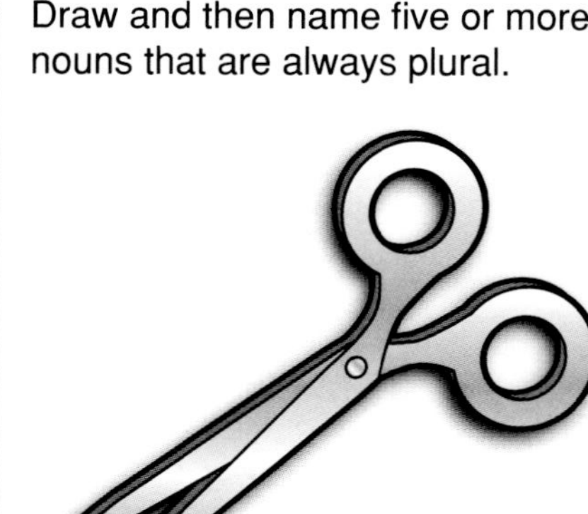

TEC44056

How to use: Display this page or give each student a copy of this page (or one card at a time) to work on during free time.

BRAIN BOOSTERS

LANGUAGE ARTS

Brain Booster 1

How many sets of homonyms can you spell using the letters in HALLOWEEN? Example: won, one

HALLOWEEN

TEC44057

Brain Booster 2

Does a fish know it's wet? Write your answer in a paragraph that will convince your best friend to agree with you.

TEC44057

Brain Booster 3

Start with the word *bread*. Remove one letter at a time and spell a new word. (You can rearrange the letters if you need to.) When you get to the word *a*, add one letter at a time, spelling a new word each time and ending with *water*.

bread
___ ___ ___ ___
___ ___ ___
___ ___
a
___ ___
___ ___ ___
___ ___ ___ ___
water

TEC44057

Brain Booster 4

Unscramble each word. Then rearrange the words to write an idiom someone might use if they were having a hard time.

dapled   ew   kerec

a   pu

ttiowhu   a   reew

TEC44057

Brain Booster 5

Write three imperative sentences, each containing five or fewer words.

TEC44057

Brain Booster 6

Find two pairs of rhyming words below. Use them to write a silly poem.

TEC44057

Brain Booster 7

Using the dictionary, find four or more three-syllable words that begin with the letter *t*. Write each word and its definition.

TEC44057

Brain Booster 8

Write a synonym that ends in *-ness* for each word.

A. shadow
B. courtesy
C. honesty
D. fellowship
E. equality

TEC44057

How to use: Display this page or give each student a copy of this page (or one card at a time) to work on during free time.

BRAIN BOOSTERS

LANGUAGE ARTS

Brain Booster 1

An occupation is hidden in the question below. Write three sentences or questions. Hide an occupation in each one.

Would you like a plum, Bert?

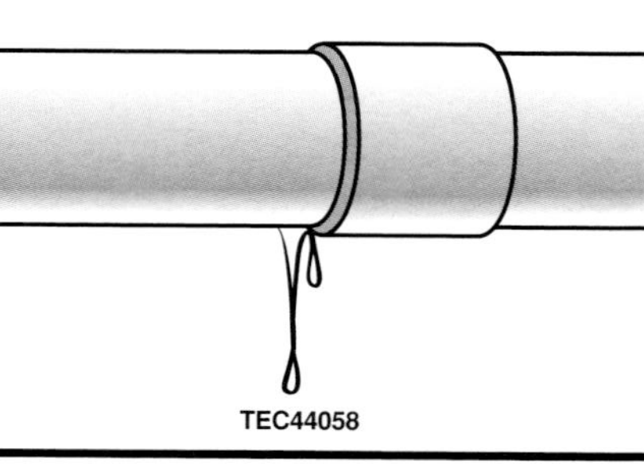

TEC44058

Brain Booster 2

For each clue, write a word that ends in ***ant.***

A. extremely large
B. far away
C. immediate
D. a baby
E. one who helps

TEC44058

Brain Booster 3

Complete this magic word square by writing a word for each clue. The words going down and across are the same.

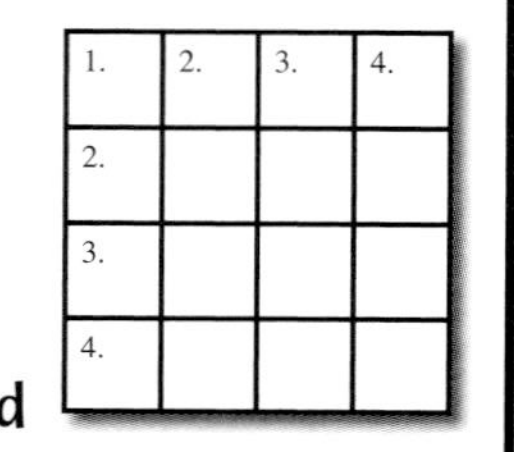

1. nearly all
2. one time
3. mark left by a wound
4. period of time in the school year

TEC44058

Brain Booster 4

Write a 15-second radio commercial to promote a new fruit drink. Use alliteration in your ad.

Buy Billy's Best Banana Blended Beverage...

TEC44058

Brain Booster 5

Write a one-syllable word for the first clue in each item. Then change the word's first letter to write the word for the second clue.

A. very warm & a folding bed
B. a body of salt water & a small, green vegetable
C. to speak & to travel on foot
D. very cool & a precious metal

TEC44058

Brain Booster 6

Write four complete sentences that describe your chair without using any of the following words: *seat, sit, legs, back.*

TEC44058

Brain Booster 7

The postal abbreviation for Maine (ME) is also a personal pronoun. For each item, write the state and its abbreviation.

A. The abbreviation for ______ is also sung as part of a musical scale.
B. The abbreviation for ______ is also the opposite of out.
C. The abbreviation for ______ is also a nickname for father.
D. The abbreviation for ______ is also a simple greeting.
E. The abbreviation for ______ is also a conjunction.

TEC44058

Brain Booster 8

List five adjectives that begin with *j* and are spelled with five letters.

J J J J J j

TEC44058

How to use: Display this page or give each student a copy of this page (or one card at a time) to work on during free time.

BRAIN BOOSTERS

Brain Booster 1

If you put all the words from the Pledge of Allegiance in alphabetical order, what would the first two words be? What would the last two words be?

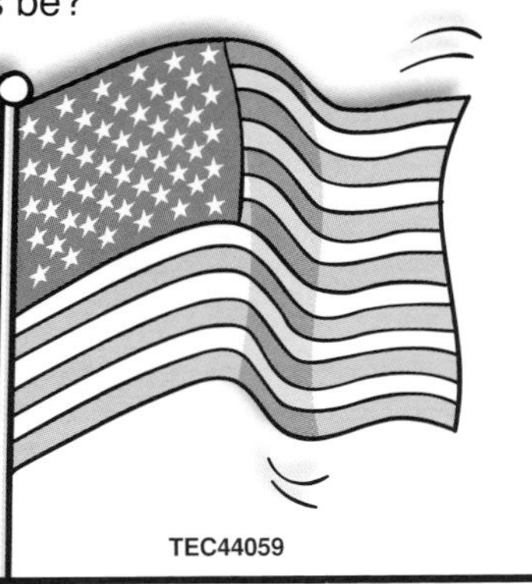

TEC44059

Brain Booster 2

Place these words in the puzzle so that each word is spelled correctly. Then draw the blank diagram and find six different words that will fit in the spaces.

bites
dread
salad
ideal
these
blind

TEC44059

Brain Booster 3

Write a Valentine's Day greeting using only three-letter words. Then write another Valentine's Day greeting using only five-letter words.

TEC44059

Brain Booster 4

Figure out what each abbreviation in the statements stand for.

Example:
There are 64 S on a C. (There are 64 **s**quares on a **c**heckerboard.)

A. There are 12 N on the face of a Cl.

B. There are 11 Pl on a S team.

C. There are 3 Wh on a Tri.

TEC44059

Brain Booster 5

Without rearranging the letters, take away one letter at a time from each word to spell a different word. Keep going until you have a one-letter word.

Example:
hoards – s = hoard – o = hard – r = had – h = ad – d = a

A. beard
B. dinner
C. paint

TEC44059

Brain Booster 6

List five or more words that can be pronounced in two different ways without changing the spelling. Then write a sentence to show the meaning of each word.

Example:

The old pipes were made of **lead**. I'll **lead** you to your seat.

TEC44059

Brain Booster 7

Make a list of 26 proper nouns that each begin with a different letter of the alphabet.

Example:

Arizona, Brittany...

TEC44059

Brain Booster 8

For each phrase below, think of a two-word rhyme.

Example:
A *sanitary legume* is a *clean bean*.

A. a seat for a rabbit
B. a skinny arm or leg
C. a large hairpiece
D. a noisy, large gathering of people

TEC44059

How to use: Display this page or give each student a copy of this page (or one card at a time) to work on during free time.

BRAIN BOOSTERS

LANGUAGE ARTS

Brain Booster 1

Unscramble the four words. Then place them in the grid so the last letter of each word is the first letter of the next.

A H R S   W S O H

T R S A   I H W T

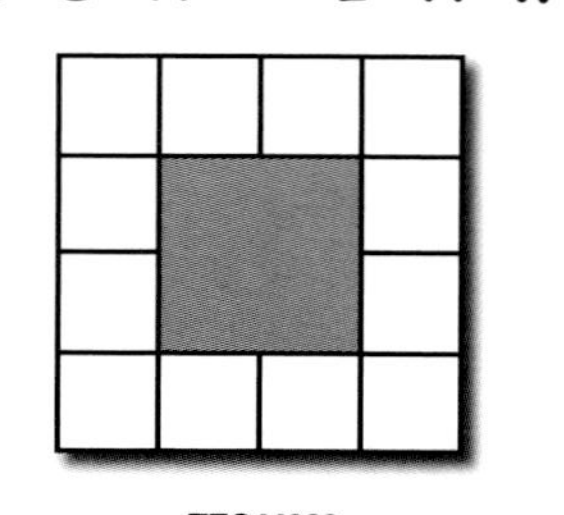

TEC44060

Brain Booster 2

Find ten words that are misspelled below. Write each word, spelling it correctly.

The inventer was begining to get discouragd. His eigth atempt at makeing a new proccess for purifyng elaments had faild.

TEC44060

Brain Booster 3

List five words that can be used as both nouns and verbs. Write one sentence for each word, using the word as a noun and as a verb.

I will play the part of Captain Hook in our class play, *Peter Pan*.

TEC44060

Brain Booster 4

Name eight or more foods that are orange colored.

TEC44060

Brain Booster 5

Find the mystery two-syllable word.

? ? ? ?

My first syllable rhymes with *rowed*. My second syllable rhymes with *mule*. I can sometimes be poisonous to eat. What am I?

TEC44060

Brain Booster 6

Look at the names of this capital city and US state.

L A [N S I N] G

M I C [H I G A] N

Write the rest of each city and state name.

A. [L A N / E O R]

B. [U N E / A S K]

C. [R A N / E N T]

D. [I D E / S L A]

TEC44060

Brain Booster 7

If you take the middle letter out of *metal*, you spell *meal*. Make a list of six more five-letter words from which you can take away the middle letter and spell another word.

metal

↓

meal

TEC44060

Brain Booster 8

Find two words that are synonyms hidden in each row of letters.

A. josadpfglumk

B. edgyefnervoush

C. taleapspringt

D. reachangesserevisenm

TEC44060

How to use: Display this page or give each student a copy of this page (or one card at a time) to work on during free time.

BRAIN BOOSTERS

LANGUAGE ARTS

Brain Booster 1

Write the word forms of numbers 1–10 in alphabetical order. Next, write the word forms of 10, 20, 30, 40, 50, 60, 70, 80, 90, and 100 in alphabetical order. Then combine the lists so that all the words are in alphabetical order.

TEC44061

Brain Booster 2

Write two four-letter words, one five-letter word, two six-letter words, and one seven-letter word that are synonyms for *small*. Then write one four-letter word, two five-letter words, one six-letter word, two seven-letter words, and one eight-letter word that are synonyms for *huge*.

SMALL **HUGE**

TEC44061

Brain Booster 3

Rearrange the letters *e, g, h, n, r, t, t, s,* and *s* to write the longest English word that only has one vowel. Then rearrange the letter sets below to write two words that each have five consonants in a row.

a b c e h i l p r t

e g h h i s t

TEC44061

Brain Booster 4

Draw a two-column chart labeled as shown and sort the words into the columns. Then choose one word from each column and explain your choices.

favored, snobbish, assertive, wealthy, pushy, educated, aggressive, conceited, prosperous, dynamic

Seems Positive	Seems Negative

TEC44061

Brain Booster 5

Make a list of 12 or more vivid verbs that name things you can do at a lake, a river, an ocean, or a swimming pool.

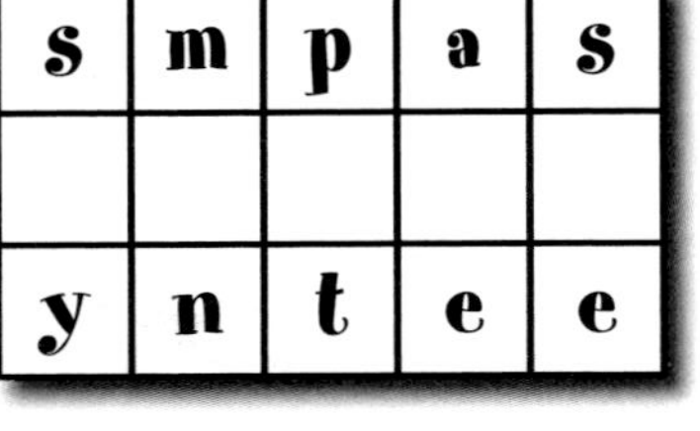

TEC44061

Brain Booster 6

Write a word that matches each definition below. For each word, use only the letters shown.

A. not fresh
B. stories
C. to take without permission
D. the smallest

e s t l a

TEC44061

Brain Booster 7

Write a letter in each box so that you will spell five common three-letter words going down and the five-letter name of a fruit going across.

s	m	p	a	s
y	n	t	e	e

TEC44061

Brain Booster 8

For each set of words shown, write three words that are related and rhyme with the original set.

Example: guess, snow, baby
yes, no, maybe

A. bread, kite, glue

B. worst, beckoned, heard

C. seas, horn, parrots

TEC44061

How to use: Display this page or give each student a copy of this page (or one card at a time) to work on during free time.

Use as center or free-time activities.

Capitalizing

YOUR MOVE

Rewrite each sentence below, correcting the capitalization errors.

1. Taylor is going to the chicago Chess championship.
2. She started playing Chess in second grade.
3. Taylor's first match is Saturday, the fifteenth, at 8:00.
4. She is scheduled to play josh wagner, a canadian player.
5. Taylor's Coach, abby McQueen, believes taylor will win the Championship.

One sentence has four errors, one has three errors, one has two errors, one has one error, and one has no errors.

TEC44056

Using a glossary

A SUPER SOURCE

Open a textbook to its glossary.
Choose a word and copy its entry.
Next, find the word in a dictionary and copy its entry.
How are the entries the same? How are they different? Draw a Venn diagram and compare the glossary and dictionary entries.

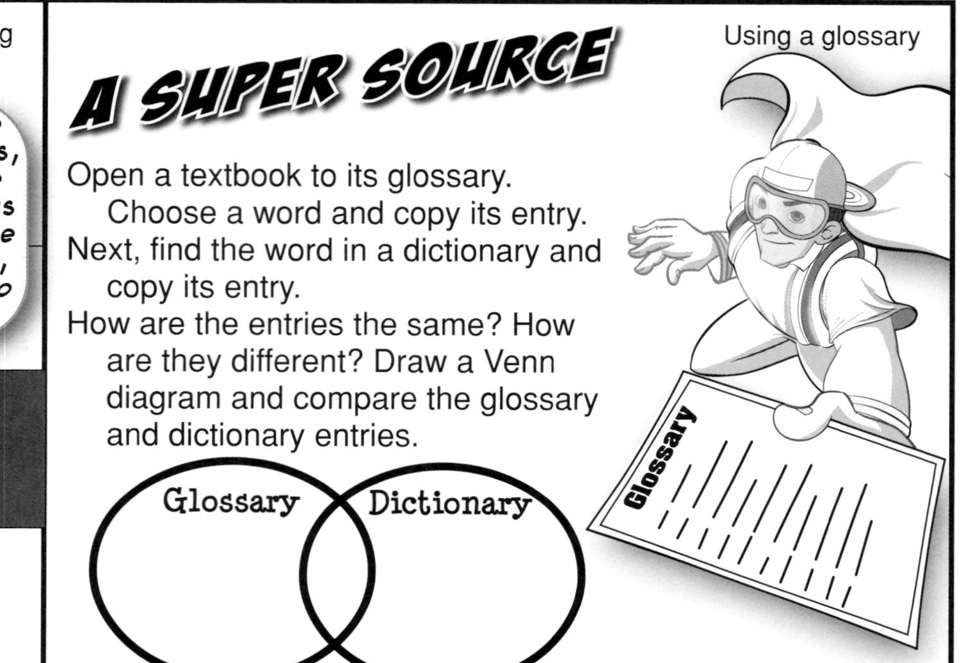

TEC44056

Sensory words

MAKE IT VIVID!

Draw five circles and label them *sight, touch, hearing, smell,* and *taste.* Sort the words shown into the circles. (Some words may be used more than once.) Then, using words that appeal to your senses, write a paragraph that describes the most disgusting thing you ever ate.

gritty
crinkled
sour
gooey
pungent
crunchy
musty
slimy
fuzzy
tasteless
smoky
fluffy
spongy
colorless
crackle
gurgle
murky
hiss
pop
burning
bitter
shimmering
salty
slosh
splash
peppery
dry
tart

TEC44056

Similes

IN OTHER WORDS

Write the simile from each sentence and draw a picture that illustrates it. Then tell what the simile really means.

1. Ms. Lane flits like a butterfly from desk to desk.
2. Anthony jogs as slow as a snail.
3. Emily's braces are as colorful as a rainbow.
4. Alexis's bus is so crowded she feels like a sardine.
5. Ryan's backpack is as heavy as a ton of bricks.
6. Mr. Ruiz's yellow tie is as bright as the sun.

TEC44056

Similes, metaphors

A Spooky Night

Copy each sentence starter and complete it with a simile or metaphor.

1. The jack-o'-lantern's smile is ___.
2. The moon glows ___.
3. With every step, the leaves crunch ___.
4. The street lights flickered ___.
5. All the neighborhood dogs howl ___.
6. The chilly breeze is ___.

Hint: A simile compares two things using *like* or *as*: She was as mad as a hornet. A metaphor compares two different things without using *like* or *as*: The thunderstorm was an angry beast.

TEC44057

Responding to a prompt

Whodunit?

Imagine that you find a bunch of strange footprints in your yard. Copy the organizer shown and fill it out with details about what might have walked all over your yard. Then write a short story about the mystery creature.

Who?
What?
How?
?
Where?
Why?
When?

TEC44057

Informational text features

Thumbing Through

1. Write the title of the book and the date it was published.
2. On what page does the table of contents begin? The index?
3. Draw a Venn diagram. Use it to compare the book's index and table of contents.

Index | Table of Contents

4. How many pages are in the book's glossary? How is the glossary different from a dictionary?
5. Find an example of each feature below. Copy the example and list the page on which you find it.

   A. boldface print
   B. color print
   C. bulleted list
   D. subheading
   E. italicized text
   F. caption

TEC44057

Explanatory writing

Tell It Like It Is

Pretend you've just been visited by an alien from outer space. It wants to know how to celebrate Thanksgiving Day on Earth. List the steps the alien should follow in order to have a happy Thanksgiving.

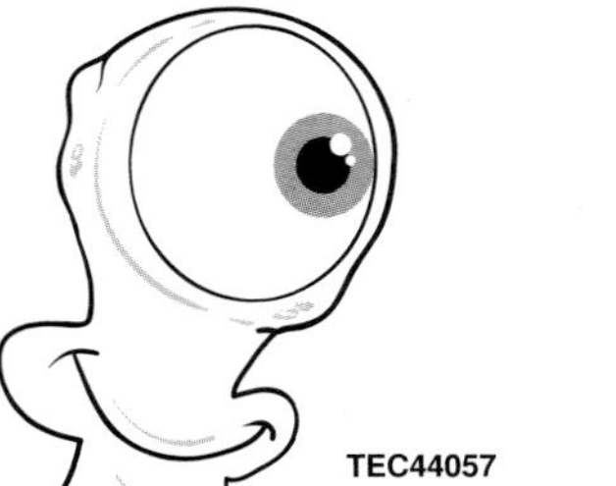

TEC44057

Language Arts Activity Cards

Use as center or free-time activities.

Hyperbole

RAINING CATS AND DOGS

Illustrate each sentence. Then tell what is being exaggerated.

1. My school bus is so old; it has wooden wheels instead of tires!
2. We'll be standing in line for years.
3. I'm so hungry; I could eat a house!
4. I need a new bike; my bike's a hundred years old.
5. Derek has a ton of money.

TEC44058

Suffixes *-ible, -able*

COMFORTABLE?

Copy each word below and underline the suffix *-ible* or *-able*. Then tell what you think the word means.

Hint: The suffixes *-ible* and *-able* can mean *fit for*, *can be done*, or *liable to*.

dependable	**renewable**
edible	**responsible**
flexible	**sensible**
horrible	**terrible**
impossible	**uncomfortable**
laughable	**visible**
likable	**washable**
predictable	**workable**

TEC44058

Sentence fragments

REINDEER GAMES

Add a subject, predicate, or both to fix each fragment below.

A. Rudolph's bright red nose.
B. Following Dasher, Prancer, and Vixen.
C. Eight reindeer pulling a bright red sleigh.
D. Too foggy to fly.
E. And then, Donner and Blitzen.
F. Comet and Cupid anxiously.

TEC44058

Writing a persuasive letter

Powers of Persuasion

Write a letter to convince the principal that students at your school should use laptops instead of textbooks.

First, brainstorm three good reasons the principal should agree with you.
Next, make a list of facts and opinions to support each reason.
Then write a strong lead paragraph to introduce your opinion.
After that, for each reason, write a paragraph that includes supporting facts and opinions.
Finally, write a concluding paragraph that restates your opinion and encourages the principal to agree with you.

TEC44058

Problem and solution

WORKING IT OUT

Choose a main character. Then choose a problem. How can this character solve the problem? Write a story about how the character solves the problem.

MAIN CHARACTERS

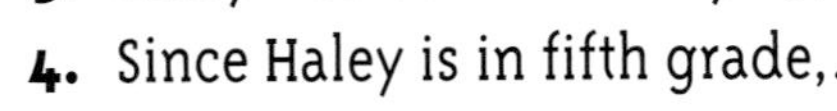
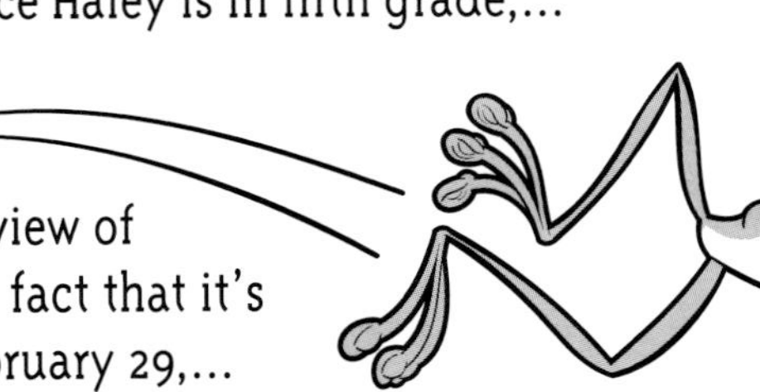

PROBLEMS

- My hamster, Hubert, chewed up my homework!
- I can't find my uniform, and the game starts in 30 minutes!
- My mom finally said I could have a cat, but I can't stop sneezing!

TEC44059

Cause and effect

WHAT A LEAP!

Copy and complete each sentence starter. Then circle the cause and underline the effect.

1. Because leap year is every four years,...
2. The year 2012 is a leap year, so...
3. Haley was born February 29, 2000,...
4. Since Haley is in fifth grade,...
5. In view of the fact that it's February 29,...

TEC44059

Word analysis

Ancient Origins

Look up each boldfaced term in the sentences below. Three of the words have been used incorrectly. If the boldfaced word in the sentence is not correct, copy the sentence and circle the boldfaced word. Then tell why the word is incorrect.

1. Feeding the dog is the most **Herculean** of my daily chores.
2. Anita really has the **Midas touch**; she earned $250.00 selling lemonade last summer.
3. You can use my **atlas** to look up your math vocabulary words.
4. Trying to clean my sister's room is a **titanic** task.
5. It's a good idea to **panic** every morning before school.

TEC44059

Verbs, collective nouns

All Together!

Write ten different sentences. For each one, choose a collective noun and a verb. Use them to write a silly sentence.

Hint: Most collective nouns are considered single units, so the verb will be singular.
The ***Flock*** of seagulls finally ***finds*** the fish.

Noun	Verb
audience	collapse
band	crawl
bunch	dunk
family	find
flock	fly
group	gnaw
herd	gripe
set	hobble
swarm	parade
team	rally

TEC44059

Language Arts Activity Cards

Use as center or free-time activities.

Editing for capitalization

Of Capital Importance

There are no capital letters in the paragraph below. Rewrite the paragraph, correcting 30 capitalization errors.

washington, dc, is the united states capital. this unique city is not part of any of the country's 50 states. when it was time to choose a permanent location for the nation's government, the members of congress had a hard time agreeing on a site. northerners didn't want the capital to be in the south. southerners didn't want it to be in the north. congress passed the residence act of 1790, which gave president washington the power to choose the spot. he chose land north of the potomac river that belonged to maryland and land south of the potomac river that belonged to virginia. both states turned their land over to the federal government. then the city was named for the president, and the area around it was called the district of columbia, abbreviated as dc.

TEC44060

Using a thesaurus

Pick of the Bunch

Using a thesaurus, look up each word. For each word, find three or more synonyms and at least one antonym. Draw a three-column chart, label it as shown, and list the words you find.

Word	Synonyms	Antonym(s)
silly	ditzy, frivolous, scatterbrained	serious

cold clean sad

bright pretty ask

TEC44060

Research

Up Close and Personal

Copy the questions below. Use reference materials to answer them. Then write a want ad on behalf of a grizzly bear that needs a new home. In the want ad, describe the perfect habitat that has everything the bear needs.

1. About how big is an adult male grizzly bear? An adult female?
2. What are five of the main things a grizzly bear eats?
3. How do grizzly bears spend winter?
4. How have people affected grizzly bears?

TEC44060

Descriptive writing

Alien Encounter

Pretend you are a reporter for the space journal *Solar News Flash*, and you've been assigned to cover the First Annual Intergalactic Conference on Planet Alpha I. Draw and complete an organizer like the one shown to describe the most interesting delegate you meet at the conference. Then write a short article describing the alien ambassador and add a captioned picture of it in action at the conference.

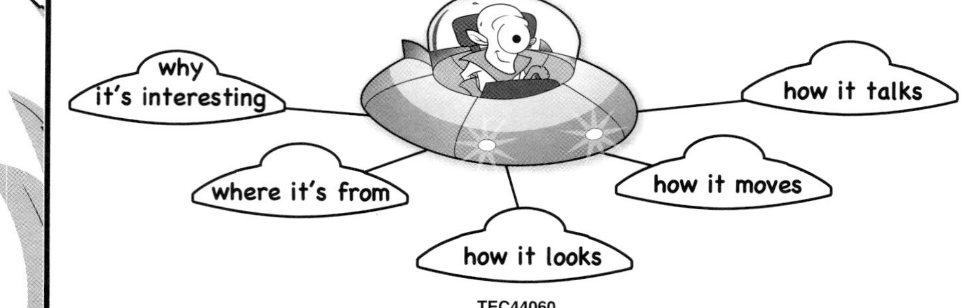

TEC44060

©The Mailbox® • TEC44060 • April/May 2012 • Key p. 308

Language Arts Activity Cards

Use as center or free-time activities.

Greek and Latin roots, affixes

Rooting Around

For each Greek or Latin root below, list two or more words that include the root. Then write each word's definition.

astr (star)
fract (to break)
auto (self)
graph (writing)
bene (good)
junct (to join)
dict (to say)
struct (to build)
eco (house)
techn (skill or craft)

TEC44061

Main idea

MAIN IDEA CAPERS

Choose a current reading selection. Think about what the author wanted to share with his or her readers. Then create a cartoon that shows the main idea and three or more supporting details.

TEC44061

Prepositional phrases

Out of the Box

Write ten or more sentences that tell where the hamster might be in relation to the box. Use a prepositional phrase in each sentence and then underline the phrase.

The hamster nibbled through the box.

in, on, around, behind, from, near, beside, beyond, inside, past, beneath, by, onto, out of, under, outside, over, up to

TEC44061

Narrative writing

WHAT A RIDE!

You've just been picked to be one of the first 25 people to ride the Zombie Coaster. It's a brand-new ride, and it's supposed to be one of the top-ten scariest roller coaster rides in the world. The owners have invited 24 others and you to ride the Zombie Coaster before it opens to the public. Imagine that it's the night before your ride. How do you feel? What are you thinking? Write an email to your best friend about the upcoming ride.

TEC44061

6 Simply Super Ideas for Reading & Language Arts

1 Pop Goes the Punctuation!

Punctuation

This review booklet packs a punch! Before starting, designate the punctuation rules for which students are held accountable. Then guide each child to review the rules and follow the directions shown to make his own reminder booklet.

Patricia Twohey, Smithfield, RI

Materials: construction paper, scissors, glue, stapler

Directions:

1. For each punctuation rule, make a 6" x 2" rectangular page and a 1" x 4" strip.
2. On each page, record one rule and write a sentence that illustrates it.
3. Then accordion-fold one strip and draw the matching punctuation mark on the top section. Glue the strip to the matching page.
4. To assemble the booklet, cut out one 12" x 2" rectangle and fold it over the pages to make a cover. Staple the pages inside the cover and title the booklet "Pop Goes the Punctuation!"

2 An Acrostic Reminder

Character analysis

Use this kid-friendly acrostic to help students examine a story's main character. Display the acrostic shown and use the questions to analyze the main character in a current class reading. Then have each child copy the acrostic on a strip of sturdy paper to make a bookmark that's also a handy reminder.

Patricia Twohey

Connect (Who does the character remind you of?)
Heart (What does the character feel?)
Appearance (What does the character look like?)
Relationships (How does the character relate to other characters?)
Actions (What does the character do?)
Conflict (What problem does the character face?)
Talk (What does the character say?)
Event (Which story event is the most important for the character?)
Resolution (How does the character resolve the problem?)

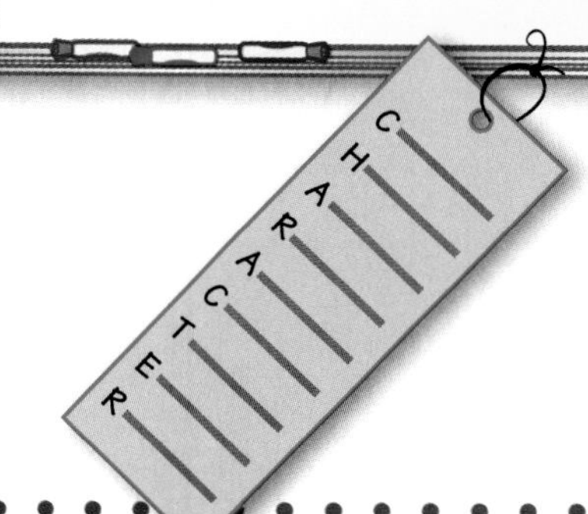

3 What's on the Menu?

Spelling

Use a menu of activities to help sharpen students' spelling skills! Post exercises that can be used with any spelling list, such as those shown. Assign each task a number. Then start class by having a student roll a die to determine the day's spelling practice.

adapted from an idea by Satina Smith, Timber Drive Elementary, Garner, NC

Spelling Activities Menu

Roll of 1 = Write each word. Then write the word again but draw a star after each syllable.
Roll of 2 = Create a word search using all the words on your list. Then solve it.
Roll of 3 = Write a story using all the words on your list. Underline each word.
Roll of 4 = Write the words on your list in alphabetical order. Then circle each silent letter.
Roll of 5 = Write each word. Then write the word's part or parts of speech.
Roll of 6 = Write each word. Then write a fraction that tells how many of the word's letters are vowels.

4 Connect the Dots!

Literature response

For this idea, program a copy of page 62 with the dates book reports will be due this year. Then copy the page for each child and put the pages in a binder. Several weeks before each due date, have each student choose and circle a genre on her page. Next, have the child select a matching book, record its title, and connect the title and genre dots. Then the student chooses a project, circles it, and connects the genre to the project and the project to the due date. She records the information in her planner, returns the page to the binder, and starts reading!

LaVone Novotny, Liberty Elementary, Caledonia, OH

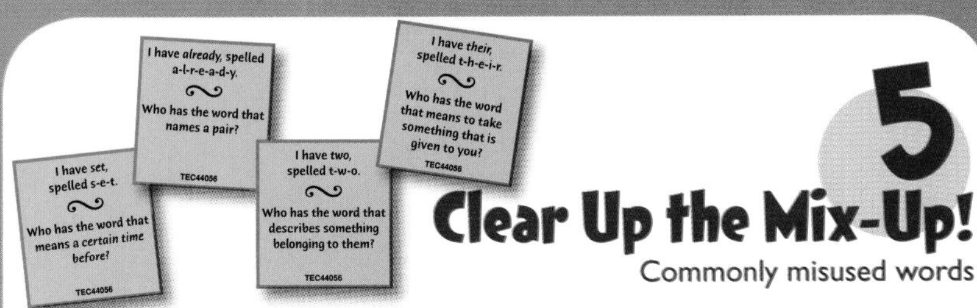

5 Clear Up the Mix-Up!

Commonly misused words

Want to help students differentiate words that are often confused? Try this small-group game. Have the students in each group cut apart the cards from a copy of page 63. Next, have the students shuffle and deal the cards so that each player has the same number. To play, one student reads aloud the question on one of his cards. The player with the card that answers the question reads the answer and then reads the question on his card. Play continues until all the cards have been read. If all the students' matches are correct, the last question will match the answer from the first card.

LaVone Novotny

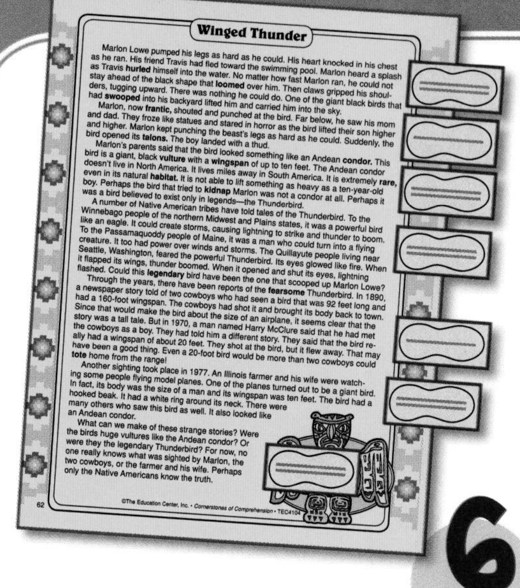

Winged Thunder

Marlon Lowe pumped his legs as hard as he could. His heart knocked in his chest as he ran. His friend Travis had fled toward the swimming pool. Marlon heard a splash as Travis **hurled** himself into the water. No matter how fast Marlon ran, he could not stay ahead of the black shape that **loomed** over him. Then claws gripped his shoulders, tugging upward. There was nothing he could do. One of the giant black birds that had **swooped** into his backyard lifted him and carried him into the sky.

Marlon, now **frantic,** shouted and punched at the bird. Far below, he saw his mom and dad. They froze like statues and stared in horror as the bird lifted their son higher and higher. Marlon kept punching the beast's legs as hard as he could. Suddenly, the bird opened its **talons.** The boy landed with a thud.

Marlon's parents said that the bird looked something like an Andean **condor.** This bird is a giant, black **vulture** with a **wingspan** of up to ten feet. The Andean condor doesn't live in North America. It lives miles away in South America. It is extremely **rare,** even in its natural **habitat.** It is not able to lift something as heavy as a ten-year-old boy. Perhaps the bird that tried to **kidnap** Marlon was not a condor at all. Perhaps it was a bird believed to exist only in legends—the Thunderbird.

A number of Native American tribes have told tales of the Thunderbird. To the Winnebago people of the northern Midwest and Plains states, it was a powerful bird like an eagle. It could create storms, causing lightning to strike and thunder to boom. To the Passamaquoddy people of Maine, it was a man who could turn into a flying creature. It too had power over winds and storms. The Quillayute people living near Seattle, Washington, feared the powerful Thunderbird. Its eyes glowed like fire. When it flapped its wings, thunder boomed. When it opened and shut its eyes, lightning flashed. Could this **legendary** bird have been the one that scooped up Marlon Lowe?

Through the years, there have been reports of the **fearsome** Thunderbird. In 1890, a newspaper story told of two cowboys who had seen a bird that was 92 feet long and had a 160-foot wingspan. The cowboys had shot it and brought its body back to town. Since that would make the bird about the size of an airplane, it seems clear that the story was a tall tale. But in 1970, a man named Harry McClure said that he had met the cowboys as a boy. They had told him a different story. They said that the bird really had a wingspan of about 20 feet. They shot at the bird, but it flew away. That may have been a good thing. Even a 20-foot bird would be more than two cowboys could **tote** home from the range!

Another sighting took place in 1977. An Illinois farmer and his wife were watching some people flying model planes. One of the planes turned out to be a giant bird. In fact, its body was the size of a man and its wingspan was ten feet. The bird had a hooked beak. It had a white ring around its neck. There were many others who saw this bird as well. It also looked like an Andean condor.

What can we make of these strange stories? Were the birds huge vultures like the Andean condor? Or were they the legendary Thunderbird? For now, no one really knows what was sighted by Marlon, the two cowboys, or the farmer and his wife. Perhaps only the Native Americans know the truth.

62 ©The Education Center, Inc. • *Cornerstones of Comprehension* • TEC4104

6 In a Nutshell

Summarizing

Here's a quick tip for guiding students to summarize their reading instead of retelling it. To begin, assign a short reading selection and give each child a sticky note for each of the selection's paragraphs. Next, have the student draw a peanut shape on each sticky note and place the note next to a paragraph. After the child reads each paragraph, he identifies its main topic, jotting a word or two inside the peanut. (The shape's limited space encourages the student to be brief.) When the student finishes the selection, he uses his notes to write a summary that recaps his reading in a nutshell!

Patricia Twohey, Smithfield, RI

Name ______________________

Date ______________________

CONNECT THE DOTS!

BOOK TITLE	BOOK GENRE	BOOK REPORT PROJECT	DUE DATE
	autobiography	poster to advertise the book	
	biography	letter to the author	
	diary or journal	comic strip about the climax	
	fable	poem that describes book's main idea	
	fantasy	timeline of important events	
	historical fiction	alternate ending	
	informational	scrapbook about important details	
	legend	multimedia summary	
	mystery	news article about the book	
	mythology	model that explains book's information	
	narrative	script for play about book	
	play	diagram of important process from book	
	poetry	flyer that encourages others to read the book	
	realistic fiction	diorama of most important scene	
	science fiction	song about story's theme or main idea	
	tall tale	puppet show about book	

Note to the teacher: Use with "Connect the Dots!" on page 61.

Easily Confused Words Cards

Use with "Clear Up the Mix-Up!" on page 61.

I have *set*, spelled s-e-t.

Who has the word that means *a certain time before?*

TEC44056

I have *already*, spelled a-l-r-e-a-d-y.

Who has the word that names a pair?

TEC44056

I have *two*, spelled t-w-o.

Who has the word that describes something belonging to them?

TEC44056

I have *their*, spelled t-h-e-i-r.

Who has the word that means *to take something that is given to you?*

TEC44056

I have *accept*, spelled a-c-c-e-p-t.

Who has the word that is a punctuation mark used to separate items in a series?

TEC44056

I have *comma*, spelled c-o-m-m-a.

Who has the word that means *at that time?*

TEC44056

I have *then*, spelled t-h-e-n.

Who has the word that means *a dry area without many plants?*

TEC44056

I have *desert*, spelled d-e-s-e-r-t.

Who has the contraction for *they are?*

TEC44056

I have *they're*, spelled t-h-e-y-'-r-e.

Who has the word for a baseball player who throws the ball to the batter?

TEC44056

I have *pitcher*, spelled p-i-t-c-h-e-r.

Who has the word that means *to stop doing something?*

TEC44056

I have *quit*, spelled q-u-i-t.

Who has the word used to compare two things?

TEC44056

I have *than*, spelled t-h-a-n.

Who has the word for being in a deep state of unconsciousness?

TEC44056

I have *coma*, spelled c-o-m-a.

Who has the word that means *to take a seat?*

TEC44056

I have *sit*, spelled s-i-t.

Who has the words that mean that everything has been prepared?

TEC44056

I have *all ready*, spelled a-l-l r-e-a-d-y.

Who has the word for a photograph or painting?

TEC44056

I have *picture*, spelled p-i-c-t-u-r-e.

Who has the word for sweet food often eaten after a meal?

TEC44056

I have *dessert*, spelled d-e-s-s-e-r-t.

Who has the word that means that something is left out?

TEC44056

I have *except*, spelled e-x-c-e-p-t.

Who has the word that means *to misplace something?*

TEC44056

I have *lose*, spelled l-o-s-e.

Who has the word that means *in that place?*

TEC44056

I have *there*, spelled t-h-e-r-e.

Who has the preposition that means *toward?*

TEC44056

I have *to*, spelled t-o.

Who has the word that means *not making any noise?*

TEC44056

I have *quiet*, spelled q-u-i-e-t.

Who has the word for talking in a normal voice?

TEC44056

I have *aloud*, spelled a-l-o-u-d.

Who has the word that describes something we own?

TEC44056

I have *our*, spelled o-u-r.

Who has the word that means *not firmly attached?*

TEC44056

I have *loose*, spelled l-o-o-s-e.

Who has the word that means *also?*

TEC44056

I have *too*, spelled t-o-o.

Who has the word that means that you have permission?

TEC44056

I have *allowed*, spelled a-l-l-o-w-e-d.

Who has a present tense form of *be?*

TEC44056

I have *are*, spelled a-r-e.

Who has the word that means *to have thrown?*

TEC44056

I have *threw*, spelled t-h-r-e-w.

Who has the preposition that means *in one side and out the other?*

TEC44056

I have *through*, spelled t-h-r-o-u-g-h.

Who has the word that means *to put something in a place?*

TEC44056

A Way with Words

Want your students to use easily confused words the right way? Check out these creative ideas!

Easily Confused Words

aloud, allowed	miner, minor
ate, eight	oar, ore, or
bear, bare	past, passed
blue, blew	quiet, quit, quite
bored, board	right, write
capital, capitol	sent, scent, cent
chose, choose	sit, set
desert, dessert	than, then
die, dye	their, there, they're
good, well	to, too, two
hole, whole	waist, waste
hour, our	ware, wear
its, it's	weather, whether
knight, night	where, were
knot, not	who's, whose
loan, lone	your, you're
loose, lose	

• Nifty Mnemonics

Give your students memory tools! First, review with students that *mnemonics* are words, sentences, or songs that can help make something easier to remember. Next, give each pair of students a copy of a mnemonic strip from page 65 and have the duo create a mini poster that advertises the mnemonic. Display students' work on a board titled "Nifty Mnemonics." **To extend the activity,** display a list of words such as those shown and challenge each twosome to create mnemonics for one set of words that will help students remember which word is which. As time allows, have each duo share its work. **Ann E. Fisher, Toledo, OH**

• Blow Out a Candle

Tired of seeing *were* and *weather* being used in place of *where* and *whether*? Try this! Have each child imagine she is holding a candle. Then lead her to repeat the words shown below. When the student says a word that begins with just *w*, very little air is expelled. So the flame on the imaginary candle would not be affected. However, when the child says a word that begins with *wh*, more air is expelled and she could blow out the flame on the imaginary candle. After the exercise, remind students to use the candle to decide whether a word needs *wh* or just *w*.

waist, waste, weather, whether, ware, way, weigh, wear, where, were, who's, whose

• A Classroom Challenge

For this week-long activity, post easily confused words, such as those shown. Also place a supply of index cards and a basket nearby. Then challenge students to find all the words in their reading during the week. When a child finds a listed word, he copies the sentence on an index card, underlines the word, and names the source. Then he signs his name, puts the card in the basket, and draws a check mark beside the matching posted word. At the end of the week, check the list and award students one extra minute of recess for every five words they found. Then use the cards to create a terrific classroom resource! Just punch holes in the cards, arrange them in alphabetical order, and slide them onto a loose leaf ring. **Ann E. Fisher**

"How could he say aloud what was in his heart?"
Redwall, page 14
Noah

"Decide whether the boldface part is the cause or the effect."
"Breakfast Banquet" worksheet
Kristen

Use with "Nifty Mnemonics" on page 64.

desert • The de**s**ert is **s**andy. (There is one ***s*** in ***s****andy* and in *de****s****ert*.)
dessert • My de**ss**ert is **s**uper **s**weet! (There are two ***s***'s in ***s****uper* ***s****weet* and in *de****ss****ert*.)
it's • **It is** time. **It's** time. (Reminder that *it's* is the contraction for *it is*.)
its • Whose? **Its**! (*Its* without an apostrophe is possessive.)
lose • **L**ost **o**bject—**s**earch **e**verywhere! (Use the words' initial letters to spell *lose*.)
loose • l**oose** g**oose** (The rhyming words have the same endings.)
sit • **Sit** down. (*Sit* means to rest in a seated position.)
set • **Set** your hat here. (*Set* means to put something in a certain place.)
their • **T**hey **h**ave **e**ight **i**cky **r**ats. (Use the words' initial letters to spell *their*.)
there • Leave **here**. Go t**here**. (The word *here* is tucked inside *there*.)
they're • **They are** home. **They're** home! (Reminder that *they're* is the contraction for *they are*.)
through • Y**ou** and Hu**gh** go thr**ough**. (*Thr****ou****gh* and *y****ou*** have *ou* vowel patterns, and *Hu****gh*** has the same ending as *throu****gh***.)
threw • I thr**ew**. It fl**ew**! (The rhyming words have the same endings.)
you're • **You are** home. **You're** home. (Reminder that *you're* is the contraction for *you are*.)
your • **Y**ou **o**wn **u**nusual **r**ats. (Use the words' initial letters to spell *your*.)

1 **Write a Song!** As a class, brainstorm a list of familiar, simple tunes, such as "Twinkle, Twinkle, Little Star." Then have each student choose one of the tunes and write new lyrics for it based on important details from the book he read.

2 **Give a character a superpower!** Have each student choose a character from his book and imagine a superpower that the character could have used. Next, guide the child to draw the character with the superpower. Then have the student write a description of the character's power and tell how the character could have used it to solve at least one of his or her problems.

8 SIMPLY AWESOME Book-Report Ideas

Want your students to create book reports that show they've read the books? Try these no-fuss ideas that can be used with any book at any time!

3 **Draw conclusions!** Have each student choose one of the following brain-stretching questions and then write her response in a letter to the author.

- How would the book change if you suddenly appeared as one of its characters?
- How would the book change if it took place in your hometown?
- How would the book change if the setting were 100 years in the future?
- How would the book change if the main character were part of your family?

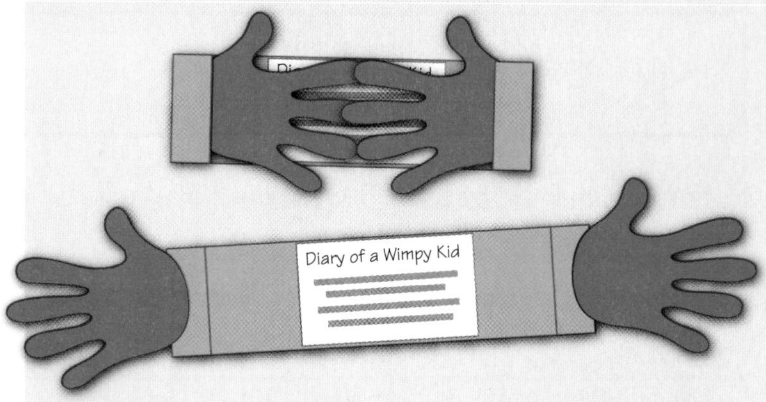

4 **Make it hands-on!** Have each student write a paragraph that describes the part of the book she found most interesting. Have her write her final copy on a large index card. Then have the child trace both of her hands on construction paper and cut out the tracings. Next, have the student glue the hand shapes to the ends of a 4" x 18" construction paper strip. Finally, have the child glue her card in the middle of the strip and fold the ends of the strip so that the hands seem to be holding the card. If desired, post students' work on a board titled "Books That Really Held Our Interest."

5 **Make a book!** Have each student develop a list of six or more story events he thinks are most crucial to the plot. Next, guide the child to illustrate each event on a separate sheet of paper. Then have him create front and back cover pages and bind the illustrations together to create a wordless picture book that retells the story.

6 **Keep a class list!** On a sheet of poster board, list your students' names, leaving plenty of blank space beside each one. Next, laminate the poster and place a wipe-off marker nearby. Each time a student finishes a book, have her write the title and author's name next to her name, add two comments about the book, and rate it (one to four stars). When the child finishes a different book, have her wipe away the first entry to make room for a new one. Show students that reading is a lifelong pleasure by including your name and an entry about a book you're reading!

7 **Make a book kit!** Have each child read a book from your classroom library. When the student finishes reading, guide her to write five questions about the book on index cards and create a corresponding answer key. Next, have the child put the cards and the book in a large resealable bag and give you the answer key to keep at your desk. Put the book kits in a basket near the classroom library and encourage students to complete them for bonus book-report credits.

8 **Entice others to read the book!** Have each student choose an exciting passage from his book and then create a 15-second ad promoting the book. Next, set aside time for each student to read his passage and present his ad.

Advertising Buzz Words

amazing	love
beautiful	magic
colossal	new
discover	proven
excellent	remarkable
fascinating	revolutionary
genuine	sensational
greatest	terrific
guarantee	tremendous
latest	wonderful

A Picture-Perfect Skill Builder

5 ways to use the picture on page 69!

Build **visual memory** skills! Display a copy of the picture for 20 seconds. Then cover it. Challenge students to list all the picture's details they can remember. Next, display the picture again for only 10 seconds. Then have students add details to their lists. Display the picture a final time and have students compare their lists with the picture. Follow up with a discussion of students' results and reactions.

Focus on **descriptive** writing! Have each student write ten descriptive sentences about what she sees in the picture. Then have each child read her most descriptive sentence aloud.

Give students practice using **strong verbs**. Guide each student to list 15 verbs that tell what characters in the picture are doing. Then have each pair of students combine their lists and work together to make sure each verb is vivid.

Guide each student to list 20 **nouns** she sees. Next, have students share their lists, identifying each noun as common or proper. Create a two-column chart of students' listed nouns. Then post the chart along with a copy of the picture and challenge early finishers to find and name all the nouns in the picture.

Have each student write an **imaginative narrative** that explains the picture. Bind students' final copies along with a copy of the picture in a class book titled "A Character-Filled Day."

Look...Observe...Examine...Scrutinize

Note to the teacher: Use with "A Picture-Perfect Skill Builder" on page 68.

6 Skill-Building Ideas to Use With Any Old Stack of Magazines

Review Parts of Speech!

Have each student choose a magazine. Next, have the child fold a sheet of paper in half and then in thirds to create six sections. Have her label each section as shown. Then challenge each student to find and cut out five or more examples for each category and glue them in place.

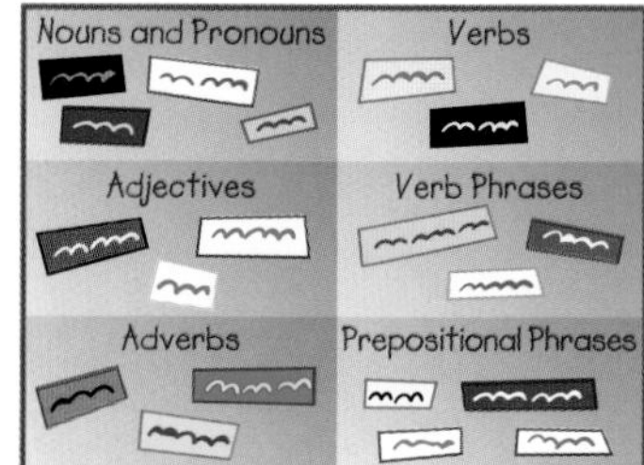

Fix Sentence Fragments!

Have each student find ten titles that are sentence fragments. Then have the child revise each one to make a complete sentence.

Find Great Lead Sentences!

Have pairs of students skim the lead sentences that have been written to grab a reader's attention. When the partners find a great lead sentence, have them highlight the sentence and tear out the page. Follow up by having each duo read aloud its mentor sentences. Then staple the pages inside a folder and place the folder of inspiration at your writing center.

Build Vocabulary!

Have each student label a page of his journal "Fab Vocab" and skim a magazine's ads to find ten attention-getting terms. Have him cut out each engaging word and glue it onto the journal page. Then guide the child to look up the word, jot its definition on the page, and name an occasion for which he might use the word. **Julie Kaiser, Floyds Knobs Elementary, Floyds Knobs, IN**

Ramp up Descriptive Writing Skills!

Cut out several interesting pictures and slide each one in a plastic page protector. Then have each student choose a picture and list as many nouns in the picture as possible. Next, have the child study the picture and add a vivid adjective to each noun. Finally, have the student write a paragraph that thoroughly describes the picture.

Reinforce Spelling Patterns!

When you introduce or review a spelling pattern, give each pair of students a magazine. Then challenge the partners to find and cut out words with that spelling pattern. Set a time limit and then have students read their words aloud. Declare the partners who found the most words the champs and give them a small prize.

(compound words)

Comprehension-Building Prompts to Use With ANY Book

Would you give this author a gold star for using colorful, interesting words? Why or why not?

Choose a story event that seems very real. Why does it seem so real?

What important events happened before this story began? Explain.

Which character in the story do you like the least? Why?

Describe the story's setting. Would the main problem be the same in another setting? Explain.

What do you think would be the main character's favorite thing to do after school? Explain.

If you went on a field trip to this story's setting, what would you be sure to bring with you? Why?

Describe an important event from the story as if you were a witness to it.

For whom do you think the author wrote this book? Explain.

Is this book easy to read, just right, or challenging? Explain.

Study the features of this text (diagrams, illustrations, bold print, titles, graphs, maps, charts, timelines, etc.). Which feature best helps you understand what you read? How does it help you?

What are three ways this book is different from the last nonfiction book you read?

Choose three fascinating facts from your reading. Paraphrase each one and then explain your choices.

Do you think the facts in this book are true? What could you do to find out? Explain.

What is the most important thing to know about this book? Explain.

Make a table of contents that lists the most important facts you have read so far.

How to use: Display the prompts after each independent reading session. Then have each child choose a prompt and write a thoughtful response.

Comprehension-Building Prompts to Use With ANY Book

Name five nouns that are important in this story. Why is each one important?

If the main character asked you to help her or him solve the story's problem, what would you do?

Find an example of figurative language in your reading. What does it describe? Does it make the story better? Explain.

What is the story about? Do you think this is the story's theme? Explain.

Is the main character telling this story? If so, why do you think the author chose to have the main character tell the story? If not, why do you think the author chose not to have the main character tell the story?

What is this story's genre? How do you know?

Folk
FANTASY
Horror
COMEDY
ADVENTURE

A common theme for children's books is how a child deals with growing up. Does that theme fit this story? Why or why not?

If you were the main character, what would you do next?

Is this text about something from the past, present, or future? How do you know?

If you made a vocabulary list for this book, which six words do you think would be most important? Why?

Choose four facts from the book. Do you believe each fact is true? Why or why not?

Could this book help a science teacher? Why or why not?

Think about the author's purpose for writing this book. What is he or she trying to accomplish? Does the author succeed? How do you know?

In an informational text, there may be questions at the end of a chapter. Write six questions about your reading. Then write the answers.

What are the three most important points from today's reading?

Fill a web with adjectives and adverbs that describe this topic.

adverb
adverb
adjective
adjective
topic
adjective
adverb
adjective
adjective

How to use: Display the prompts after each independent reading session and have each child choose a prompt and respond to it.

WRITING

WRITE NOW!

September 14, 2011
Bob Katz
28 Friendly Paws St.
Crittertown, USA
Dear Mr. Katz,
I am applying for the pet sitter position you advertised.
I have three pets (two dogs a cat), and I took care of my neig cat this summer.
I love animals and will be a t pet sitter.
Sincerely,
Jenna

"Write" for the Job

Letter of introduction

For this idea, display a copy of the classified ad clipping from the bottom of page 75. Then guide each student to choose the job in which she is most interested and for which she is most qualified. Next, guide the child to draft a letter to introduce herself and her skills. Have her type her final copy. Then post students' letters on a display titled "Need Help? We're Just 'Write' for the Job!"

Kelli Gowdy, High Point, NC

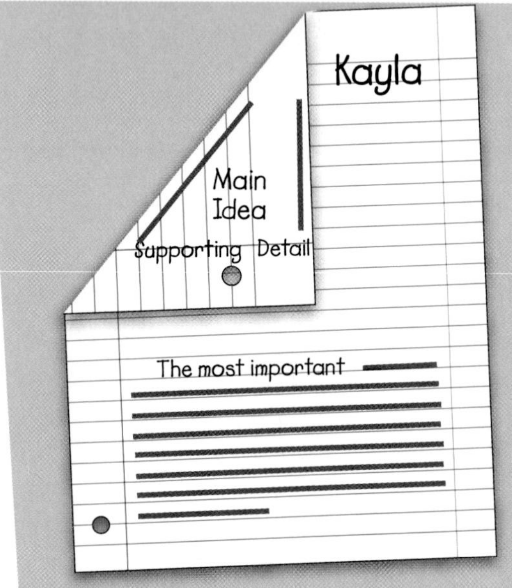

Triangle Tip

Summarizing

Want your students' summaries to focus on the main points rather than retelling everything they read? Try this! When it's time to summarize a reading selection, have each child fold the left corner of a sheet of paper down about six inches to create a right triangle. Next, guide the student to write the selection's main idea in the triangle's center. Then have the child write one supporting detail along each of the triangle's edges. After that, the child uses her triangular notes to write a one-paragraph summary on the lines below.

Ann E. Fisher, Toledo, OH

- Draw a treasure map. Then write a story about how the treasure ended up where it is.
- Draw a family of aliens and their spaceship. Then write a story about their first trip to the planet Earth.
- Draw a well-known person you admire, such as the president, an author, an athlete, an artist, or an actor. Then imagine you get to spend an entire day with the person. Write a story about the day.
- Draw your bedroom. Describe an interesting object in your room. Write a story about how you got it.
- Draw a dragon. Write a story about how you find the dragon and what you do together.

Doodle-Do!

Writing motivation, narrative writing

These fun prompts "draw" students into writing! Display one of the prompts shown and set aside ten minutes for students to draw. Then guide each child to set his drawing beside his journal and start writing in response to the prompt. Follow up by having each student take his work through the remaining steps of the writing process.

Jackie Beaudry, Getzville, NY

Have Tips; Will Write

Writing tips

Find an old suitcase or briefcase and cut out the labels from a copy of page 76. Then discuss each writing tip with students and tape its label onto the suitcase so it resembles a travel sticker. If desired, stock the case with writing materials and tuck it into a corner near your class library where it can become a portable writing center!

Ann E. Fisher, Toledo, OH

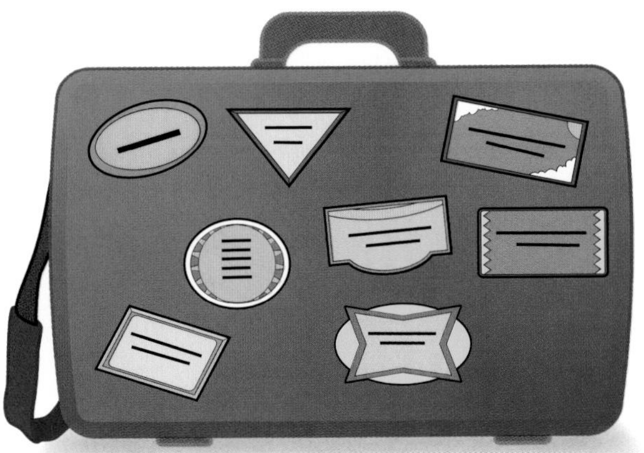

Editing's in the Bag!

Editing, revising

For these squashy reminders, purchase a container of inexpensive foam shapes. Next, review with students editing and revising tasks such as those shown. Give each child a plastic resealable bag and a foam shape for each task you want him to practice. Guide the child to use a pen to write each task on a shape and put the shapes in his plastic bag. Have the student keep the bag in his writing folder until he's ready to edit his work. Then have him take out a shape and hold on to it while he performs that task. After each task, the child sets the shape aside and draws another one. Once the student has edited his writing, he returns the shapes to the bag and writes his final copy.

Ann E. Fisher

Classified Ad

Use with "'Write' for the Job" on page 74.

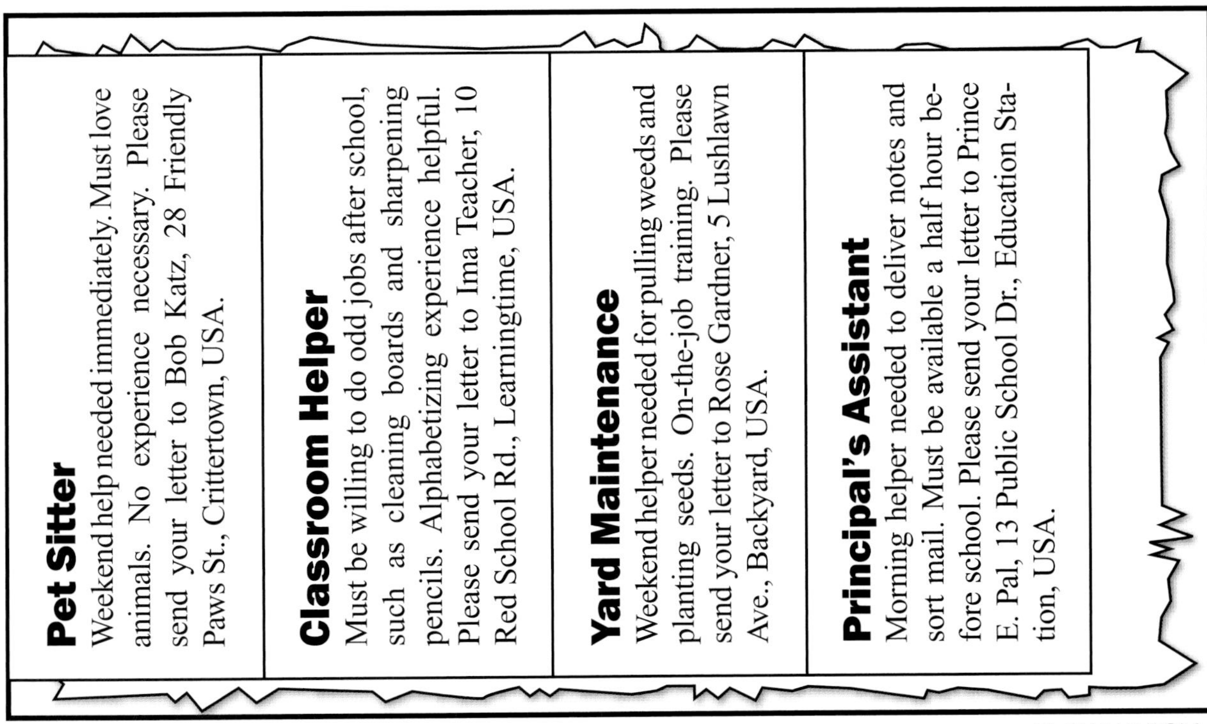

Pet Sitter

Weekend help needed immediately. Must love animals. No experience necessary. Please send your letter to Bob Katz, 28 Friendly Paws St., Crittertown, USA.

Classroom Helper

Must be willing to do odd jobs after school, such as cleaning boards and sharpening pencils. Alphabetizing experience helpful. Please send your letter to Ima Teacher, 10 Red School Rd., Learningtime, USA.

Yard Maintenance

Weekend helper needed for pulling weeds and planting seeds. On-the-job training. Please send your letter to Rose Gardner, 5 Lushlawn Ave., Backyard, USA.

Principal's Assistant

Morning helper needed to deliver notes and sort mail. Must be available a half hour before school. Please send your letter to Prince E. Pal, 13 Public School Dr., Education Station, USA.

Travel Sticker Labels

Use with "Have Tips; Will Write" on page 75.

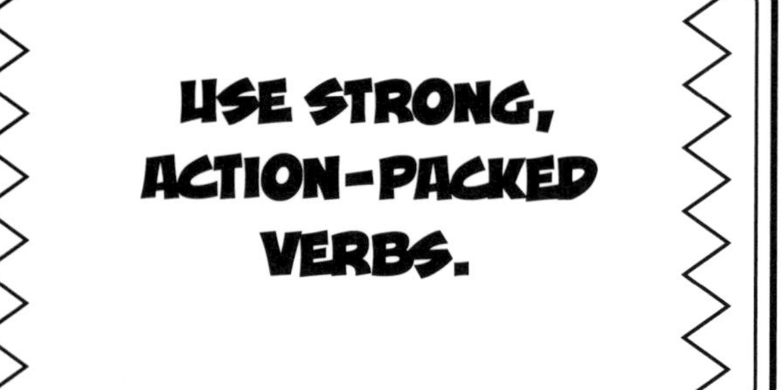

When you're writing fiction, use your imagination!

Use vivid, colorful adjectives.

Use sensory details—sights, sounds, smells, tastes, feelings!

Avoid overused words.

WRITE NOW!

It's an Adventure!

Editing

1. Its Monday and Mighty Morton, the greatest crime fighter in megalopolis, faces a challenge unlike any other
2. Nasty Ned, Mortons nemesis, has broken into the public Library and stolen all the books about nice guys and superheroes
3. where could ned have taken the books what awful fate awaits them

TEC44057

4. as Mighty morton studies the crime seen, he smells a fishy smell
5. "Aha!" he shouts I think ned took the books to the sardine cannery
6. the librarian, who is eating a sardine sandwich, tries to stop morton but he dashes out to quickly.

TEC44057

Make editing practice one of the day's highlights with the saga of Mighty Morton. Display one editing card (story installment) from page 79 each day. Have each child write and edit the sentences on her own paper. Then have students check their work as volunteers edit the displayed version. Finally, lead students to choral-read the corrected sentences and, if you have time, make predictions about the next day's escapade. **For a fun extension**, have students illustrate each episode in comic book format and then put students' illustrations together in a graphic booklet!

Carol Lawrence, Madera, CA

Who's Blogging Now?

Responding to a prompt

The Frog Blog
By Ms. Silvis's 4th Grade Class

Which do you think most farmers like better: planting or harvesting? Which would you rather do?

Ms. S.
I think farmers like planting better. It seems like it might be less work than harvesting. If I were a farmer, I think I'd rather harvest the crop.

Introduce students to blogging within the safety of your classroom. Set up a document on a class computer with a fun title and clip art so the page resembles a blog. Next, type in a prompt and post your own short response. Then introduce your classroom blog and discuss posting appropriate and positive comments. Encourage students to post their responses in their free time over the next few days. When it's time to refresh the blog, save the page in a file titled "Blog Archive." Then start a new document and post a different prompt. Simple and safe!

Maureen Silvis, Cotee River Elementary, New Port Richey, FL

Extra! Extra!

Writing a five-paragraph essay

Topic	Headline
¶ 1:	Introduction
¶ 2:	Who, When, and Where
¶ 3:	What
¶ 4:	Why
¶ 5:	Conclusion

Help students learn to write longer essays with this simple project. Have each child stack three sheets of paper an inch apart and then fold the sheets over to create a flipbook with six pages. Next, have each student label her booklet as shown and then use it to plan a newspaper article about an alien landing. If your students aren't quite ready to tackle five-paragraph essays, have them label their booklets with the parts of a good paragraph. Then have them write paragraphs that describe an alien or unidentified flying object.

Amy Payne, Clara J. Peck Elementary, Greensboro, NC

Moving at a Pretty Good Clip

Writing process

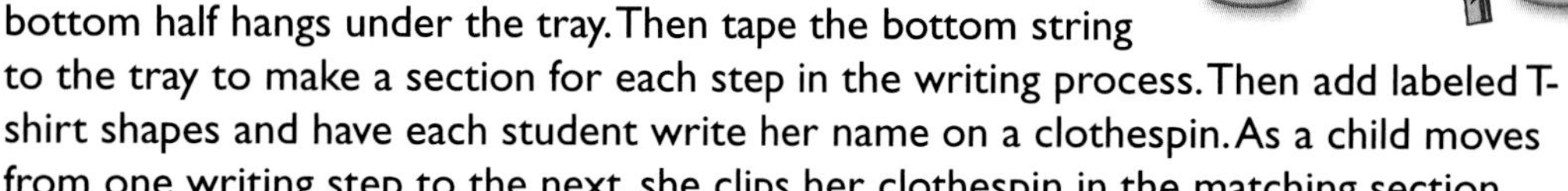

To keep track of your students' writing progress, cut a length of string twice as long as your chalkboard or white-board tray. Next, use a strong knot to tie the string ends together. Hang the string on the tray and tape it so that the bottom half hangs under the tray. Then tape the bottom string to the tray to make a section for each step in the writing process. Then add labeled T-shirt shapes and have each student write her name on a clothespin. As a child moves from one writing step to the next, she clips her clothespin in the matching section.

Amy Payne, Clara J. Peck Elementary, Greensboro, NC

"Worms dangled in Aunt Jessie's kitchen: red worms swarming over a lump of brown mud in a bowl." (*Chasing Redbird* by Sharon Creech)

Types of Strong Lead Sentences
- interesting quote
- question
- interesting fact
- dialogue
- vivid description
- onomatopoeia
- action
- riddle

Off to a Good Start

Writing a strong lead

For this idea, introduce different types of lead sentences, such as those shown. Then have each small group of students skim textbooks or trade books to find and record five lead sentences that grabbed them and two leads that did not. Next, have each group dramatically read its strong leads aloud. Guide the class to identify the sentences' strong features and sort them according to type. Then have each small group share its weak sentence examples and work with the class to make them strong. Bind students' work in a class book titled "Off to a Good Start—Strong Lead Sentences" and store the book near the rest of your classroom writing resources.

inspired by an idea from Jackie Beaudry, Getzville, NY

Back-to-Back

Description, writing a poem

Students get their inspiration from each other with this lyrical activity! Start by leading students to brainstorm adjectives that might be used to describe someone. Next, have each student tape a piece of paper to another student's back. Then have students take turns writing adjectives about each other on the papers taped to their backs. After a few minutes, have each child remove his paper. Then display the poem pattern shown and guide each student to use his classmates' notes as the basis of a poem about himself.

Amy Payne

Conner
Curious, talkative, alert, funny
Student of Ms. Payne
Classmate of Dylan, Megan, and Anna
Who is good at playing video games, multiplying, and drawing cubes
Who wonders why school starts at 8:00, why Pluto got demoted, and what's for lunch
Who hopes he'll get an A in spelling, his cousin will move closer, and lunch will be pizza
Who has learned to add fractions, get along with his sister, and bring his homework back to school
Sanders

[Student's given name]
[Four adjectives that describe the student]
Student of [teachers' names]
Classmate of [three different classmates' names]
Who is good at [three different things the student is good at doing]
Who wonders [three different things the student wonders about]
Who hopes [something the student hopes]
Who has learned [three different skills the student has learned]
[Student's last name]

1. Its Monday and Mighty Morton, the greatest crime fighter in megalopolis, faces a challenge unlike any other
2. Nasty Ned, Mortons nemesis, has broken into the public Library and stolen all the books about nice guys and superheroes
3. where could ned have taken the books what awful fate awaits them

TEC44057

4. as Mighty morton studies the crime seen, he smells a fishy smell
5. “Aha!” he shouts I think ned took the books to the sardine cannery
6. the librarian, who is eating a sardine sandwich, tries to stop morton but he dashes out to quickly.

TEC44057

7. Morton searches seven Sardine Factories but all he picks up is the stench of sardines
8. Morton cant stand the fishy smell so he takes time to have his superhero suit professionally cleaned
9. a sweet-smelling morton heads back too the libary to look for clues!

TEC44057

10. this time, morton notices that the librarian isnt very friendly In fact, she gives him the cold shoulder
11. Morton thinks her cold shoulder is a clue and he rushes write over to frigid freezers, Inc
12. There headquarters at 1001 sleet street

TEC44057

13. Mighty Morton snoops around but all he gets four his trouble is a frostbitten knows, and a bad case of the sniffles
14. back at the library, morton notices an emty potato chip bag in a trash can
15. “gadzooks! Has Nasty ned hidden the missing books in the supermarket? he asks

TEC44057

16. At the market Morton looks everywhere—even in the row with nothing but diapers Morton doesnt find Ned or a single libary book.
17. what ingenious hideout could that Evil mastermind be using
18. Alas sighs mighty morton, “I'll think about it after lunch im hungry now.”

TEC44057

19. Morton heads over to the Courthouse for his weakly lunch date with Judge Jody
20. Morton strolls into Judge Jodys office, “already talking about the case.”
21. morton stop's just in side the door to check his cape in the mirror

TEC44057

22. as Morton Pat's down a cowlick in his hair he notices movement
23. mighty morton flings his legendary lasso over his shoulder and turns around, positive hes snagged Nasty Ned
24. Instead of finding Nasty Ned morton discovers he has just nabbed judge jody, who is tied to her big leather chair

TEC44057

25. When morton yanks off the duct tape covering jodys mouth, she squeals
26. Then Judge Jody grabs mortons wrist and she drags him out the door and they race down the hall.
27. they burst into the courtroom, where they find ned sitting on a enormous pile of books

TEC44057

28. ned is holding a permanent marker and hes just about to draw mustaches on the Nice Guys and supperheroes in the books.
29. mighty Morton nabs Nasty Ned and makes him return the book's to the libary
30. this is just one more example of Mighty Mortons Marvelous work

TEC44057

Note to the teacher: Use with “It's an Adventure!” on page 77.

Write Now!

Keeping Tabs on Their Progress
Writing process

Here's a fun idea for helping students follow the writing process. Before introducing your next writing assignment, have each student draw a line across the bottom of a sheet of paper. Next, have the child divide the space into five sections, label each one with a step in the writing process, and then cut the sections apart as shown. After that, introduce the assignment and guide each student to plan her response on the page. When she's ready to write her rough draft, she tears off the "Prewriting" tab and then gets to work. As the student completes each of the remaining steps, she tears off the matching tab.

Amy Payne, Clara J. Peck Elementary, Greensboro, NC

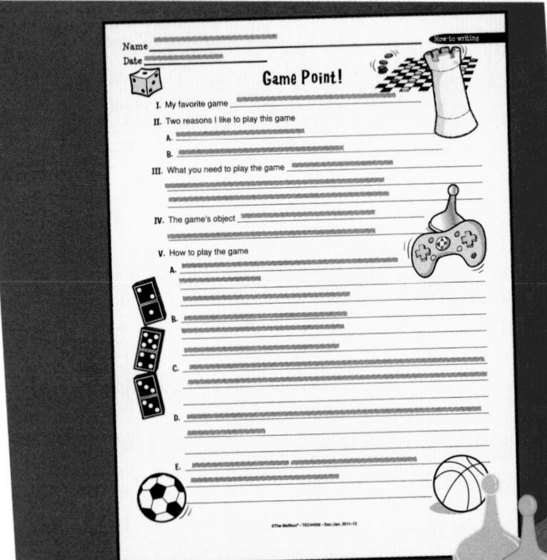

Game Point!
How-to writing

Engage your active authors with this writing topic—games! Have each student use a copy of page 81 to plan an essay that explains how to play his favorite game—card game, board game, backyard game, or sport. After the child writes his rough draft, have him read it to a partner, who pantomimes each step. If either child notices an error in the instructions, the author revises his work to correct it. When students finish their work, celebrate with an afternoon (or morning) of games. Have each student bring in the equipment required to play his game. Then rotate students, half at a time, through hosting and playing their favorite games.

Renee Silliman, Spring Shadows Elementary, Houston, TX

In the Bag
Forming and supporting an opinion

For this activity, have each student write the sentence starter shown on the front of a paper lunch bag. Then guide the child to make a bulleted list of qualities the ideal school lunch would have. Next, have the student choose the three most important qualities and circle each one. On the bag's flip side, the child writes each circled quality and adds three reasons it's important. Then he opens the bag and stands it on his desk for easy referral as he starts drafting an article that describes the ideal school lunch. At the end of each writing session, the student slides his work inside his paper bag and sets it aside until the next session. To publish his work, each student draws a lunch tray and writes his article in the sections.

Amy Payne

Name ______________________________

Date ________________

Game Point!

I. My favorite game: ____________________

II. Two reasons I like to play this game:

A. ____________________

B. ____________________

III. What you need to play the game: ____________________

IV. The game's object: ____________________

V. How to play the game:

A. First, ____________________

B. Next, ____________________

C. Then ____________________

D. After that, ____________________

E. Finally, ____________________

Note to the teacher: Use with "Game Point!" on page 80.

WRITE NOW!

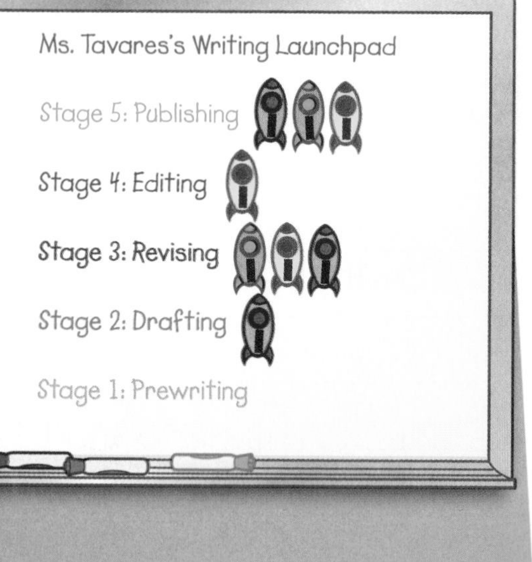

Blasting Off
Writing process

Here's an easy-to-use idea for keeping track of students' writing progress. Designate one edge of your board as your writing launchpad and label it as shown. Next, have each child personalize and cut out a copy of a rocket pattern from the bottom of page 83. Then stick a bit of magnetic tape to the back of each rocket and put the rockets on the board at the beginning of a writing assignment. When a student completes a step in the writing process, he moves his rocket to the next stage. You can check everyone's progress with a quick glance, and your students will get a kick out of blasting their way through the writing process!

Anne Tavares, Mullen Hall Elementary, Falmouth, MA

Want to use a bulletin board for your launchpad? Just have students use pushpins instead of magnets to tack their rockets to the board.

Hands-On Essays
Writing a five-paragraph narrative

For this clever organizer, have each student trace and cut out six hand shapes. Next, have the child staple the shapes together to make a booklet, labeling the top cutout with the assignment's topic or title and the story's parts as shown. Have the student label the thumb or fingers of each remaining hand with one part. Then guide the child to jot ideas for each paragraph on the matching cutout. Finally, have the student use the organized ideas to write a five-paragraph story.

Amy Payne, Clara J. Peck Elementary, Greensboro, NC

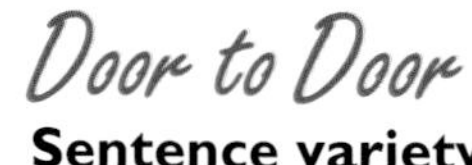

Door to Door
Sentence variety

Want your students to vary their sentences when they write? Give them a new place to practice! Cover a closet door with bulletin board paper and write a simple prompt, such as one of those shown. Next, challenge each student to write her response on the door, making sure that each sentence starts differently and is a different length. When all students have had the chance to respond and read each other's responses, cover the door with fresh paper and add a new topic.

- **A Couple of Lines About Me:** Students write about themselves.
- **Complimentary Notes:** Students write something nice about a friend, relative, place, or thing.
- **Who Knew?** Students find and write about interesting facts.

Close Encounters
Writing dialogue

Give students practice writing dialogue with this fun idea. Have each student trace the outline of his shoe on a sheet of paper. Next, have the child imagine a conversation that his toes could be having right then if they could talk. Then review the rules for punctuating dialogue and have each student write in the outline of his shoe the conversation he imagined. Follow up by having each student read his dialogue to a partner before turning in his work.

Facing Facts
Taking notes, citing sources

To focus on taking notes, have each child cut apart a copy of the cards on page 84. Then display a class textbook and have each child write the book's title on a "Print Source" card. Next, guide each student to rank the source's reliability by coloring stars. After that, choose a paragraph and have students record the page number. Then read the paragraph aloud and guide students to name the topic and paraphrase an important fact on their cards. After that, display a website relevant to the topic and repeat the steps, having each child record the site's web address along with its title on a "Website" card. Follow up by having each pair of students research the topic, using their textbooks and the website, and take notes on the remaining cards.

Amy Payne, Clara J. Peck Elementary, Greensboro, NC

Rocket Patterns
Use with "Blasting Off" on page 82.

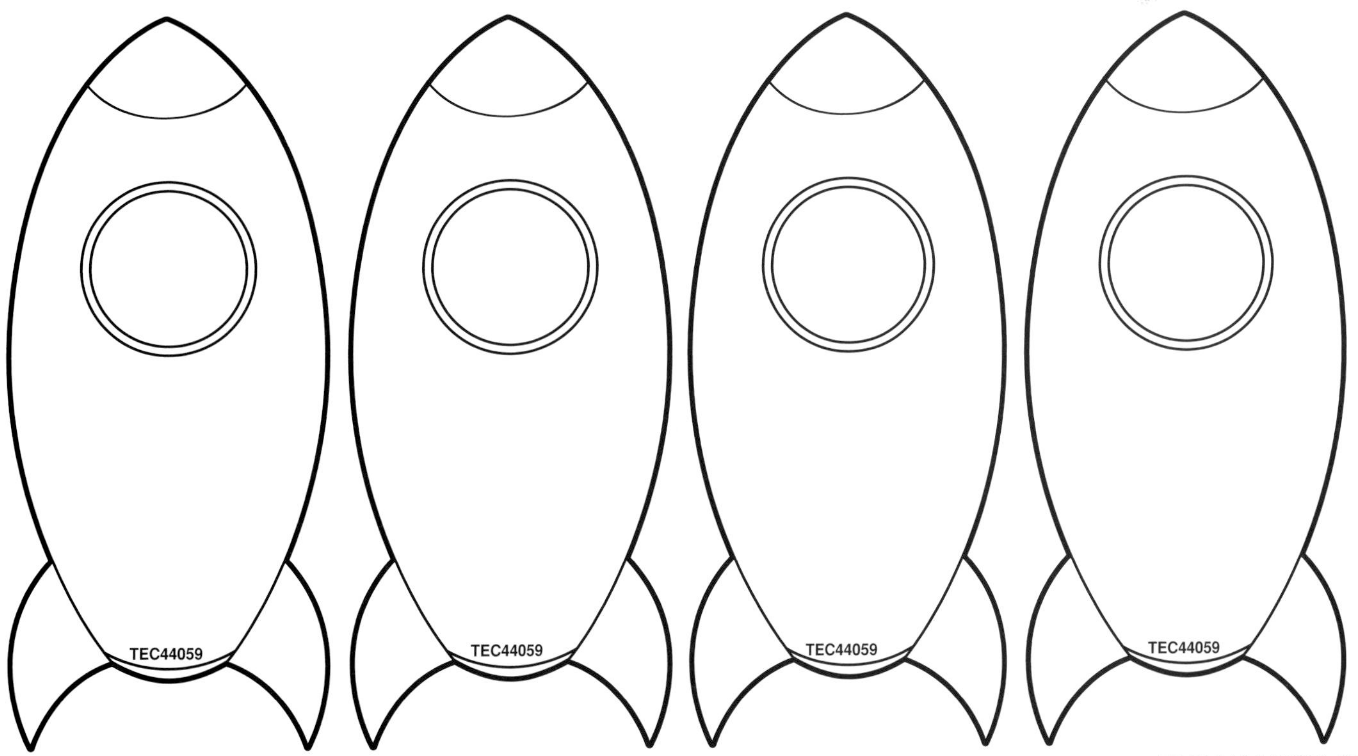

Title: ____________________
Reliability of Source: ☆☆☆☆☆☆ Page: ________
Topic: ____________________
Fact: ____________________

Print Source

TEC44059

Website

Title: ____________________
Address: ____________________
Reliability of Source: ☆☆☆☆☆☆ Date accessed: ________
Topic: ____________________
Fact: ____________________

TEC44059

Title: ____________________
Reliability of Source: ☆☆☆☆☆☆ Page: ________
Topic: ____________________
Fact: ____________________

Print Source

TEC44059

Website

Title: ____________________
Address: ____________________
Reliability of Source: ☆☆☆☆☆☆ Date accessed: ________
Topic: ____________________
Fact: ____________________

TEC44059

Title: ____________________
Reliability of Source: ☆☆☆☆☆☆ Page: ________
Topic: ____________________
Fact: ____________________

Print Source

TEC44059

Website

Title: ____________________
Address: ____________________
Reliability of Source: ☆☆☆☆☆☆ Date accessed: ________
Topic: ____________________
Fact: ____________________

TEC44059

Note to the teacher: Use with “Facing Facts” on page 83.

WRITE NOW!

Building on Details

Describing an event, revising

This activity does double duty—students practice revising *and* writing detailed descriptions! In advance, copy and cut apart the cards from page 86 so there is a set of cards for each group of four students. Then give each group card 1 and have students choral-read the paragraph. Next, lead students to choral-read the revised paragraph on card 2 and identify its changes. Repeat with cards 3 and 4. Then have the students in each group read the paragraph on card 5 and rewrite it to include more details. Have each group share and explain its revisions and then revise the paragraph one more time. After that, have each student revise the paragraph on card 6 and share her work with her group.

For a great follow-up, have each child choose card 4, 5, or 6; imagine the rest of the event; and write five or more paragraphs that describe it.

A Writing Helper

Editing

Introduce students to a colorful character, Ed I. T., whose primary goal is sharing editing tips. Copy page 88 for your files and then display the mini poster on page 87 to introduce the tips. Guide students to apply the tips as they edit a current piece of writing. Then post the page at your writing center for a daily editing reminder. As students apply the tips, give special recognition to the young writers whose work reflects excellent editing.

adapted from ideas by Jacqueline Beaudry
Getzville, NY, and Jewell F. Stewart, Ellsworth, ME

Do ocean plants have flowers?

Land and Water Plants Compared
Big Cats and Their Families
Dangerous Fish
Killer Whales—Dangerous Ocean Mammals
Mustangs—the Last of the Wild Horses

Bouncing Around Ideas

Prewriting, informational writing

Grab a beach ball or soft foam ball and post a topic such as one of those shown. Next, ask a meaningful question about the topic. Then toss the ball to a student. When she catches the ball, lead the child to ask a different thoughtful question about the topic. Record the student's question and then have her toss the ball to another student, repeating until students have generated ten or more questions. Next, help students choose the questions that will best guide research on the topic. Repeat the activity with the remaining topics and then have each pair of students choose a topic, research answers to its questions, and write a report on the topic.

Kim Minafo, Cary, NC

Note to the teacher: Use with "Building on Details" on page 85.

I know editing!

Ed I. T.

- Having trouble catching all the misspelled words in your writing? Start at the end! Read your work backward, one word at time. Then you can focus on each word, and it will be easier to spot the ones that are misspelled!

- Read your writing out loud. It helps you notice parts that don't make sense or are hard to read. (You don't have to read it really loud. Read it quietly to yourself.)

- Read your sentences one at a time. Make sure each sentence...
  - begins with a capital letter.
  - has a subject and predicate.
  - has the right ending punctuation.

- Don't expect to be able to catch all your mistakes in one reading. Read your work several times.

Note to the teacher: Use with "A Writing Helper" on page 85.

Write Now!

I think I had always wanted a horse. I'd been fascinated by them since I was little. When I was four, we used to go to some corrals near my grandmother's house and feed the horses carrots and apples. I loved petting their velvety noses. The animals were huge but gentle, and I knew I wanted one even when I was four.

(1) I really wanted a horse. (2) I was surprised when my aunt gave me a foal. (3) The first time I tried to ride my foal, I fell off. (4) I didn't give up. (5) My foal learned to trust me, and I learned to trust her. (6) I finally learned how to ride my foal. (7) Now my foal's a full-grown horse, and we go for rides every day.

One Sentence at a Time

Elaboration

Make a class supply of the paragraph strips at the top of page 89. Then have each student elaborate by writing more about what is included and implied in each sentence, without repeating information from any previous sentences or writing about anything that happens in later sentences. Lead the student to add sensory details, vivid verbs, dialogue, and specific examples. Then have him combine his elaborated sentences, adding transitions to fit them together and write a much more interesting short story. Finally, read the original story aloud and have student volunteers share their elaborated versions.

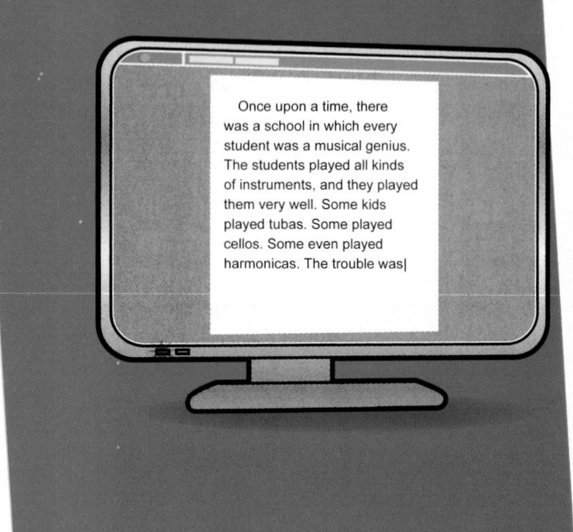

By Any Other Name

Fictional narrative

For this group activity, open a word processing document on each classroom computer. On each document, type one of the story starters from the bottom half of page 89. Next, divide students into small groups so there is one group for each computer; have each group gather at its computer and read the starter. When you say "Go," one student from the group adds a sentence. Then the next student adds a sentence and so on until every student has added at least three sentences to the story. When you say "End," the groups have five minutes to finish their stories. Then print each group's story and have the students edit it before they read it aloud.

Sharon Ciggelakis, Indiana Avenue School Number 18, Iselin, NJ

Buddy to Buddy

Informational essay

Here's a writing exercise that gives students practice interviewing and turning an interview into an interesting essay. In advance, ask the teacher of a younger class for help with this project. Next, brainstorm with your students ten questions that will help them learn interesting details about the younger students. Then have each student record the questions and use them to interview a child from the younger class. After the interview, guide each student to write an interesting essay about the child and add a colorful portrait. Then bind students' work in a fun class book and have students present it to the teacher of the younger class.

If your students have buddies from a younger class, have them interview their buddies. Then make a class supply of your students' essays, bind the essays in a book for each buddy, and have the older student read his essay to his buddy and give her a copy of the book!

Paragraph Strips

Use with "One Sentence at a Time" on page 88.

(1) I really wanted a horse. (2) I was surprised when my aunt gave me a foal. (3) The first time I tried to ride my foal, I fell off. (4) I didn't give up. (5) My foal learned to trust me, and I learned to trust her. (6) I finally learned how to ride my foal. (7) Now my foal's a full-grown horse, and we go for rides every day.

TEC44061

(1) I really wanted a horse. (2) I was surprised when my aunt gave me a foal. (3) The first time I tried to ride my foal, I fell off. (4) I didn't give up. (5) My foal learned to trust me, and I learned to trust her. (6) I finally learned how to ride my foal. (7) Now my foal's a full-grown horse, and we go for rides every day.

TEC44061

(1) I really wanted a horse. (2) I was surprised when my aunt gave me a foal. (3) The first time I tried to ride my foal, I fell off. (4) I didn't give up. (5) My foal learned to trust me, and I learned to trust her. (6) I finally learned how to ride my foal. (7) Now my foal's a full-grown horse, and we go for rides every day.

TEC44061

(1) I really wanted a horse. (2) I was surprised when my aunt gave me a foal. (3) The first time I tried to ride my foal, I fell off. (4) I didn't give up. (5) My foal learned to trust me, and I learned to trust her. (6) I finally learned how to ride my foal. (7) Now my foal's a full-grown horse, and we go for rides every day.

TEC44061

Story Starters

Use with "By Any Other Name" on page 88.

Once upon a time, there was a school in which every student was a musical genius. The students played all kinds of instruments, and they played them very well. Some kids played tubas. Some played cellos. Some even played harmonicas. The trouble was...

TEC44061

We can't believe it! It's the last day of school—one of the best days of the year! My best friend and I are riding the bus, excited about getting to school for our class party. We don't have anything to carry—no backpacks, no homework, no books, nor lunches. We are telling jokes and laughing when, suddenly, the bus driver slams on the brakes, yanks the steering wheel, and careens off course! Instead of taking us to school, he's taking us...

TEC44061

When was the last time you got a new pet? I've never had a new pet—until now, that is. I've been begging for a pet for just about forever. I've tried promising my mom I would clean up every mess. I promised I'd do odd jobs to pay for its food. I tried showing her pictures of really cuddly puppies and kittens. Nothing had ever worked. Who would have guessed that she would finally say yes and let me keep a...

TEC44061

Good grief! It's time to clean my room—again! I'm sure I just cleaned it last week, or was it last month, or was it (gasp!) last year? Mom said I can't do anything else until my room is spotless, so I might as well get started. I'd just stuff everything under my bed, but that was the first place she looked last time. Hmmmm. First, I'll...

TEC44061

Name ______________________________

Date ________________________

Spin a Story!

1. Spin to choose a story prompt.
2. Complete the organizer with story details.
3. On another sheet of paper, write the story.

Write a story about _____.

- waking up to find you are four centimeters tall
- waking up to find you are seven feet tall
- discovering you can leap 20 feet in the air
- realizing you can talk with insects
- discovering you are as strong as an elephant
- realizing you can run as fast as a cheetah

What is your first reaction?

____

____

____

What are three things you do?

1. ______________________________
2. ______________________________
3. ______________________________

What problem do you run into?

____

____

____

How do you solve the problem?

____

____

____

Do you change back to your former self? ______________________________

What do you learn about yourself? ______________________________

____

____

____

How to use: Have each student use a copy of the page to plan and then write a fictional narrative.

Name ____________________

Date ____________________

What an Impact!

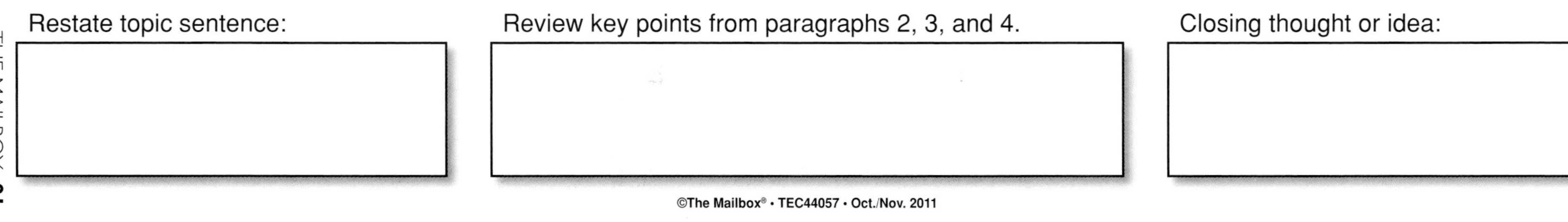

Imagine an unidentified flying object has landed on your school. The UFO's friendly crew wants to take back to their planet an example of Earth's most important invention. Use the organizer to plan an essay about the invention you would suggest.

Introduction (Paragraph 1)

Main idea: Earth's most important invention is ____________________.

The invention's most important feature is ____________________.

Its second most important feature is ____________________.

Its third most important feature is ____________________.

Body (Paragraph 2)

The invention's most important feature:

Details and examples:

Body (Paragraph 3)

The invention's second most important feature:

Details and examples:

Body (Paragraph 4)

The invention's third most important feature:

Details and examples:

Conclusion (Paragraph 5)

Restate topic sentence:

Review key points from paragraphs 2, 3, and 4.

Closing thought or idea:

Name ______________________________

Date ______________

Who Did It?

Word Bank

mystifying
baffling
peculiar
weird
secretive
puzzling
strange
curious

Read the word bank. Choose an event.
Write a story that explains the mysterious school event.
As you write, think about the events that introduce the mystery and lead up to its explanation.

Events

- Lunch is a fizzy, burping, purple goo.
- The principal is singing the morning announcements.
- Your teacher just asked you to make more noise when you walk down the hall.

How to use: Have each student use a copy of this page to plan and then write an imaginative narrative.

Name ____________________

Date ____________________

Supporting an opinion

Now Featuring...

1 Prompt

The owner of the In-Your-Face movie theater, Holly Wood, has just made a major announcement. “For the next three months,” she said, “this theater will show only 3-D movies.” After that, Ms. Wood will check ticket sales and decide whether to make the decision permanent.

2 Plan

How do you feel about Holly Wood’s decision to show only 3-D movies?

What are three reasons you feel this way?

1.

2.

3.

What are three facts that support your opinion?

1.

2.

3.

3 Write

Use your answers to write an email to Holly Wood that states your opinion about showing only 3-D movies. Use facts and reasons to persuade Ms. Wood to care about your opinion.

August Writing Prompts

 This month is American Adventures Month. Would you rather spend a week at a fancy beach hotel or spend a week camping in the wilderness? Why?	 August is National Inventor's Month. Pretend you just invented the Handy Homework Helper. Write a letter to the president of Crackerjack Gadgets. Persuade her to start selling your machine.
 Write a letter to the month of August. Will your letter have kind words for the month, or will you complain about it?	 August can seem like the hottest month of the year. Make a list of the ten best ways to cool off on a hot day.
 A 1980s fad was to have a rattail, a lock of hair that was longer than the rest of one's hair. If rattails were a fad today, would you grow one? Why or why not?	 At a rally on August 28, 1963, Martin Luther King Jr. gave his "I have a dream" speech. There were 250,000 people at the rally. Why do you think so many people were there? Explain.
 What was the most boring day of your summer? Describe the day and how you felt about it. Use words such as *dreary*, *ho-hum*, *humdrum*, *mind-numbing*, *monotonous*, *slow*, *tedious*, and *wearisome*.	 Write the title of your favorite book. Draw a circle around it. Draw five spokes coming from the circle and write a reason you like the book on each one. Then write an ad for the book.
 Write the rest of this story. I have always wanted to know what was in the trunk in my grandma's attic. I could hardly believe it when she handed me the key and said, "Go ahead. Open it."	 What was the best day of your summer? Describe the day and how you felt about it. Use words such as *fascinating*, *out of the ordinary*, *exciting*, and *satisfying*.

September Writing Prompts

The first day of September is National No Rhyme (Nor Reason) Day. It's a day to honor words that don't rhyme. Make a list of 15 or more words that don't have any rhymes.	 September is National Honey Month. What is the sweetest thing you've ever eaten? Describe it.
 Imagine that school started at 1:00 PM and ended at 7:00 PM. Would this schedule be better or worse than your current schedule? Why?	 It's Happy Cat Month! Write a story about a miserable cat that grows to be delighted by the story's end.
 The piano is the most popular musical instrument in America. Plan a party to celebrate National Piano Month (September). Describe the decorations, snacks, and games you'd choose.	 What is your favorite food? Write an email to convince your principal that this food should be served in the lunchroom at least once a week.
 If you went to lunch with an alien, would you be willing to try its favorite food? Why or why not?	 Write three paragraphs that explain how to safely ride a school bus.
 Write a letter to your teacher about field trips. In your letter, tell her how you feel about field trips. Then share three or more places you'd like to go on field trips.	 Which fall activity do you most enjoy—jumping in a pile of fall leaves, watching a football game, hiking with your family, or something else? Describe your favorite fall activity. Use all your senses.

October Writing Prompts

Fall is a great time for a warm cup of soup. Describe your favorite soup. How does it look, smell, and taste? Do you slurp it by the spoonful or sip it from a cup?	October is Children's Magazine Month. Create your own magazine. What would it be called? What would its theme be? What kinds of articles, cartoons, and puzzles would you feature?
Do you startle easily or is it hard to scare you? Write a story about a time someone or something scared you.	Imagine that, in the spirit of Columbus Day (October 12), the president of the United States asks your class to explore your state. Write a short play about where you go and what you find.
For Fire Prevention Week (October 9–15), write five tips for keeping your home safe from fire.	Declare a day in October as Massive Monster Day. Plan a parade to celebrate Massive Monster Day. Then describe the parade.
Imagine waking tomorrow and finding that your hair has turned the colors of autumn leaves. What do you think? What do you say? What do you do? Write about your day.	Which do you think most farmers like better: planting or harvesting? Explain. Which would you rather do? Why?
Ping! Ping! It's popcorn popping! Make a list of ten things you recognize just by the sound or sounds they make. Then tell which sound you most love to hear and which one you dread.	What jobs or chores do you have at home? Describe your least favorite chore and tell why you don't like it.

November Writing Prompts

Write the rest of this story: "When I heard, 'I'm really sorry! I can't pick you up for another hour, so you'll have to stay…'"	Would you rather have breakfast served to you in bed or eat breakfast at a restaurant? Why?
Imagine a scarecrow that you might build. Then describe it from head to toe.	Write ten steps that explain what your family does on a typical Thanksgiving Day.
November is Aviation History Month. Which would you rather pilot: a hot-air balloon, helicopter, glider, or jet? Explain.	Write a fable or an imaginary story that explains why we eat *ears* of corn and *heads* of lettuce.
Imagine that you want to be the next mayor of your town. Write a speech that will convince your fellow citizens to vote for you.	List five people for whom you are thankful. Then tell why each person is special to you.
In honor of Veterans Day (November 11), design a medal that could be given to those who have served in the armed forces. Then explain what your design means.	As we get closer to winter, many people trade their short-sleeve shirts for long-sleeve ones and then add sweaters or jackets. Which season do you prefer: fall or winter? Explain.

December Writing Prompts

You have found a very special magical pen. What can it do that no other pen can do? Write a story about how you find it and what you do with it.	Describe a toy that was your favorite when you were a small child. Why did you like it so much?
What would it be like to live in a life-size gingerbread house? Describe the outside and inside of this scrumptious abode.	Imagine you are planning your family's holiday dinner. Make a list of main dishes, side dishes, and desserts you would serve. Use vivid adjectives and specific nouns to name each item.
Like a snowflake, each person is unique, one of a kind. Describe something you have, know, or do that no one else has, knows, or does.	Mrs. Claus never gets credit for her hard work! Write a speech honoring Mrs. Claus and the things she does.
On December 15, the Bill of Rights will be 220 years old. If you could write a constitutional amendment that would give kids a new right, what would it be? Explain.	What is your least favorite thing about winter? Why?
Invent a new way for Santa to travel on Christmas Eve. Explain how it would work.	In your opinion, what would be the best way to spend the last six hours of the year? Write a note that will convince your parents to let you do just that.

January Writing Prompts

Choose a famous person who is often in the news. Write five New Year's resolutions you think he or she should make.	Dr. Martin Luther King Jr. wanted to make the world a better place. He believed all people should have equal rights. Describe one thing you think could make the world a better place.
Imagine you are an elf applying for a job helping Santa Claus get ready for Christmas 2012. Write a letter to Santa that will convince him to hire you.	Every year, people all over the world jump into an icy lake, a river, an ocean, or a swimming pool and go for a quick swim. Would you ever do that? Why or why not?
List five tasks that are harder to do in winter than in any other season. Then list five tasks that are easier to do in winter than in any other season.	Some people celebrate Popcorn Day on January 19. Make a list of ten or more foods that are noisy to make or noisy to eat. Then tell which one you like best.
Imagine you and your family have been asked to babysit a polar bear cub for the weekend. Write a story about it.	January 24 is Belly Laugh Day. It's a day to celebrate laughter. When would you be more likely to laugh out loud: when you are talking with friends or when you are reading a funny book? Explain.
Invent an object that will keep you warm on the coldest winter day. Then write a commercial that will encourage others to buy it.	If you were a cookie, what kind of cookie would you be? Why? Explain.

February Writing Prompts

✓ Do you think Groundhog Day should be a national holiday? Why or why not?	✓ Which US president (living or deceased) would you most like to meet? Why?
✓ Imagine you own a cupcake, cookie, or candy store. Describe a special treat that you will sell for Valentine's Day.	✓ In honor of the shortest month of the year, write about a shortcut you take that makes your life easier.
✓ Shirley Chisholm was the first African American congresswoman. Her parents told her, "Keep your head high. Always give the best you have within you to give. Somebody will recognize it in the future." Do you agree? Why or why not?	✓ Write a three- to five-paragraph short story that will make your readers laugh.
✓ Make a list of ten things you like. Next, make a list of ten things you love. Then use your lists to tell how *like* and *love* are different.	✓ What is your favorite type of book to read, such as historical fiction, realistic fiction, mystery, informational, or graphic novel? Write a letter to convince your school librarian to order more of this type of book.
✓ What do you think it means to "put your heart into" something you do? Describe something you put your heart into.	✓ Imagine that you are hiking in a nearby forest. What is the most interesting thing you see? Describe it.

March Writing Prompts

✓ Write the rest of this story: I could hardly believe it when I found a baby giraffe on my doorstep.	✓ What is the farthest you would ride a bicycle? Where would you go? What would be the most difficult part of the trip?
✓ Write a fable that explains how spring, the season, got its name.	✓ It's time for spring cleaning! Write six or more steps that explain how to clean your desk, room, or backpack.
✓ The term *March Madness* is used to describe the national college basketball tournament that takes place this month. Would you rather watch a basketball game or play in one? Explain.	✓ If you used the idiom "go fly a kite," you would probably be telling a person who was bugging you to leave you alone. How do you think this idiom got started? Explain.
✓ Imagine that, like a hibernating animal, you fell asleep in November and woke up in March. What do you do as soon as you wake up? Why?	✓ Eleanor Roosevelt once said, "The future belongs to those who believe in the beauty of their dreams." What do you dream of when you dream of your future? Describe it.
✓ Would you rather be in a St. Patrick's Day parade or watch a St. Patrick's Day parade? Explain.	✓ Make a list of five or more words that begin with silent letters. Then use the words in a free-verse poem.

April Writing Prompts

For National Card and Letter Writing Month, write a letter to invite your favorite celebrity to come speak at your school.	Write a story that begins with the following sentence: I know I'm covered in mud; just let me explain.
Imagine that, on your first night of spring break, everything goes wrong. Describe what happens.	If you could choose, would you rather take your next family trip in a car, on a plane, in a boat, on a train, or on a bus? Explain.
With spring, out come the bugs. Do insects creep you out, or do you love the little creatures? Explain.	It's National Humor Month! What is the funniest thing you've seen lately? Describe it!
Make a list of ten tips that will help anyone be healthy, strong, and fit.	Write three or more lines to complete a poem that begins "Flowers, flowers everywhere...." (Your poem can rhyme, but it doesn't have to.)
Describe your dream house.	Make a list of ten things you can do on a rainy day. Then list ten things you can't do on a rainy day.

May Writing Prompts

May 8 is No Socks Day. Draw a Venn diagram and compare the benefits and drawbacks of going without socks.	Do you like to go on picnics? Why or why not?
What do you think is the most difficult thing about being a mom, dad, or guardian? Why?	Spring is the best season of the year! Write five reasons that explain why you agree or disagree with that statement.
Imagine that everyone's homework is missing. You are a detective called in to solve the mystery of the missing homework. Write a story about how you find it.	Imagine that you've won a contest to take your family on a dream vacation this summer. How will you break the news to your family? Where will you go, and what will you do?
Write a persuasive speech to convince other students in your school to always wear bicycle helmets when they ride bikes.	What is something you love to do now but will probably not enjoy in two years? Describe it.
You've just won the Best Photo of the Year award. Describe your winning snapshot and how you got it.	Make a list of 20 verbs. Cross out the five weakest verbs and write five more. Then circle the five strongest verbs.

June Writing Prompts

Pretend you are a meteorologist for a television station. A surprise snowstorm has just hit your town, and it's June! What do you tell your viewers?	Make a list of ten or more activities you are planning for this summer.
You have just landed on a planet in a galaxy far from Earth. You have landed in the playground of a school. What do you see? Describe it.	Which of the US flag's nicknames do you like best: Old Glory, Stars and Stripes, or The Star-Spangled Banner? Why?
How do you choose a book to read? Do you read the first page? Do you read the last page? Do you skim the pictures? Do you study the cover? Do you read about the author? Explain.	What was the best lunch you had at school this year? Draw a picture and then describe what it looked like, its texture, how it smelled, and what it tasted like.
Imagine the principal gives you $300 and puts you in charge of the end-of-the-year party for your grade. What kinds of snacks, drinks, and games do you choose? What will be the easiest part of planning the party? What will be the hardest?	If you could travel anywhere you wanted this summer, where would you go? Who would you take with you? How would you get there? What would you do there? How long would you stay?
Would you rather have a summer job working at the zoo, the pet store, the mall, or the swimming pool? Explain your choice.	The first 19 days of June are still technically spring days. Label one side of a Venn diagram "Looks Like Spring" and the other side "Looks Like Summer." Then find details for all three sections.

July Writing Prompts

If you could attend a large-scale sporting event, what would you go to? Would you rather be a participant or a member of the audience?	You are sitting on a scuba-diving boat as it putts out to sea. You've been taking scuba-diving lessons for two weeks, and this is your first dive in the actual ocean. How do you feel? What do you do? Explain.
We have days to honor mothers, fathers, and grandparents. Now it's time to honor our aunts and uncles. Write a letter to an aunt or uncle who is special to you.	List ten or more foods that you tend to eat more of in the summer than during the rest of the year. Then rank the foods from your favorite to your least favorite.
July is Ice Cream Month. Invent a new flavor of ice cream and give it a creative name. Write a description of the ice cream that's sure to make others want to try it!	Which would you rather explore: the world's highest mountain or the world's deepest ocean? Explain.
What is your absolute favorite thing to do in the summer? Imagine you are grown and remembering this activity. Describe the memory of the activity from the viewpoint of your adult self.	If you could change one thing about this school year, what would you change? Why?
Imagine you are sleeping outside while on a summer camping trip. Before you fall asleep, you look up into the starry sky and see something unusual. What happens?	What question would you ask if you got to meet with the president of the United States for five minutes? Why would you ask this question?

A Report-Writing Adventure

Directions:
1. Spin to name the beneficial bug you will research.
2. Spin to find your research focus.
3. Take notes as you research the topic.
4. Use your notes to write an article about the bug.

Writing Tips

- In the first paragraph, state your main idea.
- Use words and sentences that will attract your reader's attention.
- Write three or more paragraphs, including facts and details that support your main idea.
- In your conclusion, summarize the facts and details as you restate your main idea.

HEY, WHY ISN'T MY NAME ON THERE?

Beneficial Bugs

wolf spider
dung beetle
praying mantis
predaceous stink bug
yellow jacket
ladybug
lacewing
earthworm

Research Focus

how the bug protects itself
the bug's habitat
things about the bug that make you say "ewww!"
the bug's life cycle
the bug's predators
how the bug's helpful

Writing Activity Card: Use at a center or for free time. Provide note cards and access to research materials.

Math

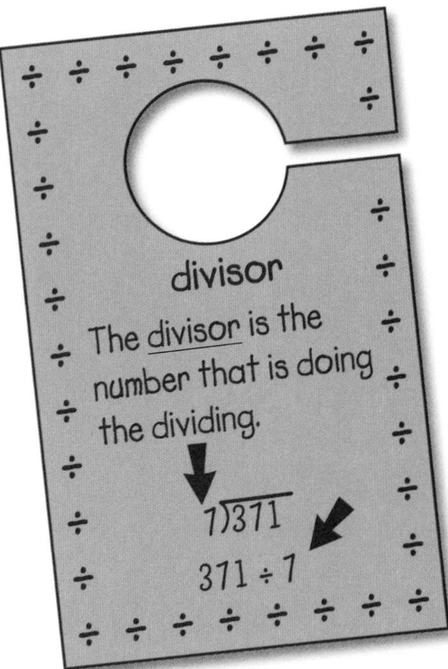

Hanging on Every Word

Math terms

Want to build your students' math vocabularies? Use student-made door hangers to highlight important terms. Assign each student a different word or phrase and have her look it up in her textbook's glossary. Next, have the child record, explain, and illustrate the term on card stock, a large index card, or a colorful sheet of foam cut in the shape of a door hanger. Then have each child share her work before dangling it from a classroom doorknob or a cupboard handle. Regularly rotate the door hangers to highlight different terms.

adapted from an idea by Colleen Dabney
Williamsburg, VA

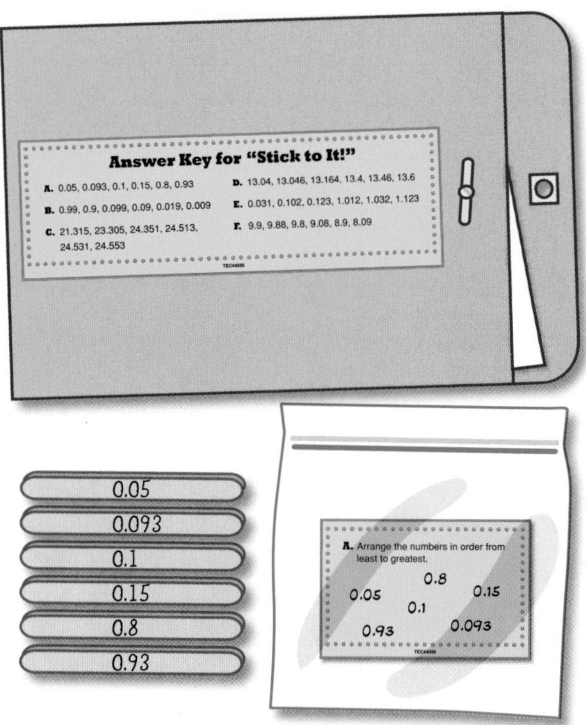

Stick to It!

Comparing, ordering decimals

To prepare this hands-on activity, copy and cut apart the direction and answer key cards from page 104. Next, label sets of six wooden craft sticks with the decimals shown on each direction card. Put each set of sticks and its matching card in a plastic resealable bag. Then glue the key onto a manila envelope and slide the bags into the envelope. A student chooses a bag and takes out its sticks. He lines up the decimal points and orders the numbers as guided. Then the child records his work, returns the sticks to the bag, and takes another bag. When the student finishes, he checks his work using the key and then returns each bag to the envelope.

Jennifer Otter
Oak Ridge, NC

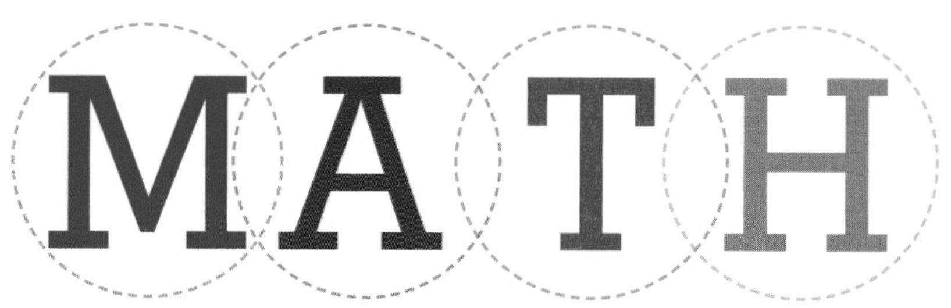

Problem-Solving Tactics

Problem solving

Help your students approach word problems in an organized manner. First, display a copy of the flowchart from page 105 and then read a word problem aloud. Use the chart to clarify the problem's question and find its solution; repeat with several word problems. Then post a copy of the chart as a reminder to take a tactical approach when solving word problems!

Jennifer Kaste
Rancho Viejo Elementary
Yuma, AZ

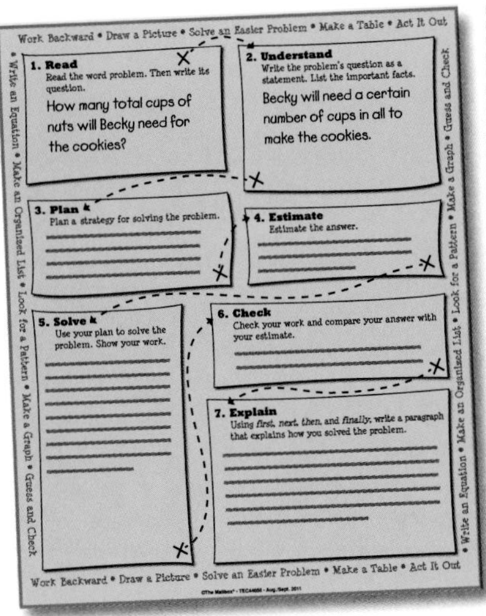

Work Backward • Draw a Picture • Solve an Easier Problem • Make a Table • Act It Out

1. Read
Read the word problem. Then write its question.
How many total cups of nuts will Becky need for the cookies?

2. Understand
Write the problem's question as a statement. List the important facts.
Becky will need a certain number of cups in all to make the cookies.

3. Plan
Plan a strategy for solving the problem.

4. Estimate
Estimate the answer.

5. Solve
Use your plan to solve the problem. Show your work.

6. Check
Check your work and compare your answer with your estimate.

7. Explain
Using *first, next, then,* and *finally,* write a paragraph that explains how you solved the problem.

Write an Equation • Make an Organized List • Look for a Pattern • Make a Graph • Guess and Check

Work Backward • Draw a Picture • Solve an Easier Problem • Make a Table • Act It Out

It's All in the Details

Division, place value

To prepare this lively whole-class review, write clues such as those shown on separate index cards and put the cards in a bag. Have each pair of students draw a card. Then post a division problem and guide students to solve it. Next, have each duo compare its card with the quotient. If the quotient meets the card's qualification, the partners read their clue aloud and explain the match. Repeat with a different problem. Then have each pair pass its clue card to another twosome, and give students two new problems to solve. Continue as time allows.

Jennifer Otter
Oak Ridge, NC

Quotient Clues

The quotient is divisible by three.

The quotient is divisible by five.

The quotient is divisible by nine.

The quotient is an even number.

The quotient is an odd number.

The digit in the quotient's tens place is its smallest digit.

All the quotient's digits are different.

The sum of the quotient's digits is an odd number.

The sum of the quotient's digits is an even number.

There are two even digits in the quotient's number.

Along These Lines

Lines, angles

Create a kid-size model to reinforce line and angle concepts. Use masking tape on your classroom floor to form parallel, perpendicular, and intersecting lines. Next, draw and label the intersecting points on the tape. Then guide students to identify lines, rays, line segments, angle measurements and angle types, using the floor diagram.

Mary Porosky
All Saints Catholic School
Canton, MI

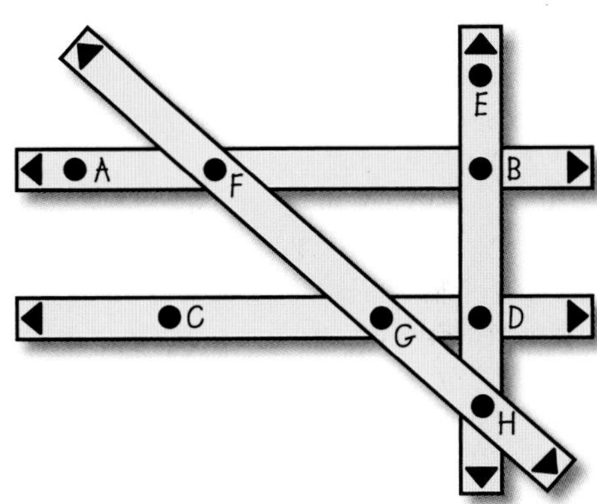

Direction and Answer Key Cards

Use with "Stick to It!" on page 102.

A. Arrange the numbers in order from least to greatest.

0.8 0.05 0.15 0.1 0.93 0.093

TEC44056

B. Arrange the numbers in order from greatest to least.

0.09 0.009 0.9 0.99 0.019 0.099

TEC44056

C. Arrange the numbers in order from least to greatest.

21.315 24.513 24.351 24.531 24.553 23.305

TEC44056

D. Arrange the numbers in order from greatest to least.

13.04 13.6 13.4 13.164 13.46 13.046

TEC44056

E. Arrange the numbers in order from least to greatest.

0.031 0.123 1.012 1.123 1.032 0.102

TEC44056

F. Arrange the numbers in order from greatest to least.

9.08 9.8 8.9 8.09 9.9 9.88

TEC44056

Answer Key for "Stick to It!"

A. 0.05, 0.093, 0.1, 0.15, 0.8, 0.93

B. 0.99, 0.9, 0.099, 0.09, 0.019, 0.009

C. 21.315, 23.305, 24.351, 24.513, 24.531, 24.553

D. 13.6, 13.46, 13.4, 13.164, 13.046, 13.04

E. 0.031, 0.102, 0.123, 1.012, 1.032, 1.123

F. 9.9, 9.88, 9.8, 9.08, 8.9, 8.09

TEC44056

Work Backward • Draw a Picture • Solve an Easier Problem • Make a Table • Act It Out

• Write an Equation • Make an Organized List • Look for a Pattern • Make a Graph • Guess and Check

1. Read
Read the word problem. Then write its question.

2. Understand
Write the problem's question as a statement. List the important facts.

3. Plan
Plan a strategy for solving the problem.

4. Estimate
Estimate the answer.

5. Solve
Use your plan to solve the problem. Show your work.

6. Check
Check your work and compare your answer with your estimate.

7. Explain
Using *first, next, then,* and *finally,* write a paragraph that explains how you solved the problem.

Guess and Check • Make a Graph • Look for a Pattern • Make an Organized List • Write an Equation •

Work Backward • Draw a Picture • Solve an Easier Problem • Make a Table • Act It Out

Note to the teacher: Use with "Problem-Solving Tactics" on page 103.

"Class-y" Geometry

Geometry vocabulary

Your students are sure to understand and remember important terminology when they act it out! Have each small group of students define a different set of geometry terms, recording the definitions on separate index cards. Then challenge the students in each group to figure out how they can form each line, set of lines, angle, or shape. Snap a photo of the students in each formation. Then, on each print, trace the formation in permanent marker and post the pictures on a board titled "Geometry in Action!" Follow up with this fun assessment: display the photos without definitions and have students name and define each formation.

Debbie Cassell, Spiller Elementary, Wytheville, VA

Swat!

Fractions

For this fast-paced class game, obtain two inexpensive flyswatters and write fractions on the board. Then divide the class into two teams. Give the first person in line for each team a flyswatter and announce a question with a fraction answer. The first student to swat the correct answer earns a point for her team. After each question, the students at the board go to the end of the line, and the next students in line step up to the board. When time's up, declare the team with more points the day's winning Fraction SWAT Team.

Colleen Dabney, Williamsburg, VA

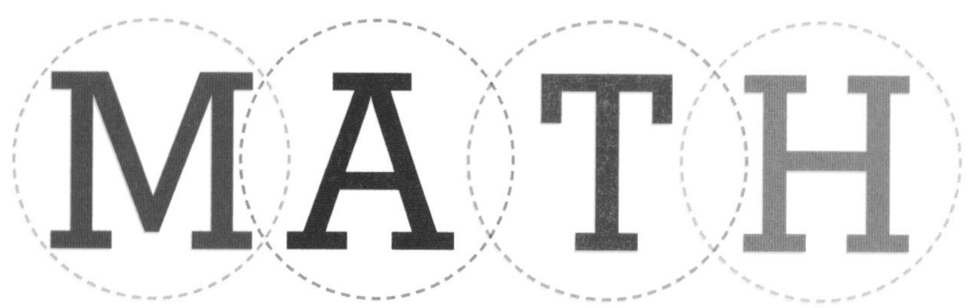

tips & tools

A Factor Race

Multiplication, factors

Use this small-group game to give students practice naming factors. Copy page 108 for every four students in your class. Then give the students in each group two dice and have them follow the directions shown.

Jennifer Otter, Oak Ridge, NC

Directions:

1. Choose a climbing path.
2. When it's your turn, roll two dice. Add the numbers you roll. If the sum is a factor of the next number on your path, name the factor pair. The player to your left uses a calculator to multiply the factors. If you are correct, shade the climbing hold.
3. If the sum is not a factor of the next number or if you cannot correctly name the factor pair, your turn is over.
4. The first player to reach the top of the wall wins.

Eight times seven equals fifty-six.

Switched-Up Sudoku

Two-digit multiplication

Here's a unique practice game for two-digit multiplication. Give each pair of students the solution to a Sudoku puzzle from a newspaper, a puzzle book, or the Internet. Also give the duo a die, different-color markers, and a calculator. To play, one partner rolls the die and finds that number on the grid. She circles the number and three more connecting numbers. Then she multiplies the first two digits by the next two. The student's partner checks her work on the calculator. If she's correct, she shades the squares; if she's incorrect, she erases her circle. Then her partner takes a turn.

Colleen Dabney, Williamsburg, VA

1	2	3	4	5	6	7	8	9
4	5	6	7	8	9	1	2	3
7	8	9	1	2	3	4	5	6
2	3	1	6	7	4	8	9	5
8	7	5	9	1	2	3	6	4
6	9	4	5	3	8	2	1	7
3	1	7	2	6	5	9	4	8
5	4	2	8	9	7	6	3	1
9	6	8	3					

Luis

52
x 83
156
4160
4,316 ✓

Grace

16
x 74
64
1120
1,184 ✓

Company's Coming!

Making a line graph

Capitalize on those daily interruptions by having students graph them! Have each student label the tally chart on a copy of page 109 with the times that match your schedule. Then, beginning with the first interval, have each student make a tally mark for each classroom visitor, adult or child, during that hour. Near the end of the day, have each student total his tallies and graph the data, making a line graph on his page. Next, lead students to discuss their graphs and the trends they notice. **To extend the activity**, have each student graph your classroom visits all week and then create a line graph that compares the daily totals or guide the class to create a double line graph that compares the number of morning and afternoon visitors.

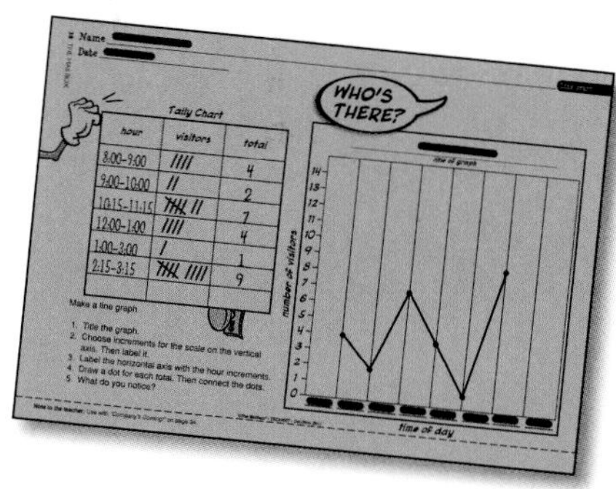

A FACTOR RACE

Note to the teacher: Use with "A Factor Race" on page 107.

Name ______________________________

Date ______________

WHO'S THERE?

Tally Chart

hour	visitors	total

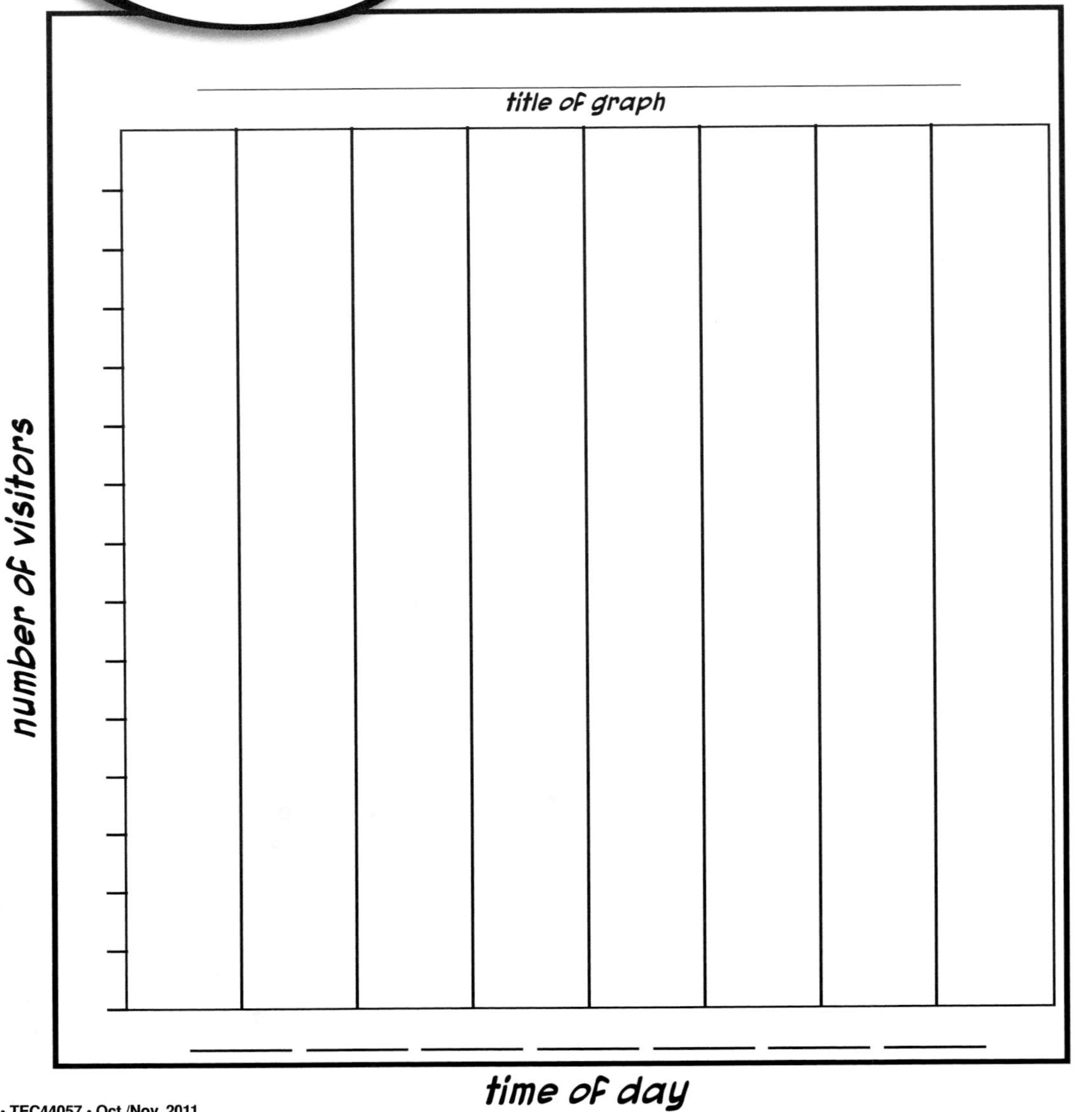

title of graph

number of visitors

time of day

Make a line graph.

1. Title the graph.
2. Choose increments for the scale on the vertical axis. Then label it.
3. Label the horizontal axis with the hour increments.
4. Draw a dot for each total. Then connect the dots.
5. What do you notice?

Note to the teacher: Use with "Company's Coming!" on page 107.

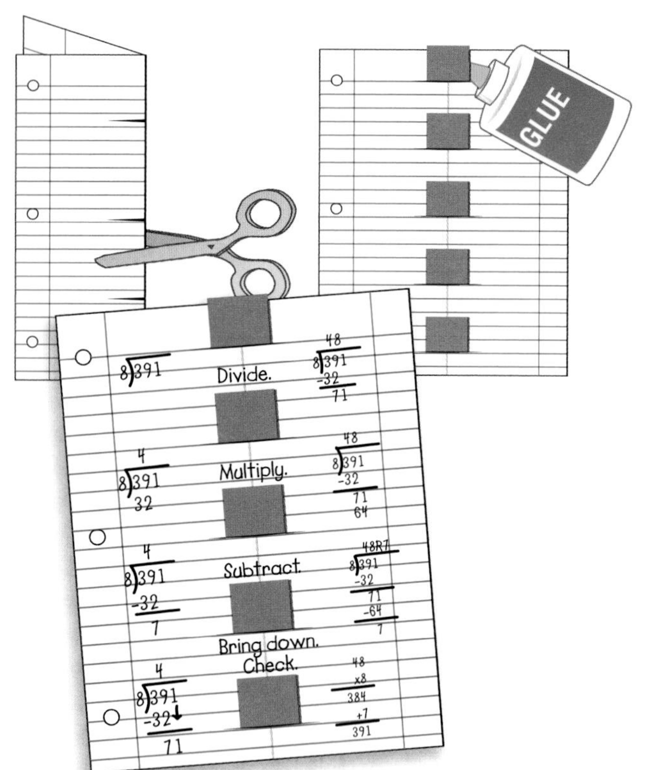

Weaving in Understanding

Division

Help students keep track of the steps in long division with this eye-catching reminder. First, have each child fold a sheet of paper in half and cut nine one-inch slits along the fold (about one inch apart). Next, have the student weave a colorful paper strip through the slits, glue the strip in place, and label her paper as shown. Then have the child write a division problem beside the first label. Guide each student to solve the problem, having her practice the process by rewriting the problem for each successive step. Finally, have the child check her work by multiplying the quotient and the divisor and adding any remainder. Then have her keep the page as a handy reminder.

Colleen Dabney, Williamsburg, VA

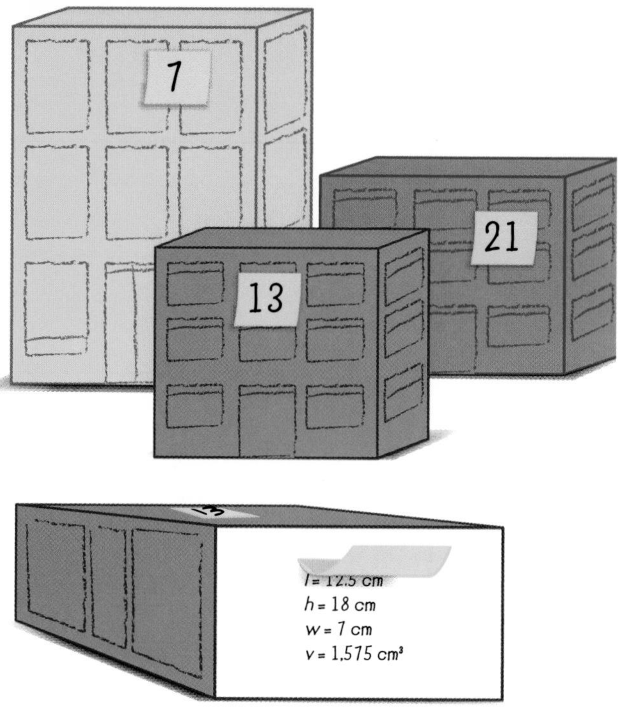

Volume With a View

Volume

For this idea, have students bring in small empty boxes from household products, such as cereal, baking soda, or pasta. Next, have each pair of students choose two different-size boxes, cover them with construction paper, and decorate them so they look like buildings. Then guide the partners to measure each building and calculate its volume. Have the pair write the measurements and volume on the bottom of the box and then cover the measurement with a sticky note. Number the buildings and place them on a shelf to create a cityscape that doubles as a center. At the center, a student chooses four buildings, records each one's number, measures each box, and calculates its volume. He records his work and then peeks under each sticky note to check it.

Colleen Dabney

If your students aren't ready to multiply fractions, have them measure in centimeters instead of inches.

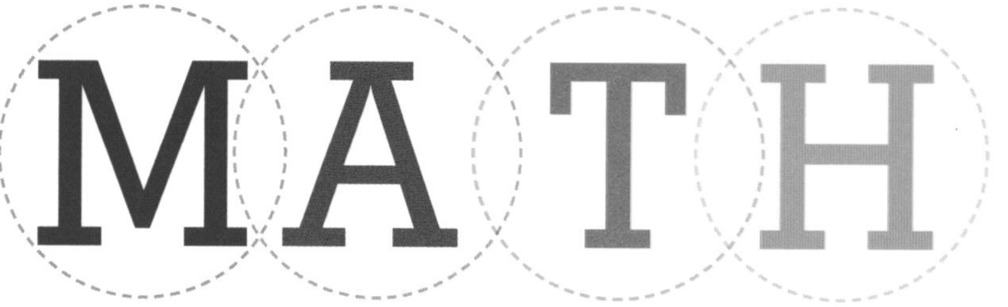

tips & tools

Five That Fit

Mean, median, mode, range

Instead of giving your students another worksheet to practice finding statistical landmarks, try this! Post a set of statistics (the range, mean, median, and mode) for a mystery set of data. Then guide students to guess and check different values until they find five numbers that have the posted set of landmarks. Next, challenge each small group of students to find five different numbers that fit the statistics. Discuss students' results. Then post additional sets of statistical landmarks and challenge each group to find five that fit each set.

Jennifer Otter, Oak Ridge, NC

Statistical Landmarks				Data
Range	*Mean*	*Median*	*Mode*	*(Numbers may vary.)*
9	8	8	8	3, 8, 8, 9, 12
9	9	8	8	6, 8, 8, 8, 15
11	11	10	7	7, 7, 10, 13, 18
11	8	6	5	5, 5, 6, 8, 16
6	5	6	6	2, 3, 6, 6, 8

"Cup-standing" Possibilities

Probability

For this idea, label five different-size or different-shape disposable cups A to E. Next, guide students to predict whether each cup, dropped from three feet high, is more likely to land on its side, its bottom, or upside down. Have each child record her predictions on a copy of page 112. Then give each small group a cup and a yardstick. Direct the students in each group to hold the cup even with the yardstick and then drop the cup. Have each child tally the results on her copy of page 112. Then have the students in the group take turns repeating the drop and tallying the results until they've dropped the cup 50 times. Next, have each group share its results. Guide the students in the rest of the class to record the results, discuss them, and draw conclusions about what's most or least likely to happen when you drop a cup!

Partner Practice

Simplest form

Here's a game that gives students lots of practice reducing fractions. Each pair of students needs a copy of page 113, writing paper, and different-colored pencils or markers. Then guide the partners to follow the directions shown.

Jennifer Otter

Directions:

1. Fold the answer key under the page. When it's your turn, choose a fraction from the top section and write it on your paper.
2. Reduce the fraction to its simplest form and have your partner check the key.
3. If you are correct, cross out the fraction you chose and shade a box on the grid with the reduced fraction. If you are not correct, your turn is over.
4. Earn points by shading four connecting boxes in the shapes shown. When all the fractions in the top section have been crossed out, tally your points. The player with more points wins the game.

Name ______________________________ Date ______________________________

"Cup-standing" Possibilities

Predictions:

I think it is most likely that cup A will land ____________________.

I think it is most likely that cup B will land ____________________.

I think it is most likely that cup C will land ____________________.

I think it is most likely that cup D will land ____________________.

I think it is most likely that cup E will land ____________________.

Results:

Cup ___ lands on its side.	Cup ___ lands on its bottom.	Cup ___ lands upside down.

In 50 drops, cup A landed ______________________________ most often.

In 50 drops, cup B landed ______________________________ most often.

In 50 drops, cup C landed ______________________________ most often.

In 50 drops, cup D landed ______________________________ most often.

In 50 drops, cup E landed ______________________________ most often.

Conclusions:

____

____

____

____

____

 Note to the teacher: Use with "'Cup-standing' Possibilities" on page 111.

Ferreting Out Simplest Form

$\frac{13}{15}$ $\frac{18}{30}$ $\frac{6}{9}$ $\frac{3}{18}$ $\frac{45}{50}$ $\frac{8}{32}$ $\frac{30}{45}$ $\frac{27}{72}$

$\frac{28}{32}$ $\frac{75}{100}$ $\frac{10}{21}$ $\frac{49}{63}$ $\frac{15}{30}$ $\frac{40}{50}$ $\frac{8}{16}$

$\frac{35}{56}$ $\frac{10}{12}$ $\frac{12}{36}$ $\frac{33}{55}$ $\frac{21}{56}$ $\frac{21}{30}$ $\frac{3}{24}$ $\frac{35}{42}$

$\frac{42}{72}$ $\frac{12}{35}$ $\frac{16}{40}$ $\frac{16}{20}$ $\frac{60}{96}$ $\frac{25}{28}$ $\frac{14}{21}$

$\frac{1}{3}$	$\frac{5}{6}$	$\frac{1}{6}$	$\frac{3}{5}$	$\frac{4}{5}$	$\frac{13}{15}$	$\frac{5}{8}$	$\frac{9}{10}$	$\frac{1}{2}$	$\frac{1}{8}$	$\frac{3}{8}$	$\frac{1}{4}$
$\frac{1}{2}$	$\frac{25}{28}$	$\frac{2}{3}$	$\frac{5}{6}$	$\frac{7}{9}$	$\frac{4}{5}$	$\frac{2}{3}$	$\frac{10}{21}$	$\frac{3}{8}$	$\frac{7}{10}$	$\frac{5}{8}$	$\frac{1}{3}$
$\frac{3}{4}$	$\frac{7}{8}$	$\frac{12}{35}$	$\frac{3}{5}$	$\frac{7}{12}$	$\frac{2}{5}$	$\frac{1}{3}$	$\frac{5}{6}$	$\frac{1}{6}$	$\frac{3}{5}$	$\frac{4}{5}$	$\frac{13}{15}$
$\frac{5}{8}$	$\frac{9}{10}$	$\frac{1}{2}$	$\frac{1}{8}$	$\frac{3}{8}$	$\frac{1}{4}$	$\frac{1}{2}$	$\frac{25}{28}$	$\frac{2}{3}$	$\frac{5}{6}$	$\frac{7}{9}$	$\frac{4}{5}$
$\frac{2}{3}$	$\frac{10}{21}$	$\frac{3}{8}$	$\frac{7}{10}$	$\frac{5}{8}$	$\frac{1}{3}$	$\frac{3}{4}$	$\frac{7}{8}$	$\frac{12}{35}$	$\frac{3}{5}$	$\frac{7}{12}$	$\frac{2}{5}$

Scoring

(Figures can be reflected [flipped] or rotated [turned on a point].)

= 1 point = 5 points = 5 points = 10 points = 10 points = 15 points

Answer Key for "Ferreting Out Simplest Form"

$\frac{3}{24} = \frac{1}{8}$
$\frac{3}{18} = \frac{1}{6}$
$\frac{8}{32} = \frac{1}{4}$
$\frac{16}{40} = \frac{2}{5}$
$\frac{6}{9} = \frac{2}{3}$
$\frac{12}{36} = \frac{1}{3}$

$\frac{27}{72} = \frac{3}{8}$
$\frac{21}{56} = \frac{3}{8}$
$\frac{12}{35}$ is in simplest form.
$\frac{10}{21}$ is in simplest form.
$\frac{15}{30} = \frac{1}{2}$
$\frac{8}{16} = \frac{1}{2}$

$\frac{33}{55} = \frac{3}{5}$
$\frac{18}{30} = \frac{3}{5}$
$\frac{30}{45} = \frac{2}{3}$
$\frac{14}{21} = \frac{2}{3}$
$\frac{42}{72} = \frac{7}{12}$
$\frac{35}{56} = \frac{5}{8}$

$\frac{60}{96} = \frac{5}{8}$
$\frac{21}{30} = \frac{7}{10}$
$\frac{75}{100} = \frac{3}{4}$
$\frac{49}{63} = \frac{7}{9}$
$\frac{40}{50} = \frac{4}{5}$
$\frac{16}{20} = \frac{4}{5}$

$\frac{13}{15}$ is in simplest form.
$\frac{28}{32} = \frac{7}{8}$
$\frac{10}{12} = \frac{5}{6}$
$\frac{35}{42} = \frac{5}{6}$
$\frac{25}{28}$ is in simplest form.
$\frac{45}{50} = \frac{9}{10}$

Note to the teacher: Use with "Partner Practice" on page 111.

gallon

$\frac{1}{2}$ gallon | $\frac{1}{2}$ gallon

quart | quart | quart | quart

pint | pint | pint | pint | pint | pint | pint | pint

cup | cup | cup | cup | cup | cup | cup | cup | cup | cup | cup | cup | cup | cup | cup | cup

Going With the Flow

Capacity

Help each of your students remember the relationship between gallons, quarts, pints, and cups with a sheet of paper and five simple steps. After guiding each child to follow the steps shown, have her tuck the page into her binder as a handy reminder.

Directions:

1. Turn a sheet of paper so that its long edges are at the top and bottom. Then draw five horizontal lines one inch apart on the page. Write "gallon" on the top line.
2. Fold the paper in half so the short ends meet. On the second line, draw a line to separate the sections and then label each part "$\frac{1}{2}$ gallon."
3. Refold the paper and fold it in half again. On the third line, draw three lines to separate the sections and then write "quart" in each one.
4. Refold the paper and fold it in half once more. On the fourth line, draw seven lines to separate the sections and label each eighth "pint."
5. Refold the paper and fold it in half one last time. On the fifth line, draw 15 lines to separate the sections and label each 16th "cup." Then cut off the extra paper.

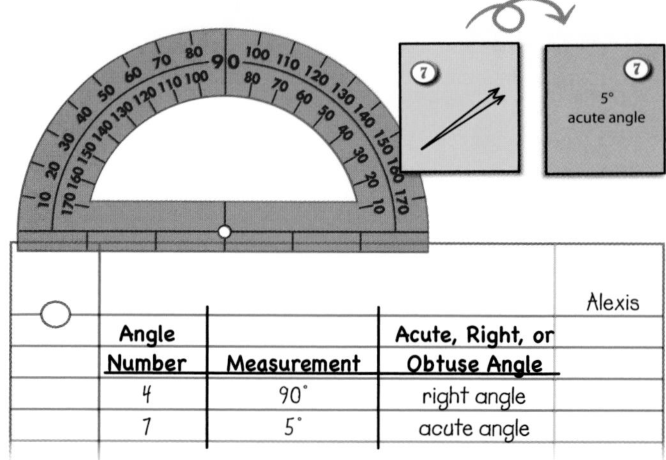

What's the Angle?

Measuring angles

For this activity, cut apart a copy of the angle cards on page 116 and use the answer key below to label the back of each card for self-checking. Next, give each student a card and have her take out a protractor. Then have the child measure the card's angle, record its measurement, and classify it as acute, right, or obtuse before flipping the card to check her work. When the student finishes, she trades cards with another student who is ready and repeats the steps. Continue as time allows or until every student has measured all the angles.

Leah Hurwitz, Yeshiva of Spring Valley, Monsey, NY

Answer Key

1. 60° acute angle
2. 35° acute angle
3. 120° obtuse angle
4. 90° right angle
5. 115° obtuse angle
6. 45° acute angle
7. 5° acute angle
8. 175° obtuse angle
9. 110° obtuse angle
10. 80° acute angle
11. 125° obtuse angle
12. 20° acute angle
13. 40° acute angle
14. 105° obtuse angle
15. 150° obtuse angle
16. 165° obtuse angle
17. 85° acute angle
18. 10° acute angle
19. 70° acute angle
20. 90° right angle
21. 12° acute angle
22. 136° obtuse angle
23. 93° obtuse angle
24. 51° acute angle
25. 108° obtuse angle
26. 54° acute angle
27. 89° acute angle
28. 127° obtuse angle
29. 68° acute angle
30. 149° obtuse angle

tips & tools

First and "Four-most"

Problem solving, order of operations

Looking for a fun way to build your students' mathematical proficiency? Try this! Explain that each of the numbers 1–10 can be obtained by using only the digit 4 and addition, subtraction, multiplication, and/or division. Next, show students the solution for getting the number 1. (See chart below.) Then challenge each pair of students to use only the digit 4 to find solutions that equal the numbers 2–10. Remind students to use parentheses if they need to. After students finish, set aside time for them to share and compare their solutions.

Possible Solutions

$1 = (4 \div 4) + 4 - 4$

$2 = (4 \times 4) \div (4 + 4)$

$3 = (4 + 4 + 4) \div 4$

$4 = (4 \div 4) \times 4$

$5 = 4 \div 4 + 4$

$6 = (4 + 4) \div 4 + 4$

$7 = 4 + 4 - (4 \div 4)$

$8 = (4 \times 4) - 4 - 4$

$9 = (4 \div 4) + 4 + 4$

$10 = (44 - 4) \div 4$

Challenge your early finishers to find another digit that can be used to equal the numbers 1–10.

The Domino Factor

Fractions, mixed review

For this small-group game, put a set of dominoes, a die, and a copy of page 117 at a center. Then have groups of two to four students rotate through the center, playing the game and building strong fraction skills.

Jennifer Otter
Oak Ridge, NC

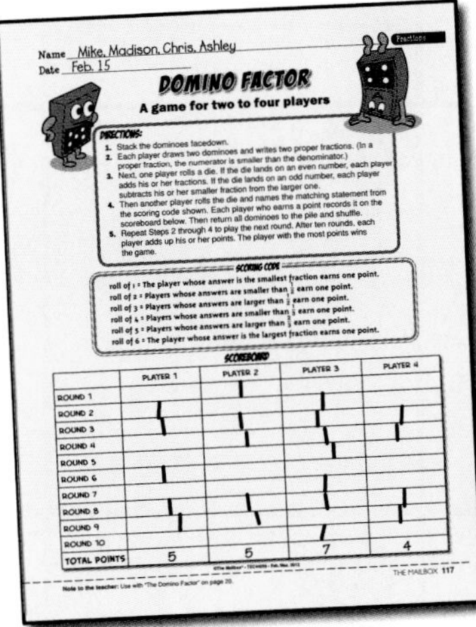

Fractions

Name Mike, Madison, Chris, Ashley
Date Feb. 15

DOMINO FACTOR

A game for two to four players

DIRECTIONS:

1. Stack the dominoes facedown.
2. Each player draws two dominoes and writes two proper fractions. (In a proper fraction, the numerator is smaller than the denominator.)
3. Next, one player rolls a die. If the die lands on an even number, each player adds his or her fractions. If the die lands on an odd number, each player subtracts his or her smaller fraction from the larger one.
4. Then another player rolls the die and names the matching statement from the scoring code shown. Each player who earns a point records it on the scoreboard below. Then return all dominoes to the pile and shuffle.
5. Repeat Steps 2 through 4 to play the next round. After ten rounds, each player adds up his or her points. The player with the most points wins the game.

SCORING CODE

roll of 1 = The player whose answer is the smallest fraction earns one point.
roll of 2 = Players whose answers are smaller than $\frac{1}{2}$ earn one point.
roll of 3 = Players whose answers are larger than $\frac{1}{2}$ earn one point.
roll of 4 = Players whose answers are smaller than $\frac{1}{3}$ earn one point.
roll of 5 = Players whose answers are larger than $\frac{2}{3}$ earn one point.
roll of 6 = The player whose answer is the largest fraction earns one point.

SCOREBOARD

	PLAYER 1	PLAYER 2	PLAYER 3	PLAYER 4
ROUND 1		|	|	
ROUND 2	|	|	|	|
ROUND 3	|		|	|
ROUND 4		|	|	
ROUND 5				
ROUND 6	|		|	
ROUND 7		|	|	|
ROUND 8	|	|		|
ROUND 9	|		|	
ROUND 10				
TOTAL POINTS	5	5	7	4

©The Mailbox® • Feb./Mar. 2012

THE MAILBOX 117

Note to the teacher: Use with "The Domino Factor" on page 20.

Right on the Money

Decimal computation

Got an assortment of receipts cluttering your car or bag? Gather them up and put them to work! First, cover any personal information with a dark marker or correction tape. Then put the receipts in an envelope along with two dice. A student rolls the dice and then takes that number of receipts. Next, the child finds the combined sum of the receipts. Depending on the student's skills, have him complete additional tasks such as those shown.

Colleen Dabney
Williamsburg, VA

Receipt Tasks

- Add the receipts' totals to find their sum.
- Add the receipts' totals to find their sum. Take a different receipt. Subtract this receipt's total from the sum.
- Add the receipts' totals to find their sum. Roll one die. Multiply the sum by that number.
- Add the receipts' totals to find their sum. Divide the sum by the number of receipts you added.

Angle Cards

Use with "What's the Angle?" on page 114.

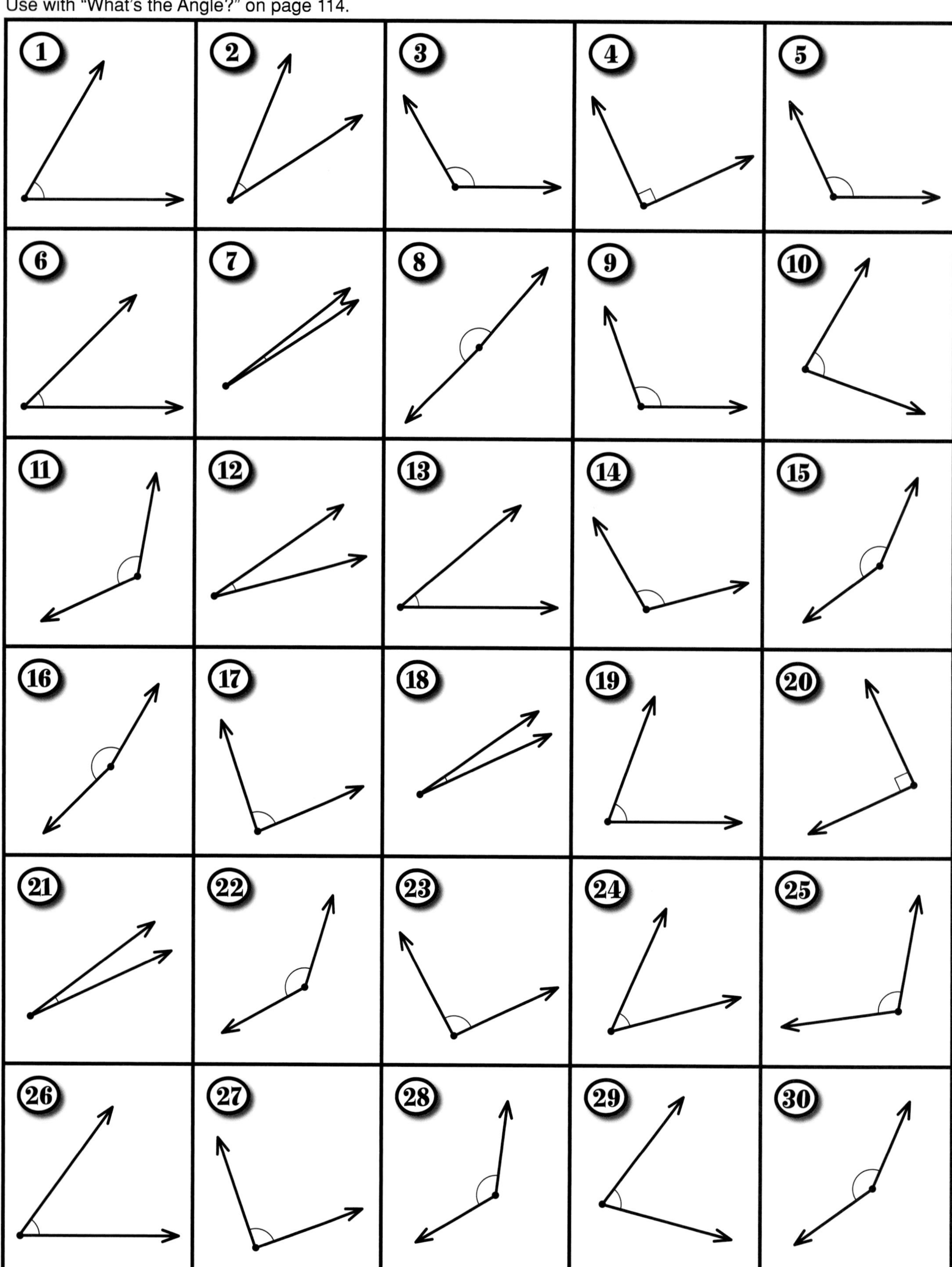

Names ____________________

Date ____________________

DOMINO FACTOR

A game for two to four players

DIRECTIONS:

1. Stack the dominoes facedown.
2. Each player draws two dominoes and writes two proper fractions. (In a proper fraction, the numerator is smaller than the denominator.)
3. Next, one player rolls a die. If the die lands on an even number, each player adds his or her fractions. If the die lands on an odd number, each player subtracts his or her smaller fraction from the larger one.
4. Then another player rolls the die and names the matching statement from the scoring code shown. Each player who earns a point records it on the scoreboard below. Then return all dominoes to the pile and shuffle.
5. Repeat Steps 2 through 4 to play the next round. After ten rounds, each player adds up his or her points. The player with the most points wins the game.

SCORING CODE

roll of 1 = The player whose answer is the smallest fraction earns one point.
roll of 2 = Players whose answers are smaller than $\frac{1}{2}$ earn one point.
roll of 3 = Players whose answers are larger than $\frac{1}{2}$ earn one point.
roll of 4 = Players whose answers are smaller than $\frac{1}{3}$ earn one point.
roll of 5 = Players whose answers are larger than $\frac{2}{3}$ earn one point.
roll of 6 = The player whose answer is the largest fraction earns one point.

SCOREBOARD

	PLAYER 1	PLAYER 2	PLAYER 3	PLAYER 4
ROUND 1				
ROUND 2				
ROUND 3				
ROUND 4				
ROUND 5				
ROUND 6				
ROUND 7				
ROUND 8				
ROUND 9				
ROUND 10				
TOTAL POINTS				

Note to the teacher: Use with "The Domino Factor" on page 115.

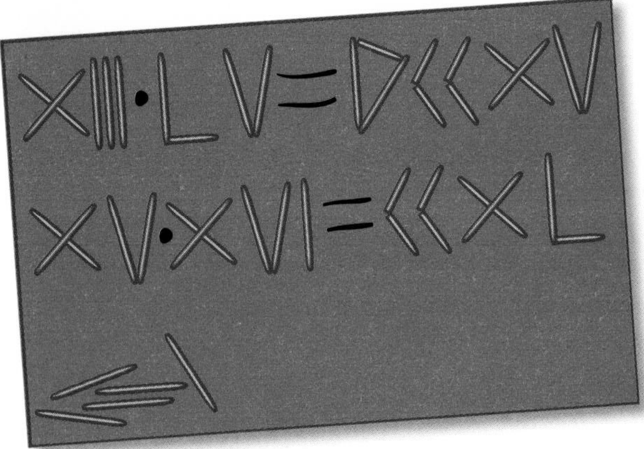

Sticking to the Facts

Computation, using roman numerals

Set up this hands-on center with a box of toothpicks, a list of roman numeral equivalents, a set of problems such as those shown, 12" x 18" construction paper, and glue. A student chooses a problem and solves it. Next, the child re-creates the equation in roman numerals, using toothpicks and glues the toothpicks in place. (Have the student break toothpicks in half to make X, L, D, and C.) Have the child repeat the process with three more problems. To accommodate long equations, have a student glue or tape together two sheets of paper.

Roman Numerals

I = 1	L = 50
IV = 4	C = 100
V = 5	D = 500
VI = 6	M = 1,000
IX = 9	V = 5,000
X = 10	

13 x 55	359 x 12
15 x 16	26 x 139
44 x 21	59 x 27
61 x 24	108 x 19
218 x 14	141 x 27

From a Different Angle

Types of angles

Each student will need a ruler, a compass, unlined paper, and his imagination for this skill-building activity! Review angle basics and then post the warm-up challenges shown. Have each student choose and complete three warm-up challenges. Then have each child demonstrate his skills by completing the final challenge as guided below.

Warm-up Challenges

- Draw a flower that has eight different acute angles. Label each angle with its exact measurement.
- Draw a doghouse that has only right angles. Label eight angles.
- Draw an alien that has four different obtuse, three right, and two different acute angles. Label each angle with its exact measurement.
- Draw a picture of the front of your house. Then list the number of acute, right, and obtuse angles that are in your picture. Label each angle with its exact measurement.
- Draw a picture of the ultimate playground equipment that has only acute and obtuse angles. Label each angle with its exact measurement.

The Final Challenge

Draw a picture of your dream house, labeling each angle with the exact measurement, so that it contains the following:

- two different acute angles that are less than 45 degrees
- two different acute angles that are greater than 45 degrees
- two different obtuse angles that are less than 150 degrees
- two different obtuse angles that are greater than 150 degrees
- three right angles

tips & tools

Compare and Keep

Comparing fractions and decimals

For this partner game, have each pair of students cut apart the cards from a copy of page 120. One student shuffles the cards and deals half to her partner. Each player stacks her cards facedown. To play, each student turns over one card. The player whose card has the greater value keeps both cards. If the cards have the same value, both players keep their cards. After both students turn over their last cards, they count to see who has more cards, and then they shuffle all the cards and play another round as time allows.

Adapted from an idea by Jennifer Otter
Oak Ridge, NC

Taking Aim

Division

Are your students' division skills on target? Find out with these quick assessments. Choose a skill and then have each child write five division problems that meet the listed qualifications. After a student creates a problem, direct her to explain how she arrived at the example and checked to make sure her work was correct.

For division:

Create a division problem for each description.

- It has a three-digit dividend, a one-digit divisor, and no remainder.
- It has a four-digit dividend, a four-digit quotient, and a remainder of 1.
- It has a three-digit dividend, a two-digit quotient, and a remainder of 3.
- It has a quotient of 34 with a remainder of 32.
- It has a two-digit divisor and a dividend greater than 3,000.

I Spy

Coordinate grids

Need to introduce your students to four-quadrant coordinate grids? Try this! Have each student fold a sheet of graph paper in half twice and then trace each fold, creating *x*- and *y*-axes. Next, have the child label each axis and then draw a two-unit by four-unit rectangle in each quadrant. Then have each student record the ordered pairs that describe each rectangle's vertices, explaining to students how to write ordered pairs with negative numbers. Follow up by having each pair of students take turns naming coordinates to spot the vertices of each other's hidden rectangles. If a student names an ordered pair that does not match one of his partner's vertices, have him draw an *x* on his own grid at that point. When a student names a matching coordinate, have him circle the point. When time's up, the student who finds more vertices wins.

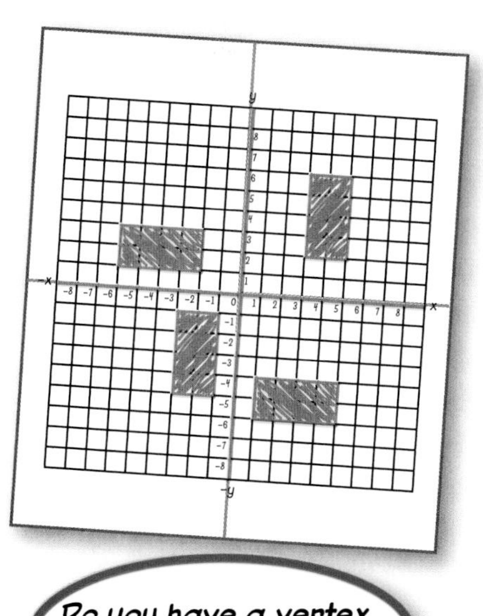

Do you have a vertex at negative two, two?

Fraction and Decimal Cards

Use with "Compare and Keep" on page 119.

0.019 TEC44060	$\frac{1}{8}$ TEC44060	0.3 TEC44060	$\frac{7}{100}$ TEC44060	$\frac{1}{10}$ TEC44060	$\frac{1}{5}$ TEC44060
$\frac{23}{100}$ TEC44060	$\frac{1}{4}$ TEC44060	$\frac{3}{10}$ TEC44060	$\frac{1}{3}$ TEC44060	0.75 TEC44060	$\frac{5}{8}$ TEC44060
$\frac{3}{5}$ TEC44060	$\frac{2}{3}$ TEC44060	$\frac{7}{10}$ TEC44060	$\frac{3}{8}$ TEC44060	$\frac{3}{100}$ TEC44060	$\frac{4}{5}$ TEC44060
0.6 TEC44060	0.01 TEC44060	0.99 TEC44060	0.125 TEC44060	$\frac{7}{8}$ TEC44060	0.4 TEC44060
$\frac{9}{10}$ TEC44060	0.05 TEC44060	0.08 TEC44060	0.09 TEC44060	$\frac{2}{5}$ TEC44060	0.15 TEC44060
0.2 TEC44060	0.22 TEC44060	$\frac{5}{6}$ TEC44060	0.33 TEC44060	0.25 TEC44060	0.48 TEC44060
$\frac{3}{4}$ TEC44060	0.5 TEC44060	0.625 TEC44060	$\frac{99}{100}$ TEC44060	0.67 TEC44060	$\frac{1}{2}$ TEC44060
$\frac{33}{100}$ TEC44060	0.02 TEC44060	$\frac{1}{6}$ TEC44060	0.9 TEC44060	0.875 TEC44060	0.65 TEC44060

An Educated Guess

Estimating

Here's a quick activity that's sure to stimulate students' estimation skills. Display a thick book and ask students to guess how many pages it has. Next, put a bookmark in the second half of the book, announce the page numbers on either side of the bookmark, close the book, and display it again. Then guide students to use the bookmark's placement to estimate the total number of pages in the book. Encourage students to share their estimates and explain their reasoning. After that, repeat the process with another book, having students record their estimates and write about their reasoning. Follow up with other quick activities such as those shown.

- Show a shoebox lid with a math connecting cube in one corner. Ask students to estimate the number of cubes it would take to cover the bottom of the box lid. Then repeat with a different-size box lid.
- Show a stack of ten pennies with a ruler lying nearby. Ask students to estimate the number of pennies it would take to make a five-inch stack. Then repeat with a stack of ten nickels.
- Ask students to estimate your height to the nearest centimeter. Then ask students to estimate the principal's, nurse's, another teacher's, or custodian's height to the nearest centimeter.

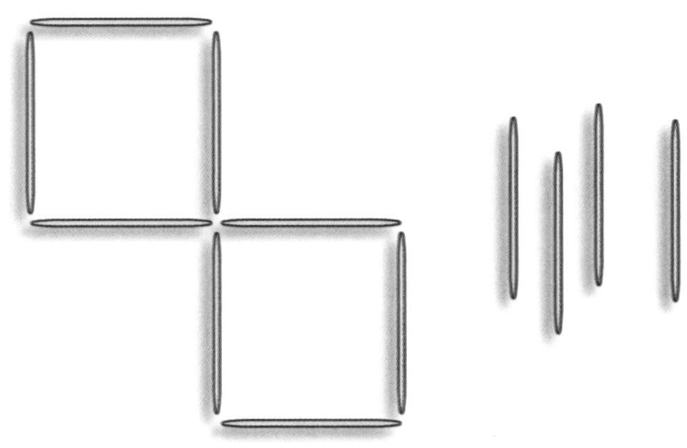

To the Point

Problem solving

For this idea, display the toothpick puzzles on page 123, explain the differences between moving and removing toothpicks, and then give each student 12 toothpicks. Next, lead students to solve the first puzzle. Then have each child fold a sheet of paper into ten sections and, in the top section, draw a diagram of the first puzzle's solution. Next, challenge students to solve the rest of the puzzles, drawing a diagram of each solution.

tip Challenge each early finisher to create a new puzzle. Then have her draw a diagram on an index card, write the puzzle's directions on the card, and show the solution on the card's flip side. Then put students' cards in a bag along with 12 toothpicks and keep the puzzles handy for other early finishers.

tips & tools

Domino Magic Squares

Problem solving

For this hands-on challenge, provide a set of dominoes, the diagram, and the magic square challenges shown. Then have each child choose a magic square challenge and find dominoes that complete it. When a child solves a magic square, have her draw a diagram of her solution and describe her process before tackling the next square. (Students' answers will vary.)

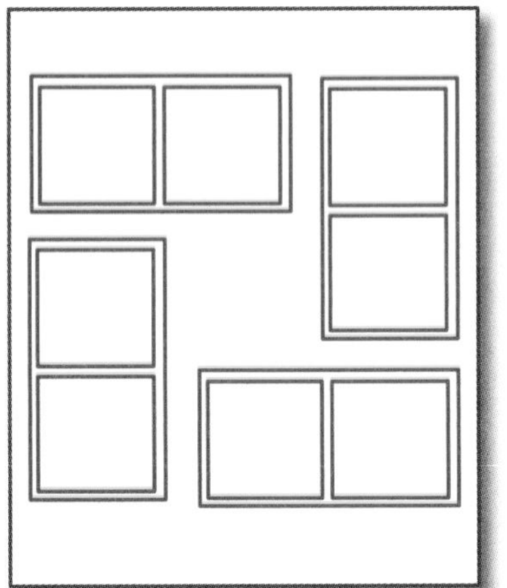

Magic Square Challenges

Each side adds up to 6.
Each side adds up to 9.
Each side adds up to 12.
Each side adds up to 15.

Each side adds up to 9.

A Summer Harvest

Rounding decimals

To help students remember rounding rules when it's time to round decimals, introduce a fun reminder such as the one shown. Then have students practice rounding decimals by playing the partner game from page 124. Have each pair of students cut apart the cards on a copy of page 124 and then follow the directions on the page to play.

adapted from an idea by April Harold
Ghent Elementary
Ghent, WV

Find the place;
Then look next door.
Four or less?
Just ignore.
Five or greater?
Add one more!

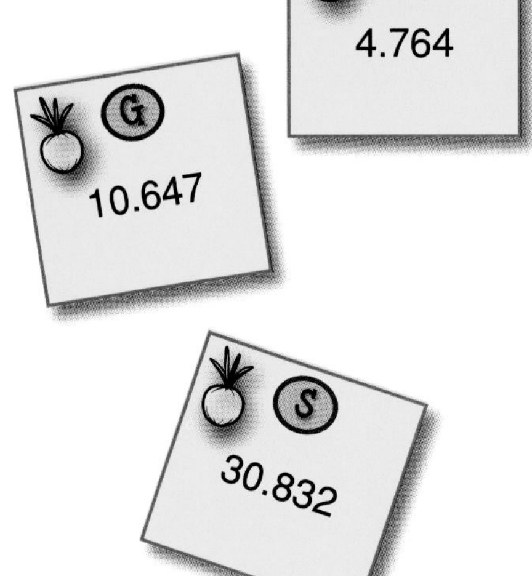

What's the Problem?

Multiplying, dividing fractions

Here's a different approach for giving students practice multiplying or dividing fractions. For multiplication, choose a multiplication problem and give students the product. Then challenge each child to find fraction factors that equal this product. For division, give students the quotient and challenge each child to find a fraction divisor and a whole number dividend. Once a student writes a problem for each answer, challenge him to find another set of factors or a divisor and dividend with the same answer. As time allows, have students discuss their processes in small groups.

The product is $4\frac{2}{5}$; what's the problem? ($2\frac{3}{4} \times 1\frac{3}{5}$)

The quotient is $\frac{3}{4}$; what's the problem? ($1\frac{1}{5} \div 1\frac{3}{5}$)

Pointy Puzzlers

Hint: *Remove* means to take a toothpick away from a figure. *Move* means to move a toothpick to a different position.

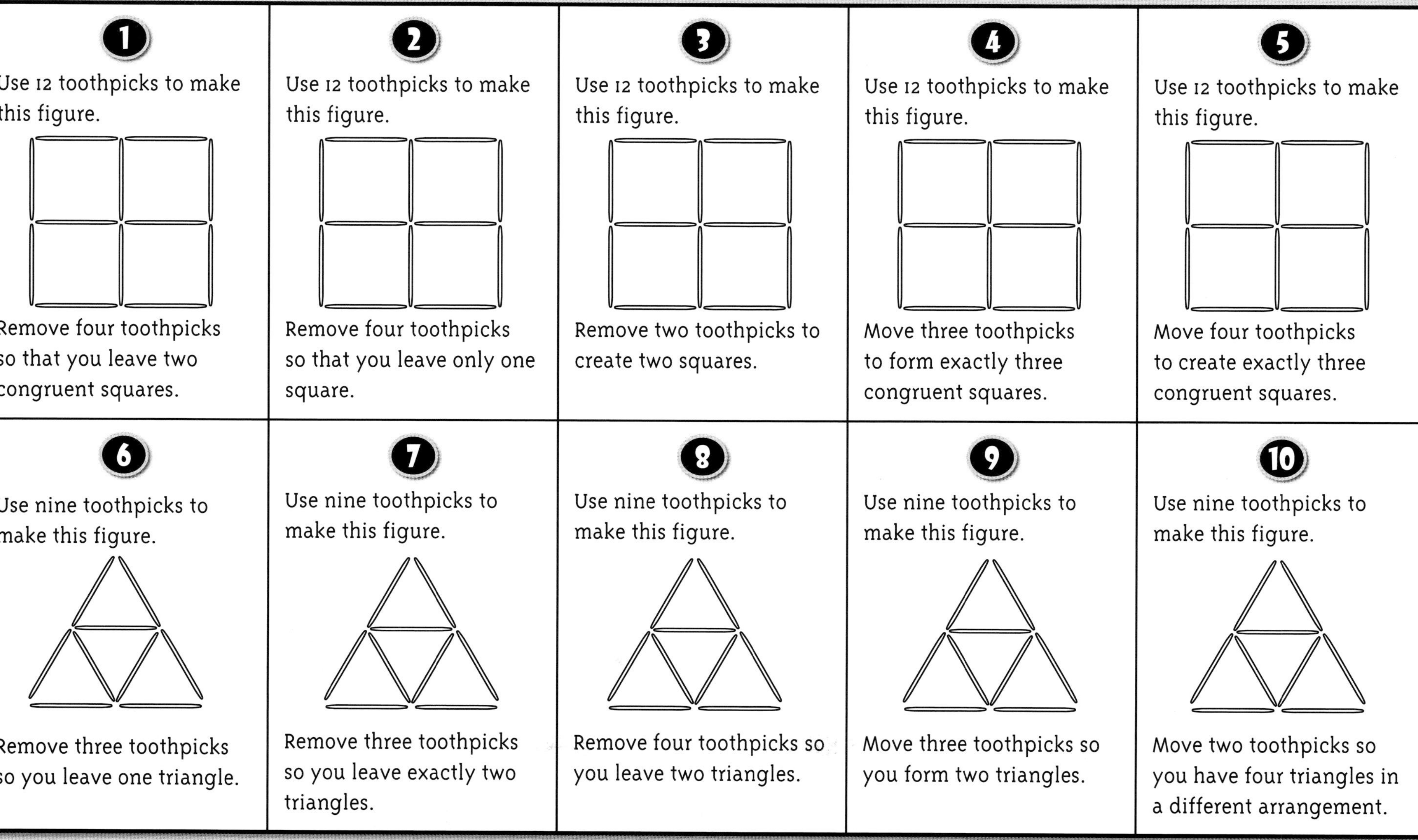

1 Use 12 toothpicks to make this figure. Remove four toothpicks so that you leave two congruent squares.

2 Use 12 toothpicks to make this figure. Remove four toothpicks so that you leave only one square.

3 Use 12 toothpicks to make this figure. Remove two toothpicks to create two squares.

4 Use 12 toothpicks to make this figure. Move three toothpicks to form exactly three congruent squares.

5 Use 12 toothpicks to make this figure. Move four toothpicks to create exactly three congruent squares.

6 Use nine toothpicks to make this figure. Remove three toothpicks so you leave one triangle.

7 Use nine toothpicks to make this figure. Remove three toothpicks so you leave exactly two triangles.

8 Use nine toothpicks to make this figure. Remove four toothpicks so you leave two triangles.

9 Use nine toothpicks to make this figure. Move three toothpicks so you form two triangles.

10 Use nine toothpicks to make this figure. Move two toothpicks so you have four triangles in a different arrangement.

Note to the teacher: Use with “To the Point” on page 121.

A Summer Harvest

Directions:

1. Stack the cards facedown. Fold the key behind the directions.
2. When it's your turn, draw a card. Record the number and then round it according to the code.
3. Have your partner check the key. If you're correct, keep the card. If you're not correct, return the card to the bottom of the pile and erase your answer.
4. Keep playing until the numbers on all the cards have been rounded correctly. The player with more cards wins.

Rounding Code

onion = round to nearest whole number
carrot = round to nearest tenth
turnip = round to nearest hundredth

TEC44061

Answer Key for "A Summer Harvest"

A.	12	P.	5
B.	8.1	Q.	27.5
C.	2.21	R.	69.39
D.	19	S.	31
E.	14.2	T.	55.1
F.	6.66	U.	1.23
G.	11	V.	6
H.	49.4	W.	6.3
I.	33.28	X.	11.41
J.	82	Y.	1
K.	6.9	Z.	2.5
L.	6.74	AA.	7.09
M.	5	BB.	30
N.	21.3	CC.	15.5
O.	23.11	DD.	8.58

TEC44061

A (onion) 12.248 TEC44061	B (carrot) 8.106 TEC44061	C (turnip) 2.211 TEC44061	D (onion) 18.552 TEC44061	E (carrot) 14.222 TEC44061	F (turnip) 6.656 TEC44061
G (onion) 10.647 TEC44061	H (carrot) 49.412 TEC44061	I (turnip) 33.282 TEC44061	J (onion) 81.615 TEC44061	K (carrot) 6.877 TEC44061	L (turnip) 6.739 TEC44061
M (onion) 4.764 TEC44061	N (carrot) 21.284 TEC44061	O (turnip) 23.107 TEC44061	P (onion) 4.944 TEC44061	Q (carrot) 27.454 TEC44061	R (turnip) 69.385 TEC44061
S (onion) 30.832 TEC44061	T (carrot) 55.107 TEC44061	U (turnip) 1.234 TEC44061	V (onion) 6.354 TEC44061	W (carrot) 6.288 TEC44061	X (turnip) 11.407 TEC44061
Y (onion) 1.144 TEC44061	Z (carrot) 2.482 TEC44061	AA (turnip) 7.085 TEC44061	BB (onion) 30.125 TEC44061	CC (carrot) 15.548 TEC44061	DD (turnip) 8.576 TEC44061

Note to the teacher: Use with "A Summer Harvest" on page 122.

Names ____________________

Date ____________________

Up, Up, and Away!

A Game for Two to Four Players

Directions:

1. When it's your turn, use a pencil to circle a product that has not been circled on a cloud.
2. On the hot-air balloon, find and circle two factors that equal the product. Another player checks your answer with a calculator.
3. If you're correct, color the factors with your colored pencil or crayon. If you're not correct, erase your circles. Your turn is over.
4. When all the products on the clouds have been used, the game is over. The player who colors the most factors wins.

3 2 2 2 2
4 3 3 3 3 3 4
4 4 4 4 4 4 5
4 4 5 5 5 5 6
5 5 5 5 5 6 6
6 6 6 6 6 6 6
6 6 7 7 7 7 7
7 7 7 7 7 8 8
8 8 8 8 8 8 8
8 8 8 8 9 9 9
9 9 9 9 9 9 9
10 10 10 10 10 11
11 11 11 12 12 12
12 12 12 12 12

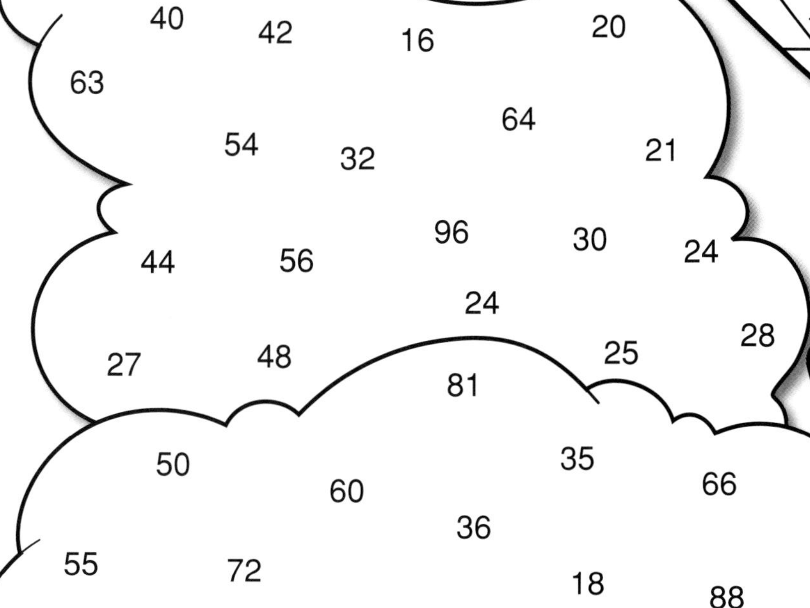

50 60 35 66 36 55 72 72 18 88 48 45 49 40 20 60 24 36 30 16 18

56 36 30 48

How to use: Each group of students needs a calculator, a copy of the page, pencils, and different-color pencils or crayons.

It's Icing on the Cupcake!

Directions for four players:

1. Choose a column. Write your name at the top.
2. When it's your turn, spin both spinners.
3. Write the numbers as a fraction, and then reduce it to simplest form.
4. At the end of each round, determine which player has the smallest fraction. That player circles the fraction. If there is a tie, both players circle their fractions.
5. Continue until all rounds have been played. The player with the most circled fractions wins!

$\frac{1}{12}$	$\frac{1}{10}$	$\frac{1}{8}$	$\frac{1}{6}$	$\frac{1}{5}$	$\frac{1}{4}$	$\frac{3}{10}$	$\frac{1}{3}$	$\frac{3}{8}$	$\frac{1}{2}$	$\frac{3}{5}$	$\frac{5}{8}$	$\frac{2}{3}$	$\frac{7}{10}$	$\frac{3}{4}$	$\frac{4}{5}$	$\frac{5}{6}$	$\frac{7}{8}$	1	$1\frac{1}{5}$	$1\frac{1}{4}$	$1\frac{1}{3}$	$1\frac{1}{2}$	$1\frac{2}{3}$	$1\frac{3}{4}$	2	$2\frac{1}{3}$	$2\frac{1}{2}$	3	$3\frac{1}{2}$

	Player 1	Player 2	Player 3	Player 4
Round 1				
Round 2				
Round 3				
Round 4				
Round 5				
Round 6				
Round 7				
Round 8				
Round 9				
Round 10				
Total Circled Fractions				

 How to use: Each small group needs two paper clips and a copy of this page.

Names ____________________

Date ____________________

JUMP, LEAP, HOP, SOAR!

A Game for Two Players

Directions:

1. Choose a path.
2. In turn, **multiply** two mixed numbers from the bushes. Show your work on a separate sheet of paper.
3. If the **product** is on your path, cross it out.
4. The first player to cross out each product on his or her path wins!

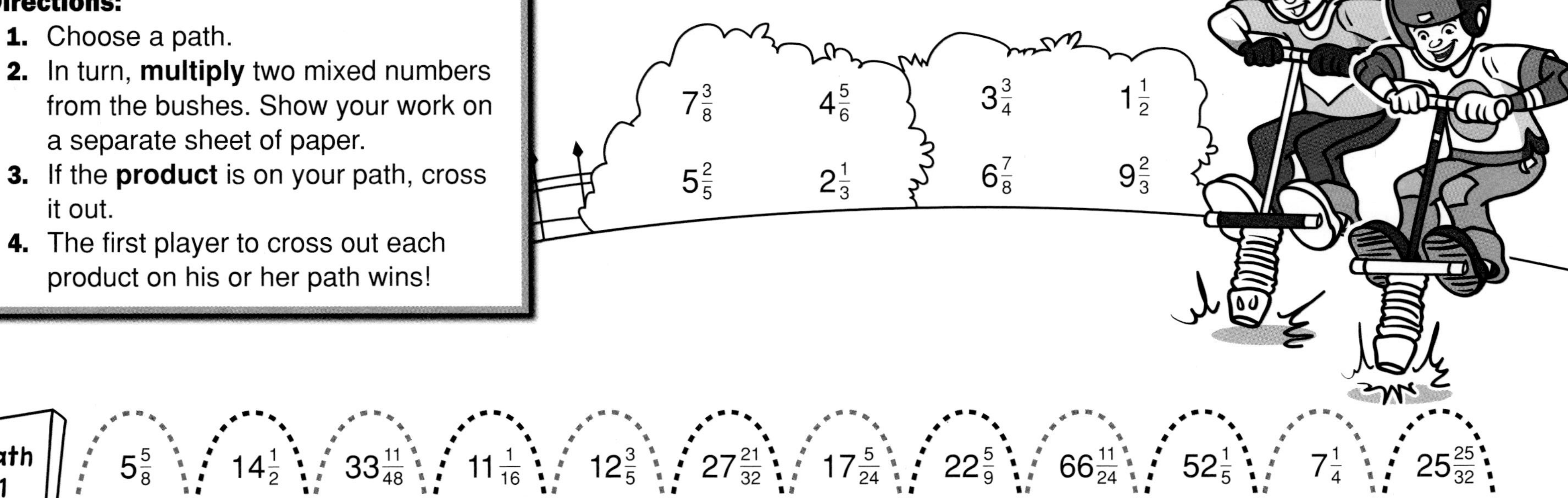

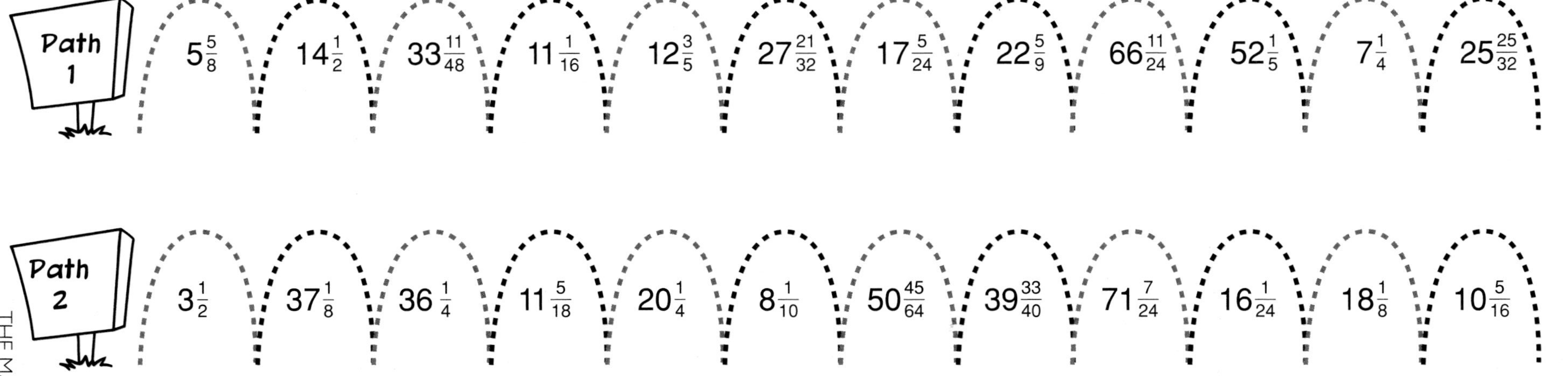

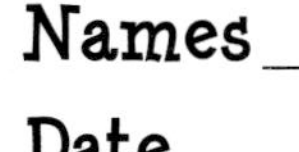

Names ____________________

Date ____________________

Catch a Wave!

A Game for Two Players

Directions:

1. When it's your turn, put your marker on Start. Then spin the spinner.
2. Divide the number in the box by the number you spin. Show your work on another sheet of paper. Your partner uses a calculator to check your quotient.
3. If you are correct, follow the arrows and move the number of boxes that equal your divisor. If your quotient was incorrect, do not move your marker. The first player to reach the island is the winner.

Start ⇨	26.03 ⇨	5.641 ⇨	12.86 ⇨	962.5 ⇨	7.039 ⇨	15.38 ⇩
78.13 ⇨	6.245 ⇨	3.157 ⇨	0.142 ⇨	9.405 ⇨	16.08 ⇩	36.72 ⇩
⇧ 327.8	321.9 ⇨	2.484 ⇨	92.02 ⇨	5.628 ⇩	91.07 ⇩	0.824 ⇩
⇧ 6.578	⇧ 35.57	49.45 ⇨	(island)	52.16 ⇩	1.927 ⇩	24.19 ⇩
⇧ 4.058	⇧ 25.11	⇧ 1.635	⇦ 70.09	⇦ 2.432	53.46 ⇩	3.728 ⇩
⇧ 5.125	⇧ 43.52	⇦ 22.61	⇦ 2.384	⇦ 6.335	⇦ 3.504	431.2 ⇩
⇧ 49.68	⇦ 18.81	⇦ 23.53	⇦ 10.65	⇦ 33.04	⇦ 1.995	⇦ 714.8

How to Use Each pair of students needs two game markers, a paper clip, and a copy of the page.

Name ______________________________

Date ______________________

Adventures in Moving

Solve each equation. Then write the solution in the matching box.

1. $p + 16 = 44$

2. $75 - g = 62$

3. $e \div 3 = 14$

4. $124 = l \times 4$

5. $m \times 5 = 90$

6. $8 = 88 \div j$

7. $a + 35 = 62$

8. $51 - h = 28$

9. $85 = d \times 5$

10. $78 - n = 47$

11. $95 = 5 \times c$

12. $b \div 3 = 12$

13. $61 = 39 + o$

14. $9 = k \div 5$

15. $f + 58 = 79$

16. $51 - i = 39$

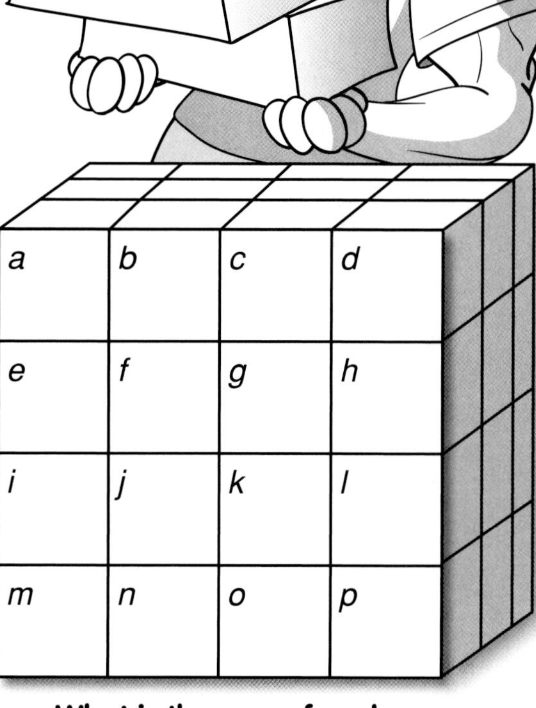

What is the sum of each row and column? _____ (If your answers are correct, the sums will all be the same.)

Bonus: Is 15 a reasonable estimate for the solution of $8 \times q = 128$? Why or why not?

Name ______________________________

Date ____________________

"It's a Roundup!"

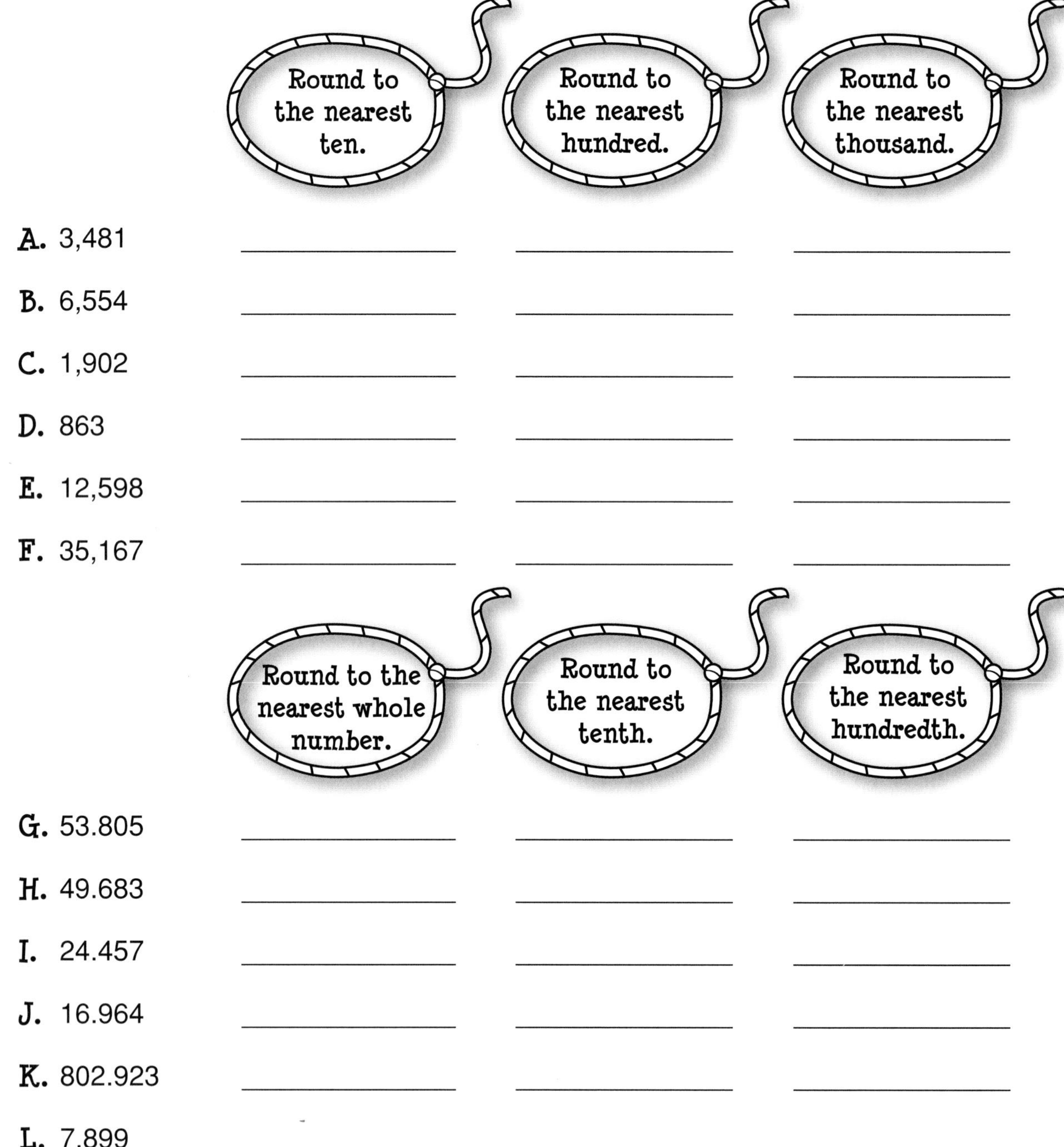

	Round to the nearest ten.	Round to the nearest hundred.	Round to the nearest thousand.
A. 3,481	________	________	________
B. 6,554	________	________	________
C. 1,902	________	________	________
D. 863	________	________	________
E. 12,598	________	________	________
F. 35,167	________	________	________

	Round to the nearest whole number.	Round to the nearest tenth.	Round to the nearest hundredth.
G. 53.805	________	________	________
H. 49.683	________	________	________
I. 24.457	________	________	________
J. 16.964	________	________	________
K. 802.923	________	________	________
L. 7.899	________	________	________

Bonus: Round these numbers to the nearest thousandth.

4.05716	15.28082	2.6399
6.21012	3.70983	29.9147

Name ____________________

Date ____________________

Unidentified Flying Objects

I. Using the spaceship, tell whether the line segments in each listed pair are **intersecting**, **parallel**, or **perpendicular**.

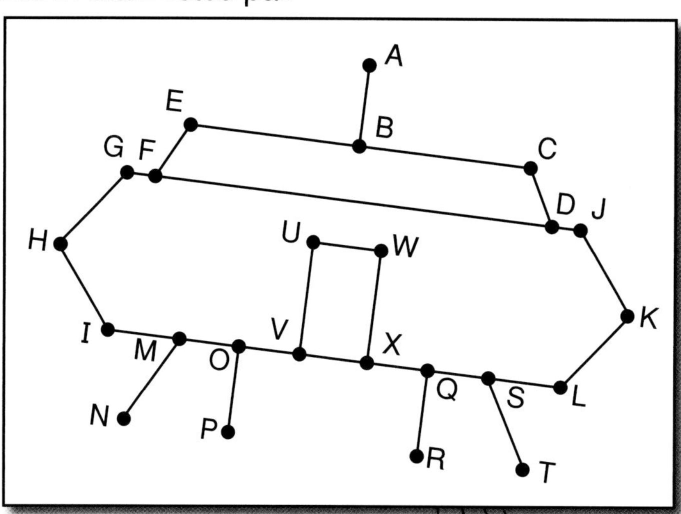

1. $\overline{AB}$ is perpendicular to $\overline{EC}$
2. $\overline{FD}$ ____________________ $\overline{IL}$
3. $\overline{UV}$ ____________________ $\overline{MQ}$
4. $\overline{CD}$ ____________________ $\overline{FJ}$
5. $\overline{HI}$ ____________________ $\overline{GH}$
6. $\overline{OQ}$ ____________________ $\overline{UW}$
7. $\overline{ST}$ ____________________ $\overline{XL}$
8. $\overline{WX}$ ____________________ $\overline{UW}$
9. $\overline{GH}$ ____________________ $\overline{KL}$
10. $\overline{OP}$ ____________________ $\overline{ML}$

II. Using the spaceship, tell whether each angle listed is an **acute**, an **obtuse**, or a **right** angle.

11. $\angle GFE$ ____________________
12. $\angle WXS$ ____________________
13. $\angle FDC$ ____________________
14. $\angle NMO$ ____________________
15. $\angle TSL$ ____________________
16. $\angle ABC$ ____________________

III. Cut out the boxes below and match each one to its definition. Then glue it in place.

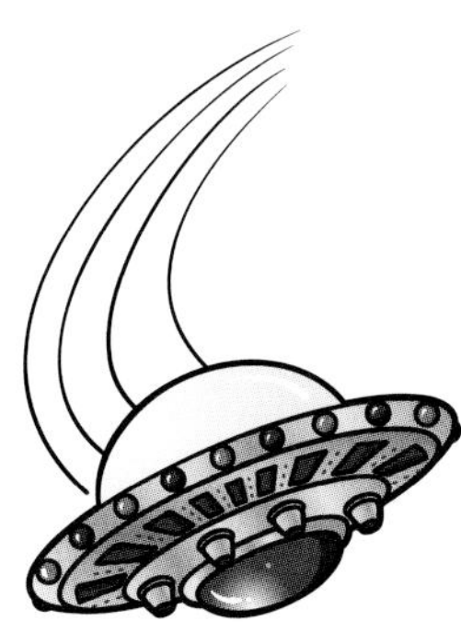

17. polygon with four congruent sides and four right angles	18. polygon with three sides and three angles	19. polygon in which opposite sides are the same length and parallel
20. quadrilateral with two pairs of congruent, parallel sides and four right angles	21. quadrilateral with just two parallel sides	22. parallelogram with four sides, all equal in length

Bonus: Draw a spaceship that has the line segments listed below. Label each point.

- four parallel line segments
- two intersecting line segments
- two perpendicular line segments

square

rectangle

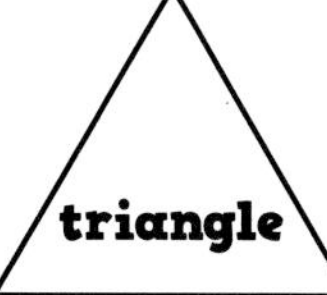

parallelogram

trapezoid

rhombus

Name ____________________

Date ____________________

DOUBLE YOUR SAVINGS!

Little's Vittles
We will redeem every coupon at face value. (No limits!)

Edie's Edibles
We will double the value of any coupon worth 60 cents or less. (You may redeem up to six coupons per visit.)

Chloe's Culinary Corner
We will triple the value of any coupon worth 60 cents or less. (You may redeem up to four coupons per visit.)

A — **50¢** off one box of **Sunny's Sun-Dried Raisins**

B — Save **$1.00** off any bottle of **Supersour Pickles.**

C — Save **55¢** on any multipack of **Breakfast in a Bag.**

D — **75¢** off one can of **Nut Nibblers**

E — **80¢** off two **Might Muscle** bars

F — **Save 45¢** on your favorite ***Gooey Granola*** bar.

G — Save **$2.00** on three bottles of **Wonder Water**.

H — **60¢** off one box of **Snackers Crackers**

I — **25¢** off one pack of **Gobs-a-Gum**

Fill out the chart to show each coupon's value at each store. Then circle the coupons Cora should use to save the most at each store.

At which store could Cora save the most money using coupons?

____

	COUPONS									
Store	A	B	C	D	E	F	G	H	I	Total Savings
Little's Vittles	$0.50									
Edie's Edibles	$1.00									
Chloe's Culinary Corner	$1.50									

Name ______________________

Date ______________

Every Which Way

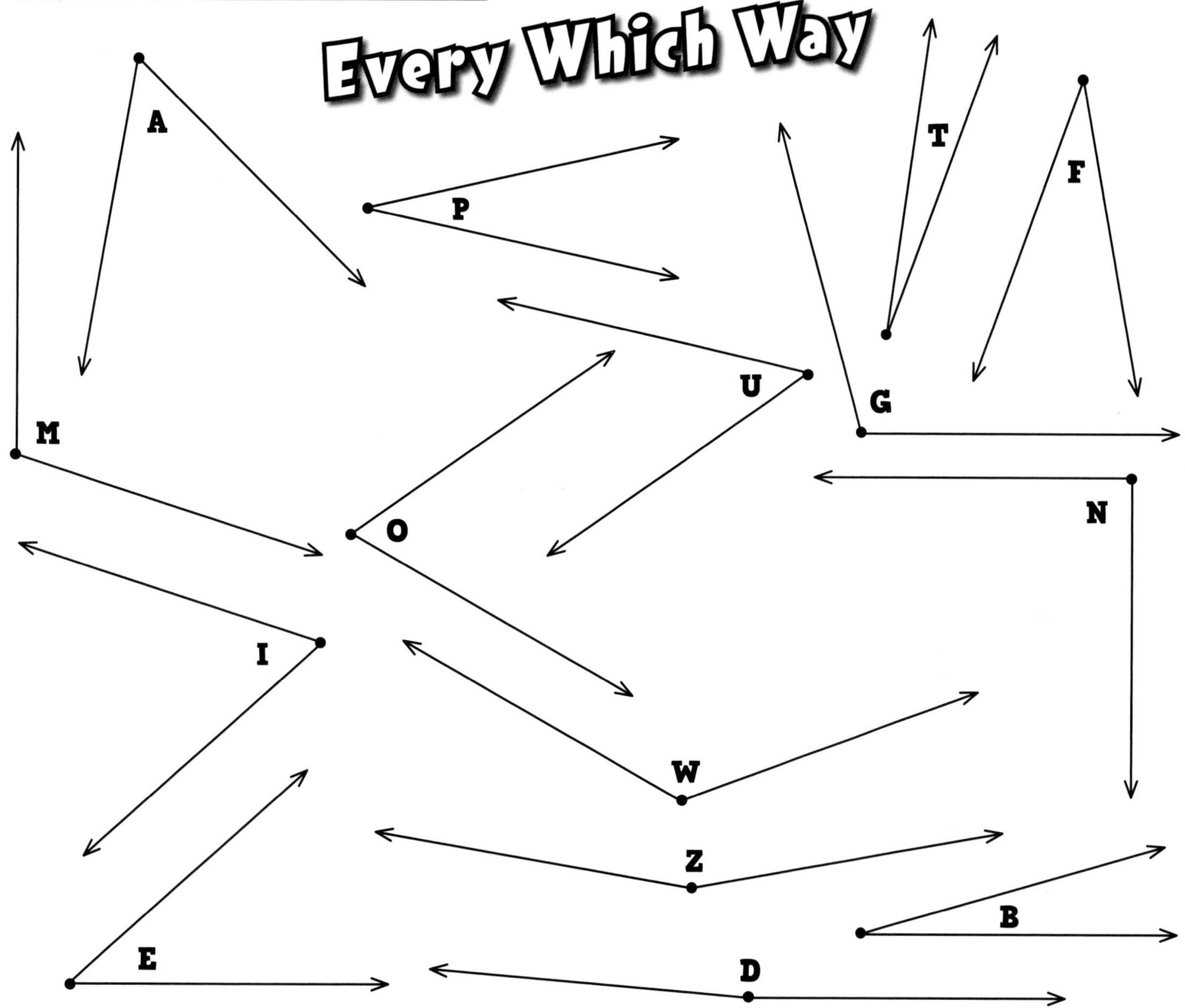

Part 1: Measure each angle. Write each angle's letter next to its matching measurement.

12° = _____	16° = _____	25° = _____	30° = _____	42° = _____
48° = _____	55° = _____	60° = _____	65° = _____	90° = _____
105° = _____	108° = _____	130° = _____	160° = _____	175° = _____

Part 2: Make each statement true. Cross out the incorrect word. Then add the correct one.

1. Angles P, B, and F are obtuse angles.
2. Angle N is a straight angle.
3. Angles G and Z are acute angles.
4. Angles M, G, W, and Z are right angles.
5. Angle I is one degree smaller than angle O.
6. Angle T is the largest angle.
7. Together, angles A and I would form an acute angle.
8. Obtuse angles F and T would both fit inside a right angle.

Bonus: Sort the angles above according to whether they are acute, right, or obtuse.

Name ______________________________

Date ____________________

A Magical Getaway

Solve. Write your answer in simplest form. Then cross off the answer on the hat.

A $1\frac{1}{4} + 2\frac{2}{3}$

B $5\frac{2}{3} + 1\frac{1}{3}$

C $5\frac{1}{3} + 2\frac{4}{5}$

D $4\frac{1}{8} + 1\frac{1}{5}$

E $8\frac{5}{12} + 6\frac{1}{4}$

F $4\frac{1}{8} + 1\frac{5}{8}$

G $7\frac{1}{4} - 4\frac{1}{6}$

H $6\frac{5}{6} - 1\frac{1}{8}$

I $6\frac{1}{4} - 2\frac{3}{5}$

J $9\frac{3}{4} - 1\frac{1}{8}$

K $3\frac{3}{4} - 1\frac{1}{2}$

L $2\frac{1}{9} + 1\frac{1}{3}$

M $2\frac{7}{8} - 1\frac{1}{4}$

N $8\frac{1}{2} - 3\frac{4}{5}$

O $4\frac{1}{10} + 6\frac{2}{5}$

Bonus: Write two addition and two subtraction problems using the mixed numbers in the hat. Then solve each one.

Name ______________________

Date ______________________

Doctor, Doctor

Solve.

A $7\overline{)532}$

T $8\overline{)688}$

N $4\overline{)272}$

I $4\overline{)96}$

G $3\overline{)87}$

W 69×53

S 41×67

O 294×18

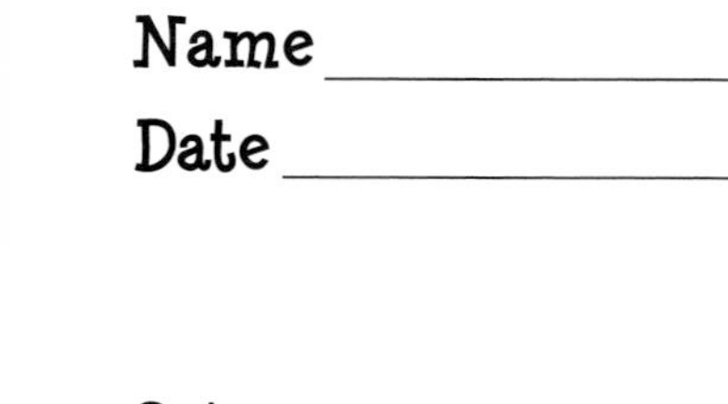

U 168×24

E 92×46

L $74\overline{)2,368}$

P 685×37

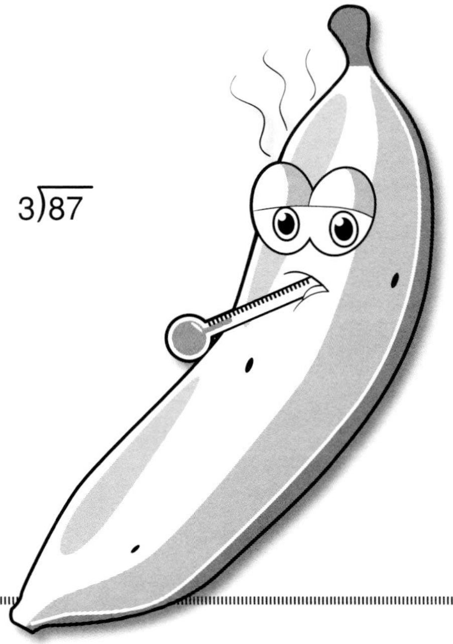

Why did the banana go to the doctor?
To solve the riddle, write each letter on its matching numbered line or lines.

___ 24 ___ 86 ___ 3,657 ___ 76 ___ 2,747

___ 68 ___ 5,292 ___ 86

"___ 25,345 ___ 4,232 ___ 4,232 ___ 32 ___ 24 ___ 68 ___ 29"

___ 3,657 ___ 4,232 ___ 32 ___ 32 !

Bonus: Multiply each quotient by the divisor to check your work.

Name ______________________________ Solving equations

Date ______________

What Happened to the Plants in Math Class?

Solve each equation. Then circle the answer in the box below.

1. $15 + x = 28$ $x =$ ______
2. $4 \cdot x = 36$ $x =$ ______
3. $x \div 9 = 21$ $x =$ ______
4. $x - 20 = 25$ $x =$ ______
5. $6 \cdot x = 66$ $x =$ ______
6. $x \div 2 = 17$ $x =$ ______
7. $21 = 7 \cdot x$ $x =$ ______
8. $x \div 9 = 11$ $x =$ ______
9. $x - 46 = 21$ $x =$ ______
10. $3 \cdot x = 12$ $x =$ ______
11. $x \div 6 = 15$ $x =$ ______
12. $7 \cdot x = 56$ $x =$ ______
13. $48 + x = 130$ $x =$ ______
14. $x - 5 = 81$ $x =$ ______
15. $38 + x = 91$ $x =$ ______
16. $x \div 3 = 12$ $x =$ ______
17. $58 - x = 41$ $x =$ ______
18. $x \cdot 12 = 72$ $x =$ ______
19. $75 + x = 125$ $x =$ ______
20. $42 \div x = 6$ $x =$ ______

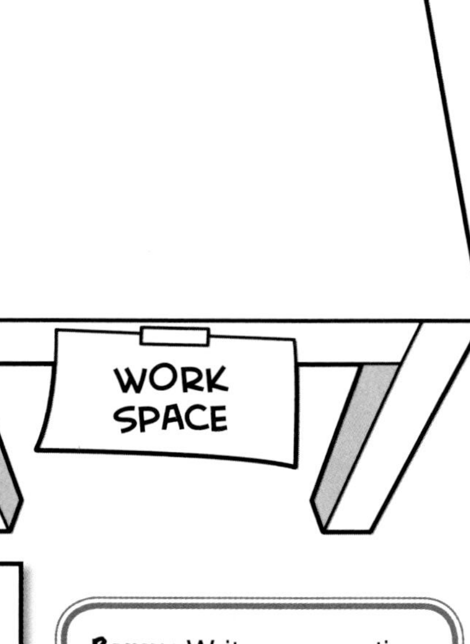

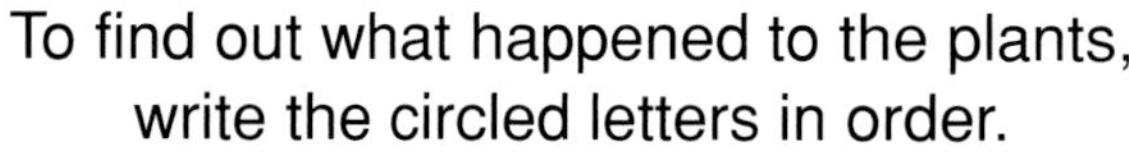

To find out what happened to the plants, write the circled letters in order.

M	TH	EY	A	A	Z	L	L	G	T
6	189	34	9	21	10	50	6	7	49
B	J	R	E	W	S	Q	D	U	O
40	5	99	4	17	11	86	25	13	55
F	A	R	E	R	T	O	O	T	S
23	3	8	45	90	18	67	53	82	36

Bonus: Write an equation for each sentence below. Then solve each equation.

x more than 17 = 56

56 divided by x = 8

_ _ _ _ _ _ _ _ _ _ _ _ _ _ _ _ _ _ _ _ _ _!

Name ____________________

Date ____________________

TIDAL CALCULATIONS

Use the table to solve the problems below.

Date	Morning High Tide	Morning Low Tide	Evening High Tide	Evening Low Tide
March 1	12:25 AM	6:55 AM	2:10 PM	7:00 PM
March 2	1:10 AM	7:40 AM	2:50 PM	7:55 PM
March 3	2:00 AM	8:25 AM	3:30 PM	9:00 PM
March 4	3:05 AM	9:15 AM	4:20 PM	10:00 PM
March 5	4:15 AM	10:00 AM	5:05 PM	11:15 PM

Lobster Buffet

BONUS: About what time might morning low tide occur on March 10?

You just never know what the tide will bring in!

1. How much time elapses between high tides on March 3? ____________
2. How many minutes later is the evening high tide on March 3 than March 2? ____________
3. How many hours and minutes later is the evening high tide on March 5 than March 3? ____________
4. How many hours and minutes is it from morning high tide until evening low tide on March 1? ____________
5. How many hours and minutes is it from morning high tide until evening low tide on March 5? ____________
6. About how many hours are there between high tides each day? ____________
7. About how many hours are there between low tides each day? ____________
8. How many hours later does evening high tide begin on March 5 than March 1? ____________
9. How many hours and minutes after morning low tide on March 1 is the evening low tide? ____________
10. How many hours and minutes are there from evening low tide on March 2 until morning high tide on March 3? ____________
11. How many hours and minutes are there from evening high tide on March 2 until morning high tide on March 5? ____________
12. About what time would morning low tide occur on March 6? Explain your answer. ____________

Name ________________________________

Date ____________________

Fore!

Solve. Then draw a tally in the chart to show the place value of the digit 4 in each product.

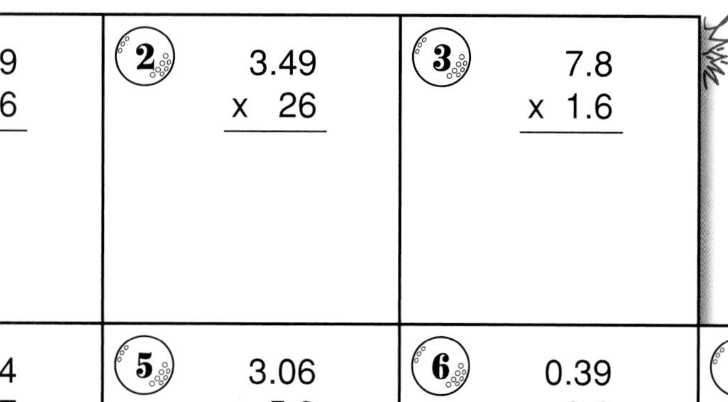

(1) 8.9 x 6	(2) 3.49 x 26	(3) 7.8 x 1.6	
(4) 6.4 x 7.7	(5) 3.06 x 5.8	(6) 0.39 x 0.6	(7) 0.06 x 0.8
(8) 6.3 x 0.18	(9) 0.405 x 6	(10) 0.985 x 76	(11) 70.06 x 0.9
(12) 0.93 x 4.4	(13) 5.04 x 3.7	(14) 0.75 x 6.2	(15) 609.7 x 5.3
(16) 91.4 x 18	(17) 0.58 x 0.3	(18) 107.3 x 0.44	

Tens	Ones	Tenths	Hundredths	Thousandths
(3)	(3)	(4)	(4)	(4)

Bonus: Fred solved the following problem. His product is incorrect. What do you think he did wrong? Explain.

67.05 x 0.3 = 2011.5

Name ____________________

Date ____________________

What Did the Otter on the Log Say to the Otter in the Water?

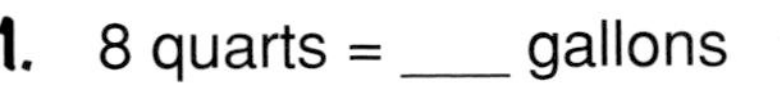

Write the amount that correctly completes each equation.

8 ounces = 1 cup	2 pints = 1 quart
2 cups = 1 pint	4 quarts = 1 gallon

1. 8 quarts = ___ gallons (L)
2. 12 cups = ___ pints (S)
3. 6 pints = ___ quarts (M)
4. 1 quart = ___ ounces (H)
5. 32 pints = ___ gallons (A)
6. 8 pints = ___ cups (U)
7. 1 gallon = ___ ounces (C)
8. 7 gallons = ___ quarts (E)
9. 16 ounces = ___ pint (J)
10. 6 cups = ___ ounces (R)
11. 2 quarts = ___ cups (O)
12. $2\frac{1}{2}$ quarts = ___ ounces (T)
13. 2 gallons, 3 quarts = ___ quarts (E)
14. $2\frac{1}{2}$ pints = ___ ounces (R)
15. $1\frac{1}{2}$ gallons = ___ cups (E)
16. 24 pints = ___ quarts (O)

Workspace

To answer the riddle, write each letter on its matching line or lines below.

___ ___ ___ ___ ___ ___ ___ ___ ___ ___ ___ ___ ___
1 16 6 80 128 4 2 2 3 28 80 32 24

___ ___ ___ ___ ___ ___ ___ ___ ___ ___ ___!
32 8 80 80 11 40 12 80 80 28 48

Bonus: Complete each equation.

A. 25 quarts = ___ gallons

B. $1\frac{1}{2}$ gallons = ___ ounces

C. 2 quarts, 6 ounces = ___ cups

Name ____________________

Date ____________________

What a Game!

Multiply. Write each product in simplest form. Then cross it out in the boxes below.

1. $\frac{7}{8} \times \frac{2}{5} =$
2. $\frac{4}{5} \times \frac{3}{10} =$
3. $\frac{1}{2} \times \frac{9}{10} =$
4. $\frac{5}{12} \times \frac{3}{10} =$
5. $\frac{3}{4} \times \frac{2}{3} =$
6. $\frac{9}{10} \times \frac{3}{5} =$
7. $\frac{1}{2} \times \frac{5}{6} =$
8. $\frac{2}{5} \times \frac{7}{10} =$
9. $\frac{5}{8} \times \frac{1}{2} =$
10. $\frac{3}{8} \times \frac{2}{3} =$
11. $\frac{1}{2} \times \frac{7}{8} =$
12. $\frac{3}{4} \times \frac{1}{2} =$
13. $\frac{3}{8} \times 6 =$
14. $\frac{3}{5} \times 15 =$
15. $8 \times \frac{1}{3} =$
16. $21 \times \frac{5}{8} =$
17. $\frac{1}{2} \times 3 \times \frac{2}{5} =$
18. $\frac{1}{4} \times \frac{3}{8} \times 6 =$
19. $\frac{3}{5} \times \frac{5}{6} \times 12 =$
20. $8 \times \frac{7}{8} \times \frac{1}{4} =$

Bonus: Complete the following statement. Then give three examples that support your statement.
When you multiply a whole number by a fraction, the product…

All the fans left!
That's the answer. To find the question, write in order the words you did not cross out.

What $2\frac{2}{3}$	How $\frac{27}{50}$	Why $\frac{2}{7}$	Do $2\frac{1}{4}$	you $\frac{6}{25}$	did $\frac{3}{4}$	the $\frac{7}{8}$	get $\frac{9}{16}$
from 6	temperature $\frac{5}{9}$	popcorn $\frac{1}{2}$	in $\frac{9}{14}$	the $\frac{3}{10}$	peanuts $\frac{3}{5}$	because 9	stadium $\frac{5}{6}$
pitcher $\frac{5}{12}$	threw $\frac{3}{8}$	rise $\frac{9}{28}$	before $\frac{7}{20}$	after $\frac{3}{11}$	glove $\frac{5}{16}$	the $\frac{8}{11}$	winning $\frac{9}{20}$
in $13\frac{1}{8}$	the $\frac{7}{25}$	ball $\frac{11}{21}$	ninth $\frac{1}{4}$	game $\frac{7}{18}$	inning $\frac{1}{8}$	was $1\frac{3}{4}$	over $\frac{7}{16}$

____

____

Name ____________

Date ____________

Game On!

Complete the table.

Player	Rank	Games Won	Games Lost	Number of Games Played	Ratio of Games Won to Games Played
I ♡ GAMES	1	15	10	25	$\frac{15}{25}$ or $\frac{3}{5}$
NEWGMR	2	12	9		
NBR1	3		8	18	
QUICKDRAW	4	17	15		
GAMEPRINCSS	5		8	17	
JOYFUL1	6	9		18	
TOPDOG	7	10	11		
RDY2PLAY	8	5	10		
GAMEKING	9	7		22	
ROCKY	10		19	27	

Bonus: If all the players play ten more games and each player wins four of the games, will the players ranked in the top five stay the same or change? Explain.

Use the table to solve each problem below.
Write each answer on another sheet of paper.

1. Which players win more than half of the games they play?
2. QuickDraw has won seven more games than NBR1. Why does NBR1 have a higher ranking?
3. If GameKing plays five more games and wins three of the games, will his ranking change?
4. Which player's ratio of wins to the total number of games played is closest to $\frac{5}{8}$?
5. Which player's ratio of wins to the total number of games played is $\frac{1}{3}$?
6. Which player's ratio of losses to the total number of games played is closest to $\frac{3}{4}$?
7. If GamePrincSS plays ten more games and wins seven of them, will her ranking change?
8. Which three players have won 40 games among them?
9. How many games altogether have all the players played?
10. What is the ratio of the total number of wins to the total number of games the players have played?

Name ______________________________

Date ______________________

A Firework Finale

Part 1.

Name the points that are in each quadrant.

Quadrant I

____

Quadrant II

____

Quadrant III

____

Quadrant IV

____

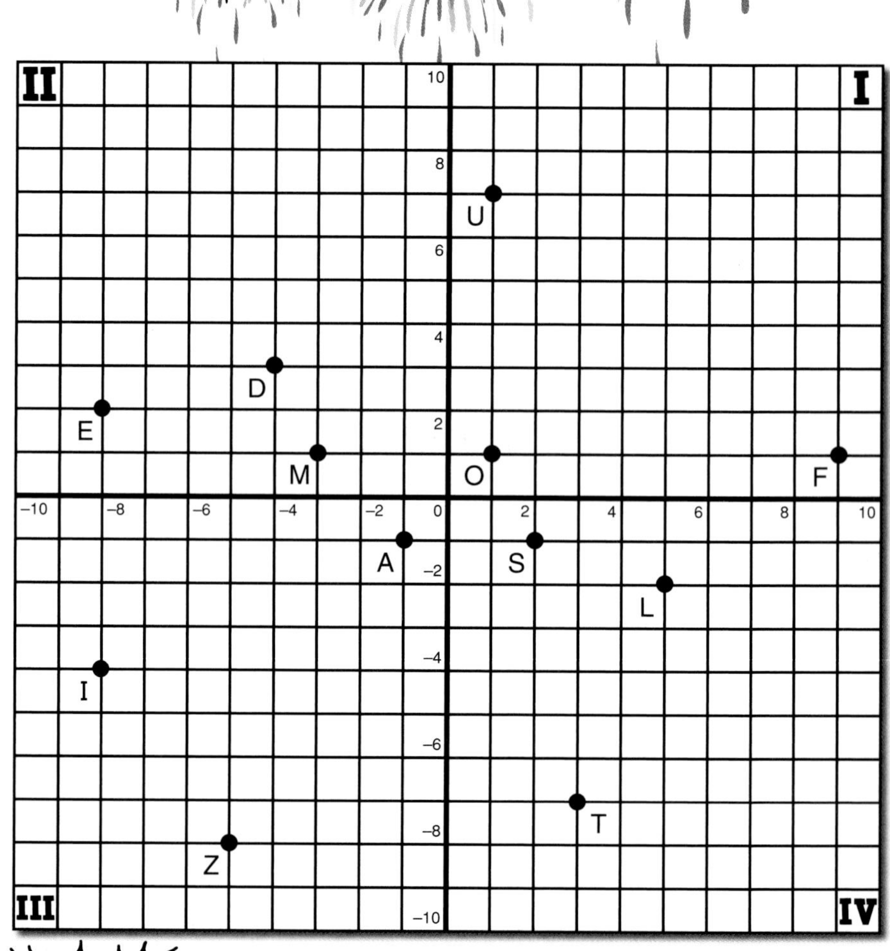

Part 2.

Write the ordered pair that describes each letter's location on the grid.

Point	Coordinates
A	(-1, -1)
D	
E	
F	
I	
L	
M	
O	
S	
T	
U	
Z	

Part 3. Find out what one firework said to another by writing each letter on the line or lines above the matching ordered pair.

I ' ___ ___ ___ ___
(–8, –4) (–3, 1) (–1, –1) (5, –2) (5, –2)

___ ___ ___ ___ ___ ___ ___
(9, 1) (–8, –4) (–5, –8) (–5, –8) (5, –2) (–8, 2) (–4, 3)

___ ___ ___ !
(1, 1) (1, 7) (3, –7)

Bonus: Plot six new points on the grid, putting at least one point in each quadrant. Label the points B, C, J, K, N, and P and then record each point's coordinates.

Name ____________________

Date ____________________

Pick and Practice

Pick _____ activities to do.
When you finish an activity, color its number.

1 Copy the diagram shown and add the missing labels. Then define each label.

_____ { 1 ⟶ _____
2 ⟶ _____

2 Write a statement to describe the shaded part of each drawing.

A.

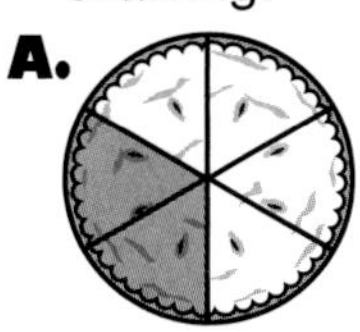

B.

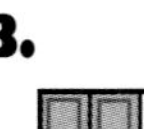

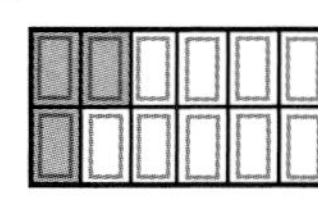

C.

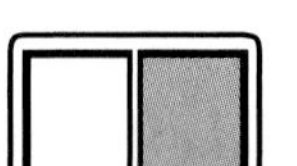

D.

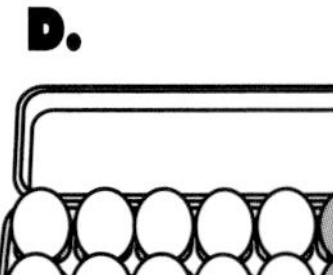

3 These drawings show parts of sets. Make each drawing whole by adding the missing part or parts.

A. $\frac{2}{3}$ of the eggs for a recipe

B. $\frac{1}{6}$ of a set of books

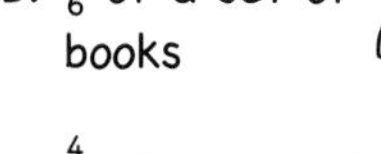

C. $\frac{4}{5}$ of the marbles are inside the circle

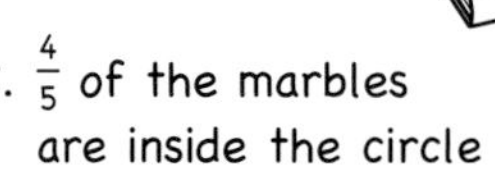

4 Write <, >, or = to compare each set of fractions.

A. $\frac{2}{3}$ $\frac{1}{2}$ $\frac{5}{7}$ $\frac{3}{8}$ $\frac{4}{16}$ $\frac{1}{4}$

B. $\frac{1}{3}$ $\frac{1}{2}$ $\frac{2}{5}$ $\frac{2}{3}$ $\frac{1}{3}$ $\frac{2}{6}$

5 Draw the number line shown. Write each fraction on your number line in the correct position.

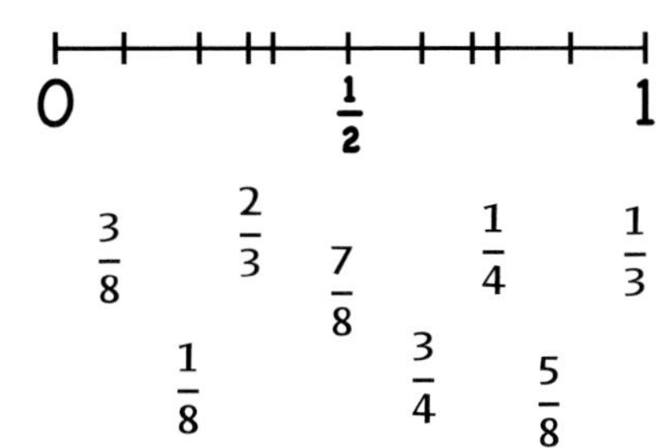

$\frac{3}{8}$ $\frac{2}{3}$ $\frac{7}{8}$ $\frac{1}{4}$ $\frac{1}{3}$ $\frac{1}{8}$ $\frac{3}{4}$ $\frac{5}{8}$

6 Circle the fractions that are not in simplest form. Then write an equation such as $\frac{5}{40} = \frac{1}{8}$ to name the equivalent fractions.

$\frac{9}{12}$ $\frac{1}{4}$ $\frac{4}{8}$ $\frac{1}{3}$ $\frac{4}{16}$ $\frac{10}{15}$ $\frac{3}{9}$ $\frac{5}{8}$ $\frac{1}{2}$ $\frac{3}{4}$ $\frac{2}{3}$ $\frac{15}{24}$

7 Draw a diagram that illustrates each pair of equivalent fractions.

Example: $\frac{1}{3} = \frac{2}{6}$

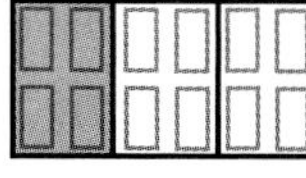

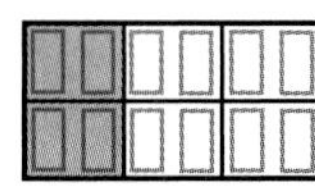

$\frac{1}{4} = \frac{2}{8}$

$\frac{3}{4} = \frac{9}{12}$

$\frac{2}{3} = \frac{10}{15}$

8 Add the missing numerator or denominator to complete each pair of equivalent fractions.

$\frac{1}{3} = \frac{6}{?}$ $\frac{7}{8} = \frac{21}{?}$

$\frac{3}{5} = \frac{?}{15}$ $\frac{5}{12} = \frac{?}{60}$

$\frac{4}{9} = \frac{?}{27}$ $\frac{8}{15} = \frac{24}{?}$

9 Create a mini poster that explains how to find an equivalent fraction for this fraction.

$$\frac{3}{8}$$

Independent practice grid: Program the student directions on a copy of this page with the number of activities to be completed. Then copy the page for each student.

Name ______________________________

Date ____________________

Pick and Practice

Pick _____ activities to do.

When you finish an activity, color its number.

Number and Geometric Patterns!

1 Find the pattern. Then describe it.

1, 1, 2, 3, 5, 8, 13, 21, 34

2 Find the pattern. Then describe it.

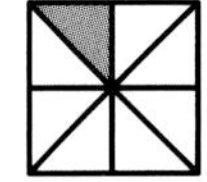 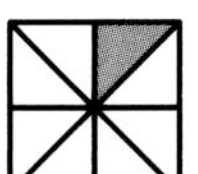 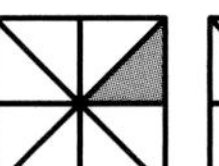 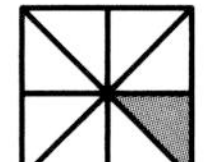

3 Find the pattern. Then write the next four numbers.

A. 3, 7, 11, 15, __, __, __, __

B. 10, 25, 40, 55, __, __, __, __

C. 51, 48, 45, 42, __, __, __, __

D. 1, 3, 4, 6, 7, 9, __, __, __, __

4 Find the pattern. Then draw the next three figures.

A. ◐ ◑ ◐ ◑ ...

B. △ □ ⬠ △ ...

C. | L ⊔ ⊔‾ ⊔⊓ ...

D. — + ✕ ✳ — ...

5 Find the pattern and complete the table. Then describe the pattern.

45	**19**	**64**
31	**89**	**120**
63		**72**
47	**16**	
	29	**84**

6 Find the pattern. Then complete each sign.

Cookies
3 .... $1.50
6 .... $3.00
8 ....
12 ....

Pretzels
2 .... $2.50
4 .... $5.00
6 ....
9 ....

Cupcakes
2 .... $5.50
3 .... $8.25
4 ....
9 ....

7 In each mystery bag, there are three game tokens and six prize tickets. Finish the chart to find out how many tokens and tickets will be in five bags.

Bags	Tokens	Tickets
1	3	6
2	6	12
3		
4		
5		

8 Create a pattern using one or more of these shapes. Explain the pattern's rule and show eight steps.

Example:

9 Find the pattern. Then draw the sixth and seventh steps.

Independent practice grid: Program the student directions on a copy of this page with the number of activities to be completed. Then copy the page for each student.

Name ______________________________
Date ______________________

Pick and Practice

Pick _____ activities to do.

When you finish an activity, color its number.

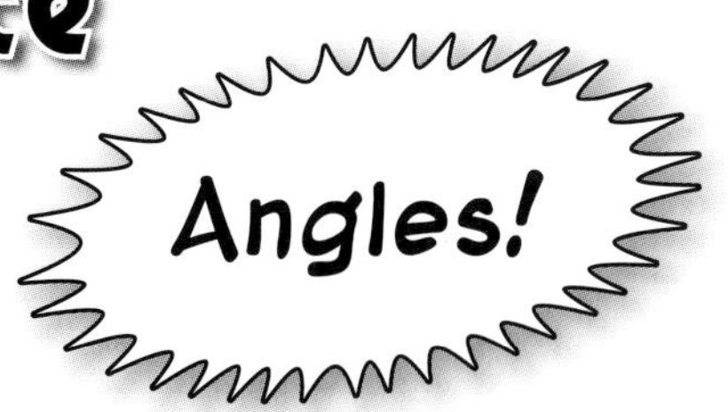

1 Make a list of ten or more everyday items that have acute angles. For each item, sketch or describe the acute angle(s).	**2** Cut a sheet of paper into six sections. On each section, write one of the terms. Put the pages in alphabetical order and staple them together. Then use words and diagrams to define each term. **ray** **right angle** **angle** **obtuse angle** **vertex** **acute angle**	**3** Make a list of ten or more everyday items that have obtuse angles. For each one, sketch or describe the obtuse angle(s).
4 Draw a Venn diagram labeled as shown. Then complete it to compare and contrast acute, right, and obtuse angles. 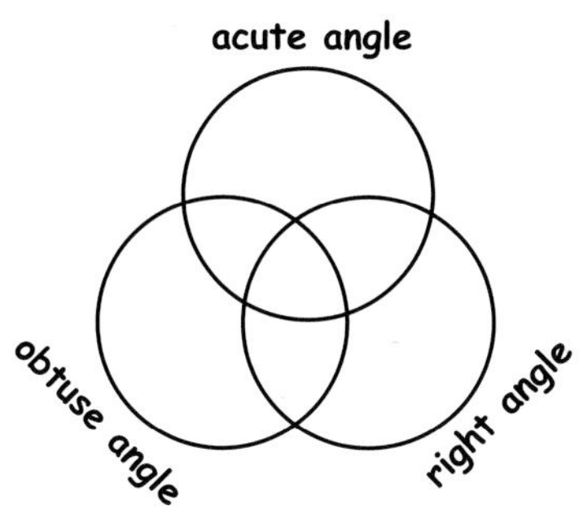	**5** Write a paragraph that explains how to measure an angle using a **protractor**. 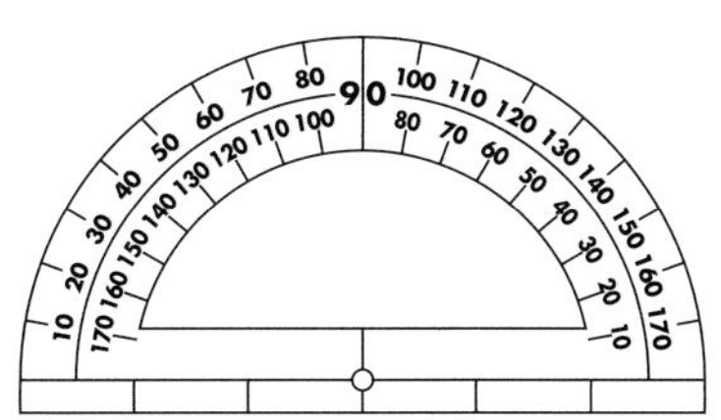	**6** Fold a sheet of paper four times, making each fold random. Next, open the paper and trace the fold lines. Then choose four vertices and measure and label the angles around each one. What do you notice? Explain. 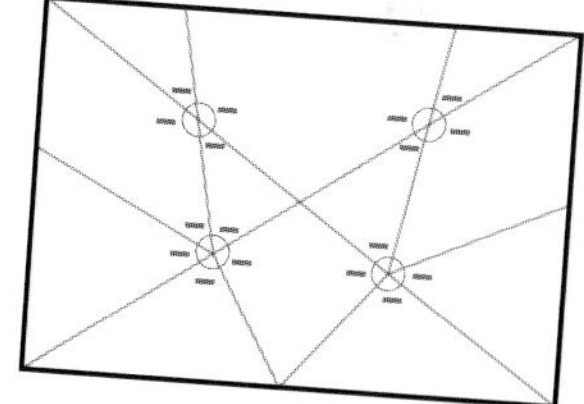
7 Cut a sheet of paper into six sections. On each section, write one of the terms. Put the pages in alphabetical order and staple them together. Then use words and diagrams to define each term. **straight angle** **protractor** **reflex angle** **congruent angles** **degree** **central angle**	**8** Carefully trace around a bowl to draw a circle. Then divide the circle into six sections. Measure each angle. Then find the sum of all the angle measurements. 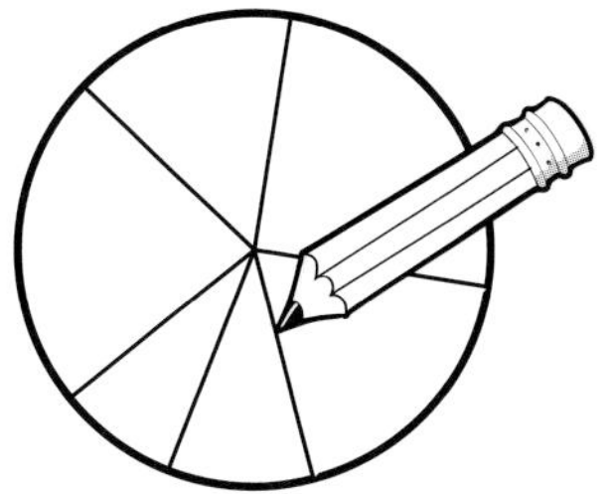	**9** In some sports (for example, diving), an athlete's actions may be described in terms of degrees he or she turns, flips, or rotates. Name and describe or diagram five athletic actions, skills, or tricks with names or descriptions that include a number of degrees.

Independent practice grid: Program the student directions on a copy of this page with the number of activities to be completed. Then copy the page for each student.

Math in Minutes Math in Minutes

Name ______________________________

LEVEL A

MEASUREMENT

1 Jana purchased an 8" x 10" picture frame. She wants to glue 2" apple shapes around its border. How many apple shapes will she need to cover the space? How do you know?

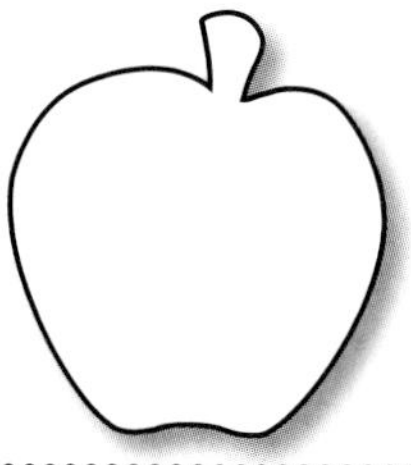

NUMBER AND OPERATIONS

2 In which numbers below is the value of the eight greater than or equal to eight thousand? Explain how you know.

8,573,261 **1,480,752** **500,837,650**

12,708 **623,578,913** **1,114,003,897**

GEOMETRY

3 Which letters in the words shown have parallel line segments? Which letters have perpendicular line segments? Which have both? Which have neither? Explain your answers.

LINE SEGMENT

MEASUREMENT

4 Stephen has been studying for 25 minutes. It is now 1:30 PM. What time did he start studying? How do you know?

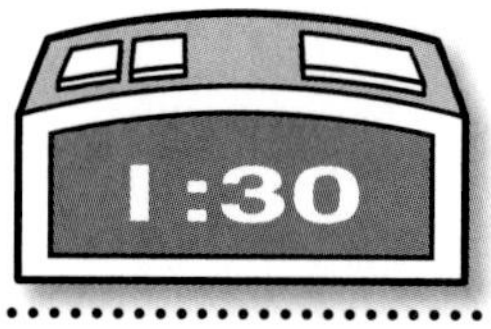

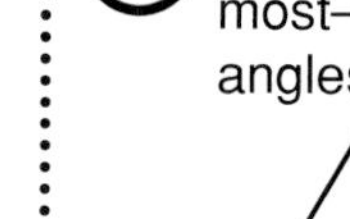

NUMBER AND OPERATIONS

5 Which person spent the closest to $100 without going over that amount? Explain your answer.

Gabe bought two pairs of jeans for $29.80 each and one hoodie for $44.30.

Taneka bought two pairs of jeans for $35.99 each and a top for $16.59.

Alecia bought four sweaters for $19.99 each and a top for $14.99.

ALGEBRA

6 Which of the numbers shown would make this inequality true? Explain your choices.

$$2x < 17$$

0, 1, 2, 3, 4, 5, 6, 7, 8, 9, 10

Name ______________________________

LEVEL B

NUMBER AND OPERATIONS

1 Solve each equation. How did you find your answers?

A. $\frac{11}{8} - n = \frac{3}{4}$ B. $\frac{1}{2} + n = \frac{3}{4}$ C. $\frac{1}{4} \cdot n = \frac{3}{4}$

NUMBER AND OPERATIONS

2 A student ticket to the museum costs $3.00. All 35 students in Mr. Adam's class plus 7 adults bought tickets. The total cost is $136.50. What is the price of one adult ticket? Explain.

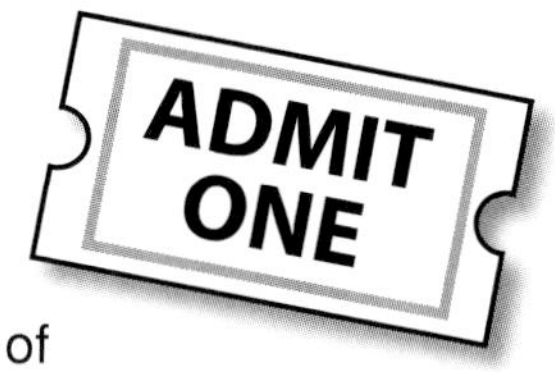

MEASUREMENT

3 Ms. Brown has 25 students and four computers in her classroom. She schedules 85 minutes each day, Monday through Friday, for students to use the computers. To be fair, how many minutes each week will a student get to use a computer? How do you know?

GEOMETRY

4 In the triangles shown, which angle occurs most—acute, obtuse, or right? Which angle or angles occur least? Explain.

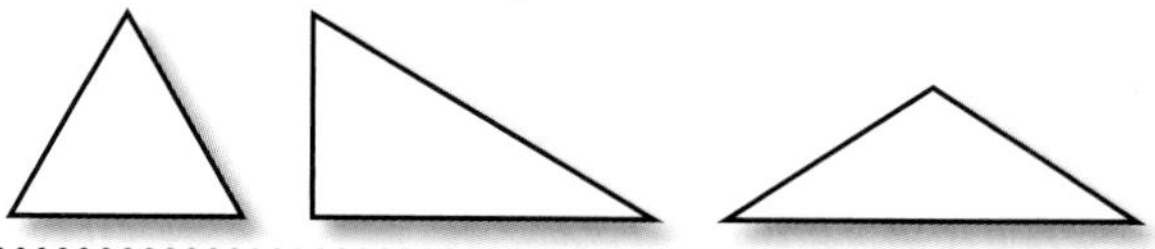

DATA ANALYSIS AND PROBABILITY

5 Terra put the following clothes on her bed. How many possible outfits can she create? How did you find your answer?

shorts, jeans, or a skirt
white top or yellow top
blue sweater, green sweater, or red sweater

NUMBER AND OPERATIONS

6 On Monday, 16 of Ms. Diaz's students bought their lunches. This is $\frac{2}{\ }$ of her class. The rest of the class brought sack lunches. How many students are in the class? How many brought sack lunches?

 How to use: When a student solves a problem, he shades its circle.

Math in Minutes Math in Minutes

Name ______________________________

LEVEL A

NUMBER AND OPERATIONS

1 Seth added these fractions. Explain his mistakes.

$\frac{3}{4} + \frac{1}{2} = \frac{4}{6}$ $\frac{2}{5} + \frac{4}{5} = \frac{6}{10}$

NUMBER AND OPERATIONS

2 Round the cost of these bike accessories to the nearest dollar.

helmet = $35.99 light = $8.75 bell = $6.19
gloves = $23.39 backpack = $15.69

If Kyra has $100.00, will she have enough money to buy all the accessories? How do you know?

NUMBER AND OPERATIONS

3 Ms. Jensen has 23 students in her class. She bought a package of 250 disposable drinking cups. If Ms. Jensen serves her entire class one cup of juice a day, how long will one package of cups last? Explain your answer.

MEASUREMENT

4 Which estimates are reasonable? Explain each choice.

length of a plastic fork	14 mm	14 cm
height of a door	2.5 m	2.5 km
depth of your math book	4 cm	4 dm
liquid in a paper cup	100 mL	100 L

ALGEBRA

5 Extend each pattern. Which was the hardest? Why?

A. 1, 30, 59, 88, ___, ___, ___
B. 111, 94, 77, 60, ___, ___, ___
C. 1, 5, 30, 210, ___, ___, ___

DATA ANALYSIS AND PROBABILITY

6 Which has greater odds of occurring: flipping a coin and getting heads or rolling an even number on a toss of a die? Explain your answer.

Name ______________________________

LEVEL B

NUMBER AND OPERATIONS

1 Write <, >, or = to compare each set. Which fraction or decimal is the greatest overall? How do you know?

$\frac{1}{4}$ ___ 0.213 $\frac{2}{5}$ ___ 0.407 $\frac{1}{8}$ ___ 0.125

NUMBER AND OPERATIONS

2 Which quotient do you think will be larger? Why? Solve to find out.

913 ÷ 48

or

714 ÷ 16

NUMBER AND OPERATIONS

3 Jacob has $3.00 after buying three puffer fish and two guppies with $25.00. If puffer fish cost $5.00 each, how much is a guppy?

MEASUREMENT

4 Farmer Pinkett needs fencing. If fencing costs $20.00 for each eight-foot section, which pen will cost more to fence? How do you know?

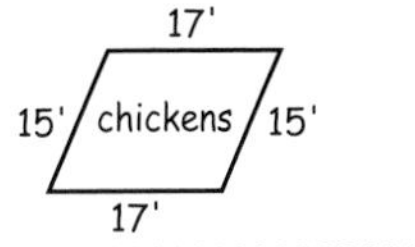

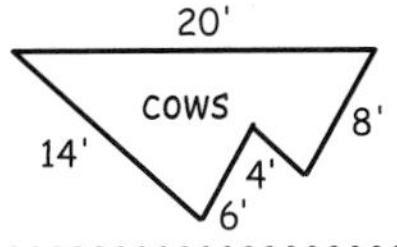

ALGEBRA

5 Write an algebraic expression for the statement shown and then solve it. How did you find your answer?

Two times a number minus three is nine.

DATA ANALYSIS AND PROBABILITY

6 For this set of numbers, which is highest: the mean, the median, or the mode. How do you know?

3 2 1 8 4 4 5 2 15 2

How to use: When a student solves a problem, he shades its circle.

Math in Minutes Math in Minutes

Name ____________________

LEVEL A

NUMBER AND OPERATIONS

1 Name the whole numbers that come immediately before and after the mixed number, fraction, and decimal. Draw pictures to explain your solutions.

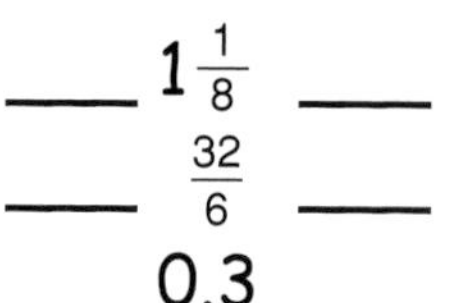

____ $1\frac{1}{8}$ ____

____ $\frac{32}{6}$ ____

____ 0.3 ____

NUMBER AND OPERATIONS

2 Find one number that will make all of the equations true. How do you know you're right?

3.28 x n = 32.8 **.138 x n = 1.38**

51.16 x n = 511.6 **0.06 x n = 0.6**

GEOMETRY

3 Zach told his classmates that two horizontal lines can be both parallel and perpendicular. Is he correct? Explain.

...parallel and perpendicular!

DATA ANALYSIS AND PROBABILITY

4 Ava's dad shows her four \$1.00 bills, two \$10.00 bills, three \$20.00 bills, and one \$50.00 bill. He shuffles them behind his back. Then he has Ava close her eyes and pick one bill. What is the probability she will pick the \$50 bill? Explain.

NUMBER AND OPERATIONS

5 Which sum is larger? How do you know?

A. $\frac{3}{8} + \frac{1}{2} + \frac{1}{4}$

B. $\frac{1}{8} + \frac{1}{2} + 1$

MEASUREMENT

6 An inch is approximately 2.5 centimeters. Sarah's new pencil is $7\frac{1}{2}$ inches long. About how many centimeters long is Sarah's pencil? How did you find your answer?

Name ____________________

LEVEL B

NUMBER AND OPERATIONS

1 Gabe bought four bags of candy to fill a piñata. He paid with a \$20.00 bill and was given \$7.44 in change. How much did each bag of candy cost? How did you find your answer?

NUMBER AND OPERATIONS

2 If x must be a whole number, which statement has more possible solutions? Why?

A. $x < 27$

B. $x > 27$

GEOMETRY

3 How many line segments can you draw using only Points A and B? How many rays can you draw using Points A and B? Explain.

NUMBER AND OPERATIONS

4 Use the numbers shown and addition, subtraction, multiplication, or division, to equal 18, 4, and 29. Tell how you find each answer.
Example: (8 + 7) x 3 = 45

8 **7** **3**

MEASUREMENT

5 Chef Jackie finishes baking 50 loaves of bread two hours and five minutes before she opens her shop at 9:30 AM. She turns her ovens off one hour and 40 minutes after she finishes the bread. When does she turn the ovens off? Explain.

ALGEBRA

6 Which three numbers in this function table are wrong? How do you know?

Rule: 4x + 1	
Input	Output
0	4
1	2
3	17

 How to use: When a student solves a problem, he shades its circle.

Math in Minutes Math in Minutes

Name ________________________________

LEVEL A

Operations and Algebraic Thinking

1. Find the number that completes each problem. How did you find it?

$$(n \div 2) - 28 = 2$$
$$n - (2 \bullet 29) = 2$$
$$n \div 30 = 2$$

Measurement and Data

2. The area measurement for each of three different rectangles is 48 square units. Find a possible length and width of each rectangle.

area = length x width

Number and Operations

3. Which has a greater sum—the even numbers between 4 and 12 or the odd numbers less than 10? Explain.

even odd

Measurement and Data

4. Ms. Stevens estimates that each of her 26 students will drink two cups of punch during the class party. If Ms. Stevens makes three gallons of punch, will she have enough for all her students? Why or why not?

Geometry

5. Draw and name the shape that matches each description.

A. Both of my bases are circles, but my face is rectangular.
B. I have six faces.
C. I have just one vertex.

Operations and Algebraic Thinking

6. Taylor just celebrated her tenth birthday. Taylor is five years younger than three times her sister's age. How old is Taylor's sister? How do you know?

Name ________________________________

LEVEL B

Operations and Algebraic Thinking

1. I am a division problem. My quotient is 23 with a remainder of 2. My divisor is 7. What is my dividend? Explain.

Number and Operations

2. Of the 24 valentines Matt received, $\frac{1}{3}$ had candy, $\frac{1}{6}$ had stickers, and $\frac{1}{12}$ had coupons for free doughnuts. How many of each item did Matt receive? How do you know?

Number and Operations

3. Predict which equation will have a product that is closest to one. Explain.

A. $0.09 \times 0.08 = n$
B. $0.9 \times 0.5 = n$
C. $0.008 \times 9 = n$

Operations and Algebraic Thinking

4. Find the pattern in the numbers shown. Then tell what the tenth and 16th numbers in the sequence will be. How did you find your answers?

51, 60, 69...

Geometry

5. Study the envelope's angles. Name two pairs of angles that are congruent. Explain.

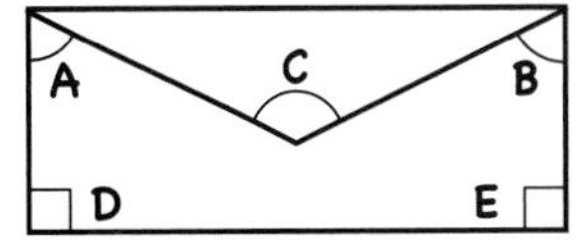

Measurement

6. Estimate the distance in feet from your desk to the main door in your classroom. If you walk this distance eight times a day for one week, how far do you think you will have walked by the end of the week? Explain.

How to use: When a student solves a problem, he shades its circle.

Math in Minutes Math in Minutes

Name ______________________________

LEVEL A

Number and Operations

1 Round each factor to the nearest ten. Which problem's product is closer to 11,000? How do you know?

A. 198×45
B. 133×86

Number and Operations

2 Missy Terious bought a ticket for 15 lunches. Each ticket cost \$3.67. Missy paid with three of the same bills, and she got \$4.95 back in change. What bills did Missy use? How did you get your answer?

Measurement

3 April's kite is 100 feet in the air. If a meter is just over a yard in length, about how many meters of string are there between April and her kite? Explain.

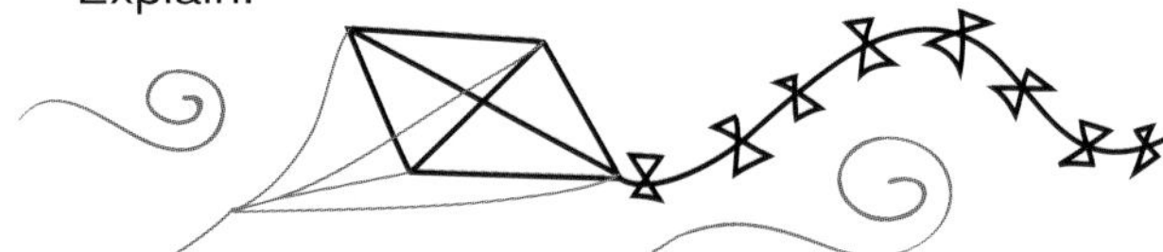

Operations and Algebraic Thinking

4 Maynard is trying to earn a 90-point average in spelling. So far, Maynard has earned a 92, an 87, and an 83. What score does Maynard need to earn on his fourth test to have a 90-point average? Explain how you found your answer.

$$(92 + 87 + 83 + s) \div 4 = 90$$

Probability

5 How many lunch combinations are possible with the following choices? How do you know?

- beef taco, chicken taco, or veggie taco
- salad or fruit
- tea, juice, or milk

Name ______________________________

LEVEL B

Number and Operations

1 Eight has the smallest value in which number? How do you know?

48.032
10.0816
13.805

Number and Operations

2 Copy the statement and add <, >, or = to complete it. Then explain your thinking.

$0.072 \div 4 \bigcirc 0.432 \div 6$

Measurement

3 It is 4:20 PM. Brook ate lunch four hours and 35 minutes ago. What time did she eat lunch? How do you know?

Operations and Algebraic Thinking

4 In which of these equations would x have a value greater than 20? How did you find your answer?

A. $x + 11 = 22$
B. $x - 17 = 21$
C. $3x = 25$
D. $x/2 = 12$

Measurement

5 Which angle is larger—A or B? Explain your answer.

A B
30° 60°

How to use: When a student solves a problem, he shades its circle.

Math in Minutes Math in Minutes

Name ______________________

LEVEL A

ALGEBRA

1 Complete each pattern. Then describe the pattern's rule.

A. 103, 118, 133, ___, ___, ___
B. 0.10, 1, 10, ___, ___, ___
C. 3,125; 625; 125; ___; ___; ___

MEASUREMENT

2 If you weighed yourself in the United Kingdom, you might use stones instead of pounds. A stone equals 14 pounds. How many stones would you weigh? Would your rather weigh yourself in stones or pounds? Explain.

NUMBER AND OPERATIONS

3 Chip is buying ice cream cones for himself and his three best friends. A single-scoop cone costs \$2.79. Can Chip pay for the cones with a ten dollar bill? Why or why not?

NUMBER AND OPERATIONS

4 Holly's practicing for a hoop-spinning contest. On average, she twirls the hoop 42 times per minute. Today, Holly counted 725 revolutions of her hoop as she twirled. Did she practice for at least a quarter of an hour? How do you know?

NUMBER AND OPERATIONS

5 A one-year subscription to Mitch's favorite monthly magazine costs \$29.95. A single issue of the magazine costs \$4.99. How much will Mitch save if he orders the subscription instead of buying the magazines one at a time? Explain.

PROBABILITY

6 Poppy has a green, a pink, and a blue leash for her puppy. She also has a polka-dot collar and a striped collar for the puppy. How can you find all the different collar and leash combinations Misty can make? Explain.

Name ______________________

LEVEL B

NUMBER AND OPERATIONS

1 At 10:00 AM, Sal leaves for the beach. The trip is 282 miles. Sal stops for a half-hour lunch break at noon. If Sal drives an average of 68 miles per hour, will he get to the beach by 2:30? Why or why not?

NUMBER AND OPERATIONS

2 A restaurant's biggest seller is a wood-grilled quarter-pound burger*. The restaurant sells 110 of these burgers on Friday, 150 on Saturday, and 70 on Sunday. How many pounds of hamburger do they use? Explain how you know.

* Each burger is made from ¼ pound of hamburger.

ALGEBRA

3 How many of the variables below equal ten? How do you know?

$2a = 12$
$\frac{1}{2}b = 20$
$58 - c = 48$
$d + 5 = 50$

MEASUREMENT

4 The mass of a nickel is five grams. Estimate the mass of a penny, dime, quarter, and half dollar. Explain.

NUMBER AND OPERATIONS

5 What whole number, when multiplied by $\frac{1}{4}$ and then multiplied by $\frac{1}{3}$, equals four less than one-half dozen? How did you find your answer?

NUMBER AND OPERATIONS

6 Sue said, "I spent exactly $\frac{1}{4}$ of my day at the library, $\frac{1}{3}$ of it in class, $\frac{1}{8}$ of it eating and riding the bus, and $\frac{1}{3}$ of it sleeping." Is Sue telling the truth? Why or why not?

...and then...

How to use: When a student solves a problem, he shades its circle.

MIND BUILDERS

MATH

MIND BUILDER 1

How many five-pound bricks can be hauled in a truck that can hold half a ton of weight?

TEC44056

MIND BUILDER 2

What is the smallest number that can be evenly divided by 3, 4, 7, and 9?

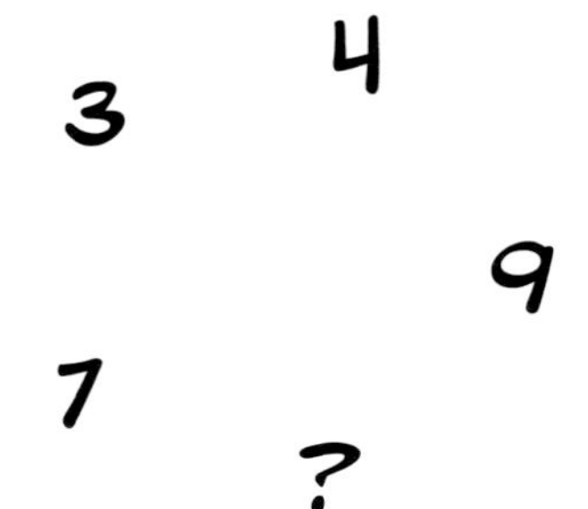

TEC44056

MIND BUILDER 3

Ms. Jones has one black pen and five red pens. Each pack of pens includes two black pens and one red pen. How many packs of pens should Ms. Jones buy to have more black pens than red pens?

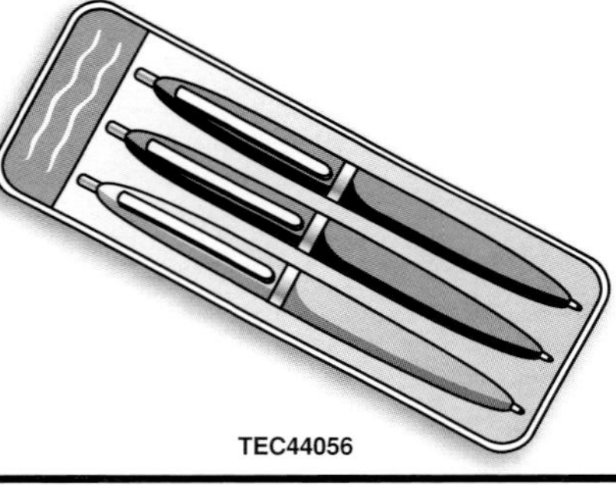

TEC44056

MIND BUILDER 4

Write five different subtraction problems that have a difference of 392. Use only four-digit numbers in your problems.

$$n - x = 392$$

TEC44056

MIND BUILDER 5

Arrange these roman numerals in order from least to greatest.

MXXII

DCCCLXV

MCMV

DCCCLXIX

TEC44056

MIND BUILDER 6

Apples cost $0.15 more per pound than bananas. Kumquats cost $0.10 more per pound than plums. Plums cost the same per pound as bananas. What is the difference in price per pound between kumquats and apples?

TEC44056

MIND BUILDER 7

Which figures can be traced without lifting your pencil or retracing any steps?

A.

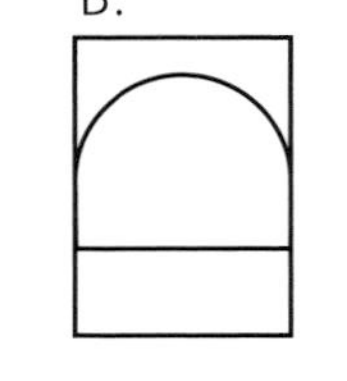

B.

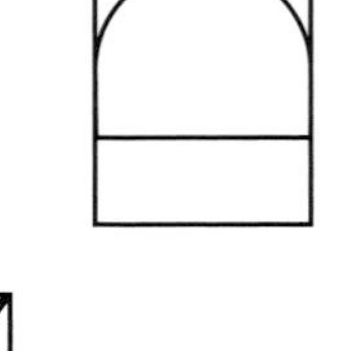

C.

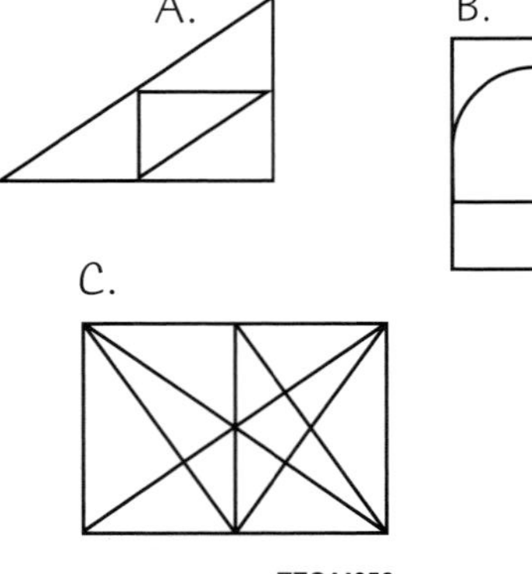

TEC44056

MIND BUILDER 8

A clock shows 9:15. It gets turned back one hour. An hour later, it gets turned ahead one hour. What time does the clock show then?

TEC44056

How to use: Display this page or give each student a copy of the page (or one card at a time) to work on during free time. Have the student solve the problems on a separate sheet of paper.

MIND BUILDERS

MATH

MIND BUILDER 1

Suppose that Z = $1.00 and Y = $2.00, all the way up to A = $26.00. Which state in each pair has the higher value?

A. Texas or Maine

B. Utah or Iowa

TEC44057

MIND BUILDER 2

Is the statement below always true, sometimes true, or never true? Give examples to support your answer.

a prime number + a prime number = an even number

TEC44057

MIND BUILDER 3

A kangaroo can run faster than a squirrel. An elephant can run faster than a squirrel but is slower than a kangaroo. A giraffe can run faster than a kangaroo. List the four animals in order from slowest to fastest.

TEC44057

MIND BUILDER 4

Which answer is largest? Smallest?

A. three times the difference of nine and two

B. twice the product of three and four

C. five times the sum of three and one

D. four times the difference of ten and three

TEC44057

MIND BUILDER 5

Each side of each kennel is five yards long. How much fencing will each set of kennels require?

A.

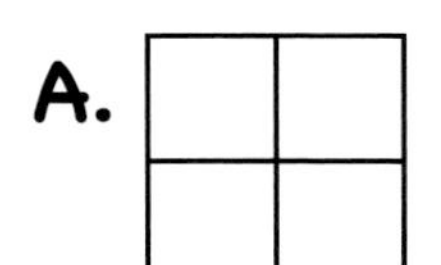

B.

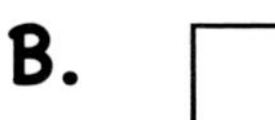

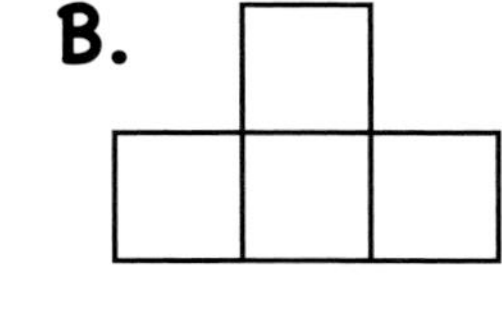

TEC44057

MIND BUILDER 6

You slept from 9:45 PM until 7:15 AM. How many minutes were you asleep?

TEC44057

MIND BUILDER 7

Put each set of measurements in order from shortest to longest.

A. 38 inches, 1 yard, $2\frac{1}{2}$ feet

B. 1,750 yards; 5,290 feet; 1 mile

C. 3 meters, 378 centimeters, 400 millimeters

TEC44057

MIND BUILDER 8

Start with 132. Reverse the digits and add the two numbers. Do the same with 346, 522, 118, and 237. What do you notice about the sums? Does 725 fit the pattern? Find three more three-digit numbers that fit the pattern.

132 + 231 = 363

TEC44057

How to use: Display this page or give each student a copy of the page (or one card at a time) to work on during free time. Have the student solve the problems on a separate sheet of paper.

MIND BUILDERS

MATH

MIND BUILDER 1

Place the digits 4, 6, 7, and 8 in this problem to make a problem with the highest possible product. Then reuse the digits to make a problem with the lowest possible product.

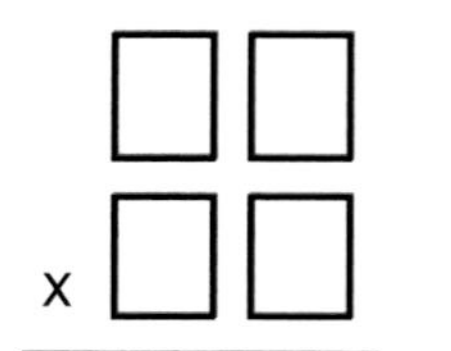

TEC44058

MIND BUILDER 2

If you rolled this cube, how many different ways could it land?

TEC44058

MIND BUILDER 3

How many six-inch floor tiles are needed to cover this floor?

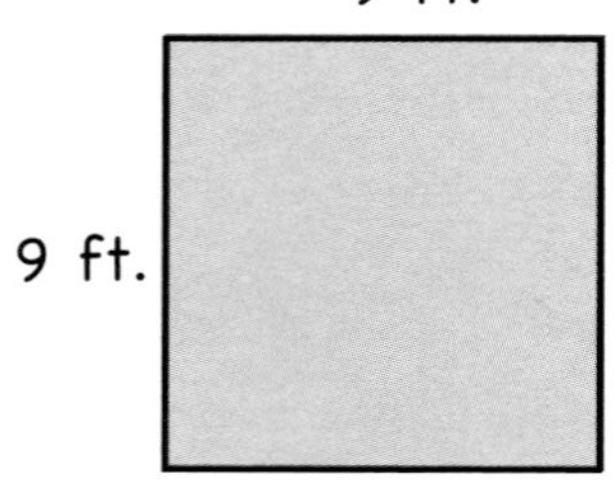

TEC44058

MIND BUILDER 4

During the first hour of a big storm, one-half inch of snow fell. The rate increased by one-half inch every hour following that for the next four hours. What was the total snowfall after five hours?

TEC44058

MIND BUILDER 5

How are these math terms alike? How are they different? Show your answers in a Venn diagram.

quadrilateral quadrant

quadruple

TEC44058

MIND BUILDER 6

There is one number between 100 and 150 that has exactly three factors. What is it?

TEC44058

MIND BUILDER 7

How many rectangles are in this shape? Hint: The answer is a prime number.

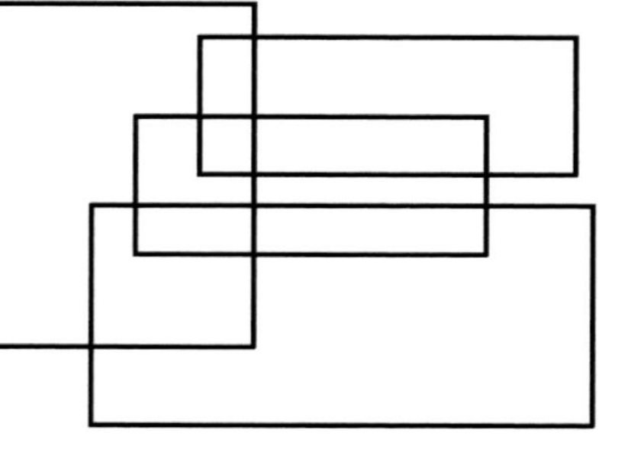
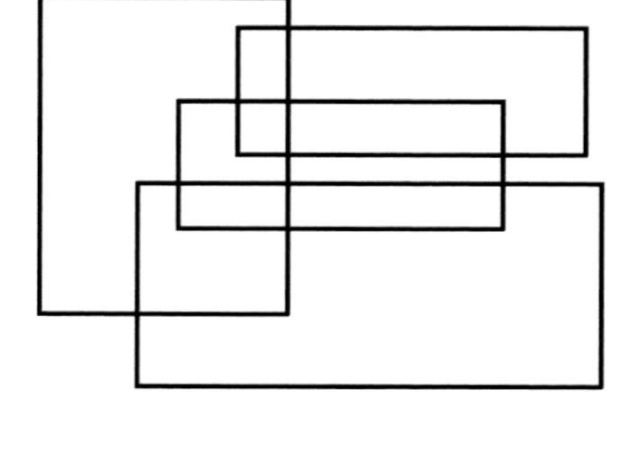

TEC44058

MIND BUILDER 8

You only have nickels, dimes, and quarters. How many different ways can you make $1.50 with exactly ten coins?

TEC44058

How to use: Display this page or give each student a copy of the page (or one card at a time) to work on during free time. Have the student solve the problems on a separate sheet of paper.

MIND BUILDERS

MATH

MIND BUILDER 1

Use the numbers 2, 3, and 4 with any operations (+, –, x, or ÷) and in any grouping to equal one, two, three, and four. See the example. How many solutions can you find for each answer?

Example:

$$3 - (4 \div 2) = 1$$

TEC44059

MIND BUILDER 2

One line divides this rectangle into two regions. Draw three more lines that will divide the rectangle into ten regions.

TEC44059

MIND BUILDER 3

Add five different whole numbers to this magic square so that the sum of each row, column, and diagonal is the same.

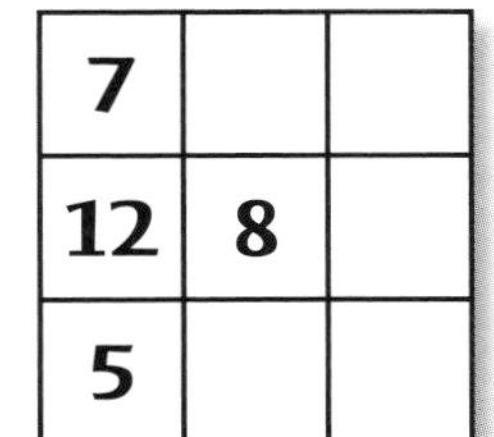

7		
12	8	
5		

TEC44059

MIND BUILDER 4

Which domino comes next in this pattern? Which domino will be the tenth domino in this pattern?

TEC44059

MIND BUILDER 5

Every time a knot is tied in a rope, the rope becomes 3 inches shorter. How many knots were tied in a $6\frac{1}{2}$-foot-long rope that now measures $4\frac{1}{4}$ feet?

TEC44059

MIND BUILDER 6

Name three factors of 72 that together have a sum of 25. Then name three different factors of 72 that also have the sum of 25.

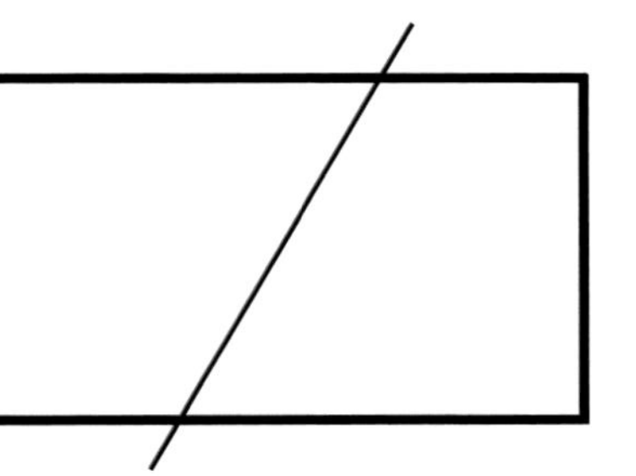

TEC44059

MIND BUILDER 7

When you write the numbers from 1 to 100, which digit do you write most often?

1, 2, 3, 4, 5...

TEC44059

MIND BUILDER 8

How many odd-numbered days are in the first three months of 2012? How many odd-numbered days will there be in the first three months of 2013?

January							February							March						
S	M	T	W	Th	F	S	S	M	T	W	Th	F	S	S	M	T	W	Th	F	S

TEC44059

©The Mailbox® • TEC44059 • Feb./Mar. 2012 • Key p. 61

How to use: Display this page or give each student a copy of the page (or one card at a time) to work on during free time. Have the student solve the problems on a separate sheet of paper.

MIND BUILDERS

MATH

MIND BUILDER 1

Bill Ding has 9 floor tiles that measure 6 inches on each side. If he arranges all of the tiles to form a square, what is the large square's perimeter? What is its area?

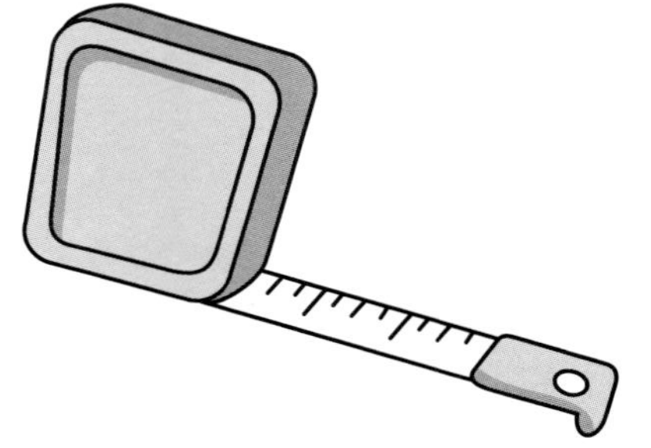

TEC44060

MIND BUILDER 2

What's the largest three-digit number that can be divided by every number less than 9 and leave no remainder?

n ÷ 8 n ÷ 7

n ÷ 6

n ÷ 5 n ÷ 4

n ÷ 3

n ÷ 2 n ÷ 1

TEC44060

MIND BUILDER 3

What number is missing in this table? Explain.

2	5	4
5	3	5
4	2	3
5	4	5
4	1	?

TEC44060

MIND BUILDER 4

If you glued five cubes together in shape A and then dipped the shape in a bucket of paint, how many of the cube faces would be painted? How many faces wouldn't be painted?

If you glued five cubes together to form shape B and then dipped the shape in a bucket of paint, how many of the cube faces would be painted? How many faces wouldn't be painted?

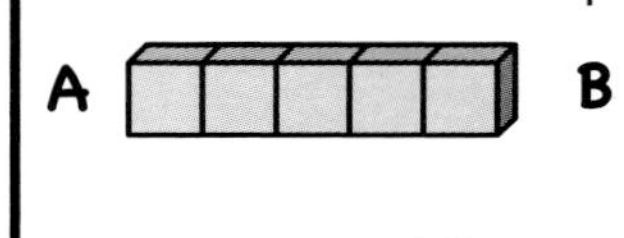

TEC44060

MIND BUILDER 5

Use scales A and B to solve for the unknown on scale C.

A. 2 bananas = 3 pears

B. 4 pears = 1 apple

C. 3 apples = ? bananas

TEC44060

MIND BUILDER 6

What is the largest two-digit number that has exactly four factors? What's the smallest?

___ ___

___, ___, ___, ___

TEC44060

MIND BUILDER 7

Arrange the numbers 5 through 13 in the circles so that the sum of each row, column, and diagonal is 27.

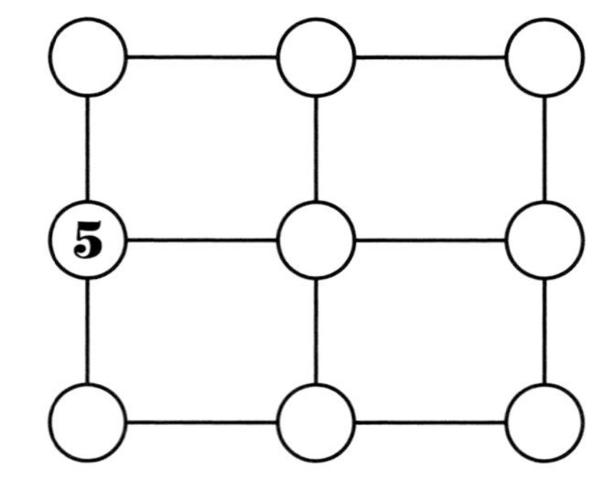

TEC44060

MIND BUILDER 8

A penny, nickel, dime, and quarter are placed in a bag. If you remove one coin without looking, what are the chances of getting a coin worth…

A. more than 10 cents?

B. less than 10 cents?

C. 50 cents?

TEC44060

How to use: Display this page or give each student a copy of the page (or one card at a time) to work on during free time. Have the student solve the problems on a separate sheet of paper.

MIND BUILDERS

MIND BUILDER 1

Flips cost $2.20. Flops cost half as much as flips. Flaps are one-half the price of flops. How much would 2 flips, 3 flops, and 5 flaps cost altogether?

TEC44061

MIND BUILDER 2

Write 12 three-digit numbers that have all the qualities listed below. How many more numbers can you write that have these qualities? Explain.

- All the digits in each number are odd numbers.
- No digit is repeated in a number.
- The middle digit in every number is 5.

TEC44061

MIND BUILDER 3

A grasshopper leaps five inches in each bound. A cricket jumps four inches at a time. By the time the two insects travel five feet, how many more jumps will the cricket have taken than the grasshopper?

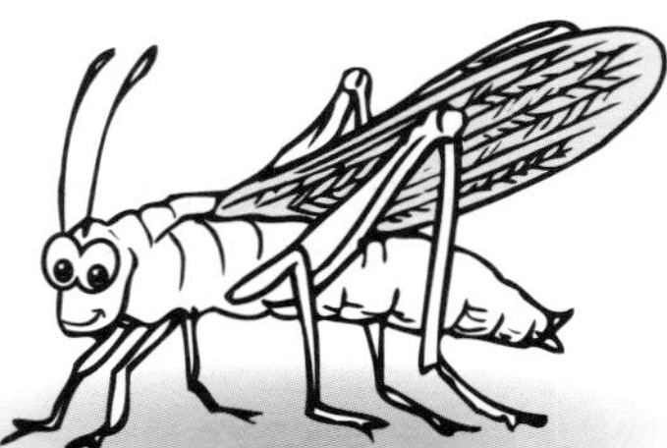

TEC44061

MIND BUILDER 4

Solve each problem. Then sort the problems according to their answers' attributes.

A. 437 + 217
B. 18,107 x 3
C. 921 - 588
D. 428 + 127
E. 10,000 - 2,346
F. 148 x 3

TEC44061

MIND BUILDER 5

At a race, there are two empty seats for every five occupied ones in a section of bleachers. If there are 35 seats in that section, how many are empty?

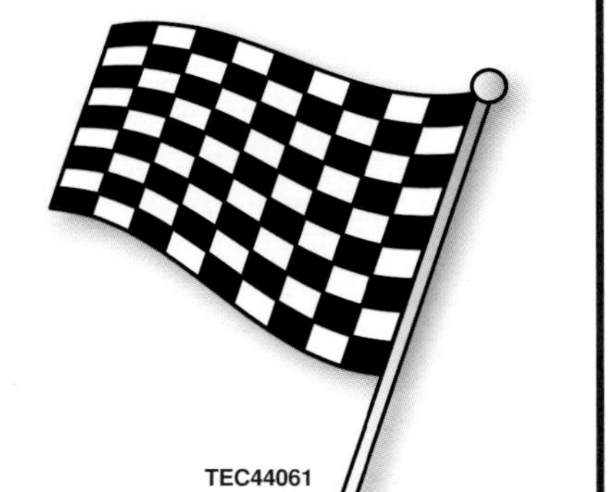

TEC44061

MIND BUILDER 6

Complete each pattern and then write its rule.

A. 100, 89, 77, 64, ___, 35, ___
B. 1, 4, 9, ___, 25, 36, ___
C. 10, 20, 40, 70, ___, 160, ___

TEC44061

MIND BUILDER 7

Follow the clues to write a ten-digit number. Use each of the digits 0–9 only one time each.

1. The thousands digit is larger than any digit in the millions period.
2. The hundreds digit plus the ones digit equals the tens digit.
3. The hundred thousands digit is the largest one.
4. The hundred millions digit plus the ten millions digit equals the millions digit.
5. The number is even.
6. 0 is beside 9.
7. The hundred millions digit is even.
8. The digits in the last three places are the three smallest prime numbers.

TEC44061

MIND BUILDER 8

Find the missing numbers.

A. 3 × 37,037 = 111,111
B. 6 × 37,037 = □
C. 9 × □ = 333,333
D. □ × 37,037 = 444,444
E. 18 × □ = 666,666
F. 27 × 37,037 = □

TEC44061

How to use: Display this page or give each student a copy of the page (or one card at a time) to work on during free time. Have the student solve the problems on a separate sheet of paper.

Use as center or free-time activities.

Place value

GOING PLACES!

Begin with 1,000,000. Then follow the steps below, changing one digit at a time. Rewrite the number each time.

1. Change the 0 in the tens place to a 1.
2. Change the 0 in the ten thousands place to a 7. (Do you have 1,070,010?)
3. Change the 0 in the ones place to a 9.
4. Change the 0 in the thousands place to a 3.
5. Change the 0 in the hundred thousands place to a 5.
6. Change the 0 in the hundreds place to an 8.
7. Change the 1 in the millions place to a 2.

Now, write five steps to change the last number to 3,073,491.

TEC44056

Division

JUST NUTTY

Solve each problem. Then arrange the quotients from smallest to largest.

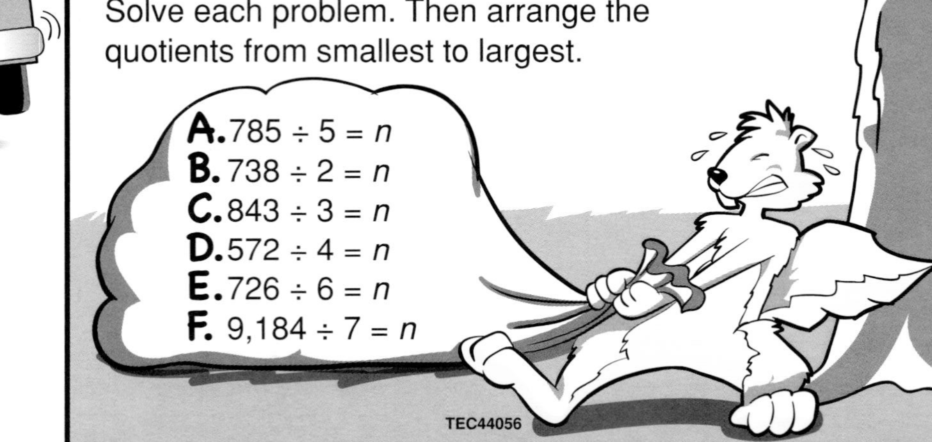

A. $785 \div 5 = n$
B. $738 \div 2 = n$
C. $843 \div 3 = n$
D. $572 \div 4 = n$
E. $726 \div 6 = n$
F. $9{,}184 \div 7 = n$

TEC44056

Subtraction, decimals

IF THE SHOE FITS

Choose a decimal from the bottom shoebox to subtract from each decimal on the top shoebox. Then find each difference.

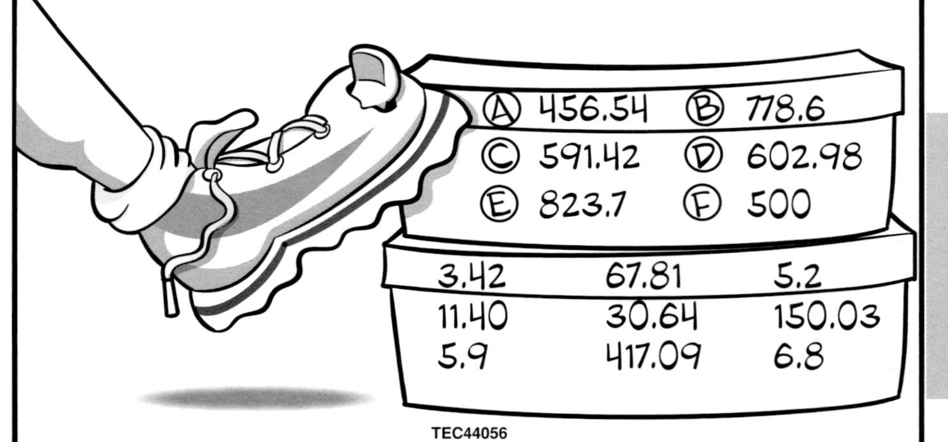

TEC44056

Measurement to one-eighth inch

Give Me a Hand!

Trace your hand on your paper. Next, use a ruler to draw the lines described below. Then measure each line to the nearest one-eighth inch and record your measurement.

1. Draw Line A from the tip of your pinkie to the tip of your thumb.
2. Draw Line B from the tip of your index finger to the tip of your thumb.
3. Draw Line C between your index and middle fingers.
4. Draw Line D from the tip of your pinkie to the tip of your middle finger.
5. Draw Line E from the tip of your pinkie to the base of your palm.
6. Draw Line F from the base of your palm to the tip of your thumb.

TEC44056

Number patterns

FLEA MARKET FINDS

Find the pricing pattern on each sign. Then copy the sign and complete the pricing.

Paperback Books
5 books for $2.50
10 books for $5.00
15 books for
18 books for
20 books for $10.00

Classic Rock CDs
2 CDs for $5.50
3 CDs for
4 CDs for
5 CDs for $13.75

Teeny Tiny Stuffed Animals
5 for $3.00
7 for
9 for $5.40
10 for
12 for

Honk if you love flea markets!

TEC44057

Metric measurement

"WEIGHT" A MINUTE!

Convert each measurement from grams to kilograms. How many kilograms are in each column? How many kilograms are there altogether?

Hint: 1 kilogram (kg) = 1,000 grams (g)

A. 2,894 g	H. 15,247 g
B. 15,422 g	I. 14,004 g
C. 124,003 g	J. 99,999 g
D. 563 g	K. 1,045 g
E. 109,604 g	L. 68 g
F. 18,947 g	M. 20,075 g
G. 955 g	N. 789 g
	O. 11,834 g

TEC44057

Naming fractions

CHAIR SHARE

There are 36 desks and chairs in the classroom. One-fourth of the chairs are blue. One-third are red, one fourth are brown, and one-sixth are yellow. One-ninth of the chairs need to be repaired.

Draw a diagram that shows the number of chairs that are blue, red, brown, and yellow.

On the diagram, circle the number of chairs that need to be repaired.

TEC44057

Multiplication

A TURKEY TROT

Winner, winner—NO turkey dinner!

5 6 7 8 9 11 12 13 14 15

Use a one-digit number and a two-digit number from the finish line tape to write a multiplication problem. Solve the problem. Repeat to solve nine more problems.

TEC44057

Math Activity Cards

Use as center or free-time activities.

Lines

Toeing the Line

Look around the room. Find four examples each of line segments that are **parallel**, **perpendicular**, and **intersecting**.
Draw and label each one.

TEC44058

Temperature

Cold Feet?

Copy and complete each statement.

1. I think it would be too cold to go outside if the temperature were ___.
2. I think it would be too hot to go outside if the temperature were ___.
3. If the temperature were 95°F, it would be a perfect day to ___, ___, or ___.
4. If the temperature were 35°F, it would be a great day to ___, ___, or ___.
5. If the temperature were 65°F, it would be a good day to ___, ___, or ___.
6. If the temperature were 0°C, it would be a great day to ___, ___, or ___.
7. My least-favorite time to be outside is when the temperature is around ___.
8. My favorite time to be outside is when the temperature is around ___.

TEC44058

Adding, subtracting fractions

GO FOR A SPIN!

- Spin this spinner two times. Record each fraction.

$\frac{2}{3}$, $\frac{1}{4}$, $\frac{5}{6}$, $\frac{7}{8}$, $\frac{3}{4}$, $\frac{1}{2}$, $\frac{3}{8}$, $\frac{3}{5}$

- Spin this spinner. Then find the sum of or the difference between the two fractions as guided.

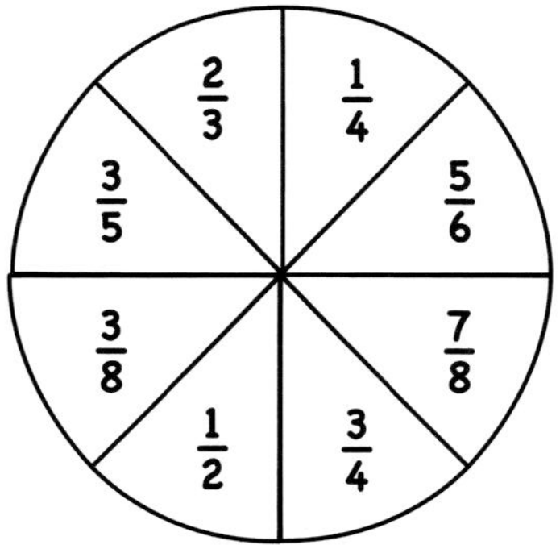

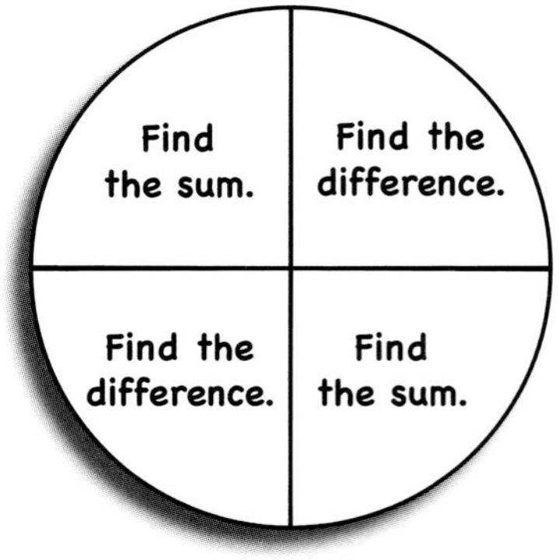

Find the sum. | Find the difference. | Find the difference. | Find the sum.

- Repeat five times to write and solve six problems in all.

TEC44058

Two-digit multiplication

PACKED WITH PRACTICE

Use the numbers on the bag to write eight different multiplication problems. Then solve each one.

45 94 47 57 73 64 28 86

TEC44058

Area

One for the Books

Choose five different books. Measure the length and width of each book's cover. Then find each book cover's area and perimeter.

perimeter = 2 • *l* + 2 • *w*

area = *l* • *w*

length (*l*)

width (*w*)

TEC44059

Division

Sweet!

Use the numbers on the candy hearts to write the rest of each division problem. Then solve each one. Use multiplication to check your quotient.

2,646 6,064 7,806 4,052 7,085

5)

6)

8)

4)

7)

TEC44059

Problem solving, logic

Cryptographers Welcome

Each symbol stands for a digit from 0 to 9. Copy the incomplete code. Figure out which digit each symbol represents. Then complete the code and write each equation, using numbers instead of symbols.

CODE

= 0	= 5
△ = 1	= 6
= 2	= 7
= 3	= 8
= 4	= 9

1. ɘ + ɘ = ɘ
2. □ + □ = △ɘ
3. □ x ₸ = △□
4. □ + ₸ = >
5. □ – ✱ = △
6. ₸ x # = ±
7. ∩ – > = △
8. ✱ + ₸ = ◇

TEC44059

Symmetry, congruency

Evenly Divided

Draw and label a four-column chart with the categories shown. Then sort each capital letter into one of the four categories.

A B C D E F G H I J K L M N O P Q R S T U V W X Y Z

TEC44059

Math Activity Cards

Use as center or free-time activities.

Problem solving, time

A Caterpillar Conference

What time does each caterpillar need to leave to get to practice on time? Show your work.

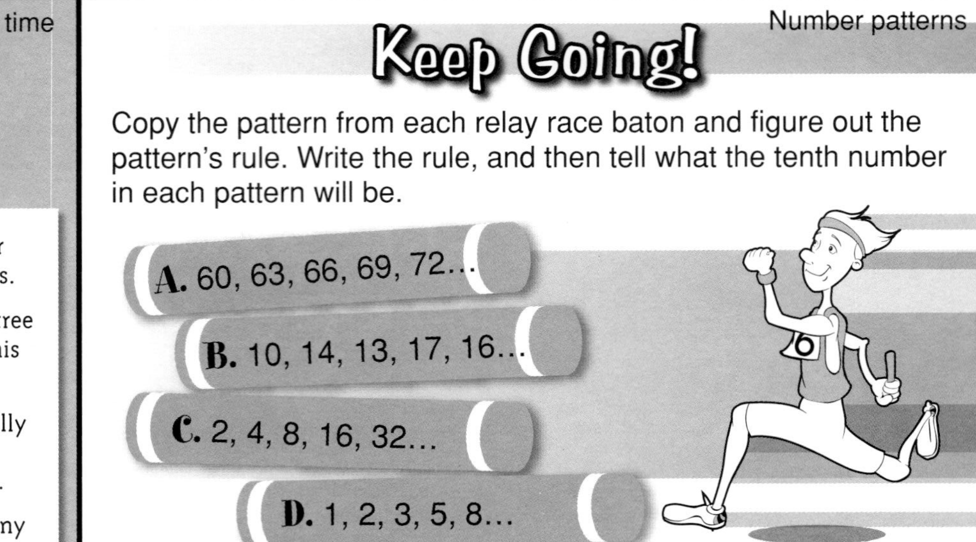

- Caitlyn has a 24-minute crawl from her branch. She'll stop for five snack breaks on her way. Each break will last five minutes.
- If he doesn't stop for any snacks, Carter can scoot across the tree in 25 minutes. He'll stop for three snack breaks though, and his breaks take six minutes each.
- Clover's bringing her little sister, Candace, with her. It normally takes Clover 17 minutes to creep across the tree. Candace will have to stop seven times for a five-minute snack at each stop.
- Calvin's going to try to get to practice without stopping for any snacks. However, he's on another tree. It will take him 22 minutes to get to the right tree. Then it will take 35 minutes to inch his way up the tree.

TEC44060

Number patterns

Keep Going!

Copy the pattern from each relay race baton and figure out the pattern's rule. Write the rule, and then tell what the tenth number in each pattern will be.

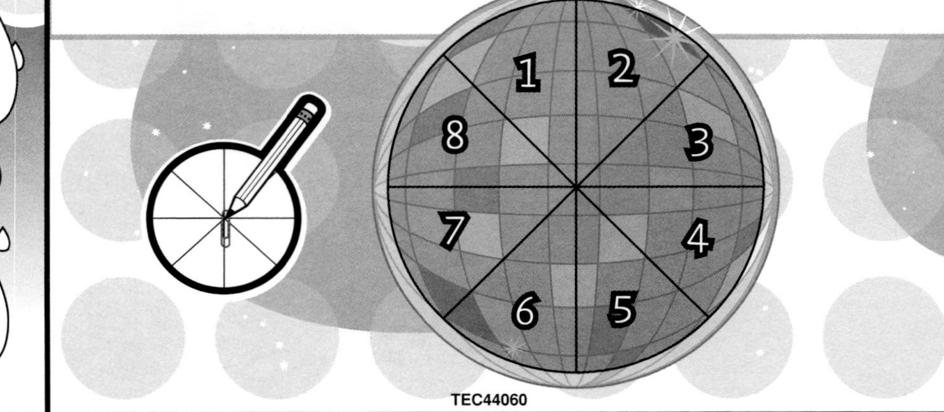

A. 60, 63, 66, 69, 72...

B. 10, 14, 13, 17, 16...

C. 2, 4, 8, 16, 32...

D. 1, 2, 3, 5, 8...

E. 5, 5, 10, 30, 120...

TEC44060

Adding fractions

April Showers

Choose a fraction. Use it and another fraction to write an equation whose sum is greater than one. Write the sum in simplest form. Repeat with each remaining fraction until you have written eight different problems.

$\frac{2}{3}$ $\frac{1}{5}$ $\frac{3}{4}$ $\frac{5}{8}$ $\frac{1}{4}$

$\frac{7}{8}$ $\frac{1}{3}$ $\frac{1}{2}$ $\frac{2}{5}$ $\frac{3}{8}$

TEC44060

Multiplying by two digits

Take a Spin!

Spin three times and write a three-digit factor using the numbers you spin. Then spin two times and write a two-digit factor using those numbers. Multiply to find the product. Repeat five times.

TEC44060

Patterns in decimal computation

HOT ON THE TRAIL

Solve each problem and tell what the answers have in common. Then write two more problems that have answers with the same patterns.

0.407 + 0.599 =

2.511 + 0.498 =

1.167 x 6 =

TEC44061

Improper fractions to mixed numbers

AT THE RACES

Make each improper fraction a mixed number to find out how many laps and fractions of laps each racer had completed.

A. Mario's tire went flat when he had completed $\frac{29}{5}$ laps.
B. Tony ran out of gas as he finished $\frac{160}{12}$ laps.
C. Jimmy was the leader for $\frac{90}{13}$ laps.
D. Willa's engine started to knock on her $\frac{900}{7}$ lap.
E. Gary bumped the wall on his $\frac{781}{8}$ lap, but he was okay and went on to win the race!

TEC44061

Converting temperatures, multiplying fractions

Getting Warmer!

Convert each temperature from degrees Fahrenheit to degrees Celsius.

Hint: To convert a temperature from Fahrenheit to Celsius, subtract 32 and then multiply the difference by $\frac{5}{9}$.

$$C = (F - 32) \cdot \frac{5}{9}$$

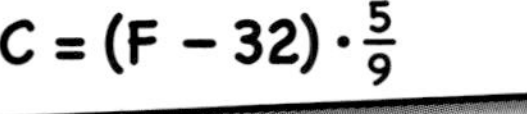
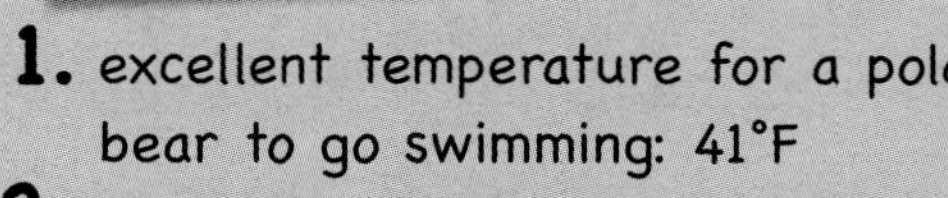
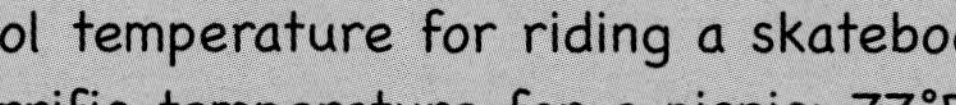

1. excellent temperature for a polar bear to go swimming: 41°F
2. super temperature for surfing: 86°F
3. great temperature for going to the swimming pool: 95°F
4. cool temperature for riding a skateboard: 68°F
5. terrific temperature for a picnic: 77°F

TEC44061

Division

Time for Grillin'

Use the numbers on the hamburgers and hot dogs to write eight different division problems. Estimate the quotient for each problem. Then solve. Compare your estimates and answers.

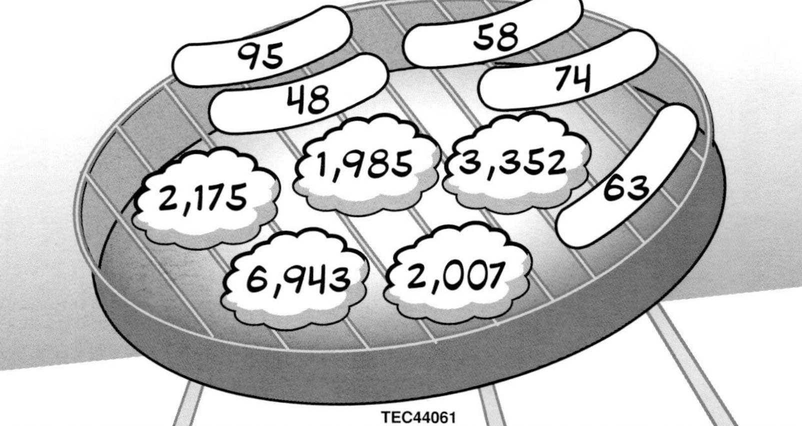

TEC44061

WHAT A DEAL!

All you need for these skill-building math games are playing cards!

Math Mind Readers

Here's a fun way to review **multiplication facts**! Divide the class into two teams and have students form two lines facing each other. In advance, remove the face cards from a deck of cards. To play, give the first player in each line a card and have him press it to his forehead without looking at the card. Next, announce the product of the numbers on the students' cards. Then have each player look at his opponent's card and call out the multiplication fact. The first player to correctly name the complete fact earns a point for his team. Play as time allows. When time's up, declare the team with more points the victor. **Ann Marie Vinson, Southampton Academy, Courtland, VA**

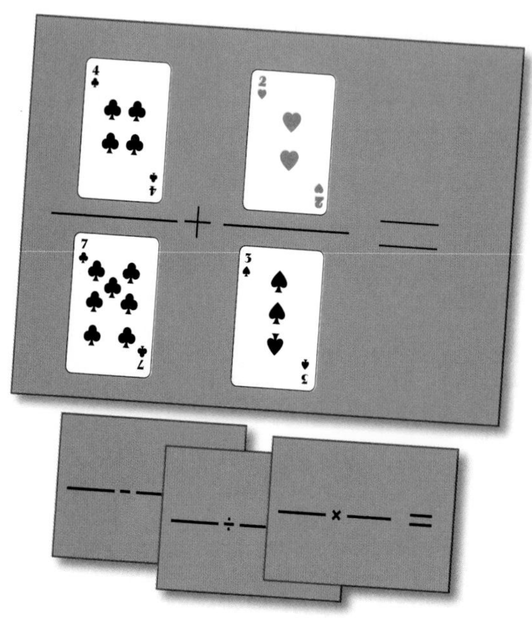

Four and More

This versatile activity gives students practice **adding**, **subtracting**, **multiplying**, or **dividing fractions** and **mixed numbers** or **improper fractions**. In advance, remove the face cards from a deck of cards and make center mats by labeling construction paper as shown for each operation. Place the mats at a center along with the cards and a supply of paper. A child takes the mat for the operation she needs to practice. Next, she places four cards facedown on the mat. Then she flips the cards and records the problem on her paper. The student solves the problem and reduces the answer to simplest form. Then she puts the cards at the bottom of the deck and takes four more cards, continuing as time allows. **Trisha Koch, Batesville Intermediate, Batesville, IN**

Eagle Eyes

With this partner game, students **identify patterns** and hone their observation skills! One player shuffles a deck of cards and then deals 25 cards facedown, making a 5 x 5 grid. The partners take turns flipping cards, one at a time. During each turn, the students look for three cards that have a pattern. When a player spots a pattern during his turn, he takes the cards, records their pattern and tallies five points. If a student fails to notice a pattern during his turn, his opponent may take the cards, record the pattern, and earn the points. The students deal three more cards to fill the empty spaces and keep playing. The first partner to earn 50 points wins. If a student can't find a pattern during his turn, he turns the cards over and his partner takes a turn.

A Penny for Your Thoughts

by Stacy Shaener
Aleph Bet Jewish Day School
Annapolis, MD

For this "cents-ible" exploration, give each student a penny. Then read aloud the questions shown. After each question, have each child record his answer.

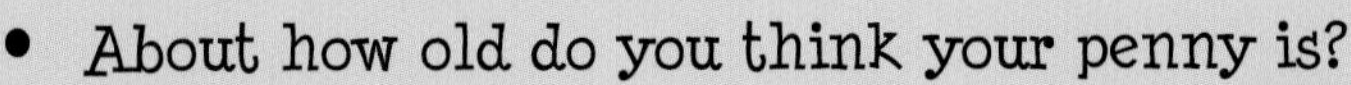

- About how old do you think your penny is?
- What year was your penny minted?
- How old is your penny?
- Was your penny minted in an even or an odd year?
- What is the expanded form of your penny's minting year?
- What is the word form of your penny's minting year?
- What is the sum of the digits in your penny's minting year?
- Are there any other years whose digits would have the same sum? What are they?
- Is your penny older or younger than you are?
- How many years older or younger than you is your penny?
- In what year did or will your penny turn 18 years old?
- When did or will your penny turn 50 years old? 75 years old? 100 years old?

MERRY MATH MINUTES

Problem-solving puzzlers that are perfect for keeping students engaged right up to the beginning of winter break!

- Give bell work a seasonal twist by displaying a puzzler at the beginning of each math lesson.
- Copy and cut apart the puzzlers. Have each pair of students take one, solve it, and then write a new question for it. After that, have each duo trade work with another pair, check each other's work, and answer the additional question.
- Post the puzzlers as extra credit challenges for early finishers.

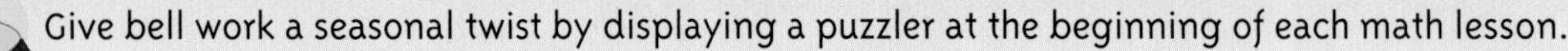

Just suppose...

1 ...it takes one yard of wrapping paper to wrap three gifts. If each student in your class were to wrap five gifts, how many yards of paper would the class need?

2 ...the Can't Stop Singing Carolers cover $2\frac{1}{2}$ miles each evening for one week. How many miles do they walk? How many miles will they walk if they go out each evening for three weeks?

3 ...you are making a nine-foot-long cranberry garland. You fit three cranberries on every inch of string. How many cranberries will you need to finish the garland? How many cranberries would you need to make two garlands?

4 ...Santa gets 75,635 letters in one week. Each letter has a $0.44 stamp on it. If the same number of letters are received each day, how much would the stamps for one day's mail have cost? How much would one day's postage be if each stamp cost $0.45?

5 ...a Christmas tree absorbs three quarts of water each day. How many quarts of water will it absorb in two weeks? How many gallons of water will it absorb in four weeks?

6 ... you light a candle at 6:30 PM and then blow out the flame at 9:15 PM. How long does the candle burn? For how many hours will the candle burn if you light it each evening for twelve days?

7 ...there are 2,948 hoofs in a herd of reindeer. How many reindeer are in the herd? Every reindeer has a full pair of antlers. How many antlers are in the herd?

8 ...it snows $7\frac{1}{2}$ feet every day for four days. On the fifth day, the sun melts $3\frac{1}{2}$ feet of the snow. However, the sixth day brings $6\frac{1}{2}$ more feet of snow! How deep is the snow? If the snow melts at least $3\frac{1}{2}$ feet a day, how many days will it take the snow to melt?

9 ...you decide to make a gingerbread house for each of your classmates. It takes $1\frac{1}{4}$ pounds of dough and $2\frac{1}{2}$ cups of icing to make each house. How much dough will you need in all? How much icing?

10 ...Santa has visited your house every Christmas Eve for 12 years. In those years, he has eaten a total of 60 cookies. About how many cookies does Santa eat at your house each year? How many will he have eaten in all if he stops by your house for six more years?

11 ... everyone in your neighborhood is coming to your house for the big day! There will be 84 hungry people in your house! How many turkeys should your parents cook? (A 14-pound turkey will serve about seven people.) How many six-serving pies should your parents bake?

12 ...each of the 84 hungry people who came to your house for dinner used two dishes, a knife, a spoon, two forks, and one glass. How many dishes and glasses are there to wash? How many pieces of silverware?

Seasonal

Read-the-Room Editing

Back-to-school, spelling

Here's an upper-grade version of reading the room that has students thinking as soon as they arrive. Before the first day of school, label supplies and furniture around the room, misspelling about half the names. Then post a greeting that lists the number of misspelled labels and challenges students to find them throughout the day. Have each child list the misspelled labels as she spots them and write their correct spellings. Near the end of the day, have students point out the misspellings and use editing marks to correct them. If desired, collect students' work and award bonus points toward future spelling assignments.

Ann E. Fisher, Toledo, OH

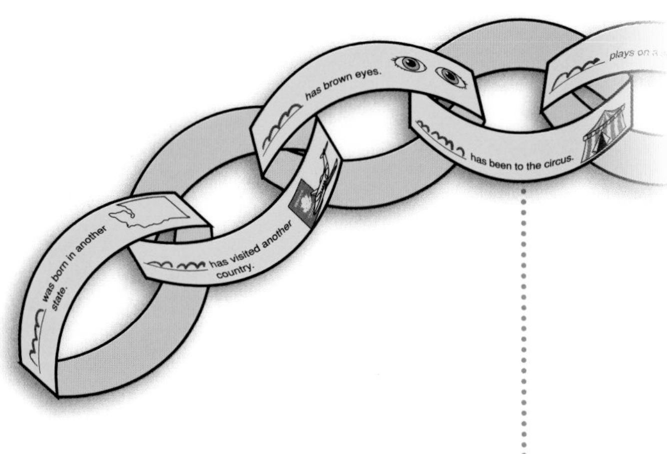

Making Connections

Back-to-school

For this getting-to-know-you activity, give each student a copy of page 170 and have him circulate the room, asking classmates to sign statement strips that describe themselves. When time is up, have each child cut out the strips and then glue them together in links to make a paper chain. After students complete their chains, use construction paper strips to link all the chains together. Then display the class chain on a board titled "Our Class Is Connected!"

Hard Workers

Similes

For this lyrical Labor Day idea, brainstorm with students a list of occupations. Next, display the simile pattern shown. Challenge students to create similes that describe the workers' occupations and their duties. Then combine students' similes into a class poem that honors the country's workforce.

Jackie Beaudry, Getzville, NY

All-Star Citizens

Citizenship, writing in response to a prompt

Commemorate Constitution Day and Citizenship Day (September 17) with a week of writing prompts that lead students to set citizenship goals. On Monday through Thursday, display a different prompt from the top of page 171 and lead students to write thoughtful responses. Then, on Friday, have each child review her responses and write five goals for being a good citizen. Next, have the student cut out a five-point star, write her name in the center, and record each goal inside a different point. Display students' work on a board titled "All-Star Citizens."

Ann E. Fisher, Toledo, OH

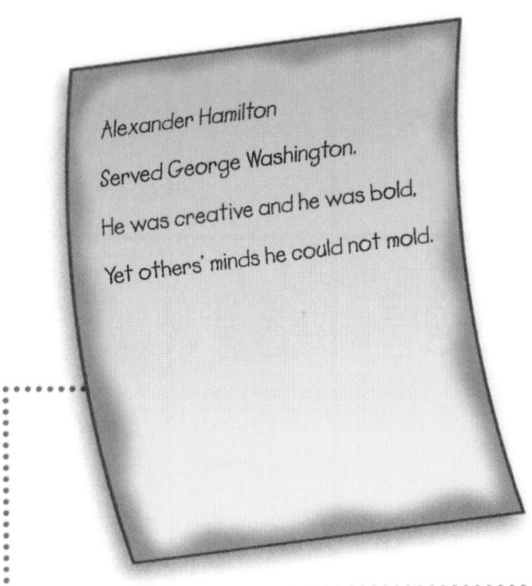

Constitutionally Creative

Writing a poem

Here's a fun way to celebrate Constitution Day and Citizenship Day (September 17). Display the clerihew poem shown. (A clerihew poem is a light poem consisting of two rhyming couplets. The name of a famous person makes one of the rhymes.) Then point out that the poem, made up of two rhyming couplets, is based on the name of one of the original signers of the United States Constitution. Next, guide each pair of students to choose a signer, research him, and then draft a clerihew poem about him. Have each duo read its poem aloud as time allows.

Getting to the Core

Rounding

Give students "a-peel-ing" practice rounding with this fall-themed activity. Review rounding rules and then have each child cut out the apple and worm patterns from a copy of the bottom of page 171. Next, have each student accordion-fold the apples vertically and glue a worm to the left side of each apple row. Then guide the child to round the numbers to the places listed on the apples.

Colleen Dabney, Williamsburg, VA

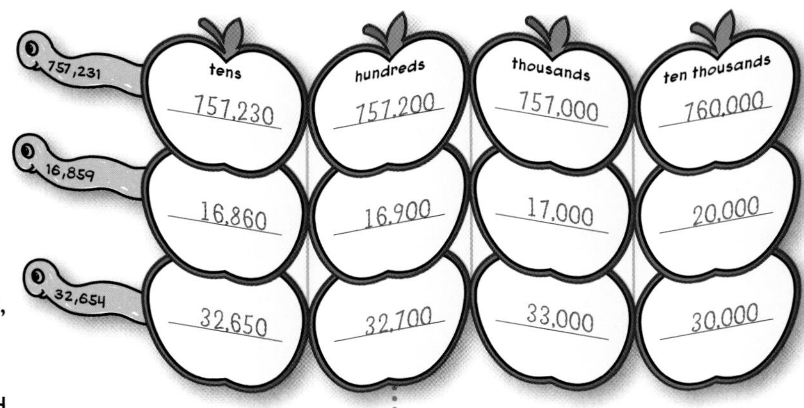

Icebreaker Strips

Use with "Making Connections" on page 168.

________ has been to a professional sports game.	Glue here.
________ has been to a concert.	Glue here.
________ has three or more siblings.	Glue here.
________ went to a different school last year.	Glue here.
________ likes to draw.	Glue here.
________ likes to read nonfiction.	Glue here.
________ plays a musical instrument.	Glue here.
________ speaks another language.	Glue here.
________ has a birthday this summer.	Glue here.
________ was born in another state.	Glue here.
________ has visited another country.	Glue here.
________ has brown eyes.	Glue here.
________ has a dog.	Glue here.
________ plays on a sports team.	Glue here.
________ has been to the circus.	Glue here.
________ likes pizza.	Glue here.
________ has a birthday this month.	Glue here.
________ is left-handed.	Glue here.

Citizenship Prompts

Use with "All-Star Citizens" on page 169.

As a citizen of the school, you are entitled to certain rights and privileges. What are your rights and privileges? What are your duties as a citizen of the school? TEC44056	If a citizen is someone who has certain rights, privileges, and duties, could you be considered a citizen of your home? Why or why not? TEC44056
Name someone you know who shows good citizenship. What are three things this person does that make him or her a good citizen? TEC44056	Do you think you are a good citizen of the country? Why or why not? TEC44056

Apple and Worm Patterns

Use with "Getting to the Core" on page 169.

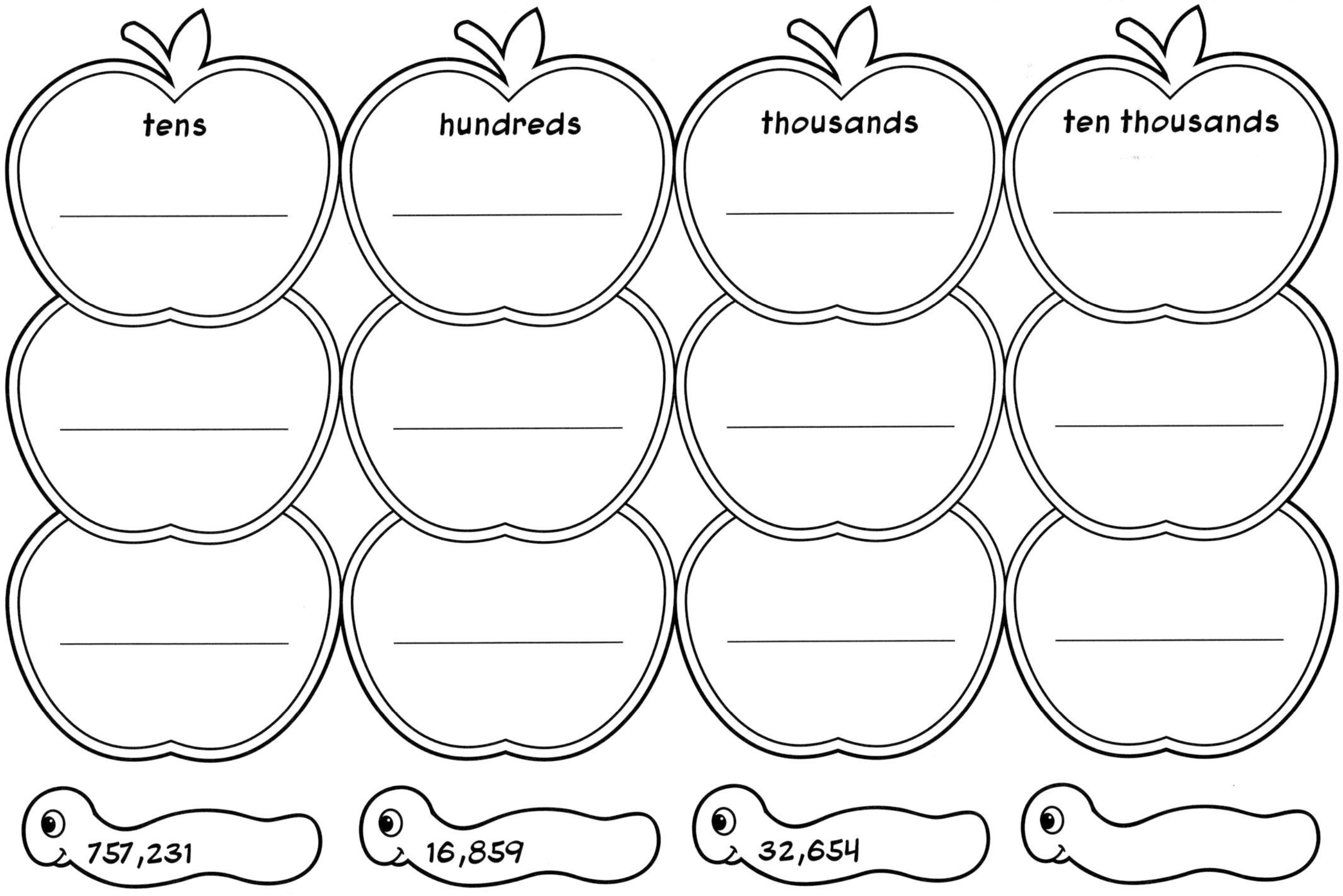

tens

hundreds

thousands

ten thousands

757,231

16,859

32,654

SKILLS FOR THE SEASON

In Fourteen Hundred Ninety-Two

Computation review

Try this fun idea for observing Columbus Day! Display the problems shown and have students solve each one. Once students realize that each problem's answer is 1,492, issue this Columbus Day dare. Challenge each child to create four problems, one for each operation, that each equal 1,492. Then have students trade papers and check each other's problems, making sure each sum, difference, product, and quotient is equal to 1,492. **Ann E. Fisher, Toledo, OH**

c = 1,492

736 + 756 = c

2,441 – 949 = c

373 x 4 = c

4,476 ÷ 3 = c

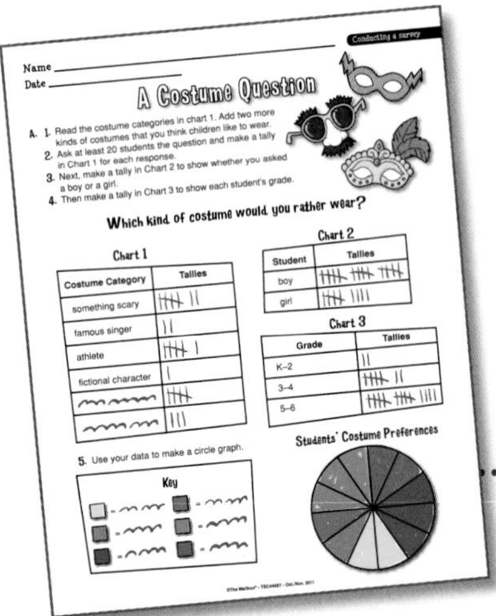

Conducting a survey

Name ____________

Date ____________

A Costume Question

A. 1. Read the costume categories in chart 1. Add two more kinds of costumes that you think children like to wear.
2. Ask at least 20 students the question and make a tally in Chart 1 for each response.
3. Next, make a tally in Chart 2 to show whether you asked a boy or a girl.
4. Then make a tally in Chart 3 to show each student's grade.

Which kind of costume would you rather wear?

Chart 1

Costume Category	Tallies
something scary	𝍸 ||
famous singer	||
athlete	𝍸 |
fictional character	|
	𝍸
	|||

Chart 2

Student	Tallies
boy	𝍸 𝍸 𝍸
girl	𝍸 ||||

Chart 3

Grade	Tallies
K–2	||
3–4	𝍸 ||
5–6	𝍸 𝍸 ||||

5. Use your data to make a circle graph.

Key

Students' Costume Preferences

Junior Pollsters

Conducting a survey, graphing results

Keep students focused on math instead of Halloween treats with this interactive idea. Have each child use a copy of page 174 to survey fellow students about their ideal costumes, tallying their responses. Next, have students graph their results as guided on the page. Then lead a class discussion about students' results with questions such as those shown. **Colleen Dabney, Williamsburg, VA**

According to your surveys, which kind of costume is most popular? Least popular?
According to your surveys, which kind of costume is most popular for girls? For boys?
How many fourth- and fifth-grade students prefer a costume that is not on the list?
How many students in grades below fourth prefer a costume that is not on the list?
Which kind of graph would you use to display the class's combined results? Explain.

In the End

Narrative writing

Here's a great writing activity that's just right for Halloween. First, have each student cut out a copy of the goblin feet from the bottom of page 173. Next, have the child make a construction paper hat and glue the feet to it as if the goblin is upside down in the hat. Then guide each child to outline and draft a story that ends, "That is how the goblin fell into his hat." Have the student write his final copy on lined paper trimmed to match the hat's shape and staple the page or pages to the back of the cutout. Finally, set aside time for each student to read his story aloud. **Emily Clark, Vernal, UT**

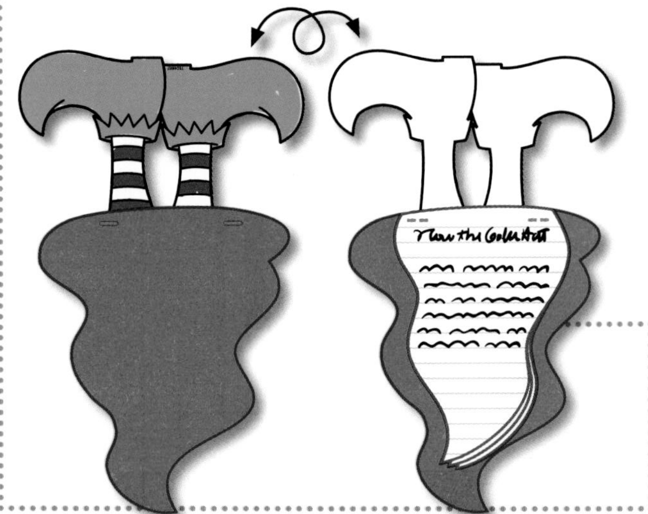

Salutations!

World Hello Day (November 21)

Promote peace in your little corner of the world by challenging students to complete these people-friendly activities.

- Greet ten people today. If you're feeling shy, remember that a smile and a nod can be a greeting.
- Write five different ways to greet someone.
- Make up a secret handshake with a friend.
- Design a card for a friend you haven't seen recently. Write a special greeting or poem inside.
- Find out how to say hello in two other languages. Teach each greeting to a friend.

Double the Dinner?

Fractions, multiplying

Want to give students real-world fraction practice? Have them imagine they are preparing stuffing, pumpkin pie, or cranberry sauce for Thanksgiving. Then give each pair of students a copy of a recipe card from page 175 and have the duo rewrite the recipe so that it will serve eight instead of four. If a twosome finishes early, have the partners rewrite the recipe one more time so that it will serve six or 12. Provide access to measuring spoons and cups to help students visualize the measurements. Then follow up by guiding students to rewrite the pie recipe so it will serve everyone in the class. Have volunteers bring ingredients and set aside class time to make and enjoy the pies. **Becky Fuentes, Rebecca A. Juneau School, Marysville, WA, and Ann E. Fisher, Toledo, OH**

Goblin Feet Pattern

Use with "In the End" on page 172.

TEC44057

Name ______________________

Date ______________

A Costume Question

1. Read the costume categories in chart 1. Add two more kinds of costumes that you think children like to wear.
2. Ask at least 20 students the question and make a tally in Chart 1 for each response.
3. Next, make a tally in Chart 2 to show whether you asked a boy or a girl.
4. Then make a tally in Chart 3 to show each student's grade.

Which kind of costume would you rather wear?

Chart 1

Costume Category	Tallies
something scary	
famous singer	
athlete	
fictional character	

Chart 2

Student	Tallies
boy	
girl	

Chart 3

Grade	Tallies
K–1	
2–3	
4–5	
6–7	

5. Use your data to make a circle graph.

Key

☐ = ☐ =

☐ = ☐ =

☐ = ☐ =

Students' Costume Preferences

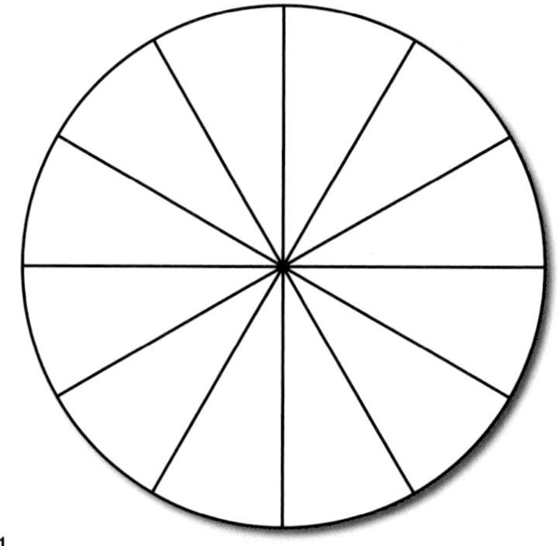

 Note to the teacher: Use with "Junior Pollsters" on page 172.

Recipe Cards

Use with "Double the Dinner?" on page 173.

Cranberry Sauce for Four

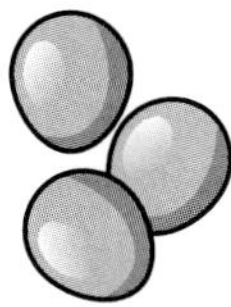

$\frac{1}{3}$ cup sugar
$\frac{1}{3}$ cup water
$1\frac{3}{4}$ cups fresh or frozen cranberries
$\frac{1}{4}$ teaspoon ground cinnamon

1. Wash the cranberries.
2. Put the water and sugar in a saucepan and bring to a boil. Stir constantly to dissolve the sugar.
3. Add the cranberries and bring to a boil again. Reduce the heat and simmer for about ten minutes or until the cranberries open up.
4. Add the cinnamon.
5. Remove the pan from the burner. Cool completely. Then keep in the refrigerator. (The sauce will thicken as it cools.)

TEC44057

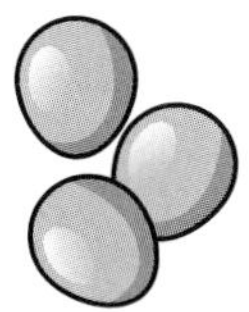

Cranberry Sauce for Four

$\frac{1}{3}$ cup sugar
$\frac{1}{3}$ cup water
$1\frac{3}{4}$ cups fresh or frozen cranberries
$\frac{1}{4}$ teaspoon ground cinnamon

1. Wash the cranberries.
2. Put the water and sugar in a saucepan and bring to a boil. Stir constantly to dissolve the sugar.
3. Add the cranberries and bring to a boil again. Reduce the heat and simmer for about ten minutes or until the cranberries open up.
4. Add the cinnamon.
5. Remove the pan from the burner. Cool completely. Then keep in the refrigerator. (The sauce will thicken as it cools.)

TEC44057

Stuffing for Four

$\frac{1}{4}$ cup butter
$\frac{1}{4}$ cup chopped onion
$\frac{1}{3}$ cup chopped celery
3 cups dry bread cubes
$\frac{1}{4}$ cup chicken broth
$\frac{1}{2}$ teaspoon ground sage
$\frac{3}{4}$ teaspoon celery salt
$\frac{1}{4}$ teaspoon ground black pepper

1. Melt the butter in a skillet. Add the onion and cook until it is tender.
2. Add the celery and cook until it is tender too.
3. Stir in the remaining ingredients.
4. Bake in an oven-proof dish at 350° for about 30 minutes.

TEC44057

Stuffing for Four

$\frac{1}{4}$ cup butter
$\frac{1}{4}$ cup chopped onion
$\frac{1}{3}$ cup chopped celery
3 cups dry bread cubes
$\frac{1}{4}$ cup chicken broth
$\frac{1}{2}$ teaspoon ground sage
$\frac{3}{4}$ teaspoon celery salt
$\frac{1}{4}$ teaspoon ground black pepper

1. Melt the butter in a skillet. Add the onion and cook until it is tender.
2. Add the celery and cook until it is tender too.
3. Stir in the remaining ingredients.
4. Bake in an oven-proof dish at 350° for about 30 minutes.

TEC44057

Pumpkin Pie for Four

$\frac{1}{3}$ cup milk
$\frac{1}{2}$ cup canned pumpkin
$\frac{1}{2}$ small package instant vanilla pudding mix
$\frac{1}{8}$ teaspoon cloves
$\frac{1}{8}$ teaspoon nutmeg
$\frac{1}{4}$ teaspoon ground cinnamon
$\frac{1}{2}$ cup frozen whipped topping
4 mini graham cracker crusts

1. Thaw whipped topping.
2. Mix the milk and pumpkin until they are smooth.
3. Add the pudding mix and spices and mix well.
4. Fold in the whipped topping.
5. Divide the mixture among the shells. Refrigerate until serving.

TEC44057

Pumpkin Pie for Four

$\frac{1}{3}$ cup milk
$\frac{1}{2}$ cup canned pumpkin
$\frac{1}{2}$ small package instant vanilla pudding mix
$\frac{1}{8}$ teaspoon cloves
$\frac{1}{8}$ teaspoon nutmeg
$\frac{1}{4}$ teaspoon ground cinnamon
$\frac{1}{2}$ cup frozen whipped topping
4 mini graham cracker crusts

1. Thaw whipped topping.
2. Mix the milk and pumpkin until they are smooth.
3. Add the pudding mix and spices and mix well.
4. Fold in the whipped topping.
5. Divide the mixture among the shells. Refrigerate until serving.

TEC44057

Flip the Dreidel?

Comparing fractions and decimals

For this partner game, have each pair of students cut apart the cards on a copy of page 178 and then spread the cards facedown. Next, have the partners take turns flipping two cards, trying to find equivalent decimals and fractions. If a player's cards are equivalent, she keeps them. If the cards aren't equivalent, she turns them back over. The students play until all the matches have been made. The player with more matches wins. If desired, have each student record her equivalent pairs. **Colleen Dabney, Williamsburg, VA**

A Tree of Treats

Mixed review

Here's a fun holiday review! Draw a holiday tree on the board. Then tape gaily wrapped treats on the tree as ornaments. When you have an extra five minutes, ask a review question. The first student to correctly answer the question gets to take a treat from the tree. The chance to earn a treat will keep everyone on their toes during the distractions of December.

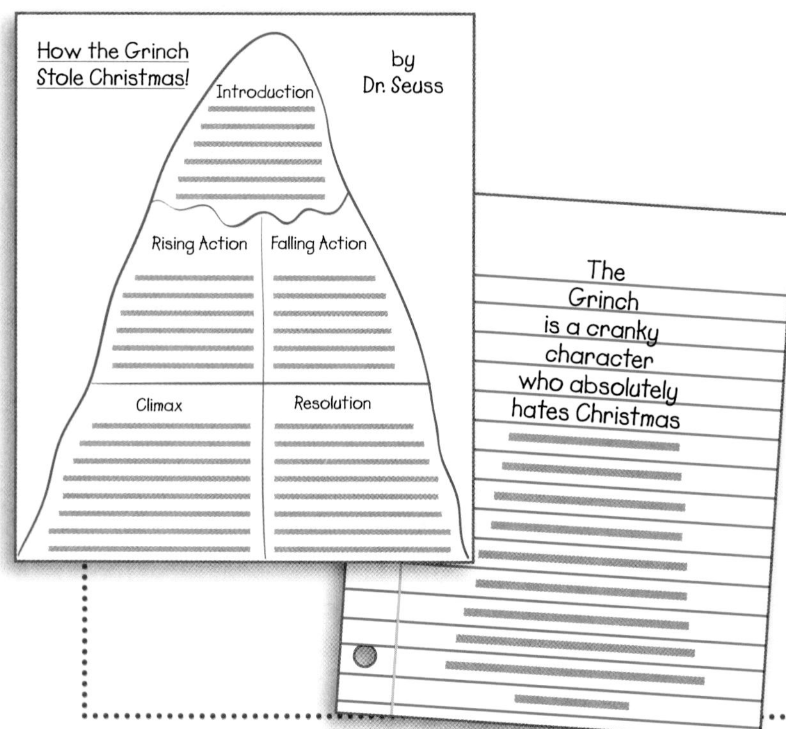

Seasonal Story Analysis

Elements of plot

Use the clearly drawn plot in Dr. Seuss's *How the Grinch Stole Christmas!* to build students' comprehension skills! Begin by having each student draw a snow-capped mountain, divide it into five sections, and label each section as shown. Next, read the book aloud and guide each child to describe the story's parts in the matching sections. Then have each child use his organizer to draft a story summary and write it in the shape of a Christmas tree. (Just have him lightly draw the outline of a tree on his paper, write the summary inside the shape, and then erase the outline when he's finished.) **LeAnne Eisner, Westwood Elementary, Novelty, OH**

Mathematical Greetings

Greatest common factor

Recycled holiday cards are the star features in this practice idea. Have each student cut a piece of construction paper to fit inside a card. Then have the child write four two-digit number pairs on the paper and glue the paper to the card as shown. Next, have the student find each number pair's greatest common factor and list it on the card's back. Then have each child trade her card with a classmate, find the greatest common factors, and then flip the card to check her work. Repeat as time allows. Or stock a center with students' cards as a self-checking challenge for early finishers. **Colleen Dabney, Williamsburg, VA**

A Gift of Words

Word origins

Commemorate Kwanzaa with this small-group activity. Display a list of English words that have African roots, such as those shown. Next, assign three words to each small group of students. Have the group look up each word, discuss and paraphrase its definition, and create a picture that shows what it is. Then have each group present its work before posting it on a colorful board titled "Words With African Roots." **adapted from an idea by Jackie Beaudry, Getzville, NY**

A New Year's Math Mingle

Midyear math review

Welcome students back to school in January with this mathematical icebreaker! Give each child a copy of page 179. Then have students ask classmates to solve and then initial different squares on the grid. To be sure students interact with as many classmates as possible, stipulate that each child may solve and initial only one or two spaces per sheet. When time's up, bring students back together and review the solutions. **Colleen Dabney**

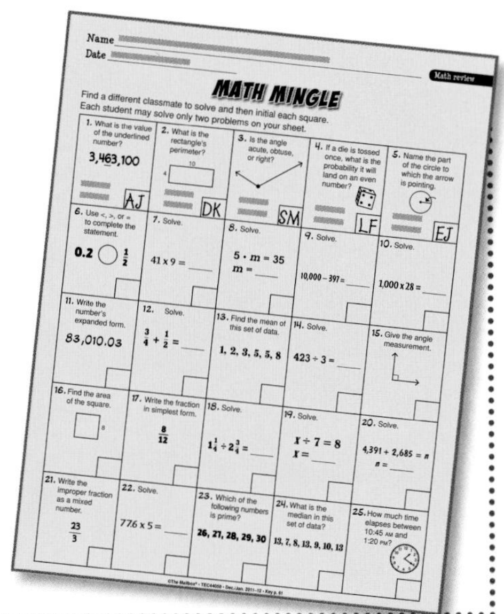

Name

Date

Math review

MATH MINGLE

Find a different classmate to solve and then initial each square. Each student may solve only two problems on your sheet.

1. What is the value of the underlined number? 3,463,100 — AJ
2. What is the rectangle's perimeter? (10, 4) — DK
3. Is the angle acute, obtuse, or right? — SM
4. If a die is tossed once, what is the probability it will land on an even number? — LF
5. Name the part of the circle to which the arrow is pointing. — EJ
6. Use <, >, or = to complete the statement. 0.2 ◯ $\frac{1}{2}$
7. Solve. 41 x 9 = ____
8. Solve. $5 \cdot m = 35$, $m =$ ____
9. Solve. 10,000 – 397 = ____
10. Solve. 1,000 x 28 = ____
11. Write the number's expanded form. 83,010.03
12. Solve. $\frac{3}{4} + \frac{1}{2} =$ ____
13. Find the mean of this set of data. 1, 2, 3, 5, 5, 8
14. Solve. 423 ÷ 3 = ____
15. Give the angle measurement.
16. Find the area of the square. (8)
17. Write the fraction in simplest form. $\frac{8}{12}$
18. Solve. $1\frac{1}{4} \div 2\frac{3}{4} =$ ____
19. Solve. $x \div 7 = 8$, $x =$ ____
20. Solve. 4,391 + 2,685 = n, $n =$ ____
21. Write the improper fraction as a mixed number. $\frac{23}{3}$
22. Solve. 77.6 x 5 = ____
23. Which of the following numbers is prime? 26, 27, 28, 29, 30
24. What is the median in this set of data? 13, 7, 8, 13, 9, 10, 13
25. How much time elapses between 10:45 AM and 1:20 PM?

Game Cards

Use with “Flip the Dreidel?” on page 176.

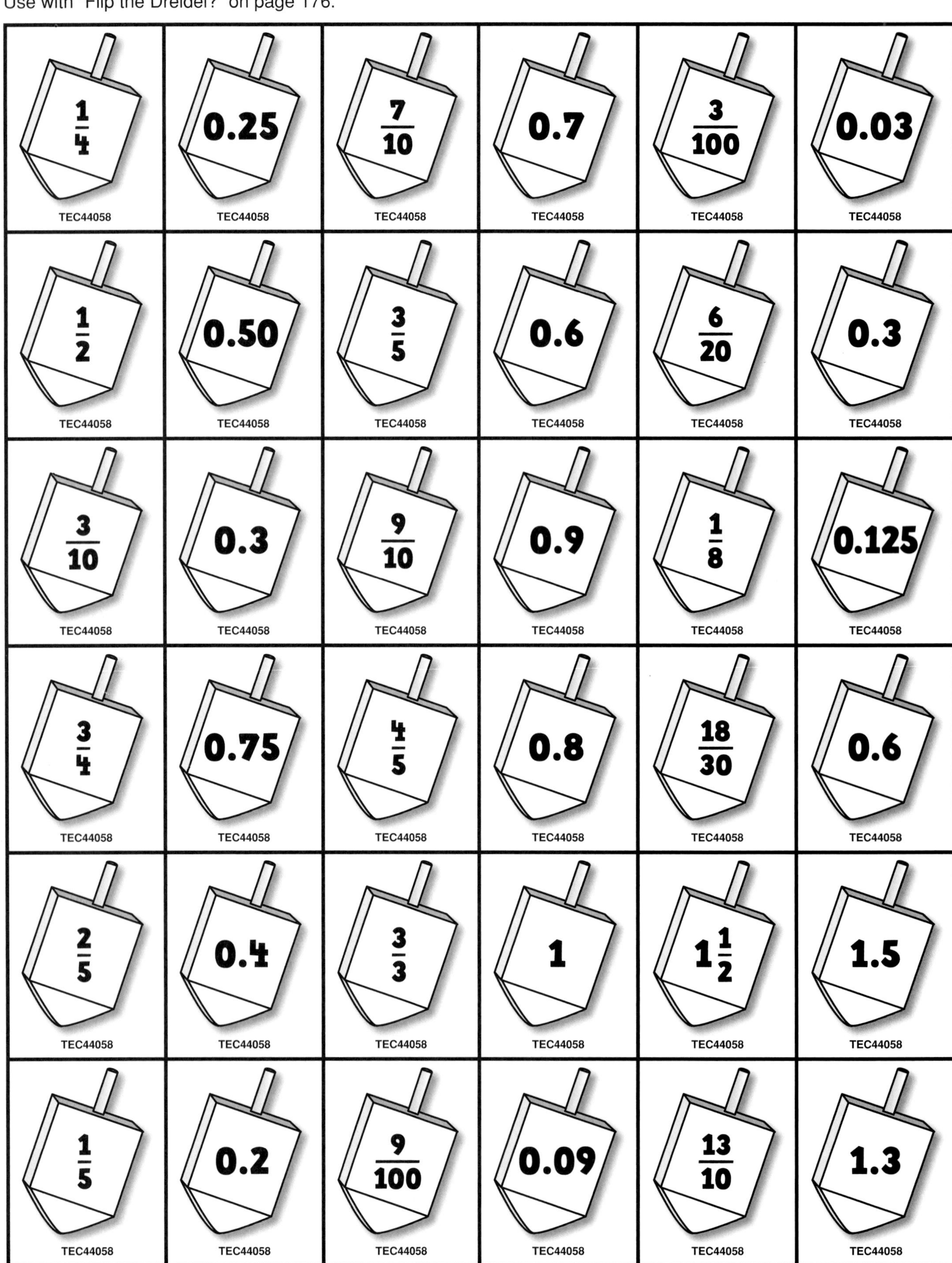

Name ______________________________

Date ____________________

MATH MINGLE

Find a different classmate to solve and then initial each square.
Each student may solve only two problems on your sheet.

1. What is the value of the underlined number?

$3{,}4\underline{6}3{,}100$

2. What is the rectangle's perimeter?

10

4

3. Is the angle acute, obtuse, or right?

4. If a die is tossed once, what is the probability it will land on an even number?

5. Name the part of the circle to which the arrow is pointing.

6. Use $<$, $>$, or $=$ to complete the statement.

$0.2 \bigcirc \frac{1}{2}$

7. Solve.

41 x 9 = _____

8. Solve.

$5 \cdot m = 35$

$m =$ _____

9. Solve.

10,000 – 397 = _____

10. Solve.

1,000 x 28 = _____

11. Write the number's expanded form.

83,010.03

12. Solve.

$\frac{3}{4} + \frac{1}{2} =$ _____

13. Find the mean of this set of data.

1, 2, 3, 5, 5, 8

14. Solve.

423 ÷ 3 = _____

15. Give the angle measurement.

16. Find the area of the square.

8

17. Write the fraction in simplest form.

$\frac{8}{12}$

18. Solve.

$1\frac{1}{4} + 2\frac{3}{4} =$ _____

19. Solve.

$x \div 7 = 8$

$x =$ _____

20. Solve.

$4{,}391 + 2{,}685 = n$

$n =$ _____

21. Write the improper fraction as a mixed number.

$\frac{23}{3}$

22. Solve.

77.6 x 5 = _____

23. Which of the following numbers is prime?

26, 27, 28, 29, 30

24. What is the median in this set of data?

13, 7, 8, 13, 9, 10, 13

25. How much time elapses between 10:45 AM and 1:20 PM?

Note to the teacher: Use with "A New Year's Math Mingle" on page 177.

Great Groundhogs!
Point of view

Want to give Groundhog Day a skill-building nod? Display the groundhog facts shown. Then have each student use the facts and her experience to write a blog entry about the holiday from a groundhog's point of view. Set aside time for each student to read her work aloud, or set up a word processing document and have each child type her blog on a separate page. Then keep the document open on a class computer for fun independent reading.

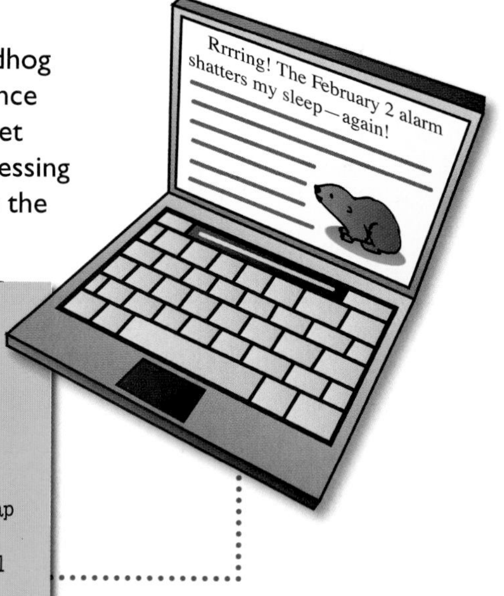

- A groundhog's body is covered with coarse, brown fur.
- Groundhogs are vegetarians. They eat clover, grass, alfalfa, and vegetables.
- They live in underground burrows or dens that they dig.
- When a groundhog spots danger, it makes a shrill whistle to warn other groundhogs and then it ducks back into its burrow.
- The legend behind Groundhog Day came from an old farmers' tradition in Europe. The old belief was that if there was a sunny day on February 2, there would be six more weeks of winter weather. It is said that when the groundhog awakens from its winter nap (hibernation), it will look for its shadow. If it sees its shadow, it returns to its burrow and sleeps for six more weeks. If the critter does not see its shadow, spring weather will come early.

Leap Year Logic
Number patterns

To introduce this mathematical exploration, explain that a person born on February 29 can technically celebrate his birthday only once every four years. Next, point out that 2012 is a leap year and challenge students to figure out how old—in leap years and in actual years—a person born February 29, 2012, will be on March 1, 2024. *(Three leap years old and 12 years old.)* Guide students to identify the pattern and plan a strategy for finding later ages. Then post the dates shown and have each student figure out the mystery person's ages in leap years and actual years.

Date	Leap Year Age	Actual Age
February 28, 2013	0	1
February 29, 2016	1	4
February 29, 2020	2	8
March 2, 2022	2	10
February 29, 2028	4	16
March 2, 2030	4	18
March 2, 2033	5	21
February 29, 2036	6	24

Stellar Research
Black History Month

For this timely research project, have each child choose an important Black American such as one of those shown. Next, have the student research the person as guided on a copy of page 182 and publish his research on the page's star banner. Then display students' work on a board titled "All-Star Research."

Ms. Rice can speak Russian.

Condoleezza Rice was born November 14, 1954, in Birmingham, Alabama.

Ms. Rice was the first African American woman to serve as the United States secretary of state.

- Hank Aaron
- Louis Armstrong
- Benjamin Banneker
- Mary McLeod Bethune
- Guion Bluford
- Carol Moseley Braun
- George Washington Carver
- Shirley Chisholm
- Frederick Douglass
- W. E. B. Du Bois
- Duke Ellington
- Althea Gibson
- Matthew Henson
- Langston Hughes
- Jesse Jackson
- Mae C. Jemison
- Martin Luther King Jr.
- Thurgood Marshall
- Garrett Morgan
- Barack Obama
- Michelle Obama
- Jesse Owens
- Tyler Perry
- Colin L. Powell
- Condoleezza Rice
- Jackie Robinson
- Wilma Rudolph
- Sojourner Truth
- Harriet Tubman
- J. C. Watts Jr.
- L. Douglas Wilder

Presidential Hometowns

Map skills, research

Here's a map challenge just right for Presidents' Day. To begin, post a large map of the United States. Also provide access to red, white, and blue construction paper; yarn; and pushpins. Next, assign each small group of students five to six presidents and have the group find each president's birthdate and birthplace. When the students find a president's facts, they record them along with the president's name on construction paper cut into a three-inch-long pennant shape. Then the students pin a length of yarn to the US map in the president's home state and tack the yarn's other end to the pennant outside the map. When students finish, compare the states where many presidents were born with states where few were born.

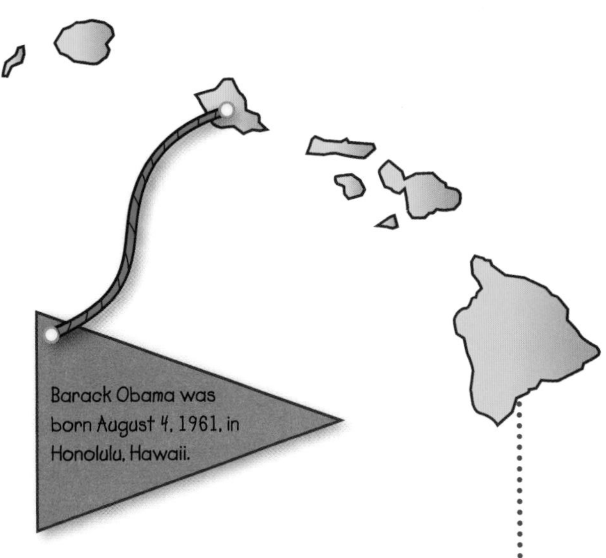

By a Woman...

Skimming, summarizing

Build reading skills and commemorate National Women's History Month with this idea. To begin, collect a supply of recent newspapers. Next, have each pair of students skim a section to find an article written by or about a woman or for women. When the partners find an article, they cut it out. Then they read the article and summarize it on an index card. After that, they post their article and summary on a board titled "Making History—Women in the News."

Top o' the Morning

St. Patrick's Day

During the week before St. Patrick's Day, post a different Irish proverb each day. Then have each student copy the proverb and illustrate or explain both its literal and its figurative meanings. If desired, have students jot their responses on green writing paper or write their responses on regular paper, using green colored pencils.

tip Have each student add "Mc" or "O'" to the beginning of her last name when she signs her work this week.

Name ______________________________

Date ______________

ALL-STAR RESEARCH

Directions:

1. Choose a famous Black American.
2. Find information that will help you answer the questions shown about this person.
3. On the star, write the person's name as well as where and when he or she was born.
4. In the space to the left, write interesting details about the person. In the space to the right, describe his or her most important accomplishment.
5. Cut out the star banner.

Where and when was he or she born?

What is the person's most significant accomplishment? (Describe it and tell why it is important.)

What are two interesting details about the person?

Researched by ______________________

Note to the teacher: Use with "Stellar Research" on page 180.

SKILLS FOR THE SEASON

Rockin' Spring Break!

Earth science, rocks

For this activity, give each student a snack-size plastic resealable bag before spring break. Then direct each child to find a rock during vacation that fits inside the bag and bring it to school on the first day back. On that day, guide each student to measure her rock, weigh it, give it the scratch test to determine its hardness, and record each characteristic on a copy of the top half of page 185. Next, have the child describe her rock's appearance and then write a story that describes what she imagines was her rock's journey through the rock cycle.
Heather Finn, Grant Line Elementary, New Albany, IN

Follow up with this **great center!** Have each student number her rock. Then put students' rocks, their descriptions, and measuring materials at a center. A child chooses a description other than her own, reads it, and then tries to identify the matching rock. She writes the rock's number and her name on a small sticky note and sticks the note on the description's flip side. As time allows, each student checks the notes on her paper and verifies or corrects other students' guesses.

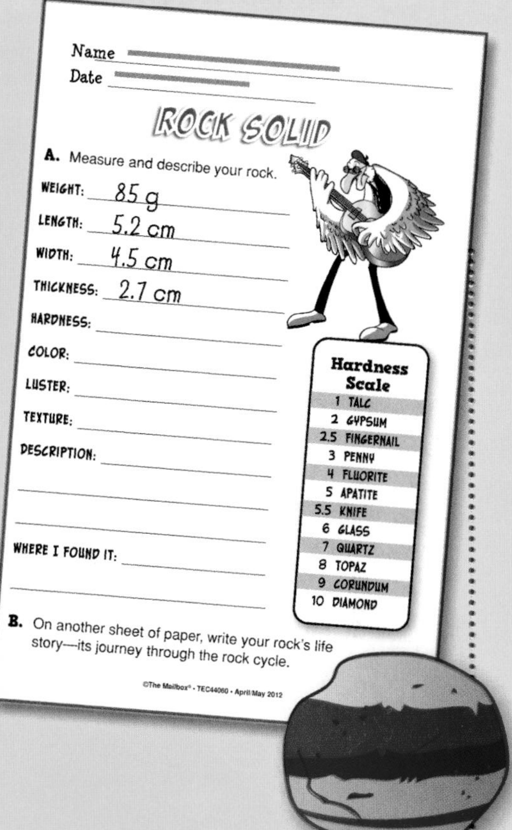

Name
Date

ROCK SOLID

A. Measure and describe your rock.

WEIGHT: 85 g
LENGTH: 5.2 cm
WIDTH: 4.5 cm
THICKNESS: 2.7 cm
HARDNESS:
COLOR:
LUSTER:
TEXTURE:
DESCRIPTION:

WHERE I FOUND IT:

Hardness Scale	
1	TALC
2	GYPSUM
2.5	FINGERNAIL
3	PENNY
4	FLUORITE
5	APATITE
5.5	KNIFE
6	GLASS
7	QUARTZ
8	TOPAZ
9	CORUNDUM
10	DIAMOND

B. On another sheet of paper, write your rock's life story—its journey through the rock cycle.

©The Mailbox® • TEC44060 • April/May 2012

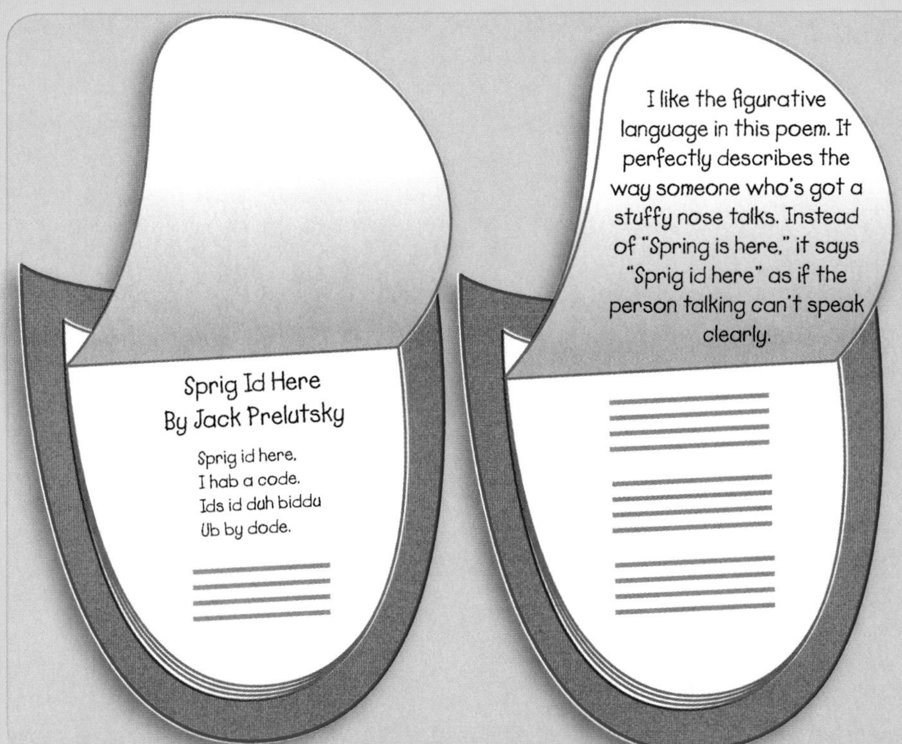

Grin 'n' Share It!

Poetry

Celebrate National Poetry Month and National Humor Month (both April) with student-made anthologies! Place books of humorous poetry at a center along with a copy of the bottom half of page 185, construction paper, unlined paper, scissors, and a stapler. Then have each student follow the directions to create a booklet and fill it with rib-tickling poems. When all students have rotated through the center, set aside time for each student to share his favorites with a small group.

"Eggs-traordinary" Practice

Decimal place value

For this handy center, label each section of a sanitized egg carton with a different place value. Then put 25 pom-poms, beans, or other small markers in the carton and place it at the center. A pair of students takes turns shaking the carton gently to redistribute the pom-poms and then opening the carton. Each student writes the number that matches the number of pom-poms in each section. Then each student writes the number in word form. The partners compare their work to check it, discuss and correct any errors, and repeat as time allows. To increase the challenge, label the sections randomly. **Heidi Gross, Avoca Central School, Avoca, NY**

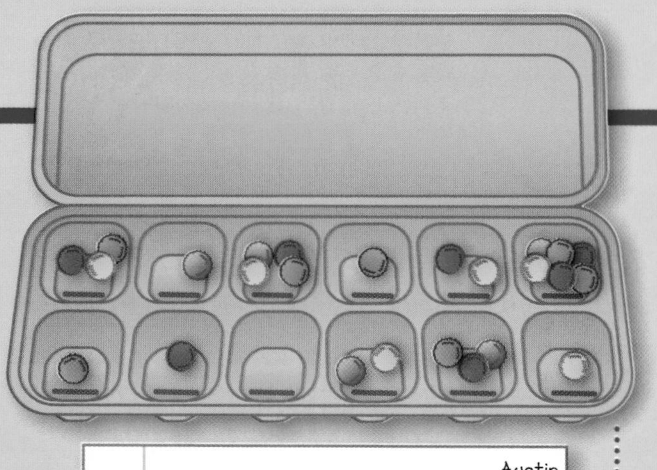

Austin

314,126.110.231

three hundred fourteen million, one hundred twenty-six thousand, one hundred ten and two hundred thirty-one thousandths

How Does Your Garden Grow?

Life science, flowering plants

To begin this spring activity, post a list of flowers that have interesting or downright silly names. Have each student choose a flower and imagine what the flower might look like if it looked just like its name. Then have the child fold a sheet of paper as shown and draw the flower she imagines on the front. Next, have each student research her flower. After that, the child opens her paper. On the left flap, she names the plant on which her flower grows and describes its habitat. On the right flap, the student describes the flower's role in the plant's life cycle. In the center, the student draws a diagram of the actual flower and tells how it got its unusual name. Then she posts her work on a board titled "Flowers by Any Other Name."

Earth-Friendly Effects

Research, persuasive writing

Here's a no-fuss idea for commemorating Earth Day. Display the sentence starters from page 186 and lead students to complete each statement. Next, guide each pair of students to choose one statement and research it to find facts that support or clarify it. Then have the partners compose a message that will convince others to make choices that will lead to earth-friendly effects. Finally, open an email document (leaving the address blank) and have each duo type and sign its message within the document. Once all the partners have added their messages, send the email to students' parents as a thoughtful Earth Day message.

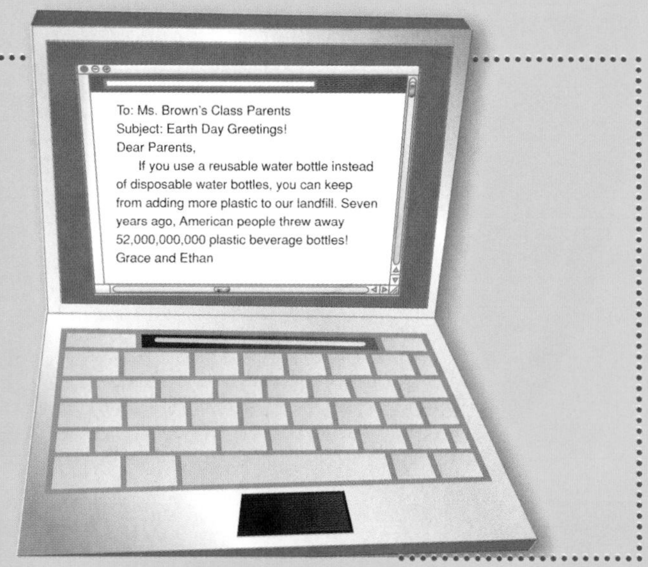

ROCK SOLID

Name ______________________

Date ______________________

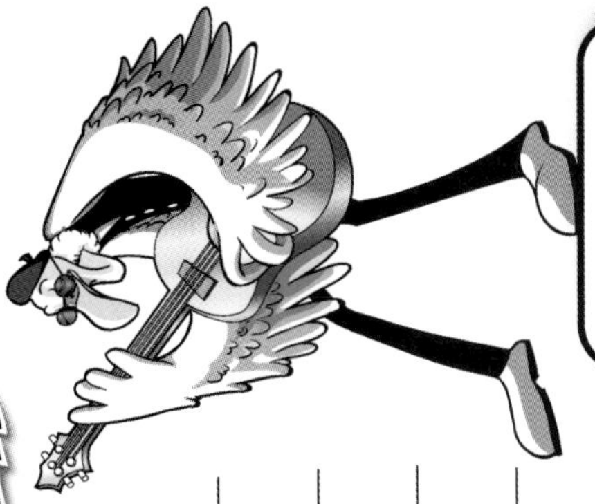

A. Measure and describe your rock.

WEIGHT: ______________________

LENGTH: ______________________

WIDTH: ______________________

THICKNESS: ______________________

HARDNESS: ______________________

COLOR: ______________________

LUSTER: ______________________

TEXTURE: ______________________

DESCRIPTION: ______________________

____

____

WHERE I FOUND IT: ______________________

____

Hardness Scale

1	TALC
2	GYPSUM
2.5	FINGERNAIL
3	PENNY
4	FLUORITE
5	APATITE
5.5	KNIFE
6	GLASS
7	QUARTZ
8	TOPAZ
9	CORUNDUM
10	DIAMOND

B. On another sheet of paper, write your rock's life story—its journey through the rock cycle.

A Rib-Tickling Anthology

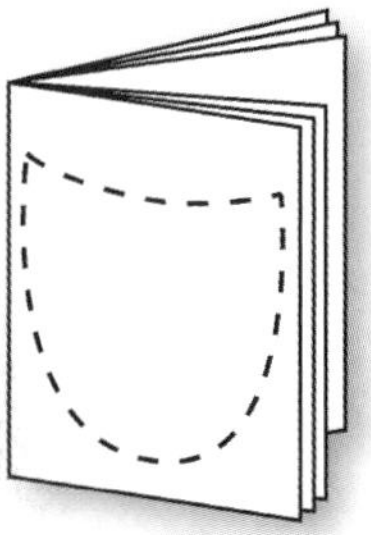

Directions

1. Stack three sheets of unlined paper and fold them in half horizontally. Draw a large mouth shape on the folded papers and cut it out to create six mouth-shaped pages.
2. Place one mouth pattern on a half sheet of construction paper. Draw around it to create a slightly larger mouth shape. Then cut it out.
3. Staple the six unlined pages to the construction paper mouth as shown. Then draw teeth on the top page and title your booklet.
4. On each blank page, copy a poem you like and record the poet's name. On the page's flip side, name one of the poet's techniques. Then give an example of the technique from the poem and describe your reaction to it.

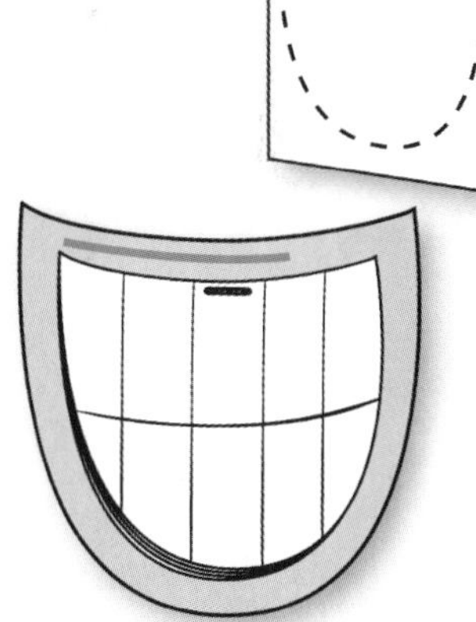

Poetic Techniques

alliteration: repetition of beginning consonant sounds

assonance: repetition of vowel sounds in words

consonance: repetition of consonant sounds anywhere in words

end rhyme: rhyming of words at the ends of lines

internal rhyme: rhyming of words within lines

onomatopoeia: words whose sounds bring to mind their meanings

repetition: repetition of a word or phrase to add rhythm or to emphasize an idea

rhythm: flow of the poem from one idea to the next

Note to the teacher: Use "Rock Solid" with "Rockin' Spring Break!" on page 183. Use "A Rib-Tickling Anthology" with "Grin 'n' Share It!" on page 183.

Name ______________________________

Date ______________

Cause-and-effect sentence starters

R U Earth Friendly?

1. If you take a short shower instead of a bath, then ______________________________
2. If you use rechargeable batteries instead of disposable ones, then ______________________________
3. If you turn off the lights in an empty room, then ______________________________
4. If you turn off the water while you're brushing your teeth, then ______________________________
5. If you and your family start a compost pile, then ______________________________
6. If you and your family use cloth bags for groceries instead of paper or plastic bags, then ______________________________
7. If you recycle metal and aluminum cans, then ______________________________
8. If you recycle newspapers, magazines, and junk mail, then ______________________________
9. If you and your family reuse glass bottles, then ______________________________
10. If you donate the clothes and toys you don't use anymore instead of throwing them away, then ______________________________
11. If you choose products that don't have excessive packaging, then ______________________________
12. If you use a reusable water bottle instead of disposable plastic water bottles, then ______________________________

Note to the teacher: Use with "Earth-Friendly Effects" on page 184.

SKILLS FOR THE SEASON

A Survival Guide

End of the year

Here's a writing activity your students are sure to love. Begin by guiding students to think about tips they could share with students who will be in your class next year. Then have each child work with a partner to brainstorm 25 or more tips that will give next year's students the inside scoop on surviving the year. The duo might write humorous as well as serious tips. When the partners finish, have each student publish their tips in a three-fold pamphlet. Collect students' work and save it until school starts in the fall. Then set the pamphlets on your new students' desks. The survival guides make great icebreakers for nervous students during the first week of school! **Sarah Watson, Marshall Greene Middle School, Birch Run, MI**

To publish their survival guides, have students type their lists in a word-processing program, using the landscape orientation. Have the duo format the page in three columns, and then print out a pamphlet that's ready to decorate and fold!

A Dose of Data

End of the year

Looking for a quick math lesson perfect for the end of the year? Post the question shown. Then draw a large three-circle Venn diagram labeled as shown. Next, have each child draw an x in the section that shows where he expects to spend most of his summer. Finally, lead students to analyze their results.

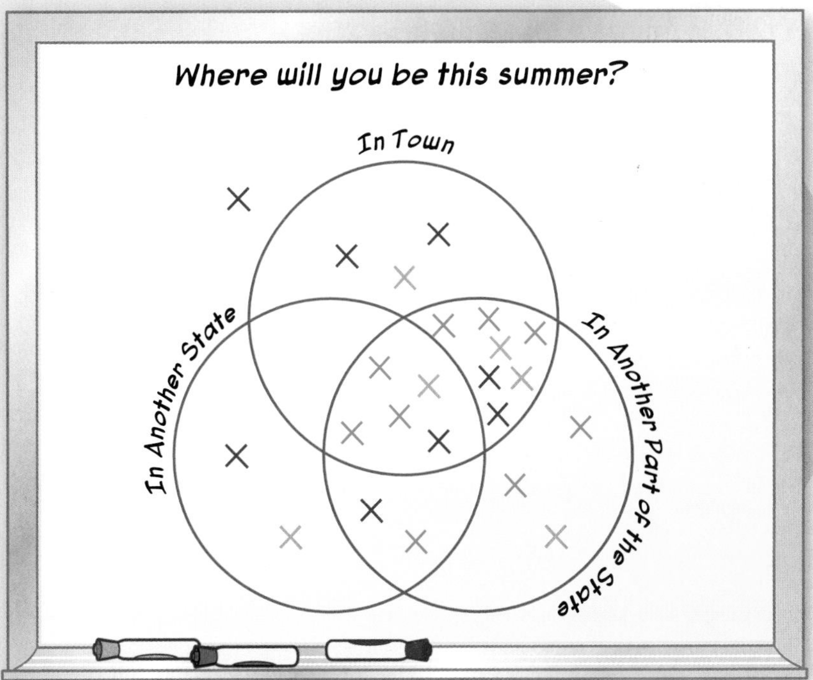

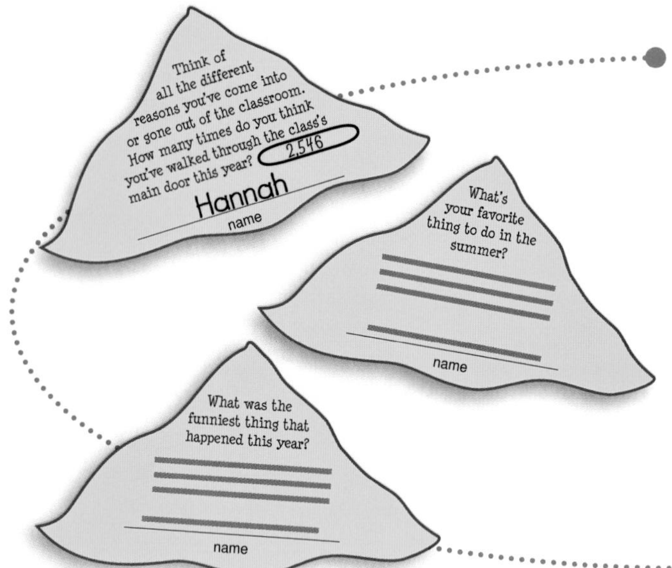

"Nacho" Ordinary Farewell!

End of the year

Celebrate a wonderful school year with a simple and tasty idea! Have students' parents send in simple nacho fixings, such as tortilla chips, refried beans, shredded cheese, shredded lettuce, diced tomatoes, chopped olives, and salsa. Then give each child a copy of page 189. Have the student answer the question on each chip card, sign her name, and cut out the card. Next, collect students' cards, put them in a big bowl, and have students assemble their nachos. As students snack on their nachos, draw chip cards from the bowl and read aloud the questions, answers, and respondents' names for a simple but fun celebration!

Student Tour Guides

End of the year

Before your students leave for the year, have them create an orientation guide for next year's students and parents! Assign each small group a specific area of your room, such as where students put their coats and bags, centers, math manipulatives, or the class library. Then have each group create a poster, slide show, or video that introduces the space or explains how to use it. Make sure each group captions its work and includes illustrations or photos. Display students' work outside your classroom or on your class website shortly before school starts to welcome and inform incoming students. **Abigail Green, McIntire Munson Elementary, Zanesville, OH**

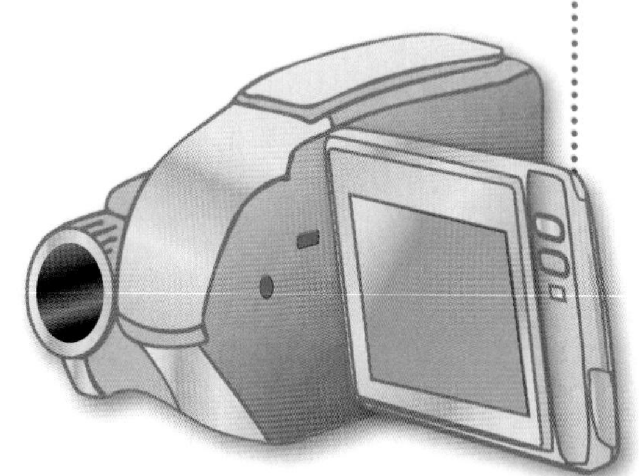

A Different Kind of Bug Collection

Summer

Here's a standard- and metric-measuring challenge that's sure to entice even the most squeamish of your students. Give each child a copy of page 190 and have him estimate each insect's length or wingspan, recording his estimate on another sheet of paper. Next, have the student measure the insects. Then post the clues shown and have students use them to name each insect. Follow up by encouraging students to notice insects this summer and practice estimating each insect's size. **To extend the activity,** have each student choose and research an insect from the list.

- The **gallnipper mosquito**, about one-half-inch long, is the biggest mosquito.
- The **bull ant** can grow up to $1\frac{5}{8}$ inches long.
- The **black carpenter ant** is large for an ant: 0.6 to 1.6 centimeters long.
- The **widow skimmer** dragonfly is usually between $2\frac{1}{2}$ and four inches long.
- The **Goliath beetle** grows to about 13 centimeters.
- The **broad-winged katydid**, a relative of the grasshopper, will be from 1.3 to 7.6 centimeters long.
- The **June bug** or **June beetle** can range from 8 to 25 millimeters.
- A **carpenter bee** is usually from 0.3 to 2.5 centimeters long.
- The **common bumblebee's** wingspan is generally one-half to $1\frac{1}{8}$ inches.
- The **crescent butterfly** has a wingspan of from $1\frac{1}{4}$ to $1\frac{3}{4}$ inches.
- A **walkingstick** can be from 15 to 20 centimeters long.

Chip Cards

Use with "'Nacho' Ordinary Farewell!" on page 188.

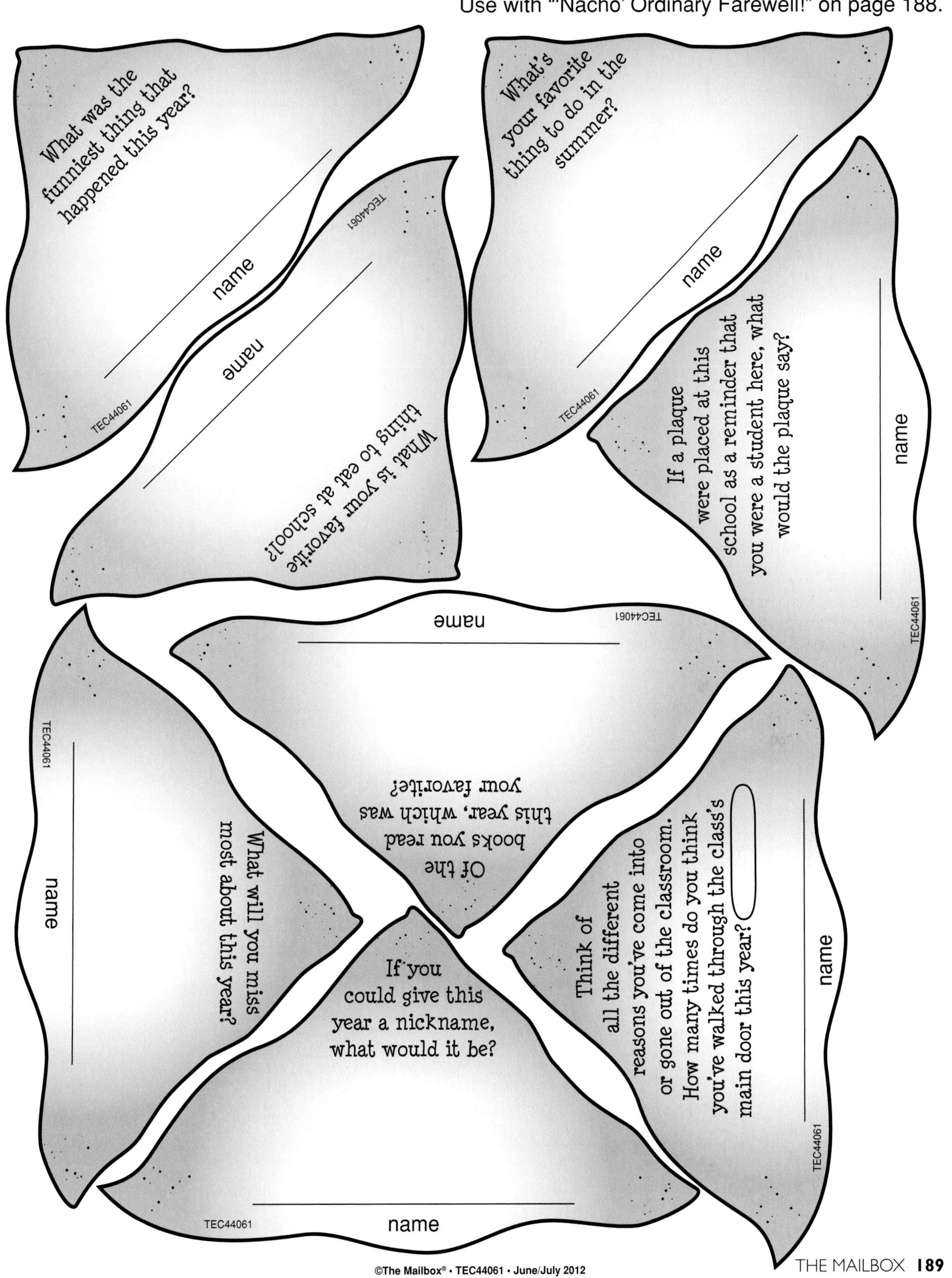

Name ____________________

Date ____________________

GUESS AND THEN MEASURE

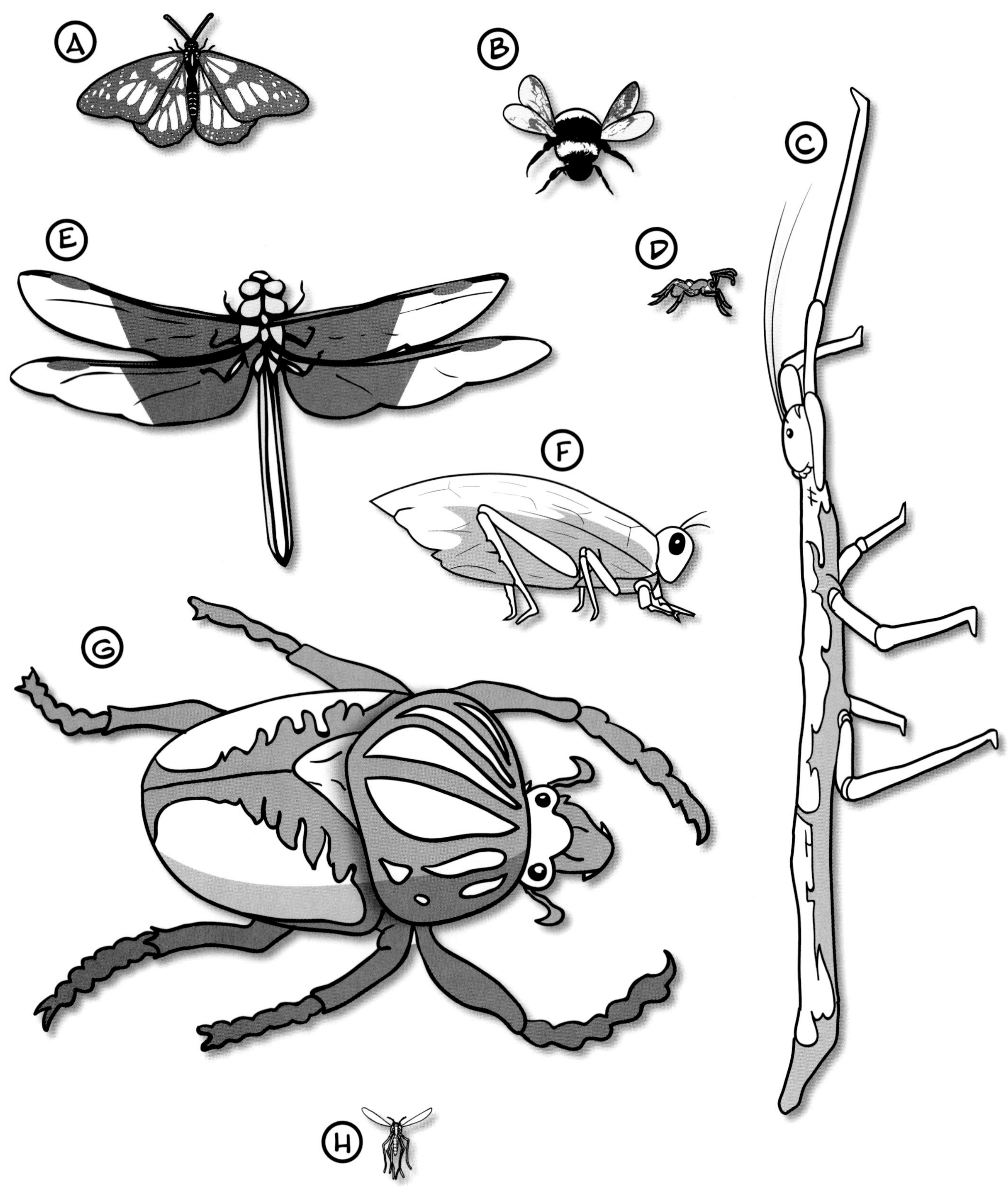

 Note to the teacher: Use with "A Different Kind of Bug Collection" on page 188.

Name ______________________________

Date ____________________

Something's Fishy!

A. Write the word or words that make each boldface contraction.

It's 1 the first day of class at Seaside School. Lily Pond, the principal, is on the intercom. "**We're** 2 going to have a great year! **We've** 3 got to work hard. Good students **don't** 4 worry about making mistakes. **Here's** 5 the reason: no **one's** 6 perfect. **You'll** 7 learn a lot if you just keep doing your best. If **there's** 8 something you **can't** 9 figure out, just ask your teacher. **You're** 10 going to learn every day! **I've** 11 high expectations this year. **Who's** 12 ready to learn?"

1. ____________________
2. ____________________
3. ____________________
4. ____________________
5. ____________________
6. ____________________
7. ____________________
8. ____________________
9. ____________________
10. ____________________
11. ____________________
12. ____________________

B. Write a contraction for each pair of boldface words.

13. ____________________
14. ____________________
15. ____________________
16. ____________________
17. ____________________
18. ____________________
19. ____________________
20. ____________________
21. ____________________
22. ____________________

Suddenly a huge, wiggly worm appears above Ms. Pond. At first, **she is** 13 startled. Then she says, "**You are** 14 not going to believe this. **I have** 15 just spotted a big, fat, juicy worm. Remember, you **should not** 16 assume that every worm is yummy. I need to focus! I **must not** 17 think about the worm. What was I saying? **Who has** 18 asked a question? **What is** 19 the chance that worm **is not** 20 attached to a treacherous hook? Maybe **I would** 21 be sorry if I took a bite, or maybe I **would not** 22 be sorry.

Bonus: Write the words that make up these contractions.
mustn't **there've** **shouldn't've** **won't** **wouldn't've**

Name ____________________

Date ____________________

Stacks of Back-to-School Stats

Study the graphs. Then answer the questions.

A. How many total students responded to the survey? ________

B. How many girls responded to the survey? ________

C. How many boys responded to the survey? ________

D. Do more girls have one sibling or no siblings? ________

E. How many more girls than boys have two siblings? ________

F. How many students have one pet? ________

G. How many boys have one or two pets? ________

H. How many students have three or more pets? ________

I. Which playground activity do the highest number of boys prefer? ____________

J. How many girls prefer either four square or running? ________

K. Which is greater, the number of boys who prefer four square or the number of girls who prefer running? ____________ How much greater? ________

L. If 18 of the students with one pet have dogs, how many of them do not have dogs? ________

M. If 7 of the boys with one pet own dogs, how many of them do not own dogs? ________

N. Are there more girls who prefer basketball or boys with two or more pets? ____________

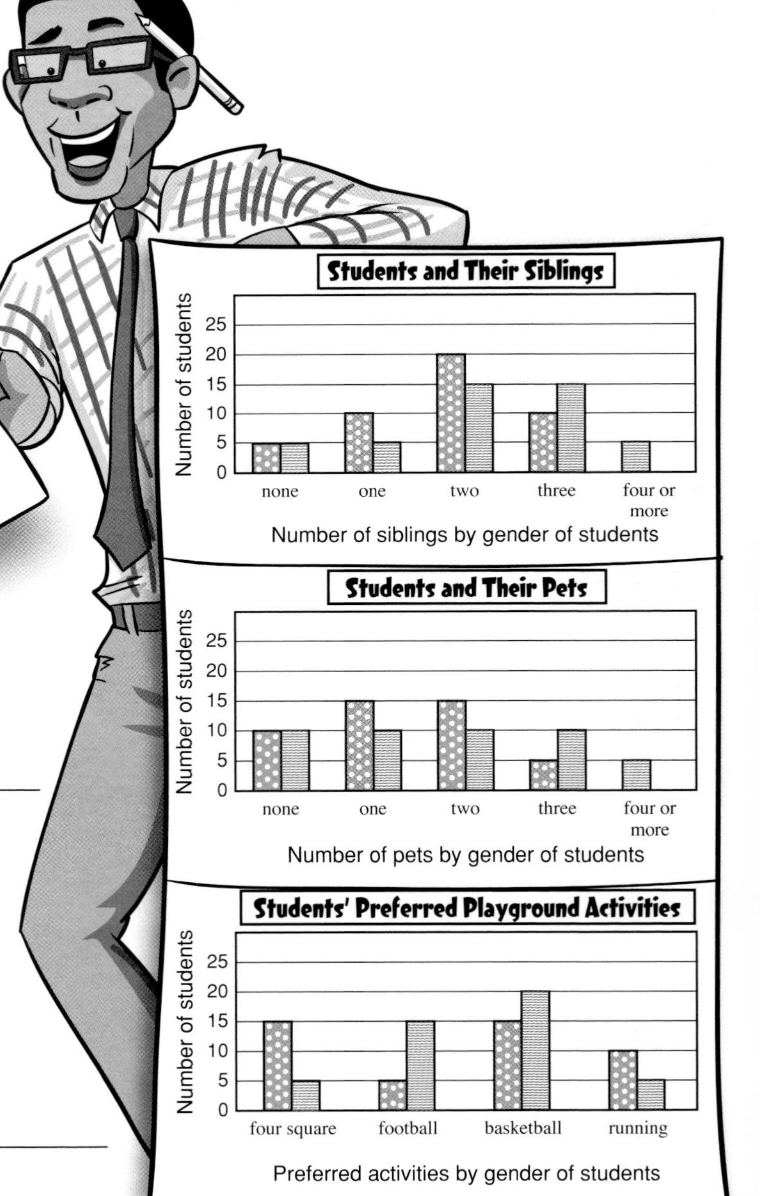

Bonus: Do you think the data would be easier to understand if it were in pie charts instead of bar graphs? Why or why not?

Name ____________________

Date ____________________

Mad for Mariachi

Complete each table. Write the rule. Then color each sombrero according to the code.

1

Input	Output
6	30
9	
18	90
4	

Rule: Multiply by 5.

2

Input	Output
60	10
36	6
72	
12	

Rule:

3

Input	Output
44	57
92	105
12	
38	

Rule:

4

Input	Output
64	55
81	
43	
59	50

Rule:

5

Input	Output
45	15
12	
63	21
27	

Rule:

6

Input	Output
6	21
17	
25	40
32	

Rule:

7

Input	Output
9	81
3	27
12	
8	

Rule:

8

Input	Output
84	21
56	
16	4
36	

Rule:

9

Input	Output
71	63
28	
39	
14	6

Rule:

10

Input	Output
100	75
62	37
59	
47	

Rule:

11

Input	Output
18	34
36	
25	41
51	

Rule:

12

Input	Output
5	35
3	
12	84
9	

Rule:

Color Code

addition = red
subtraction = yellow
multiplication = black
division = green

Bonus: Create an input-output table. Use the rule "Multiply by 12."

Name ______________________________

Date ______________________

With Citizens in Mind

Circle the prefix in each boldface word.
Then write each word's letter next to its definition.

In 1783, the American states became (A) **independent**, free from England's control. It would have been (B) **impossible** to do this without a national government. But after the American Revolution, their original government was (C) **ineffective**. The states could not work together to solve problems. There was (D) **disorder** among them. Each state was (E) **disinterested** in working with other states or as a whole country. The government could not stop the states' (F) **illicit** actions. The first government was (G) **imperfect**, and it needed to change.

In 1787, a meeting was called to fix the problems. Some people (H) **disagreed** with the need for the meeting. They thought everything was fine. During the meeting, there was often (I) **discord**. The states' delegates rarely agreed.

In time, the Constitution was written. It set up a strong national government. Some states still (J) **disliked** this written plan. They wanted it to include citizens' rights too. So amendments were added. The first ten of these are called the Bill of Rights. The amendments name the (K) **inalienable** rights of US citizens. Some amendments prevent (L) **inequality** in citizens' rights. The Constitution also outlines (M) **illegal** actions. Citizens are not permitted to (N) **disobey** the laws spelled out in the Constitution.

Many people who (O) **immigrate** to the United States agree to live under the Constitution and become citizens. Americans celebrate their citizenship and the anniversary of the Constitution's signing on September 17 each year.

_____ 1. to not agree

_____ 2. to not need help

_____ 3. not interested

_____ 4. not equal

_____ 5. to not obey

_____ 6. not perfect

_____ 7. not possible

_____ 8. not to be taken away

_____ 9. against the law

_____ 10. not legal

_____ 11. to not like

_____ 12. not effective

_____ 13. not having the same opinion

_____ 14. not having order

_____ 15. moving to live in another country

Bonus: List ten more words that have the prefixes *dis-, il-, im-, or in-*.

Name ______________________________

Date ______________________________

GOING BATTY

If a sentence is a fact, it can be proved. Shade the circle next to each sentence that is a fact. If the sentence is an opinion, circle the clue word or words. Hint: Look for clue words, such as *always, never, none, best, worst, probably,* and other emotional descriptors.

1. To survive, a vampire bat drinks animal blood.
2. Vampire bats are the worst kinds of bats.
3. A vampire bat uses its razor-sharp front teeth to cut the skin of its prey.
4. Vampire bats probably have the world's sharpest teeth.

5. Even a vampire bat's scientific name, *Desmodus rotundus,* is scary.
6. Vampire bats don't really suck an animal's blood; they lap it up from a cut.
7. Since a vampire bat has a short, thin throat, it can only swallow liquids.
8. The most interesting fact about vampire bats is that they don't live in North America.

9. It's silly to be afraid of vampire bats because they are just three inches long.
10. A vampire bat can drink about half of its body weight at once.
11. You would never want to run into a vampire bat.

12. A vampire bat's saliva keeps an animal's blood from clotting.
13. The most awful thing about vampire bats is that they drink human blood.
14. The real danger of a vampire bat's bite is that it can spread rabies or cause infection.
15. A vampire bat can walk on all fours; it can even run and hop.
16. Tigers may be scary, but vampire bats are creepy.

Bonus: Should people be afraid of vampire bats? Write a paragraph that tells what you think. Support your opinion with facts from above.

Name ____________________

Date ____________________

"HOWL-OWEEN" CARNIVAL

Figure out what each person bought at the carnival snack bar. Use the chart to work out each person's purchases.

Spooky Snacks

Hot Dog Mummy	$5.50
String Cheese Finger	$2.50
Monster's Toe Cookie	$3.00
Cup of Witch's Brew Punch	$1.50

1. BOB APPLE BOUGHT SIX ITEMS FOR $10.00.
2. CANDY BARR BOUGHT THREE THINGS FOR $10.00.
3. CRYSTAL BALL SPENT $25.00 ON EIGHT ITEMS.
4. DOUG GRAVES BOUGHT SIX THINGS FOR $25.00.
5. DR. CROAK BOUGHT SEVEN ITEMS FOR $30.00.
6. DR. PAYNE SPENT $30.00 ON ELEVEN ITEMS.
7. FRANK N. STEIN BOUGHT 18 ITEMS FOR $40.00.
8. KANDI APPLE SPENT $50.00 ON 15 ITEMS.

Bonus: The high school football coach spent $75.00 on snacks for his team at the carnival. The coach bought 28 items in all. What did he buy?

Name	Number of Hot Dog Mummies	Subtotal	Number of String Cheese Fingers	Subtotal	Number of Monster's Toe Cookies	Subtotal	Cups of Witch's Brew Punch	Subtotal	Total
Bob Apple									
Candy Barr									
Crystal Ball									
Doug Graves									
Dr. Croak									
Dr. Payne									
Frank N. Stein									
Kandi Apple									

Name ______________________________

Date ____________________

In Tribute

I. Find 16 prepositional phrases in the sentences below. Underline each one and circle the preposition. Then draw an arrow from the preposition to its object.

1. On Veterans Day, we honor our country's soldiers.
2. We honor men and women who have served in the United States Armed Forces.
3. Some people send cards to veterans, thanking and honoring them.
4. Some celebrate Veterans Day with parades.
5. During those parades, veterans may ride inside fancy cars.
6. The veterans sometimes throw candy along the route.
7. Speeches are often given about soldiers' sacrifices.
8. Some people put flowers or flags by soldiers' graves.
9. A special ceremony is held each year at Arlington National Cemetery.
10. The cemetery is across the Potomac River from Washington, DC.
11. The president places a wreath upon the Tomb of the Unknowns.
12. There are similar celebrations for veterans throughout the country.

Look for prepositions like these.
about
across
along
at
by
during
for
from
in
inside
of
on
throughout
to
upon
with

II. Complete each sentence with a prepositional phrase.

13. The soldier stands

______________________________.

14. A plane flies

______________________________.

15. The wreath is placed

______________________________.

16. The Tomb of the Unknowns is

______________________________.

Bonus: Rewrite sentences 13 through 16 with different prepositional phrases.

Name ______________________________

Date ____________________

Presidential Pardon, Please

Which turkey will the president pardon for Thanksgiving Day this year? Solve each problem. Then cross the matching product off one of the signs below. The lucky turkey is the one with more crossed-off products.

1. 75 x 32
2. 87 x 45
3. 61 x 14
4. 59 x 27
5. 91 x 47
6. 749 x 23
7. 806 x 34
8. 265 x 71
9. 482 x 29
10. 703 x 56

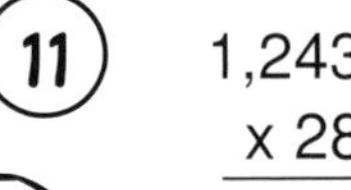

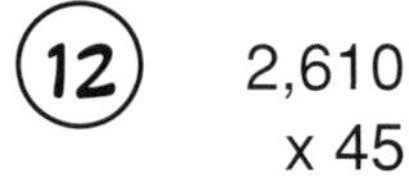

11. 1,243 x 28
12. 2,610 x 45

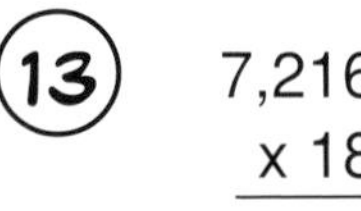

13. 7,216 x 18
14. 5,161 x 37

Pick me!

2,400	14,078
27,404	13,978
129,888	104,078
854	108,957
3,553	4,915

Pick me!

4,005	17,227
18,815	34,804
190,957	1,593
4,277	117,450
39,368	3,915

Bonus: What is the easiest part of multiplying by two digits? The hardest? Explain.

Name ____________________

Date ____________________

WINTER FUN

Use the correct forms of the verbs shown to complete the sentences. Cross out each verb as you use it.

drink know sit tell freeze drive feel wake sleep stand fall get begin rise take set say go catch fly see cut find slide keep bring eat leave

1. My Dad and I ________ ice fishing this year for the first time together.
2. This winter adventure ________ long before the crack of dawn.
3. We ________ up at 2:00 AM and piled all our gear into the van.
4. I ________ sleepy but excited about getting to the lake.
5. My dad ________ the van, and I tried to stay awake; but I ________ for most of the four-hour trip.
6. When we ________ to the lake, the sun still hadn't ________ .
7. We gathered all our gear and ________ it to the lake's edge.
8. We ________ everything down and ________ out onto the ice.
9. Before long, we ________ what we hoped was the perfect spot.
10. Then we ________ a hole in the ice with a saw we ________ from home.
11. We dropped our fishing lines into the icy water and ________ down to wait.
12. We ________ hot chocolate to keep warm.
13. When I got a nibble, I ________ up so quickly that my hot chocolate ________ on the ice.
14. The chocolate drink instantly ________ into a chocolaty slab.
15. I ignored it and yanked my fishing pole so hard that my line and something huge ________ out of the water.
16. I just ________ I had ________ an enormous fish!
17. As I reeled in my catch, I ________ that it was actually a hunk of icy moss.
18. We ________ fishing for three more hours without any success.
19. Then we ________ our lunches—frozen sandwiches and crystal-coated carrots.
20. After one more hour of ice-cold waiting, Dad ________ me he was ready to leave.
21. I jumped up from my icy seat, I grabbed my gear, and we ________ .
22. Last week, Dad asked me if I wanted to go ice fishing again; I ________ , "Thanks, but no thanks."

BONUS: Write the past tense of each verb shown below.
choose forget read shrink stride swing

Name ______________________________

Date ____________________

Hanukkah Lights

A Write <, >, or = to compare each set of fractions.

1. $\frac{3}{4}$ ◯ $\frac{1}{2}$
2. $\frac{5}{8}$ ◯ $\frac{3}{10}$
3. $\mathbf{\frac{1}{4}}$ ◯ $\frac{50}{100}$
4. $\frac{4}{10}$ ◯ $\frac{2}{5}$
5. $\frac{2}{10}$ ◯ $\frac{1}{4}$
6. $\frac{1}{8}$ ◯ $\mathbf{\frac{1}{10}}$
7. $\mathbf{\frac{7}{8}}$ ◯ $\frac{8}{10}$
8. $\frac{6}{8}$ ◯ $\frac{75}{100}$
9. $\frac{1}{2}$ ◯ $\frac{60}{100}$
10. $\mathbf{\frac{7}{10}}$ ◯ $\frac{73}{100}$
11. $\frac{9}{10}$ ◯ $\frac{9}{100}$
12. $\frac{2}{4}$ ◯ $\frac{5}{10}$

B Write <, >, or = to compare each set of decimals.

13. 0.125 ____ **0.20**
14. **0.5** ____ 0.45
15. **0.75** ____ 0.750
16. 0.90 ____ 0.09
17. 0.80 ____ 0.8
18. **0.375** ____ 0.33
19. 0.87 ____ 0.8
20. **0.625** ____ 0.65
21. 0.05 ____ 0.050
22. 0.10 ____ 0.09
23. 0.55 ____ 0.6
24. 0.85 ____ 0.875

C Write the boldfaced fractions and decimals in order below.

Name ______________________________

Date ______________________

Up on the Rooftop

Convert each measurement. Write your answer on the blank and then in the puzzle.

Across

A. 396 inches = ______ yards

C. 48 feet = ______ yards

D. 3 miles = ______ yards

E. 7 yards 5 inches = ______ inches

G. 168 inches = ______ feet

H. 756 inches = ______ yards

J. 19 feet 8 inches = ______ inches

L. 26 yards = ______ feet

N. 4 miles = ______ yards

P. 420 inches = ______ feet

Q. 22 feet = ______ inches

Down

A. 44 yards = ______ inches

B. 144 inches = ______ feet

C. 1,224 inches = ______ feet

F. 6 feet = ______ inches

G. 16 feet 5 inches = ______ inches

I. 5 yards 2 feet = ______ feet

J. 72 feet = ______ yards

K. 8 yards 15 inches = ______ inches

M. 24 yards = ______ inches

O. 7 yards 1 foot = ______ feet

Hint:
12 inches = 1 foot
3 feet = 1 yard
36 inches = 1 yard
1,760 yards = 1 mile

	A	B		C				
	D							
				E		F		
G						H	I	
		J	K				L	M
N						O		
			P			Q		

Bonus: How many feet are there in two miles?

Name ______________________________

Date ____________________

BONUS: Use your combined sentences and what you know to write an article about Martin Luther King Jr. or about a Martin Luther King Day parade.

IN THE NEWS

In each pair of sentences, words in the subject or the predicate are repeated. Combine the sentences to make one longer sentence without repetitive words. Write the new sentence under the correct title.

1. The parade will start at City Park.
   The parade will end at Lincoln School.
2. Millions of Americans supported Martin Luther King Jr.'s nonviolent campaign.
   People in other countries supported Martin Luther King Jr.'s nonviolent campaign.
3. Fire trucks from three stations are scheduled to join the parade.
   Police cars are scheduled to join the parade.
4. Over 200,000 American people joined the March on Washington in 1963.
   Over 200,000 American people listened to Dr. King speak.
5. Our mayor will be the parade's grand marshal.
   Our mayor will dedicate the new Martin Luther King Library after the parade.
6. Martin Luther King Jr. gave dynamic speeches.
   Martin Luther King Jr. was an important civil rights leader.
7. Martin Luther King Jr. organized the March on Washington.
   Other civil rights leaders helped organize the March on Washington.
8. Two local high school bands will march in the parade.
   The jazz band from City University will march in the parade.
9. As part of the March, Martin Luther King Jr. gave his "I Have a Dream" speech.
   As part of the March, Martin Luther King Jr. shared his hope that all Americans could be treated equally.
10. In honor of Martin Luther King Day, our city will host a parade.
    In honor of Martin Luther King Day, our city will offer special events.

CITY NEWS

Tenth Annual Martin Luther King Day Parade

The parade will start at City Park and end at Lincoln School.

Fast Facts About Martin Luther King Jr.

Name ______________________________

Date ______________

THEY'RE PLAYING MY SONG

Circle the misspelled word in each sentence. Then write the correctly spelled word on the line and circle it in the puzzle.

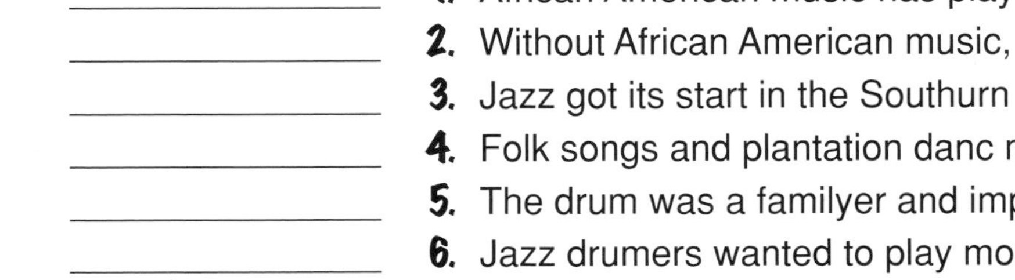

______ **1.** African American music has played an improtant role in music history.

______ **2.** Without African American music, there woud be no jazz.

______ **3.** Jazz got its start in the Southurn United States during the late 1800s.

______ **4.** Folk songs and plantation danc music were key to early jazz.

______ **5.** The drum was a familyer and important instrument in early jazz music.

______ **6.** Jazz drumers wanted to play more than one drum at a time.

______ **7.** The drum set developped as jazz music grew.

______ **8.** Wire brushes that made softer sounds were invented to use insted of drumsticks.

______ **9.** By 1900, jazz and its first famous musicians were makeing New Orleans their home.

______ **10.** Louis Armstrong became nown as the world's greatest jazz cornet and trumpet player.

______ **11.** From the mid-1930s to the mid-1940s, the latest style of jazz, swing music, became populer.

______ **12.** Ella Fitzgerald, a famus and important jazz singer, was known as the "First Lady of Song."

______ **13.** Ms. Fitzgerald was famous for being a great scat signer.

______ **14.** In scat singing, the artist woudl sing rhythmic syllables instead of words.

______ **15.** In the 1940s and 1950s, bebop and cool jaz became popular all over the world.

______ **16.** There are still meny styles of jazz, but now most artists play "straight ahead jazz," which is a modern form of bebop and swing.

```
P A T G U M F A M I L I A R
S I M P O R T A N T C L Q P
O C N C A M A K I N G T D R
U O S D T N E R E O S K E B
T M A R A A S A R J U I V A
H P K U I N S T E A D S E P
E A N M Y E C U W Z O F L O
R R O M A N Y E N Z E A O P
N E W E G I K W D O S M P U
N D N R N E W O U L D O E L
G O V S P E O U L E T U D A
E X P E R I E L C E D S H R
S I N G E R H D B L C H I C
```

BONUS: Common spelling mistakes include mixing up the order of the letters (*poeple* for *people*), leaving out letters (*were* for *where*), and writing the wrong word (*their* for *they're*). When you make spelling mistakes, what kind of mistakes do you usually make? Explain.

Name ____________________

Date ____________________

Adding and subtracting fractions

Secret Admirers

Add or subtract. Write each answer in simplest form.

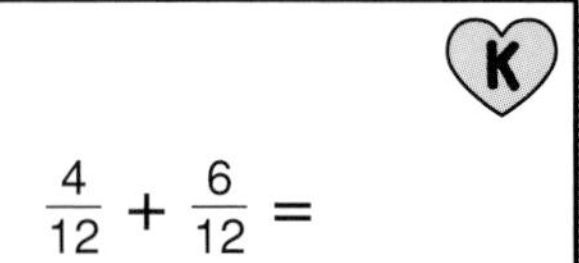

K $\frac{4}{12} + \frac{6}{12} =$	**E** $\frac{5}{6} - \frac{1}{6} =$	**H** $\frac{10}{15} - \frac{5}{15} =$
A $\frac{4}{9} + \frac{3}{9} =$	**P** $\frac{9}{18} + \frac{7}{18} =$	**D** $\frac{6}{10} + \frac{3}{10} =$
G $\frac{1}{7} + \frac{5}{7} =$	**S** $\frac{4}{12} - \frac{2}{12} =$	**C** $\frac{6}{8} - \frac{2}{8} =$
O $\frac{6}{11} - \frac{1}{11} =$	**N** $\frac{5}{6} + \frac{3}{6} =$	**W** $\frac{7}{9} - \frac{2}{9} =$
T $\frac{9}{10} - \frac{2}{10} =$	**T** $\frac{5}{8} + \frac{7}{8} =$	**M** $\frac{5}{7} - \frac{1}{7} =$
C $\frac{8}{15} + \frac{7}{15} =$	**L** $\frac{7}{14} + \frac{6}{14} =$	**I** $\frac{14}{18} - \frac{6}{18} =$

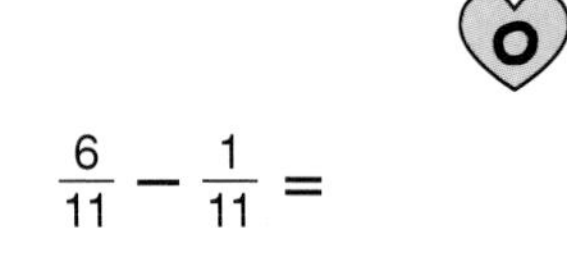

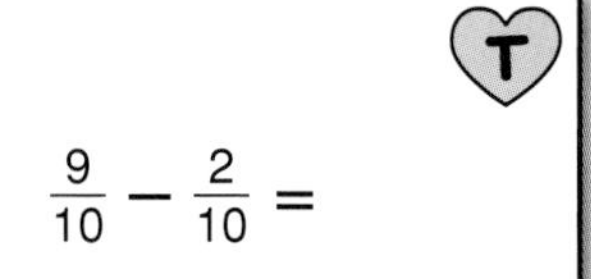

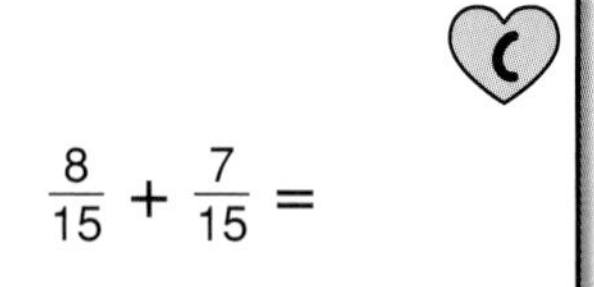

What did the valentine card say to the stamp?

To solve the riddle, write each letter on its matching numbered line or lines.

$\frac{1}{6}$ $\frac{7}{10}$ $\frac{4}{9}$ 1 $\frac{5}{6}$ $\frac{5}{9}$ $\frac{4}{9}$ $1\frac{1}{2}$ $\frac{1}{3}$ $\frac{4}{7}$ $\frac{2}{3}$, $\frac{7}{9}$ $1\frac{1}{3}$ $\frac{9}{10}$

$\frac{5}{9}$ $\frac{2}{3}$' $\frac{13}{14}$ $\frac{13}{14}$ $\frac{6}{7}$ $\frac{5}{11}$ $\frac{8}{9}$ $\frac{13}{14}$ $\frac{7}{9}$ $\frac{1}{2}$ $\frac{2}{3}$ $\frac{1}{6}$!

Bonus: Write three different addition problems that will equal 1.

Name ______________________________

Date ____________________

Positively Presidential

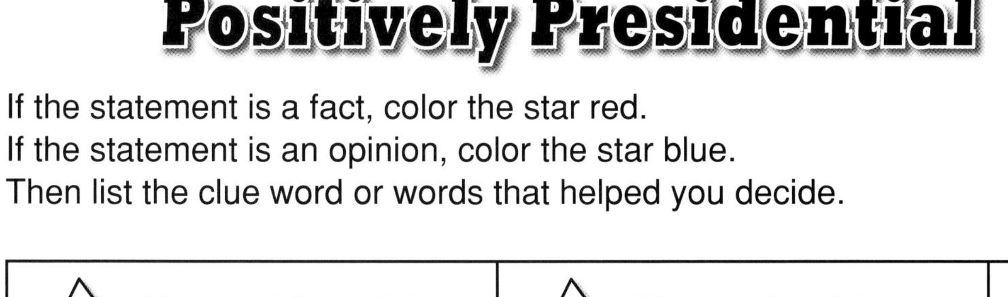

If the statement is a fact, color the star red.
If the statement is an opinion, color the star blue.
Then list the clue word or words that helped you decide.

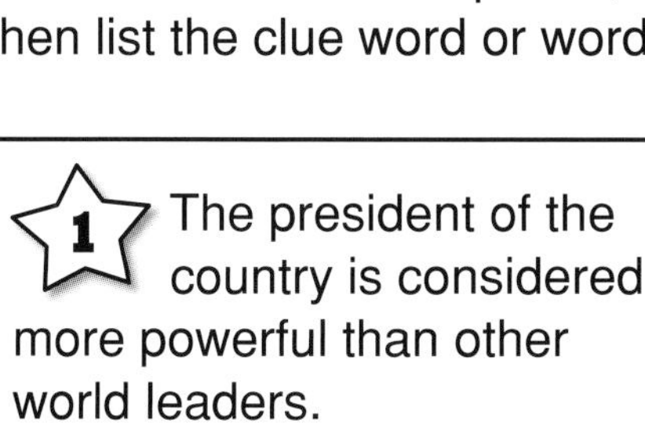

1 The president of the country is considered more powerful than other world leaders.	2 The president has too many roles and responsibilities to be able to keep everyone happy.	3 The president is in charge of the government's executive branch.
4 Since a president has such a demanding job, he shouldn't have to campaign for reelection.	5 The first president, George Washington, went to school for just seven or eight years.	6 Abraham Lincoln only went to school for a year; however, he was the country's best president.
7 On Presidents' Day, we honor all our presidents, not just George Washington and Abraham Lincoln.	8 To truly honor the country's presidents, this holiday should be celebrated for a full month.	9 To be president, a person must be at least 35 years old and have lived in the country for 14 years.
10 The worst part of the president's job is making tough choices and then making some people mad.	11 The president attends meetings, makes appearances, and travels.	12 The president is so busy that he meets with nearly 100 people every day.
13 Many presidents were once lawyers; it is clearly the best job for a future president.	14 Barack Obama, the forty-fourth president, is the country's first African American president.	15 The country's voters should elect a female president soon, before it's too late.

Bonus: Choose five statements that are opinions. Rewrite each one so it is fact.

Name ______________________________

Date ____________________

Slices of "Pi"

Using a protractor, measure each angle.

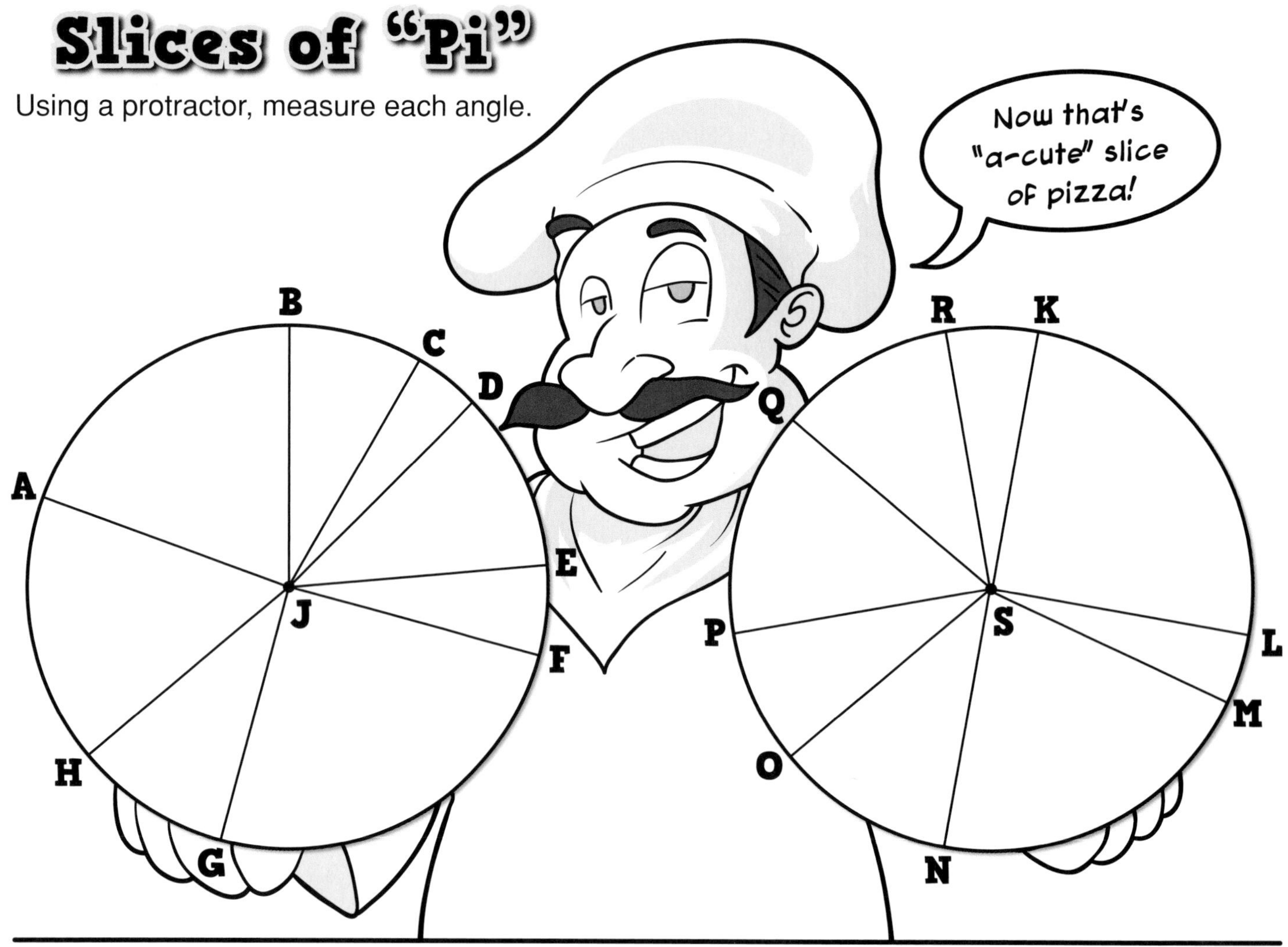

1. __________ ∠AJB	**9.** __________ ∠HJB	**17.** __________ ∠OSP
2. __________ ∠BJC	**10.** __________ ∠AJD	**18.** __________ ∠PSQ
3. __________ ∠CJD	**11.** __________ ∠AJE	**19.** __________ ∠QSR
4. __________ ∠DJE	**12.** __________ ∠GJE	**20.** __________ ∠RSK
5. __________ ∠EJF	**13.** __________ ∠KSL	**21.** __________ ∠RSL
6. __________ ∠FJG	**14.** __________ ∠LSM	**22.** __________ ∠LSO
7. __________ ∠GJH	**15.** __________ ∠MSN	**23.** __________ ∠LSN
8. __________ ∠HJA	**16.** __________ ∠NSO	**24.** __________ ∠OSR

Bonus: How much do angles FJC, CJA, AJG, and GJF measure in all?

Name ____________________

Date ____________________

IT TAKES TWO TO TANGLE!

Divide.
Shade the matching quotient.

A. 61)6,649 B. 12)3,048 C. 35)735

D. 27)2,565 E. 19)912 F. 32)832

G. 64)9,408 H. 23)667 I. 16)8,256 J. 33)4,785

K. 78)936 L. 49)9,947 M. 57)4,902 N. 45)675

O. 34)782 P. 29)2,523

12 13

15 21

23 26

29 48

86 87

95 109

145 147

203 254

442 516

Every time!

BONUS: Use the two unshaded numbers to make a division problem and then solve it.

Name ____________________

Date ____________________

Springing into Action

The subject of each sentence has been personified. Circle each subject. Then underline the word or words that give the object human traits or characteristics.

Did I put any seeds in that row?

1. After the rain, the earth breathes a sigh of relief.
2. The fresh spring air lures the gardener outside.
3. Dewdrops wink from each blade of grass.
4. The blades of the gardener's tiller grab chunks of the moist soil.
5. Seeds jump out of the packets, eager to be planted.
6. The freshly dug rows of soil swallow the seeds.
7. Trees dance merrily in the spring breeze.
8. Between each row, weeds beg to be pulled.
9. The soil crowds around the weeds' roots, refusing to let go.
10. At the end of the day, the gardener's back groans from the hard work.

BONUS: Choose three sentences. For each one, explain how the personified object is being compared to a human.

Use the object and verb on each seed packet to write a sentence with a personified object.

sun smiles

11. ____________________

wind howls

12. ____________________

butterfly kisses

13. ____________________

rocks leap

14. ____________________

rabbits tiptoe

15. ____________________

Name ______________________________

Date ________________

All Quacked Up

Use the race roster to answer the questions below.

The Great Duck Race Roster

First Race	Second Race	Third Race	Fourth Race
Don (1)	Doug (3)	Deb (2)	Dru (6)
Deb (2)	Don (1)	Dru (6)	Doug (3)
Duff (5)	Duff (5)	Darla (4)	Darla (4)

1. What is the probability that Don can win the first race? 1 out of 3, or $\frac{1}{3}$
2. What is the probability that Duff will win the second race? ______________
3. What is the probability a duck with an even number will win the third race? ______________
4. In the fourth race, what is the probability the winning duck's number will be a multiple of 3? ______________
5. In which race is it certain that a duck with an odd number will win? ______________ Explain. ______________
6. In which race would it be impossible for a duck with an odd number to win? ______________ Why? ______________
7. What is the probability that Darla will win the fourth race? ______________
8. Why would it be impossible for Don to win the third race? ______________
9. How many possible outcomes are there in each race? ______________
10. In which races is it more likely a duck with an odd number will win than a duck with an even number? ______________ Why? ______________
11. What is the probability that Darla can win the third race or the fourth race? ______________ Explain. ______________
12. If Don joined the fourth race, what is the possibility a duck with an even number will win the race? ______________ How do you know? ______________

____

impossible | unlikely | equally likely | likely | certain

Bonus: Is there a duck that has a better chance of winning a race than the other ducks? Explain.

Name ______________________________

Date ______________________

Down in the Dumps?

Volume (v) = length · width · height

Find the volume of each box.

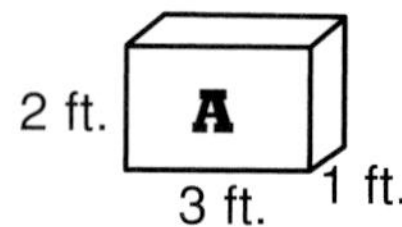

v = ______ $ft.^3$

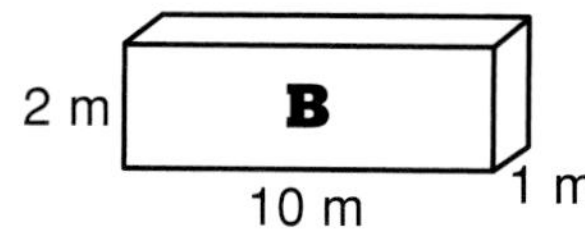

v = ______ m^3

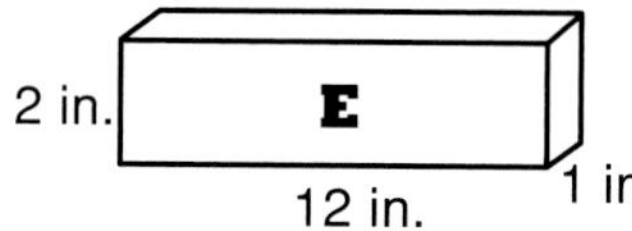

v = ______ $in.^3$

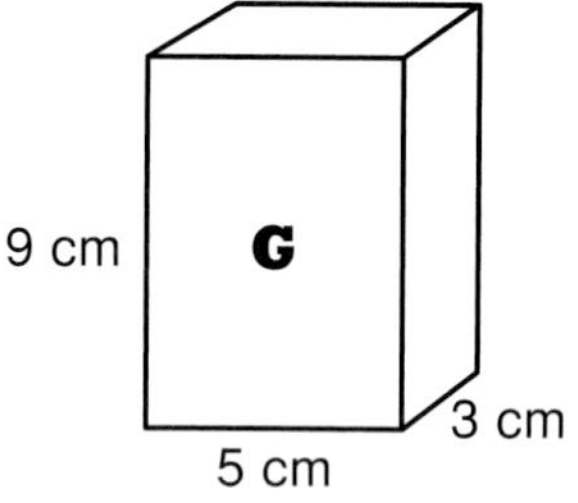

v = ______ cm^3

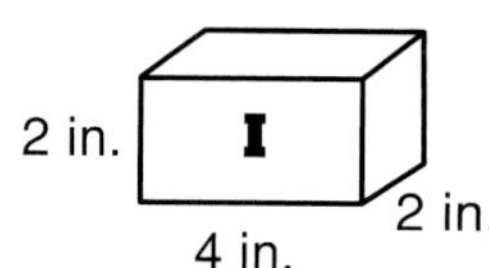

v = ______ $in.^3$

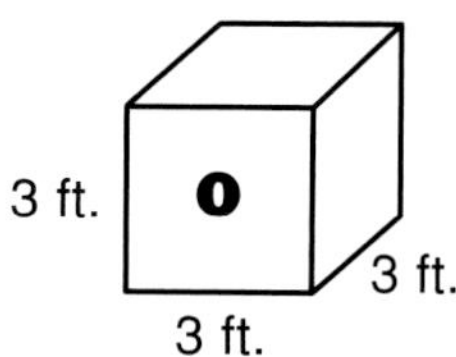

v = ______ $ft.^3$

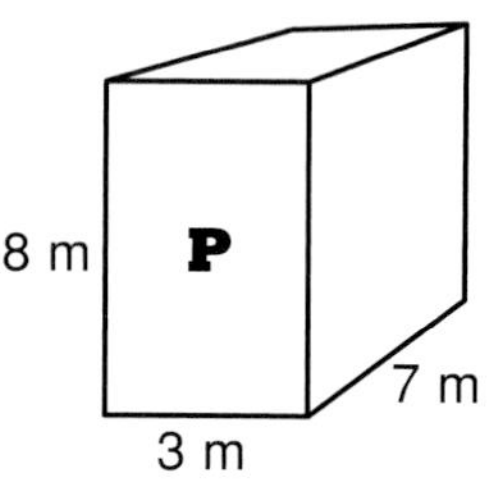

v = ______ m^3

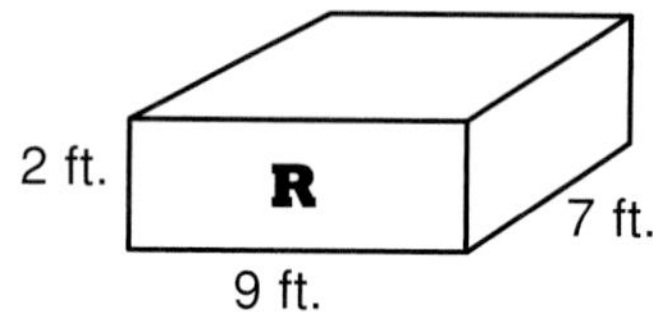

v = ______ $ft.^3$

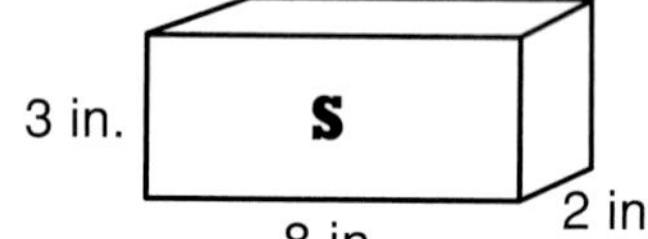

v = ______ $in.^3$

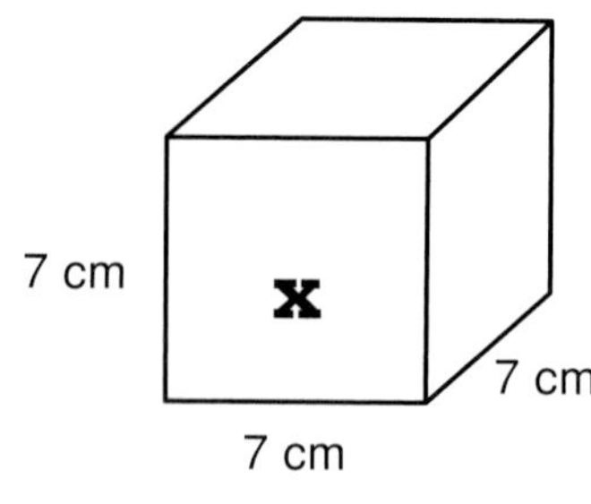

v = ______ cm^3

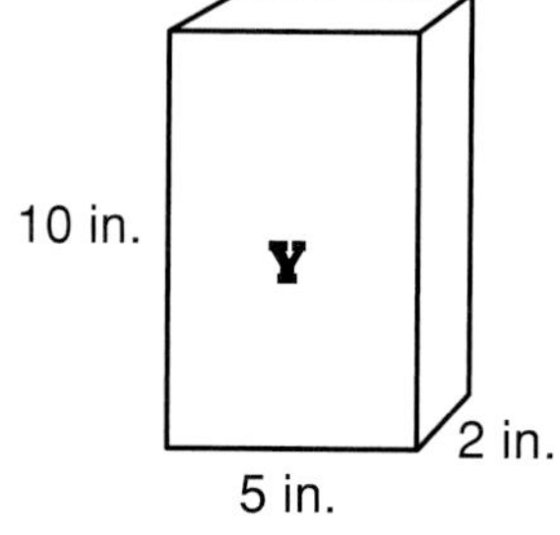

v = ______ $in.^3$

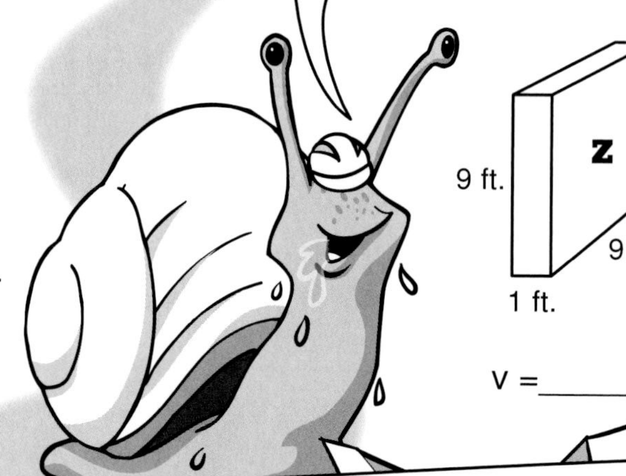

Z: 9 ft., 1 ft., 9 ft.

v = ______ $ft.^3$

What's Sully's Earth Day reminder?

To find out, write each letter on its matching numbered line or lines.

Never recycle

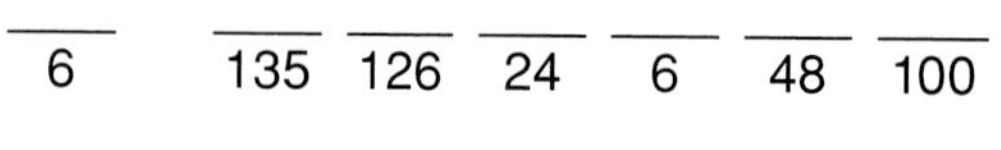

Bonus: Explain how to find the volume of the box shown. It has a square base. What is the volume?

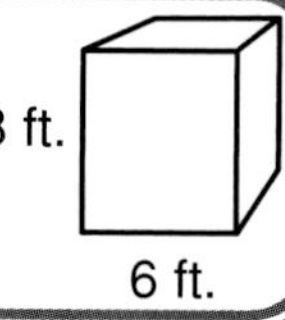

Name ______________________________

Date ______________________________

Figurative language: spoonerisms

A Dream Vacation

A spoonerism is a humorous play on words. The initial sounds of two or more words are swapped to make accidental words that are fun to read or say.

Circle the spoonerisms in each sentence.

1. Mr. Jones is telling us the difference between (cattleships) and (bruisers), but I can't concentrate.
2. My brain keeps chipping flannels between school and summer vacation.
3. My family has planned a trailing sip in July.
4. I have always dreamed about dishing with my fad.
5. I can just imagine how neat it will feel to catch my first fig bish.
6. The fish will be bo sig my dad will have to help me reel it in.
7. I can't wait until the dig bay comes!
8. All of a sudden I heard someone may ny same.
9. It was Mr. Jones, and he did hot nook lappy!
10. I felt my race furn ted as I snapped my head off the desk.
11. I tried to hide the pool druddle on my desk.
12. Then Mr. Jones said doring snisturbs his class.
13. I told him I must have been thinking about vummer sacation.
14. Well, let's just say I had learned a lood gesson.
15. It's mad banners to sleep in class.
16. I'll try not to daydream in Mr. Jones' class again, but if I do, I will sang a hign on my desk that says "Gone fishing!"

Switch the starting letters of the circled words and write the correct words on the matching numbered lines below.

(1) battleships, cruisers
(2) ______________________
(3) ______________________
(4) ______________________
(5) ______________________
(6) ______________________
(7) ______________________
(8) ______________________
(9) ______________________
(10) ______________________
(11) ______________________
(12) ______________________
(13) ______________________
(14) ______________________
(15) ______________________
(16) ______________________

BONUS: Write three of your own spoonerisms.

Name ____________________

Date ____________________

Adding and subtracting fractions and mixed numbers

Nearing the Finish

Add or subtract. Write each answer in its simplest form.
Then color the matching answer.

A. $3\frac{1}{3} + \frac{3}{4}$

B. $4\frac{2}{9} + 1\frac{2}{3}$

C. $3\frac{3}{10} - 1\frac{1}{2}$

D. $\frac{3}{4} - \frac{2}{5}$

E. $6\frac{6}{8} - 2\frac{2}{3}$

F. $7\frac{2}{5} + 4\frac{6}{7}$

G. $9\frac{1}{2} - 3\frac{5}{6}$

H. $\frac{5}{12} + \frac{1}{4}$

I. $2\frac{5}{8} + \frac{2}{16}$

J. $5\frac{2}{6} - \frac{2}{9}$

K. $8\frac{1}{7} - 4\frac{2}{3}$

L. $\frac{4}{6} + \frac{3}{5}$

M. $12\frac{9}{10} - 4\frac{4}{8}$

N. $\frac{11}{12} - \frac{1}{2}$

O. $3\frac{7}{16} + 5\frac{3}{4}$

P. $4\frac{4}{6} - 2\frac{4}{9}$

Q. $\frac{3}{14} + \frac{6}{7}$

R. $8\frac{1}{5} + \frac{8}{20}$

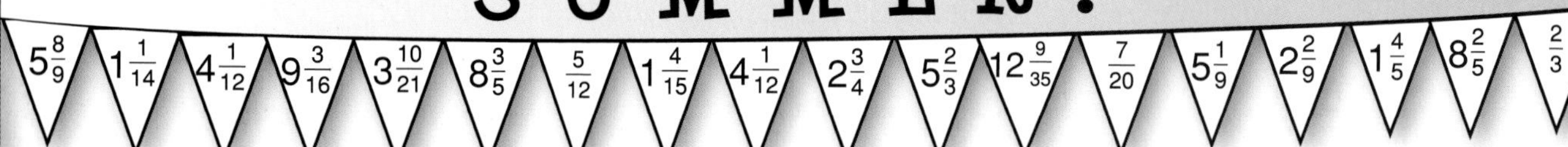

Bonus: Subtract $3\frac{4}{9}$ from $5\frac{3}{4}$. Then use addition to check your answer.

Making inferences

Name ____________________

Date ____________________

Beach Bound

Read each book description and write the letter of its genre.
Explain your choice.

1. Learn about sharks that live in the deepest parts of the ocean. ______

2. In this medieval tale, no one knows that Mary is really the knight who kills the dragon. ______

3. LeBron James gives you the inside scoop on his exciting life as a professional basketball player. ______

4. Jack Findsalot is an excellent detective determined to solve the case of the missing puppy. ______

5. Princess Bellina asks her fairy godmother to help her find a handsome prince. ______

6. The story of Jim Thorpe, one of the greatest all-around athletes ever, is sure to inspire you. ______

7. Sarah Sharp is trying to help her family survive when her father joins General Washington's unit. ______

8. Laugh as you read these silly rhymes about the funny things kids do. ______

9. A sly fox tries to outsmart the chicken farmer in this classic tale of cleverness. ______

10. Katie learns a valuable lesson about caring for her younger twin sisters. ______

11. Find out how the eagle got its wings in this Native American tale. ______

12. Jeremy can hardly believe it, but he knows he can travel through time to the future. ______

Genre Bank

A. autobiography
B. biography
C. fable
D. fairy tale
E. fantasy
F. folktale
G. historical fiction
H. mystery
I. nonfiction
J. poetry
K. realistic fiction
L. science fiction

Bonus: Write the titles of four different books you have read and name each book's genre.

Name ______________________

Date ______________________

Problem solving: division

Ballpark Munching

Solve. Show your work.

1. Sal sells snacks at the Seals baseball park. Sal has 875 hot dogs to sell during today's game. If Sal sells the same number of hot dogs during each of the nine innings, how many hot dogs will he have left at the end of the game?

2. Sal has 540 soft pretzels to sell by the end of the ninth inning. If he sells 78 pretzels each inning, during which inning will Sal run out of soft pretzels?

3. Sal makes 131 cups of popcorn. A large popcorn tub holds six cups of popcorn. How many large tubs can Sal fill?

4. Sal gets a bushel of 95 crisp, delicious apples. Sal slices each apple into ten sections and then puts six slices in a cup with yogurt sauce. How many cups of apple slices with sauce does Sal make?

5. Sal sells 900 water bottles for $2,250 total. How much does Sal charge for each water bottle?

6. Sal has 380 bags of cotton candy. He sells 93 bags each inning. In which inning will Sal have sold all the cotton candy?

7. Sal sells 748 ice cream cones by the end of the game. He sells about the same number of cones during each of the nine innings. About how many ice cream cones does Sal sell each inning?

8. Sal has 435 juice boxes at the beginning of the game. He sells the same number of juice boxes during each inning, but runs out at the end of the fifth inning. How many juice boxes does he sell each inning?

Bonus: Sal gets $245.50 in tips during the game. He always shares his tips with his employees, Sally and Sol. What would be the best way to fairly share the tips from today's game?

Name ______________________________

Date ______________________

A Thirsty Thinker

Write the number that correctly completes each statement.
Then cross out the number that is incorrect.

1	If 1 cup equals 8 ounces, then 4 cups equal ____ ounces.	16	(T)	32	(A)
2	If 3,000 pounds equals $1\frac{1}{2}$ tons, then 1 ton equals ____ pounds.	2,000	(S)	1,000	(L)
3	If $\frac{1}{2}$ cup equals 4 ounces, then 2 cups equal ____ ounces.	16	(C)	8	(E)
4	If 8 pints equal 4 quarts, then 8 quarts equal ____ pints.	4	(W)	16	(N)
5	If $\frac{1}{2,000}$ ton equals 1 pound, then 2,000 pounds equal ____ ton(s).	$\frac{1}{2}$	(A)	1	(T)
6	If 4 cups equal 1 quart, then 4 quarts equal ____ cups.	16	(O)	8	(M)
7	If 6 tons equal 12,000 pounds, then 500 pounds equal ____ ton(s).	$\frac{1}{2}$	(H)	$\frac{1}{4}$	(W)
8	If 10 cups equal 80 ounces, then 10 ounces equal ____ cups.	800	(S)	$1\frac{1}{4}$	(M)
9	If 120 seconds equal 2 minutes, then 100 seconds equal ____ minutes.	$1\frac{2}{3}$	(E)	$1\frac{1}{2}$	(A)
10	If 5 yards equal 15 feet, then 15 yards equal ____ feet.	30	(N)	45	(F)
11	If 2 miles equal 10,560 feet, then 2,640 feet equal ____ mile(s).	$\frac{1}{2}$	(R)	$\frac{1}{3}$	(C)
12	If 600 seconds equal 10 minutes, then 60 minutes equal ____ seconds.	1,000	(L)	3,600	(D)
13	If 1 mile equals 5,280 feet, then $\frac{1}{2}$ mile equals ____ feet.	2,500	(T)	2,640	(C)
14	If 6 pints equal 3 quarts, then 6 quarts equal ____ pints.	12	(I)	3	(N)
15	If 144 inches equal 4 yards, then $1\frac{1}{2}$ yards equals ____ inches.	48	(W)	54	(A)
16	If 800 ounces equal 50 pounds, then 450 ounces equal ____ pounds.	$28\frac{1}{8}$	(T)	25	(M)

Why did Lucy drink frozen lemonade before her math test?
To answer the riddle, write each letter you did not cross out on the matching numbered line or lines.

She heard __ __ (14 5) __ __ __ (7 1 2)

__ __ __ __ (8 15 12 9) __ __ __ __ (10 11 6 8)

__ __ __ __ __ __ __ __ __ __ __ ! (13 6 4 3 9 4 16 11 1 16 9)

Bonus: Complete this chart.

____ ounces = 1 cup

____ pints = 1 quart

____ ounces = 1 pound

____ pounds = 1 ton

____ feet = 1 mile

OPEN FOR Learning!

FUN IDEAS for making your open house presentation memorable and setting the tone for a great year!

Gung Ho Greeting

Have students help you create this meaningful display. In advance, cut out large construction paper letters that spell the word *teamwork*. Then cut the letters into puzzle pieces and give each child a piece. On his piece, have the student describe or draw a picture about one of his talents. Next, have students work together to assemble the puzzle. Then display it in your room or the hall. What a way to start the year!

Jennifer Ohnhaus, Elizabeth, PA

tip To streamline the puzzle assembly, use a different-color paper for each letter.

Survival Kit

Surprise families with survival kits that are custom-made for intermediate students' parents. For each student, place the items listed in a bag. Staple a note on each bag to explain the items' significance. Then put a bag on each child's desk.

Suzanne Kurasz, Veterans Memorial Elementary, Brick, NJ

world map: The world is out there. Explore it with your child, and remember that, as she begins to chart her own course, she still needs guidance.

bit of string: Raising a child is like flying a kite: let your child soar, but keep a firm grasp on the string.

penny: Penny for your thoughts? Talk to your child. Tell him what you think. Ask him what he thinks. Then listen.

playing card: We never know what life will deal us. Remind your child to play fair, win humbly, and lose graciously.

piece of paper: Give your child an outlet for negative feelings so she can let them go. When your child is frustrated, disappointed, or angry, have her write about the problem. Then have her toss the note to let her troubles go.

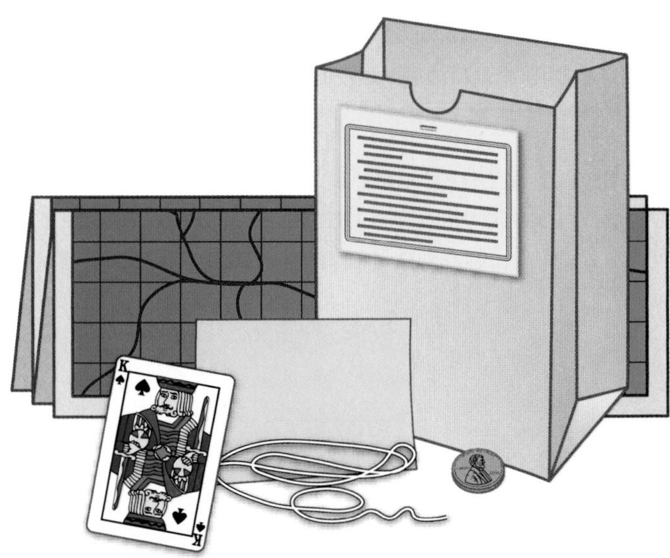

Mystery Starter

Before open house, type a question, such as the one shown, on a class computer and number a line for each student. Then have each student move the cursor to the right of the first number available and type her name and answer. When every student has answered the question, print the page and keep this printout handy. Next, delete students' names and print the page again. Put a copy of the nameless version on each child's desk before open house. As parents arrive, challenge them to identify their children's responses. Then, before parents leave, take a few minutes to match students to their answers.

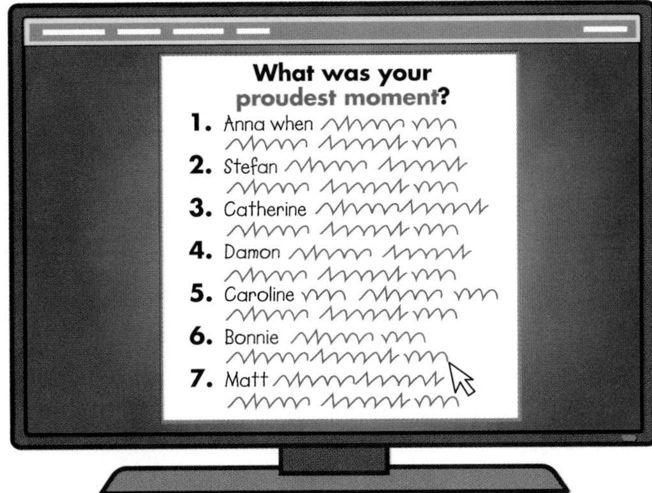

Get the Picture

Use your classroom computers to give parents a glimpse of life in your classroom. Download class photos from last year onto each computer. Then set each screensaver to show a slideshow of memorable events from the previous year. Simply turn on each computer before parents start trickling in. As an alternative, create a slideshow of previous students' technology projects. Either way, parents will get a clear picture of what to expect during the school year!

adapted from an idea by VaReane Heese, Springfield Elementary, Springfield, NE

When I Was Your Age...

Here's a fun way to engage parents at open house and your students the next day! Draw a giant Venn diagram on colorful bulletin board paper and label the circles for students today and students from yesterday. Then post the diagram, provide markers, and invite parents to jot details from their intermediate school years in the correct section. Explain to parents that your students—their children—will read the comments during class the next day. Then students will complete the diagram, sorting and recording details about their school experiences in the diagram's other sections.

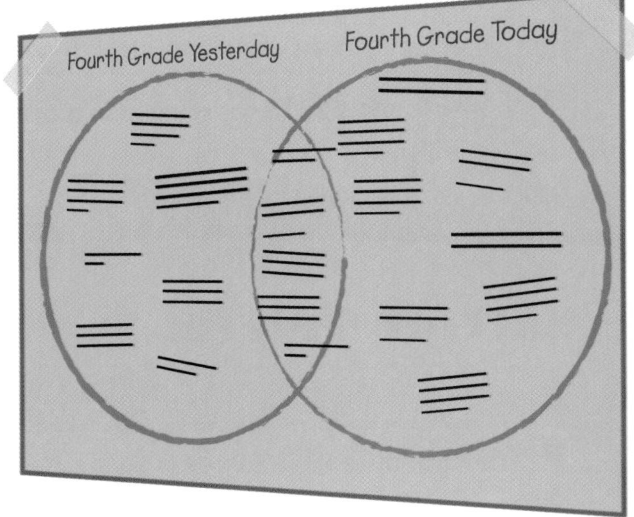

Kim Minafo, Apex, NC

It's 09-09! Isn't That Fine?

Celebrate September's Bonza* Bottler* Day (September 9) by sprinkling activities and trivia focused on the number nine throughout the day. This offbeat holiday can be celebrated any month on the date that the day and month are the same number.

Julia Alarie, Williston, VT

Bonza Activities:

- Review multiplication facts that have 9 as a factor.
- Show students how to tell whether a number is divisible by 9. *(Add up all the number's digits. If the sum is divisible by 9, then so is the number.)* Call out numbers and challenge students to decide whether they are divisible by 9.
- Have students skip-count by 9s. Challenge them to identify and describe the patterns in the numbers' ones and tens digits. *(The digits in the ones places decrease by one. The digits in the tens places increase by one.)*
- Teach students how to say *nine* in French (*neuf* [nuhf]), Spanish (*nueve* [nweh bay]), German (*neun* [noin]), and Japanese (*ku* [ku]).
- Challenge students to draw nonagons (polygons with nine sides and nine angles).

* In Australia, "bonza" is an exclamation meaning super, great, or fantastic, and "bottler" is something that's excellent.

Bottler Trivia:

- A hundred dollar bill lasts an average of nine years.
- The Grand Canal in Venice is an average of nine feet deep.
- There are nine 0s in a billion.
- There are nine Supreme Court Justices in the United States.
- New Hampshire was the ninth state admitted to the Union (1788).

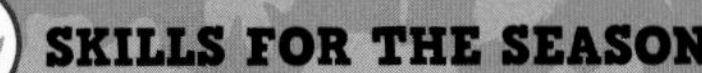

5 Fabulous Ideas for Using Fall Leaves

Take advantage of the season's offerings (lots of leaves) with these math, writing, and science ideas!

1 Create a quick measurement center!

Stock the center with different fall leaves and rulers. A student creates a recording sheet as shown. Next, she chooses five leaves and estimates each one's width and length to the nearest ⅛-inch or centimeter. Then she measures each leaf, recording the measurements. **Ann E. Fisher, Toledo, OH**

	Estimated Width	Estimated Length	Actual Width	Actual Length
Leaf #1				
Leaf #2				
Leaf #3				
Leaf #4				
Leaf #5				

2 Make a fun fall estimation jar!

Fill a see-through container with leaves. Then have each student estimate the number of leaves inside. Have the child record his educated guess and then write a paragraph that explains the process he used. When students finish, draw a line plot on the board and have each student explain his process and then plot his estimate. Finally, count the leaves, announce the number, and congratulate those students with close estimates.

3 Inspire colorful fall poetry!

Have each student choose a leaf, name it, and then personify the leaf in a bio poem about it. Guide each child to use the template shown to write a poem that creatively describes her new botanical friend. Then have each student write her final copy on a construction paper leaf cut in the same shape as her leaf.
Emily Clark, Vernal, UT

Botanical Bio Poem

____
leaf's name

____
four words that describe the leaf

Leafy sibling of __________.
Leaf who likes __________.
Leaf who needs __________.
Leaf who gives __________.
Leaf who fears __________.
Leaf who wishes __________.

____
leaf's name

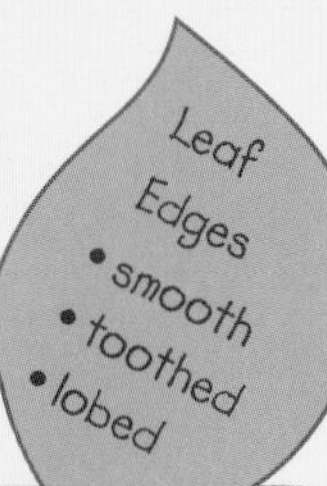

4 Explore prepositional phrases!

Tape a fall leaf to the board and write beside it "The leaf is on the board." Then identify the preposition and point out the prepositional phrase. Next, guide each pair of students to take a fall leaf, place it in a different spot, and write a sentence that describes the leaf's location. After repeating the process nine more times, the partners circle each preposition and underline each prepositional phrase.

5 Sort them according to their characteristics!

Provide a variety of leaves and a list of the different leaf types, as shown. Next, have each student choose five leaves and sketch each one. Then have the child label each leaf's edge type, the pattern of its veins, and the number of blades.

Leaf Edges	Leaf Vein Patterns	Number of Blades
smooth	pinnately veined	simple
toothed	palmately veined	compound
lobed	parallel veined	double compound
	center	

A HAUNTED HELPER

5 Ideas for using the haunted house pattern on page 221!

1 Give computation practice a seasonal twist! Program a copy of page 221 with problems students need to practice. Then copy a class supply. Keep the grading simple by having each student check her work on a calculator!

2 For fun weekly spelling practice, have each student list and then define his spelling words in the windows and door of the haunted house. For a simple center, laminate a color copy of the house and place it at a center along with wipe-off markers and copies of students' spelling lists. A student writes his words in the house's windows and door and then checks his work; if a word is misspelled, he wipes it off and tries again.

3 Have students practice writing figurative language. Guide each child to decorate a copy of the house by writing in each window and the door an example of simile, metaphor, hyperbole, personification, or onomatopoeia that describes or might be heard in a haunted house. Display students' work on a board decorated to look like a spooky street and titled "Figurative Language From 'Spook-tacular' Street." Melodee Morgan, Boulder Ridge Middle School, Menifee, CA

4 Jot seasonal writing prompts, such as those shown, on a color copy of the page. Then display the page at the beginning of language arts lessons and have each student respond to a different prompt each time.

- Would you rather carve a fat pumpkin or a skinny pumpkin? Explain.
- What is your favorite kind of candy? Describe it.
- Write five or more steps that explain how to carve a pumpkin.
- Would you like to change places with the school principal? Why or why not?
- Make a list of ten or more things that can be scary.
- Describe the inside of a pumpkin.
- Do you like to dress up in costumes? Why or why not?
- Write five steps that explain how to trick-or-treat.
- Would you like to spend Halloween at a haunted corn maze? Why or why not?
- Make a list of ten or more spooky sounds.
- Do you think teenagers should be allowed to trick-or-treat? Why or why not?
- Write a story about your best Halloween yet.

5 Post a copy of the house to motivate good behavior. Then draw a ghost in a window each time you catch your students following classroom rules or showing good effort. When all the windows are filled with ghosts, celebrate students' "spook-tacular" behavior with a popcorn party or an extra recess.

Note to the teacher: Use with "A Haunted Helper" on page 220.

Kid-pleasing ideas that celebrate winter!

An Inside Snowpal

Measurement

For this idea, have each student follow the directions shown as you read them aloud. Then display students' work on a board decked out with snowflakes and titled "Precision-Made Snowpals."

Belinda Rippon, Kiptopeke Elementary, Cape Charles, VA

Materials for each student: large sheet of white construction paper, compass, ruler

Directions

1. Use a compass to draw the snowpal's body and head. Draw 7 cm, 5.5 cm, and 3.5 cm circles, overlapping each one slightly.
2. For the eyes, draw two 1 cm equilateral triangles. Then draw a line segment from each vertex to the center of the opposite side.
3. Make the snowpal's nose by drawing a right triangle that has two 1 cm sides.
4. For the mouth, draw a trapezoid that has a 3 cm base, 1 cm nonparallel sides, and a 4 cm top.
5. In the snowpal's middle and bottom sections, draw six 1 cm square buttons.
6. For the arms, draw two 6 cm line segments. Then add three 1.5 cm line segments for the fingers.
7. To create the snowpal's hat, draw a 9 cm x 1 cm rectangle hat brim. For the rest of the hat, draw a 5 cm x 6 cm rectangle.
8. Add colorful details.

Keep It Rolling!

Narrative writing

To get these cumulative stories started, have each student draw five large snowballs on a sheet of paper and label them as shown. Then lead the child to brainstorm and record ideas for one of the categories. Next, have each student pass his paper to the next student who reads the brainstormed ideas, chooses a category, and then brainstorms and jots ideas in its circle. Have students continue passing their papers until each page is full of details. Finally, have students return their papers to the original authors, who use the details to write a snowy adventure story.

Jackie Beaudry, Getzville, NY

Math—"Snow" Much Fun!

Comparing decimals; finding range, median, and mean; multiplying decimals

Turn snowflakes into a center that gives students math practice galore! To set it up, have each student make a six-point snowflake. Then program students' snowflakes with decimals such as those shown and post them on a wintry board. As time allows, each student chooses a snowflake, records its decimals, and then arranges them from least to greatest. Next, she calculates the decimals' range, circles the median decimal, and finds the mean. Finally, the child multiplies each decimal on the snowflake's outer edges by the decimal in the center. That's a lot of practice!

Colleen Dabney, Williamsburg, VA

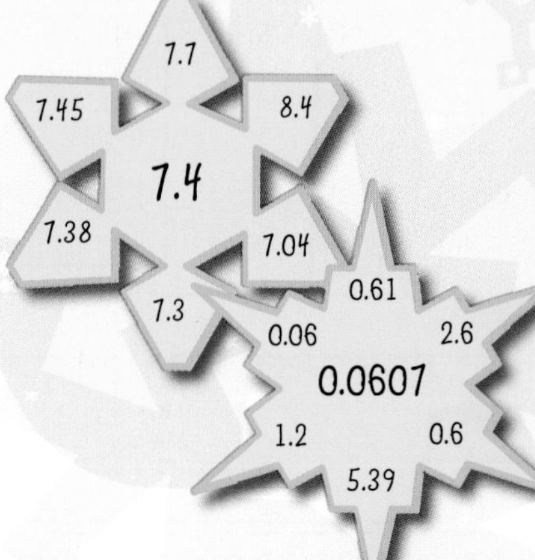

We ♥ Valentine's Day!

5 "Heart-y" cross-curricular activities!

1 Celebrate Kindness!

Help students start each day of this holiday week with kind thoughts. Before school, post a quote about being kind, such as one of those shown. Then have students copy the quote in their journals and write about what the words mean to them.

- "The man who treasures his friends is usually solid gold himself." –*Marjorie Holmes*
- "No act of kindness, no matter how small, is ever wasted." –*Aesop*
- "Great persons are able to do great kindnesses." –*Miguel de Cervantes*
- "What wisdom can you find that is greater than kindness?" –*Jean Jacques Rousseau*

2 Declare Red-Hot Writing Day!

Have students use red pens and pencils to complete their work all day. They'll love it!

3 Give It a Scientific Twist!

Have your students create science-themed valentines that reinforce important science vocabulary! Provide access to construction paper and markers. Next, explain that each student will create a Valentine's Day card that incorporates a science term. Then post a rubric such as the one shown. As each student finishes his card, use a copy of the rubric to quickly grade it. Give each child his graded rubric and then post his work on a board titled "Putting Our Hearts Into Science." *Anne Rath, Seven Springs Middle School, New Port Richey, FL*

Science-Themed Valentine Rubric	
The card has a creative science and Valentine's Day theme.	10 points
The science term is correctly spelled.	5 points
The card clearly shows the term's meaning.	10 points
The card has no errors.	5 points
Total points possible	30 points

4 Send Students on a Word Hunt!

Write commonly overused emotion words—such as *like, good, happy, glad, mad,* or *sad*—on separate construction paper hearts. Post the words on a board titled "Using Heartfelt Words." Then challenge each pair of students to find another way to describe each emotion. When students finish, have each duo read its alternatives. Record the unique and descriptive terms around the matching heart. *Karen Slattery, Dunrankin Drive Public School, Mississauga, Ontario, Canada*

5 Do Some Sweet Math!

Give each student ten or more conversation hearts and display a color code like the one shown. Next, have each child draw a diagram that shows the number and colors of her candy hearts. Then guide each student to write five probability questions about her candy sample. Have the child write the answers on the back of her paper. As time allows, have students trade their work with partners and use the diagrams to answer the questions. *Jennifer Otter, Oak Ridge, NC*

Color Code
purple = P
yellow = Y
pink = PK
green = G
white = W
orange = O

1 Popping In

Give students something to look forward to every day! Blow up a few balloons. Inside each one, place a message that will make the next day special. Then, at the end of each day, have a student who exhibited great behavior pop a balloon and read aloud the message inside.

Tomorrow is Team Day! Wear a T-shirt with your favorite team's colors!

Gimme-a-Break Day!—Enjoy ten extra minutes of recess tomorrow!

2 Picnic Weather

Say goodbye to another school year with a picnic in the schoolyard or a nearby park. If the weather gets in the way, no problem! Just cut out a large sun from yellow bulletin board paper and hang it in your classroom. Then have students spread beach towels or blankets on the floor, put on sunglasses and caps, and enjoy their picnic lunches inside!

3 A Few Words

Put restless students to work creating a display for next year's students. Have each child create a self-portrait on construction paper and cut it out. Next, have the student cut out a speech bubble and write a message on it for next year's students. The message can be advice about how to be successful or a hint about what students will learn. Then post students' work on a back-to-school display titled "A Few Words From Former Students."

4 Summer Correspondence

Encourage students to keep in touch the old-fashioned way! First, have each student staple together five index cards to make an address book and collect classmates' addresses. Then set aside time and have each student write a letter to a classmate. Next, have the child put his letter in an envelope and address it. Then collect students' envelopes, jot quick notes to any students who might not have received letters, add stamps, and mail the letters a week after school is out.

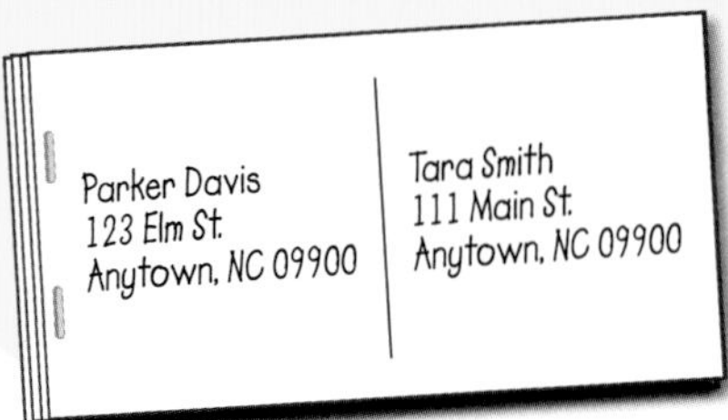

5 Purposeful Posts

For this idea, have each student bring in two stamps and two envelopes. Also collect the names and addresses of companies and organizations that send free materials to children. Then have each student choose a company and guide her to write a letter requesting materials. Have the child enclose a self-addressed, stamped envelope with her letter and mail it before school is out. Your students will love receiving the requested materials during their summer vacations, and they'll learn something about the power of the written word!

SCIENCE

simple machines, lever, fulcrum

At This Point

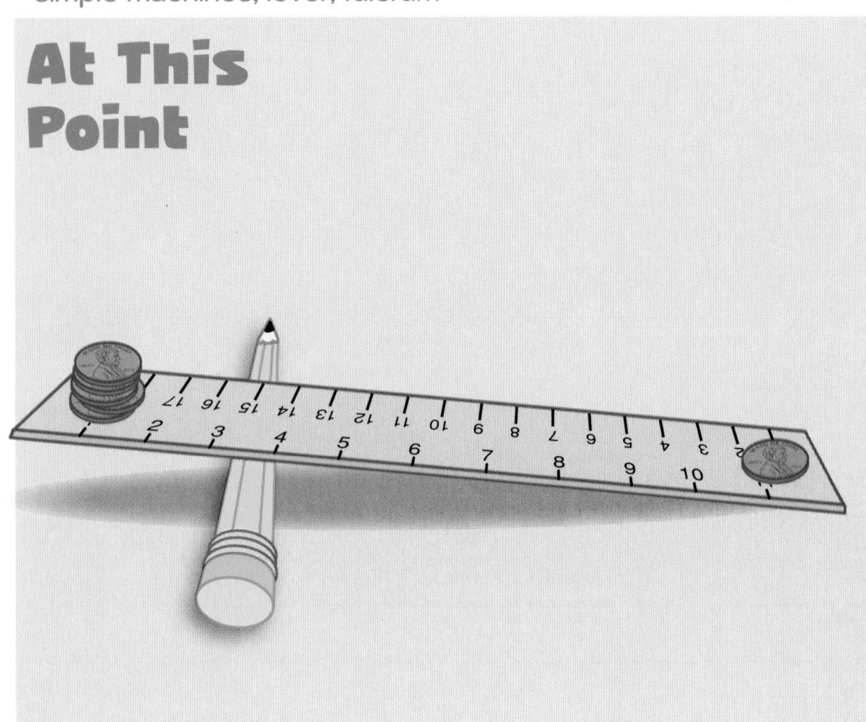

Help students explore a lever's physics with this hands-on center. Stock the center with 20 pennies, a ruler, a pencil, and tape. To make the lever, have the student tape the pencil (the fulcrum) to the underside of the ruler. Next, have her stack five pennies (the load) on one of the ruler's ends. Then have the child stack pennies on the ruler's opposite end until the number of pennies (the force) is great enough to lift the load. Have the student explore the effects of fulcrum placement by moving and taping the pencil five times to different spots along the ruler's length. Have the student record each placement and the force (number of pennies) it took to lift the load. Then guide the child to describe the exploration and draw a conclusion about a lever's fulcrum placement.

density, scientific method

On the Level

Inquiry's the name of the game with this exploration. Review with students the definition of *density* and then provide each small group with the materials listed. Next, challenge each group to decide which liquids are most dense and arrange them in order from most dense to least. Then have the students pour their liquids into a bottle in the order they've predicted. Guide each student to record his group's hypothesis and process as the liquids in the bottle settle. Once the liquids separate, have each group compare its hypothesis with its results. Then have each child record and describe the results.

¼ c. corn syrup tinted with food color
¼ c. vegetable oil
¼ c. liquid dish soap
¼ c. water tinted with a different food color
empty water bottle

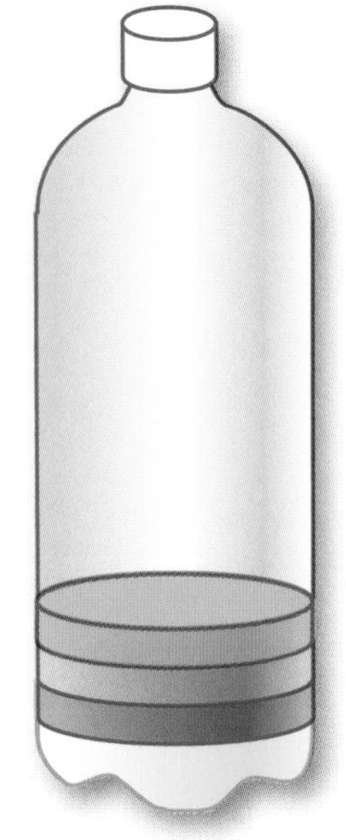

"On the Level" extension

To extend the exploration, provide each small group with small objects, such as a paper clip, piece of pasta, marble, popcorn kernel, or dried bean. Next, have the students predict which small objects are the densest and arrange them in order. Have each child record his group's hypothesis. Then have the students take turns gently dropping each object into their bottle. As the objects settle, have the students describe the process and then the results.

research, scientific and technological changes

Breakfast of Thinkers

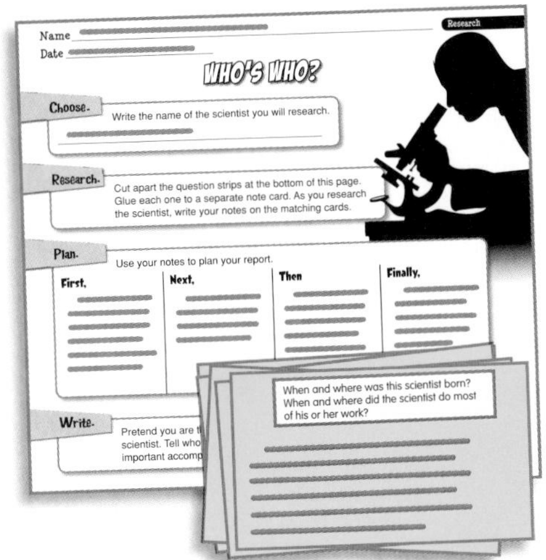

Here's a project that helps students connect with their research subjects. In advance, set a date for a morning science lesson and ask parent volunteers to provide simple breakfast foods—such as bagels, juice, and fruit—on that day. Next, announce that each child will research a scientist and then attend a breakfast as the scientist. Display the list at the bottom of this page and have each student choose a different scientist. Then have each child research and write about a scientist as guided on a copy of page 228.

On the morning of the breakfast, have students arrange their desks in rows that resemble banquet tables. Also have each child create a nametag and a placard for the scientist he researched. Then challenge each student to pretend to be the scientist throughout the breakfast. Intersperse the breakfast with students' reports, reminding students to maintain their scientific roles as they read and listen. adapted from an idea by Norma Garrett, Twin Oaks Elementary, Leesburg, GA

life cycles

My Life in the Round

To introduce this important topic, name the main stages in a human's life cycle *(infancy, childhood, adolescence, and adulthood)*. Then have each child draw a life cycle diagram that features sketches of herself at each of the stages. Next, have each child make an x on her diagram to show where she is in her life cycle. Post students' work on a board titled "Student Life Cycles." Then, as students explore other animal and plant life cycles, have them draw diagrams to illustrate those too.

SCIENTIST WHO'S WHO

Antoine Henri Becquerel	Sir Alexander Fleming	Lynn Margulis	Ernst Ruska
Niels Bohr	Robert Goddard	Matthew Fontaine Maury	Jonas Salk
Marie Curie	Alexander Graham Bell	Barbara McClintock	Matthias Jakob Schleiden
John Dalton	Robert Hooke	Gregor Mendel	Theodor Schwann
Charles Darwin	Anton van Leeuwenhoek	Luc Montagnier	Eugene Shoemaker
Thomas Edison	Otto Lilienthal	Sir Isaac Newton	Daniel Hale Williams
Albert Einstein	Joseph Lister	Louis Pasteur	Jane Wright
Enrico Fermi	Wangari Maathai	Joseph Priestley	Orville and Wilbur Wright

Note to the teacher: Use with "Breakfast of Thinkers" on this page.

Name ____________________

Date ____________________

WHO'S WHO?

Choose.

Write the name of the scientist you will research.

____

Research.

Cut apart the question strips at the bottom of this page. Glue each one to a separate note card. As you research the scientist, write your notes on the matching cards.

Plan.

Use your notes to plan your report.

First,	Next,	Then	Finally,

Write.

Pretend you are the scientist. Write a story from your point of view as the scientist. Tell who you are, why you became a scientist, and what your most important accomplishment was. Then describe how this accomplishment affected others.

When and where was this scientist born? When and where did the scientist do most of his or her work?	What is the scientist's most important accomplishment? Describe it.
What was this scientist like? What was he or she curious about? Why did he or she become a scientist?	How have the scientist's accomplishments affected others?
What problem was the scientist trying to solve and why? What did he or she do to solve the problem?	Which resource or resources did you use?

Note to the teacher: Use with "Breakfast of Thinkers" on page 227. Students will need access to research materials and six index cards.

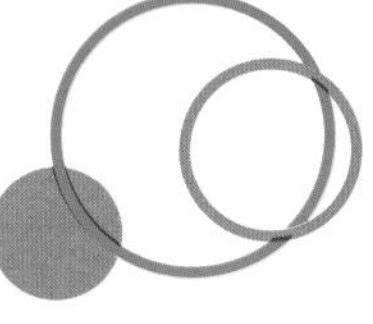

health, using data

Fast Food Figures

With this exploration, students analyze the nutritional value of their favorite fast foods. Begin by displaying a fast food restaurant's online menu. Have each student plan a lunch of up to four items from the menu and record her choices on a copy of page 231. Then display the restaurant's online nutrition information and guide students to record each item's nutritional values in Table 1 on her page. Next, guide each child to compare her lunch's nutritional totals with the recommended daily values by completing Table 2. After students complete the activity, lead them to discuss their work with questions such as those shown.

LaVone Novotny, Liberty Elementary, Caledonia, OH

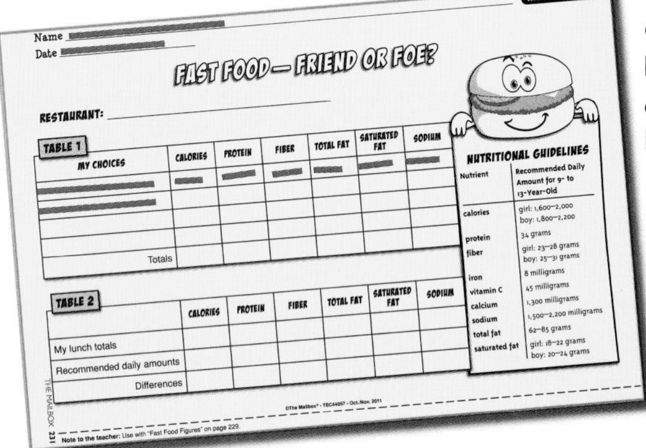

Health, using data

Name

Date

FAST FOOD—FRIEND OR FOE?

RESTAURANT:

TABLE 1

MY CHOICES	CALORIES	PROTEIN	FIBER	TOTAL FAT	SATURATED FAT	SODIUM
Totals						

TABLE 2

	CALORIES	PROTEIN	FIBER	TOTAL FAT	SATURATED FAT	SODIUM
My lunch totals						
Recommended daily amounts						
Differences						

NUTRITIONAL GUIDELINES

Nutrient	Recommended Daily Amount for 9- to 13-Year-Old
calories	girl: 1,600–2,000 boy: 1,800–2,200
protein	34 grams
fiber	girl: 23–28 grams boy: 25–31 grams
iron	8 milligrams
vitamin C	45 milligrams
calcium	1,300 milligrams
sodium	1,500–2,200 milligrams
total fat	62–85 grams
saturated fat	girl: 18–22 grams boy: 20–24 grams

©The Mailbox® • TEC44057 • Oct./Nov. 2011

THE MAILBOX 231

Note to the teacher: Use with "Fast Food Figures" on page 229.

- Imagine you have a breakfast of oatmeal, fruit, and milk. You have 350 calories, 13 grams of protein, 5 grams of fiber, 7 grams of total fat, 3.5 grams of saturated fat, and 240 mg of sodium.
  - Combine this breakfast with the lunch you planned. To stay within the values on the chart, about how much fiber should you have at your next two meals?
  - Compare your lunch totals with the breakfast data. Which meal is more nutritious?

classifying organisms

Mystery Life Forms

Give students hands-on, minds-on practice classifying organisms. First, provide access to craft materials and have each child create an organism no one has ever seen before. After he creates his critter, have the student classify it according to categories such as those shown. Then have the child give his critter a scientific-sounding name and record its characteristics on an index card. **To extend the activity**, have students sort their organisms into subgroups according to the critters' features.

- Is it a vertebrate or an invertebrate?
- Is it warm-blooded or cold-blooded?
- Does it have fur or feathers?
- Is it a carnivore or an herbivore?

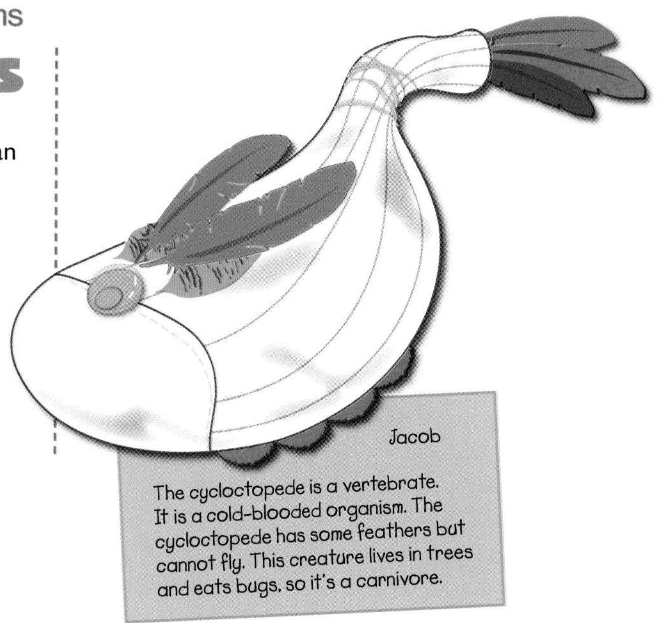

Jacob

The cycloctopede is a vertebrate. It is a cold-blooded organism. The cycloctopede has some feathers but cannot fly. This creature lives in trees and eats bugs, so it's a carnivore.

vocabulary

A Stand-up Game Show

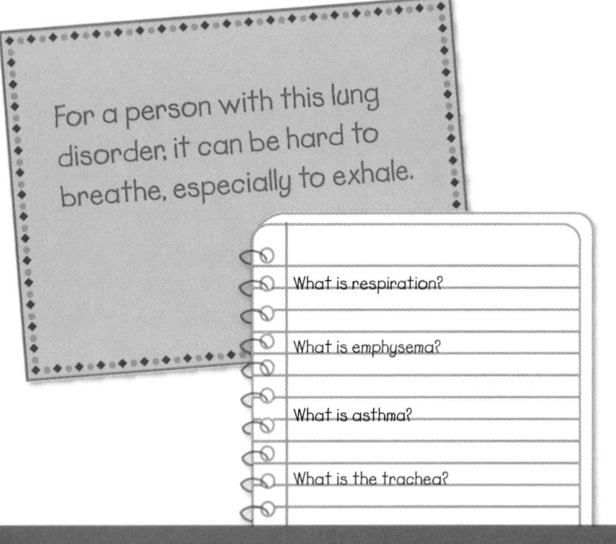

For this interactive review, post a list of ten or more vocabulary terms from a current unit of study. On separate sheets of paper, write each term's definition in the form of a Jeopardy! game show clue. Then post the clues around your room. Next, have each student record the vocabulary terms as questions, leaving space to fill in the matching clues. Set aside time for students to walk around the room, finding and recording the clues that match their terms. Follow up by reading each clue aloud and having students name the matching terms—as questions, of course! **Marciava Stovall, West Hoke Middle School, Raeford, NC**

nature of science

On the Cutting Edge

Keep yourself and your students up-to-date with this simple center idea. Stock the center with recent newspapers, surplus magazines, a binder, scissors, lined paper, and glue. At the center, a pair of students looks for an article about a recent scientific development. When the partners find an article, they read it. Then they cut it out, glue it to a sheet of paper, list the article's source and topic, and then summarize the news in a short paragraph before adding their work to the binder. Periodically, review the articles in the binder, having pairs share their work and discuss its implications with the class.

water cycle

All Wet

Guide students to explore the water cycle by having them pretend to tag and then track a water droplet as if they were studying an endangered animal. Have each small group of students draw a water droplet and give it a numbered tag. Then guide the group to create a log of their droplet's journey through the water cycle. Post vocabulary terms each group should include and encourage students to write vivid stories about the droplet's journey in their logs. Have each group share its work and then post it on a board titled "All Wet: Tracking the Water Cycle." **LaVone Novotny, Liberty Elementary, Caledonia, OH**

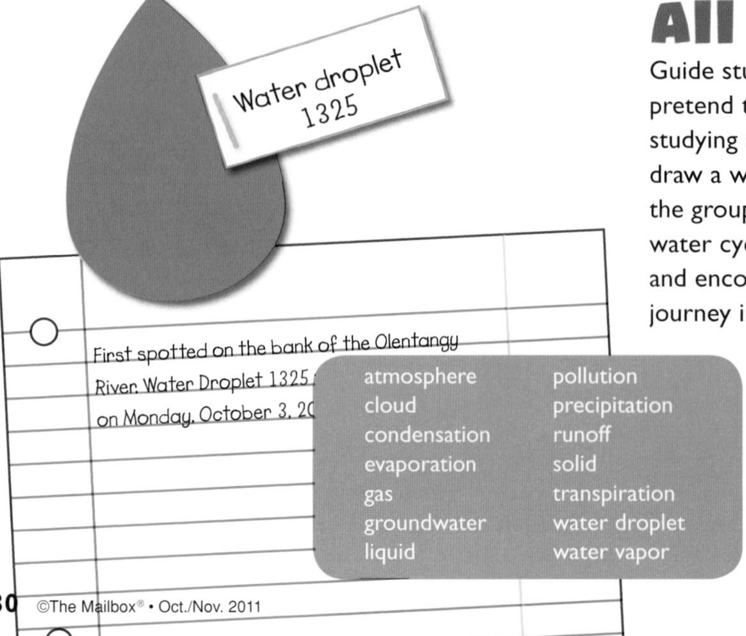

atmosphere	pollution
cloud	precipitation
condensation	runoff
evaporation	solid
gas	transpiration
groundwater	water droplet
liquid	water vapor

Grab students' interest by sharing a short article or video clip about scientists tagging and tracking an endangered animal, such as a whale or shark.

Name ______________________

Date ______________

FAST FOOD—FRIEND OR FOE?

RESTAURANT: ______________________

TABLE 1

MY CHOICES	CALORIES	PROTEIN	FIBER	TOTAL FAT	SATURATED FAT	SODIUM
Totals						

TABLE 2

	CALORIES	PROTEIN	FIBER	TOTAL FAT	SATURATED FAT	SODIUM
My lunch totals						
Recommended daily amounts						
Differences						

NUTRITIONAL GUIDELINES

Nutrient	Recommended Daily Amount for 9- to 13-Year-Old
calories	girl: 1,600–2,000 boy: 1,800–2,200
protein	34 grams
fiber	girl: 23–28 grams boy: 25–31 grams
iron	8 milligrams
vitamin C	45 milligrams
calcium	1,300 milligrams
sodium	1,500–2,200 milligrams
total fat	62–85 grams
saturated fat	girl: 18–22 grams boy: 20–24 grams

Note to the teacher: Use with "Fast Food Figures" on page 229.

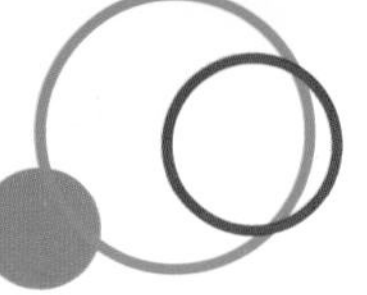

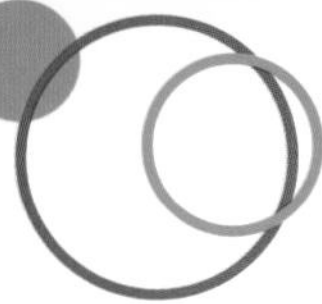
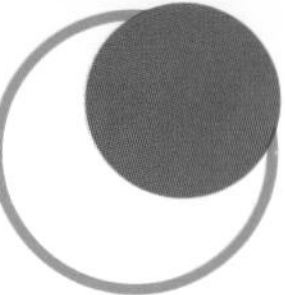

elements and compounds

Sweet Combinations

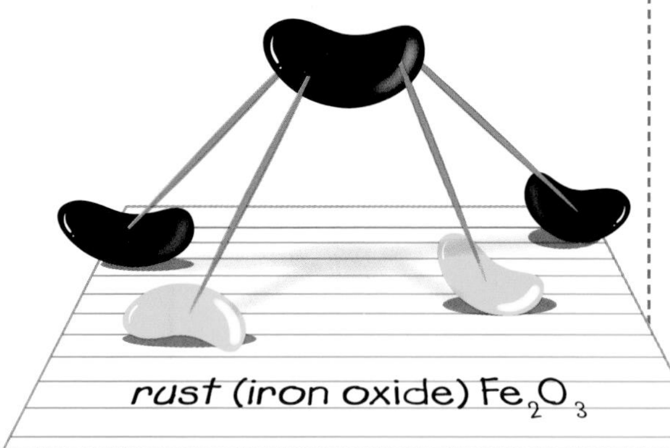

Here's a sweet introduction to chemical compounds. In advance, purchase a bag of jelly beans for every six students. Next, show students examples of common compounds. Explain that each compound is made up of the atoms of two or more chemical elements and display the chemical names from a copy of the top of page 233. Then introduce the color code for the chemical elements, pass out jelly beans and toothpicks, and guide the students in each group to assemble one molecule of each compound. **LaVone Novotny, Liberty Elementary, Caledonia, OH**

Color Code

H = red
O = black
Cl = white
Na = purple
C = orange
Fe = yellow
N = green

electric series circuit

Keep 'em Current!

Want to help students understand simple circuits? Try this! First, have each group of six students cut apart the labels on a copy of the bottom half of page 233, setting one card labeled "wire" aside. Next, have each student tape a label to her shirt. Then guide students to arrange themselves in a series circuit, as shown, holding hands to signify the wire. Have each child wearing "lightbulb B" drop her hands as if the bulb were removed from the circuit. Lead students to recognize that the circuit to both lightbulbs has been broken and neither one will be lit. Follow up by having each student cut apart the cards on the top half of a copy of page 234 and arrange them to diagram a complete series circuit. Finally, have the child glue her completed diagram in her journal and describe a series circuit and when it will or won't work.

To extend the activity, have students work in groups of seven using all the labels to create a parallel circuit. Next, have the student labeled "lightbulb B" drop her hands. Then guide students to understand that the circuit is not broken and electricity will still flow to the remaining bulb. Follow up by having each student cut apart the cards on a copy of the bottom half of page 234 and arrange them to diagram a complete parallel circuit. **LaVone Novotny**

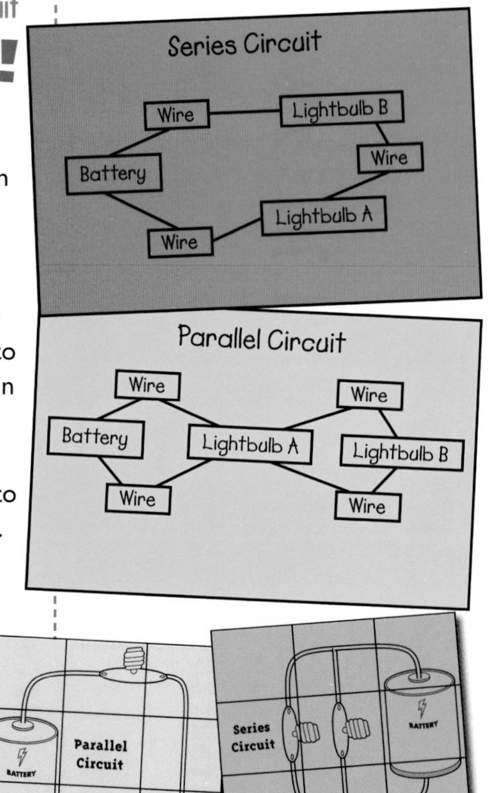

Compound and Element Names

Use with "Sweet Combinations" on page 232.

Chemical Element	Chemical Symbol
hydrogen	H
oxygen	O
chlorine	Cl
sodium	Na
carbon	C
iron	Fe
nitrogen	N

Compound Name	Formula	Common Name
water	H_2O	water
sodium chloride	$ClNa$	salt
carbon dioxide	CO_2	carbon dioxide
iron oxide	Fe_2O_3	rust
nitrous oxide	N_2O	laughing gas
hydrogen peroxide	H_2O_2	hydrogen peroxide
benzoic acid	$C_9H_8O_4$	aspirin
acetaminophen	$C_8H_9NO_2$	Tylenol pain reliever

Circuit Labels

Use with "Keep 'em Current!" on page 232.

battery	wire
wire	lightbulb A
wire	lightbulb B
wire	

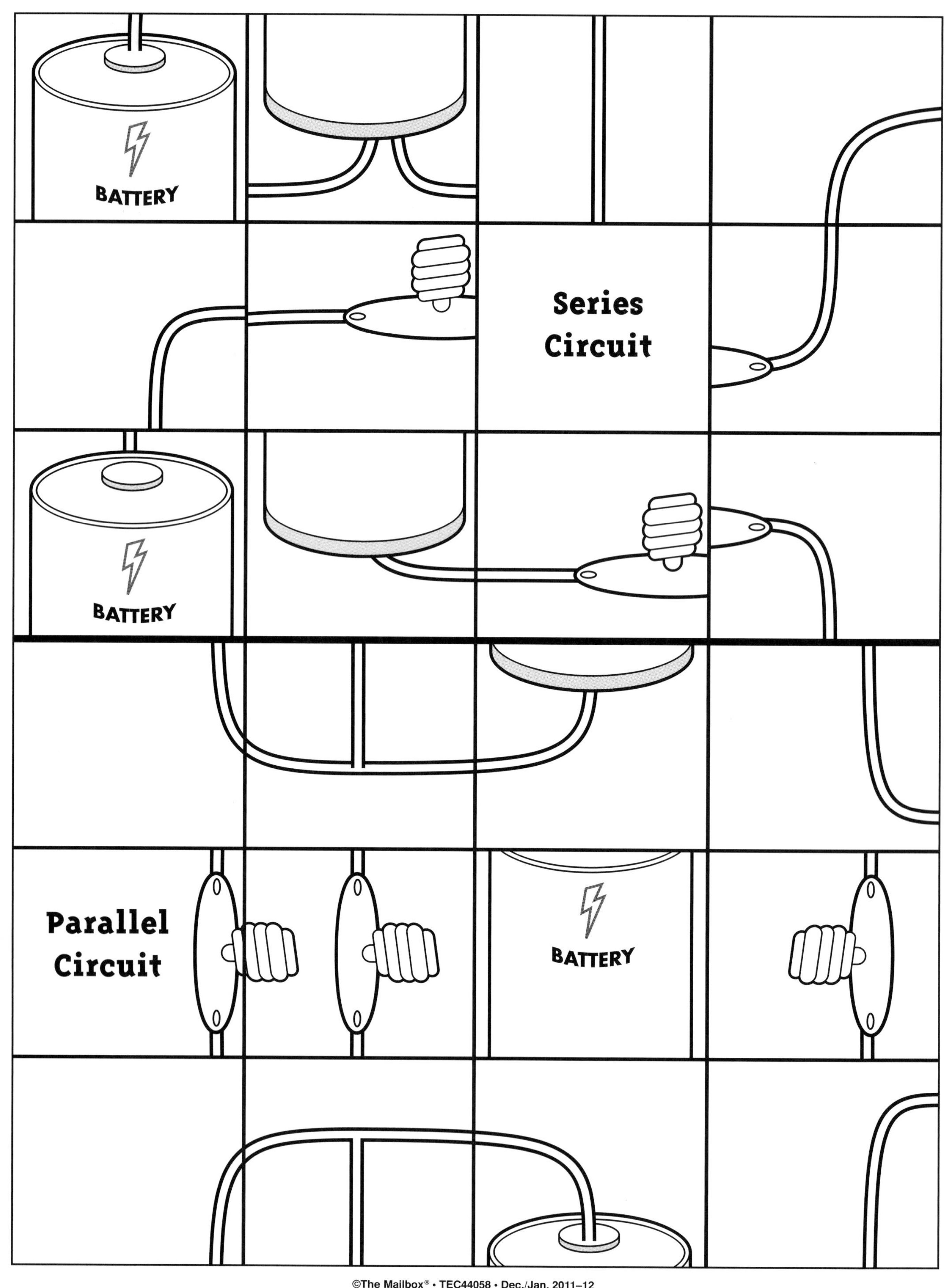

 Note to the teacher: Use with "Keep 'em Current!" on page 232. (Some cards will not be used.)

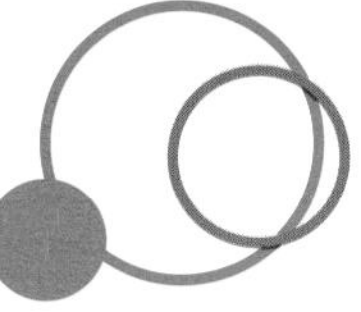

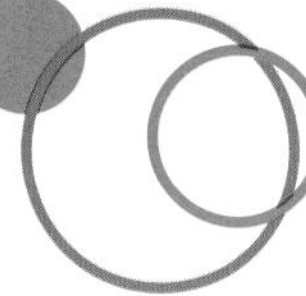
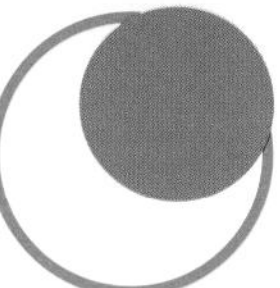

Properties of matter

A Sensory Examination

For this hands-on exploration, gather edible items, such as ice cubes, water, baby carrots, snack-size cups of flavored gelatin, soda, or fish-shaped snack crackers. Next, have each student make a chart on her paper with the categories shown. Then give each child a sample of one item and guide her to examine the example and describe its properties on her chart, making sure she doesn't ingest it before filling in each column. Encourage students to judge each item's density by comparing it to the density of an ice cube. Repeat with additional items. Then guide students to describe the similarities and differences they noticed and categorize each item as a solid, liquid, or gas.

Item	Color	Shape	Texture	Density Compared to an Ice Cube	Smell	Taste	State of Matter
ice cube	clear	oblong with a straight edge	smooth, like glass	very dense	no smell	no taste	solid
classroom air							

Sound, listening

Do You Hear...?

Help students put a scientific slant on listening. First, have students list noises they hear at school and in the classroom. Next, have students sit perfectly quiet for one full minute, listening for every sound. Then guide each child to list all the sounds he heard during the quiet minute. After that, have each student complete a Venn diagram that compares the two lists of sounds. Discuss with students reasons they heard different things and follow up by having each child repeat the activity at home.

Sedimentary and metamorphic rocks

S'mores Science

This tasty idea is sure to help students remember how different kinds of rocks are formed. Gather s'mores ingredients for your class and then guide each student to follow the steps shown. Follow up with a class discussion while students devour their rock models! **Mattie Jacobs, Golden Oak Elementary, Shafter, CA, and Vanessa Lepore, Lincoln Edison Elementary, North Las Vegas, NV**

Materials for each student: graham cracker square, 5 mini marshmallows, 2 T milk chocolate chips, plastic resealable bag

Steps:

1. Put a graham cracker square in a plastic bag and crush it, using the heel of your palm. Then add five mini marshmallows and two tablespoons of milk chocolate chips.
2. Seal the bag and gently shake it so the ingredients settle at the bottom. This mimics the settling of minerals that creates sedimentary rock. Describe your sedimentary rock model and then draw a diagram that explains how sedimentary rock is formed.
3. Hold your sedimentary parent rock between both hands for at least two minutes, gently pressing your hands against the bag. This mimics heat and pressure causing changes in a parent rock to create a metamorphic rock.
4. Study your metamorphic rock. Describe your rock model and then draw a diagram that explains how metamorphic rock is formed.
5. Research igneous rocks to find out how they are formed. Then draw a diagram that explains the formation.

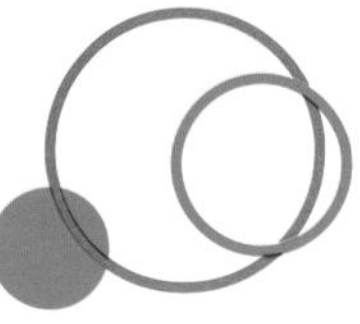

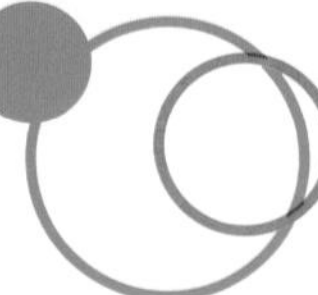

earth science, erosion

Natural Beauties

For this research project, have each child choose a natural landmark that was sculpted by weathering, such as one of those shown. Next, have the student research the landmark and identify the type or types of weathering that created it. Then guide the student to create a diagram that shows how the feature was formed and explain the process. Post students' work on a board titled "Erosion as Sculptor." **Jennifer Otter, Oak Ridge, NC**

Grand Canyon National Park
Badlands National Park
Garden of the Gods
Arches National Park
Bryce Canyon National Park
White Sands National Monument

matter

Grin and Find It

Here's an engaging activity on the properties and common forms of matter. In advance, collect the comic section from several Sunday newspapers so you have a page for each small group of students. Next, post and review vocabulary terms, such as those shown. Then give each group a page of comics and challenge the students to identify ten or more liquids, solids, and gases pictured on their page. Have the students in the group use the posted vocabulary to describe each item's physical properties. **Jennifer Otter**

color	physical properties
definite	shape
density	size
gas	solid
liquid	state
mass	volume
matter	weight

weather, wind

When the Wind Blows

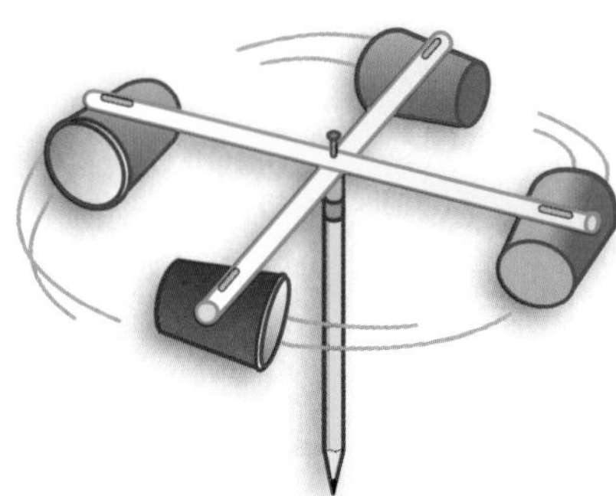

Give each pair of students the materials listed below and have them follow the directions to make a simple anemometer. Next, have each pair of students take its anemometer to a different spot on the playground. Then guide the partners to take turns holding their anemometer at arm's length and counting the number of times the different-colored cup goes around in one minute. Have each pair record its results and repeat the measurements at the same place and time each day for a week. Follow up by having students graph their results, compare them with other students' results, and then draw conclusions about the wind on your playground.

Materials for each pair of students: 2 drinking straws, pencil with its eraser, four 3-ounce disposable cups (3 matching and 1 of another color or design), straight pin, access to a stapler, stopwatch or watch with a second hand

Steps:

1. Cross the two drinking straws so they create four 90° angles. Then push the pin through the center of the straws and into the top of the pencil eraser.
2. Staple one cup onto each end of each straw. Be sure the open ends of the cups face the same direction.
3. Hold the pencil upright and position the cups about one foot from your face. Blow toward the open end of the cups to make sure the cups will spin in a breeze.
4. To measure the wind speed, count the number of times the different cup goes around in one minute.

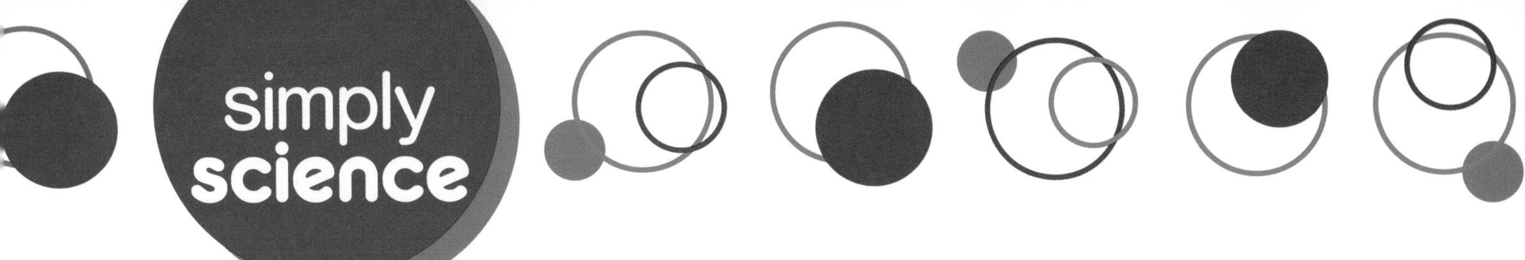

vocabulary

That's a Wrap!

Here's a great idea for an end-of-the-unit, end-of-the-semester, or even end-of-the-year review. Have each student create a glossary of science terms, trying to include a term that begins with each letter of the alphabet. Give each student a one-foot by three-foot strip of bulletin board paper for her science vocabulary scroll. Next, have the child divide her scroll into 26 sections and then write each science term and its definition in the appropriate section. Award bonus points to the child who fills all her sections (if possible) and includes the unit's important terms. Then have each student roll up her scroll and take it home as a great study tool! **Donna Jeffress, Linden Avenue Middle School, Red Hook, NY**

A
acid rain

B
biome

C
chlorophyll
climate

D

solar system

Planetary Promotion

For this activity, have each student choose and research a different planet. To share his research, have the child create a travel agent character who advertises the planet as an ideal vacation destination, including pictures and persuasive facts about the planet. The student may design a web page for the character's travel agency, write the script for an infomercial starring the character, or create a pamphlet from the character's travel agency. After students complete their projects, set aside time for them to share their work. **Laura Kegan Gallion, Christ Central Academy, Pikeville, KY**

scientific method

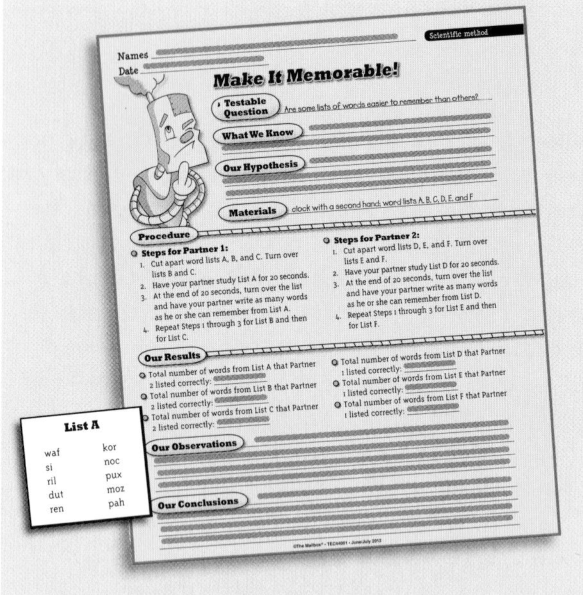

Make It Memorable!

Introduce this memory experiment by having students think about what makes information easy or difficult to remember. In the test, each student will try to remember as many words from three different lists of words as he can, but the words on the lists will be related in different ways. To begin, give each pair of students a copy of the word lists at the bottom of this page and a copy of page 239. Next, have the partners follow the steps on page 239 to test their memories and practice following the scientific method. When students finish their experiments, have them share their results and conclusions in a class discussion.

Word Lists

Use with "Make It Memorable!" on this page.

List A

waf	kor
si	noc
ril	pux
dut	moz
ren	pah

©TEC44061

List B

bat	ball
tag	run
field	base
dodge	grass
fence	play

©TEC44061

List C

bikes	ride
better	when
their	tires
are	full
of	air

©TEC44061

List D

sar	kur
fi	cew
lih	zof
ba	moz
ren	pah

©TEC44061

List E

water	ocean
sand	wave
splash	surf
jump	dive
swim	pool

©TEC44061

List F

good	books
are	like
good	friends
you	can
take	everywhere

©TEC44061

Names ______________________________

Date ______________________

Make It Memorable!

Testable Question Are some lists of words easier to remember than others?

What We Know ______________________________

Our Hypothesis ______________________________

Materials clock with a second hand; word lists A, B, C, D, E, and F

Procedure

Steps for Partner 1:

1. Cut apart word lists A, B, and C. Turn over lists B and C.
2. Have your partner study List A for 20 seconds.
3. At the end of 20 seconds, turn over the list and have your partner write as many words as he or she can remember from List A.
4. Repeat Steps 1 through 3 for List B and then for List C.

Steps for Partner 2:

1. Cut apart word lists D, E, and F. Turn over lists E and F.
2. Have your partner study List D for 20 seconds.
3. At the end of 20 seconds, turn over the list and have your partner write as many words as he or she can remember from List D.
4. Repeat Steps 1 through 3 for List E and then for List F.

Our Results

- Total number of words from List A that Partner 2 listed correctly: __________
- Total number of words from List B that Partner 2 listed correctly: __________
- Total number of words from List C that Partner 2 listed correctly: __________
- Total number of words from List D that Partner 1 listed correctly: __________
- Total number of words from List E that Partner 1 listed correctly: __________
- Total number of words from List F that Partner 1 listed correctly: __________

Our Observations

____

Our Conclusions

____

Note to the teacher: Use with "Make It Memorable!" on page 238.

Name ____________________________________

Date ____________________________

Life science, food chains, ecosystems

Pick and Practice

Pick _____ activities to do.

When you finish an activity, color its number.

1 Make an eye-catching poster that illustrates a complete **food chain**. Use pictures of plants and animals from old magazines. If you can't find an important animal or plant that completes the chain, draw it.

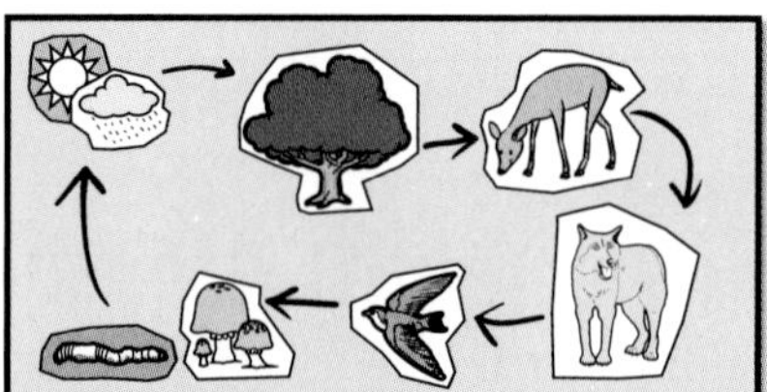

2 Choose an animal. Then write a story from that animal's perspective about life in its food chain. In your story, write about your **predators** and how you avoid them. Also write about the animals or plants that you eat. Describe your **habitat** and the challenges you face finding enough food.

3 Choose an **ecosystem** and identify its main elements—**the sun**, **nonliving parts**, **primary producers**, **primary consumers**, **secondary consumers**, and **decomposers**. Next, illustrate each element on a $2\frac{1}{4}$" x 12" construction paper strip. Then staple the strips together to make a chain that shows how the elements interact.

4 Invent an animal. Then create a shoebox diorama that shows the creature's **niche** in its habitat. On the outside of the box, illustrate the creature's life cycle and its food chain.

5 Imagine you are a scientist who discovers a new insect **species**. This insect seems to live on a diet of ants. You bring 20 of the insects back to your lab to study. However, they escape on their first night in your lab. How does this insect species affect the **ecosystem** around your community? Write six journal entries from your point of view as a scientist about what happens.

6 Choose a major city in your state. Research the city's history to find events that have changed the city's **environment**, such as land clearing, road building, or construction. Then make a timeline that describes ten or more of these major events and how they affected the environment.

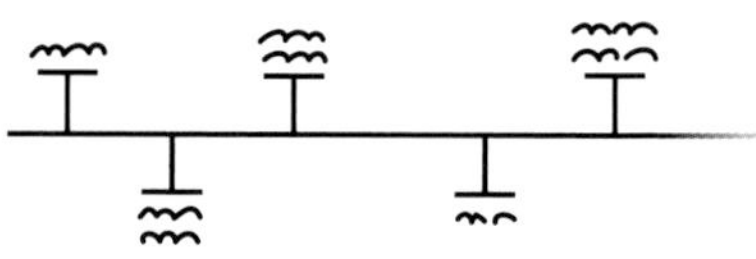

7 Choose an animal that is **endangered**, such as one of those shown. Create a presentation (a speech to the class or a digital presentation) that describes the animal, its habitat, and its food chain. Next, explain why the animal is in danger. Then suggest three actions that can be taken to help save the animal from **extinction**.

American crocodile

black-footed ferret

California condor

red wolf

8 Make a four-column table like the one shown. Then research ten **decomposers** and record facts about each **organism** in the table.

Decomposer	Type (Scavenger or Decomposer)	Type of Matter It Breaks Down	How It Affects Its Ecosystem

9 Arrange the boldfaced terms on this page in alphabetical order. Next, pick ten terms, record each one's definition, and then draw an illustration or diagram to explain or give an example of each term.

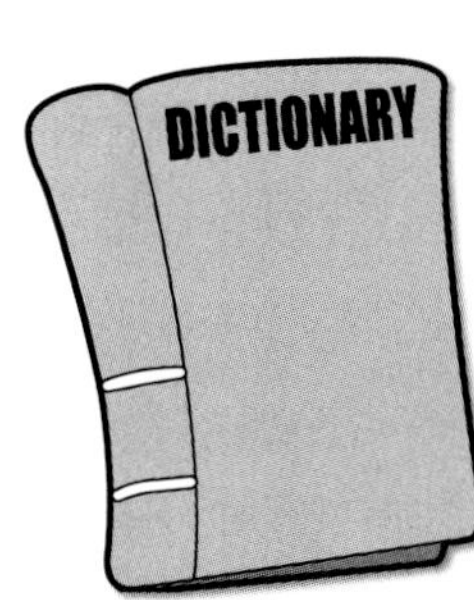

Independent practice grid: Program the student directions on a copy of this page with the number of activities to be completed. Then copy the page for each student.

Name ______________________________

Date ______________________________

Pick and Practice

Weather!

Pick _____ activities to do.
When you finish an activity, color its number.

1 Write five or more paragraphs that describe a thunderstorm you have experienced. Tell how it began, what it was like, what you did during the storm, how it ended, and what happened afterward.

2 Find out how tropical storms and hurricanes are named. Create a picture book of six or more pages that explains the process.

A Storm Named Alice

3 Use an almanac to find states that tornadoes tend to hit most. Draw a map of the United States and color each state in Tornado Alley.

Almanac

4 Fold a sheet of paper in half three times to create eight sections. Then cut the sections apart and staple them together to create a booklet of weather map symbols. On each page, draw the symbol for and define one of the following terms.

cold front	stationary front
dry line	low pressure system
occluded front	high pressure system
squall line	warm front

5 Research the warning signs of a tornado. Make a chart listing the warning signs and explaining the precautions people should take before a tornado strikes.

Warning!

6 If a severe storm warning were issued while you were at school, what would you do? Find out from your principal what your school's safety guidelines are. Create a mini poster about the guidelines that can be copied and shared with other classes.

7 Write an acrostic poem for three of the following stormy words.

rain	**twister**
hail	**wind**
lightning	**clouds**
storm	**thunder**

8 Arrange the facts shown in order of importance. Then use the facts to write a paragraph about hurricanes.

- get weaker as they move over land
- begin over a warm sea
- strongest winds and heaviest rains surround their centers
- form where sea temperatures are 82°F or higher
- winds swirl around the eye

9 Arrange the facts shown in order of importance. Then use the facts to write a paragraph about tornadoes.

- also called *twisters*
- occur mostly in spring or early summer
- have the most violent of all winds
- can form in minutes
- can form with no warning
- centers are like vacuums
- called *waterspouts* when they form over lakes or oceans

Independent practice grid: Program the student directions on a copy of this page with the number of activities to be completed. Then copy the page for each student.

Thought Stretchers

SCIENCE

Stretcher 1

The circuit diagrams below will not work. For each one, draw a diagram that shows the correct circuit.

Stretcher 2

Imagine you are a scientist being sent to the International Space Station. Plan an experiment with plants you might conduct in a weightless environment. Write a question, a hypothesis, and a description of what you would do.

Stretcher 3

Draw and label a diagram that shows the water cycle and includes the terms shown.

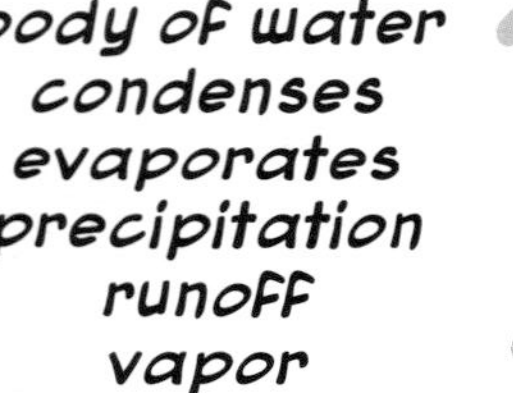

body of water
condenses
evaporates
precipitation
runoff
vapor

Stretcher 4

Choose an imaginary animal. Draw a diagram of its life cycle. Then draw a food web that shows the creature's role.

Stretcher 5

Make a three-column chart labeled as shown. Then sort the terms below into the appropriate columns. (One term will be used two times.)

Circulatory System	Respiratory System	Digestive System

arteries
blood vessels
diaphragm
esophagus
heart
large intestine
liver
lungs
mouth
nose
small intestine
stomach
trachea
veins

Stretcher 6

Make a list of every item you've used today that depends on electricity. Then make a list of every item you've used today that does not depend on electricity.

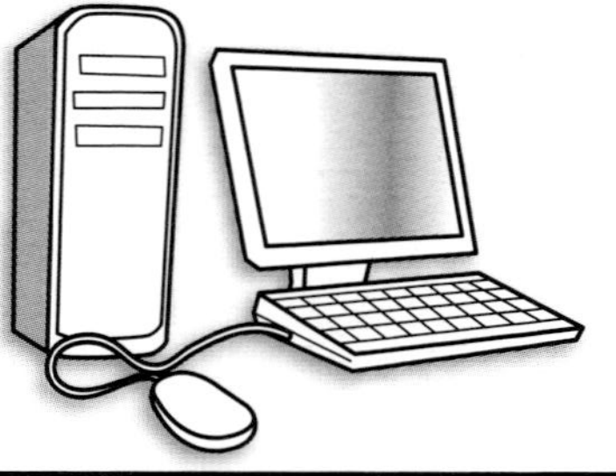

Stretcher 7

Which of the following endangered species are native to the United States?

American crocodile
Asian elephant
Asiatic lion
black-footed ferret
black rhinoceros
California condor
cheetah
Devils Hole pupfish
giant panda
imperial parrot
orangutan
red wolf
snow leopard
tiger

Stretcher 8

What would be the best way to fill a balloon with carbon dioxide? Draw a Venn diagram to compare a carbon dioxide–filled balloon with a helium-filled balloon.

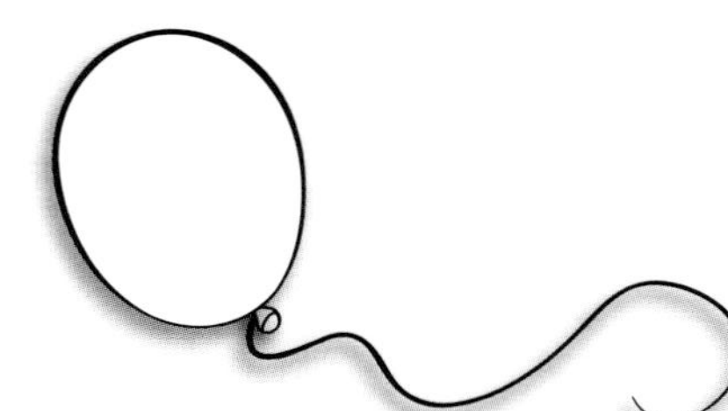

How to use: Display this page or give each student a copy of the page (or one card at a time) to work on during free time.

Social Studies

EXPLORING Social Studies

Rhinestone Roundup

Map skills, latitude, longitude

Here's a partner game that provides hands-on practice reading lines of latitude and longitude. Give each pair of students a copy of page 245, two paper clips, and different-color pencils. Then have the duo follow the steps on the page to play.

Carol Lawrence, Madera, CA

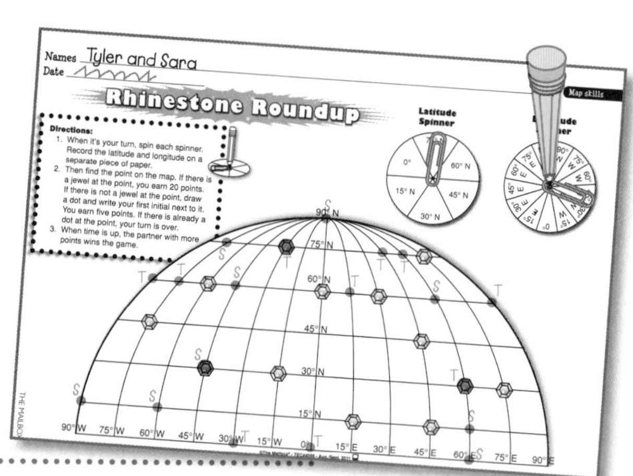

Names Tyler and Sara
Date

Rhinestone Roundup

Map skills

Directions:

1. When it's your turn, spin each spinner. Record the latitude and longitude on a separate piece of paper.
2. Then find the point on the map. If there is a jewel at the point, you earn 20 points. If there is not a jewel at the point, draw a dot and write your first initial next to it. You earn five points. If there is already a dot at the point, your turn is over.
3. When time is up, the partner with more points wins the game.

Latitude Spinner

Wade On In!

Current events

Motivate students to read about current events with this clever idea. Place a small wading pool in a corner of your classroom and keep it stocked with copies of a daily newspaper. Then have one or two students who have finished their work early sit in the pool to read and "soak up the news." Once the weather cools off, replace the pool with a sled or toboggan and blanket. Then invite students to "warm up to what's happening!"

Marsha Goode, Middletown, OH

Report in the Round

Native American history, research

For this project, guide each student to research an early Native American group, exploring topics such as those shown. To share his research, the child traces a paper plate on construction paper. He divides the circle so there is one section for each topic and then, in each section, draws a picture that represents a topic. Next, the student cuts apart each section and staples it to the paper plate's edge. The child folds up each paper piece in turn and writes about its topic on the plate. When the student finishes, he folds back each section, flips the plate, and lists his sources on the back.

Carol Lawrence

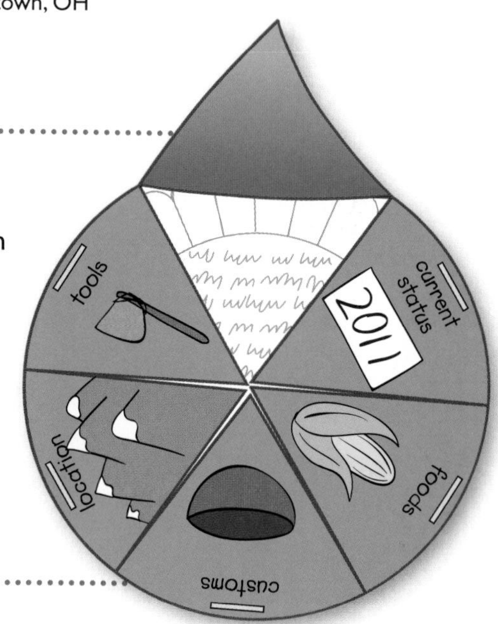

Names ______________________

Date ______________________

Map skills

Rhinestone Roundup

Directions:

1. When it's your turn, spin each spinner. Record the latitude and longitude on a separate piece of paper.
2. Then find the point on the map. If there is a jewel at the point, you earn 20 points. If there is not a jewel at the point, draw a dot and write your first initial next to it. You earn five points. If there is already a dot at the point, your turn is over.
3. When time is up, the partner with more points wins the game.

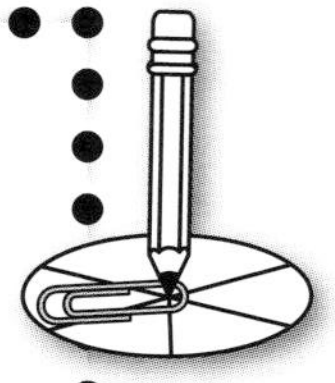

Latitude Spinner

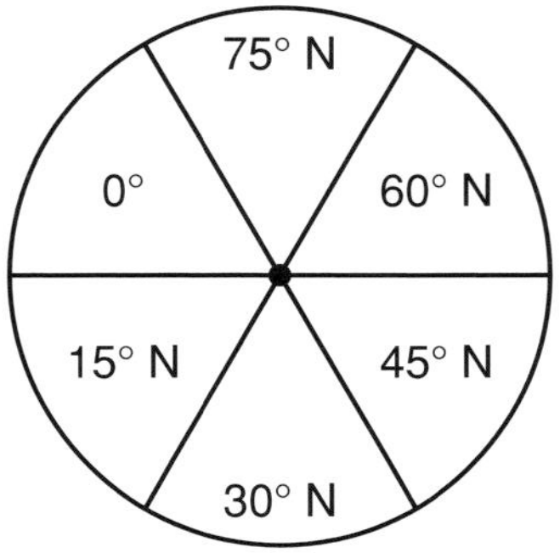

75° N, 60° N, 45° N, 30° N, 15° N, 0°

Longitude Spinner

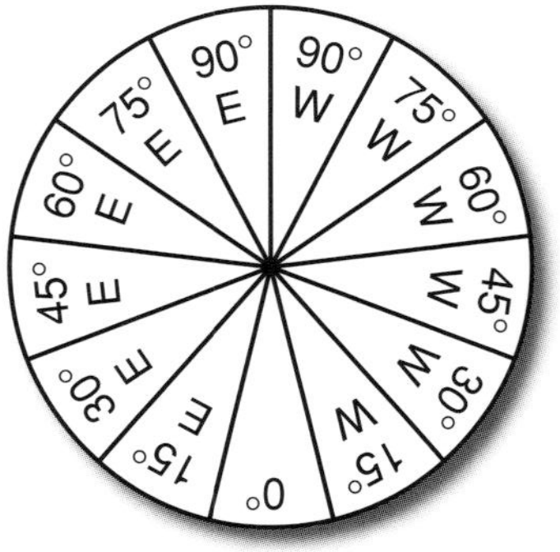

90° W, 75° W, 60° W, 45° W, 30° W, 15° W, 0°, 15° E, 30° E, 45° E, 60° E, 75° E, 90° E

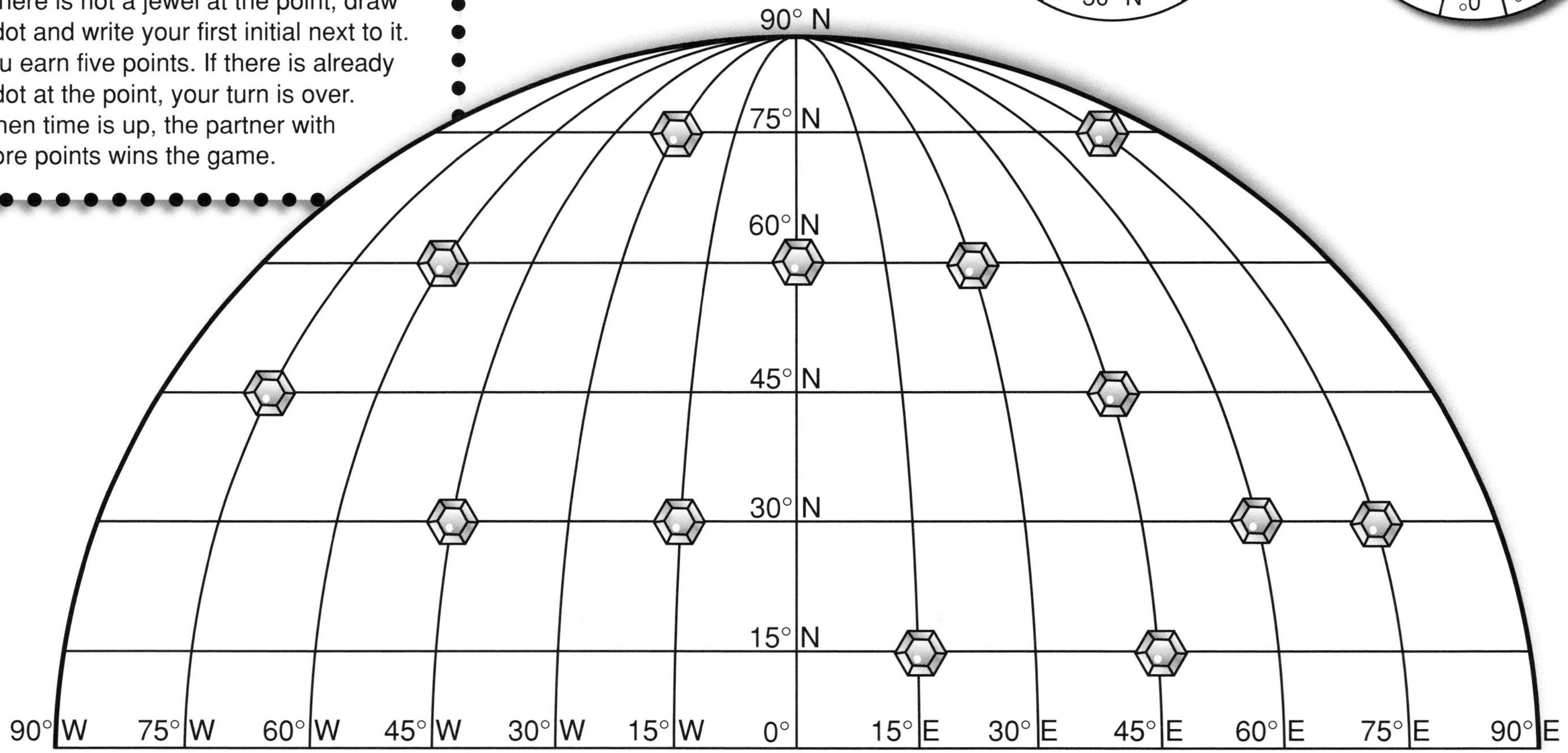

90° N

75° N

60° N

45° N

30° N

15° N

90° W 75° W 60° W 45° W 30° W 15° W 0° 15° E 30° E 45° E 60° E 75° E 90° E

Note to the teacher: Use with "Rhinestone Roundup" on page 244.

EXPLORING Social Studies

A "State-ly" Skill Builder

Using a map to gather information

For this idea, display the directions shown. Then guide each pair of students to complete the steps using a state map. **To extend the activity,** have each twosome read aloud its directions for Step 4 or 5. As the duo reads, challenge the remaining students to follow along and guess the partners' destination before they name it. **Patricia Twohey, Smithfield, RI**

Directions

1. Name the state capital and then list five of the state's major cities.
2. List five bodies of water in the state.
3. List the states, natural features, or countries along the state's north, east, south, and west borders.
4. Choose a location near the state's southern border (point A) and a location near the state's northern border (point B). Then write directions that explain how to get from point A to point B.
5. Choose a location near the state's western border (point C) and a location near the state's eastern border (point D). Then write directions that explain how to get from point C to point D.

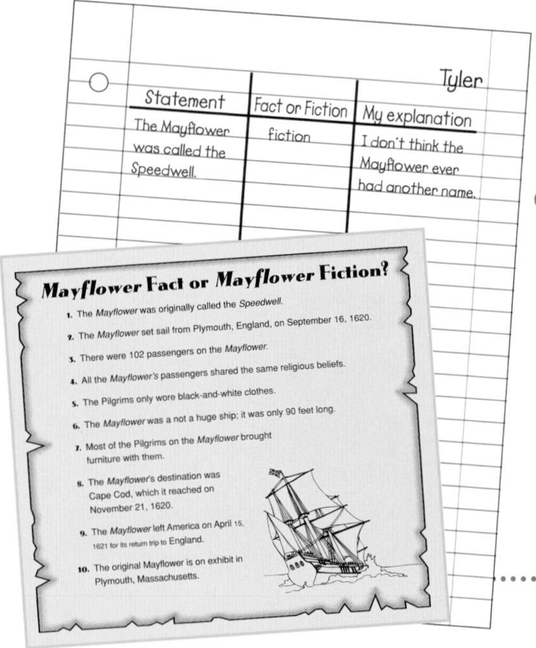

Tyler

Statement	Fact or Fiction	My explanation
The Mayflower was called the Speedwell.	fiction	I don't think the Mayflower ever had another name.

Mayflower Fact or Mayflower Fiction?

1. The *Mayflower* was originally called the *Speedwell.*
2. The *Mayflower* set sail from Plymouth, England, on September 16, 1620.
3. There were 102 passengers on the *Mayflower.*
4. All the *Mayflower's* passengers shared the same religious beliefs.
5. The Pilgrims only wore black-and-white clothes.
6. The *Mayflower* was a not a huge ship; it was only 90 feet long.
7. Most of the Pilgrims on the *Mayflower* brought furniture with them.
8. The *Mayflower's* destination was Cape Cod, which it reached on November 21, 1620.
9. The *Mayflower* left America on April 15, 1621 for its return trip to England.
10. The original Mayflower is on exhibit in Plymouth, Massachusetts.

Mayflower Fact or *Mayflower* Fiction?

History, critical thinking

Here's an idea that's sure to engage students' historical curiosity. To begin, read aloud a statement from the top half of page 247 and have each student decide whether the statement is true. Next, have the child draw a three-column chart labeled as shown. Then guide the student to write an abbreviated version of the statement, decide whether the statement is fact or fiction, record his choice, and then explain it. Repeat as time allows, saving time at the end of the session to reveal which statements are facts.

By Any Other Name

Geography, research

To set up this independent center, post the list of cities shown and provide access to research materials such as an atlas, maps, or a supervised Internet search. Next, guide each student to choose a city's name from the list and research the city to find out how it got its name and what its status is today. Then have the child use his research to write a paragraph about the city. To display students' work, post a map of the United States on a board titled "What's in a Name?—History!" Then have each student stick a push pin into the map at her city's location and post her paragraph near the map. Finally, stretch a length of yarn from the pin to the child's paragraph.

Mayflower Fact or *Mayflower* Fiction?

1. The *Mayflower* was originally called the *Speedwell.*
2. The *Mayflower* set sail from Plymouth, England, on September 16, 1620.
3. There were 102 passengers on the *Mayflower.*
4. All the *Mayflower's* passengers shared the same religious beliefs.
5. The Pilgrims only wore black-and-white clothes.
6. The *Mayflower* was a not a huge ship; it was only 90 feet long.
7. Most of the Pilgrims on the *Mayflower* brought furniture with them.
8. The *Mayflower*'s destination was Cape Cod, which it reached on November 21, 1620.
9. The *Mayflower* left America on April 15, 1621 for its return trip to England.
10. The original *Mayflower* is on exhibit in Plymouth, Massachusetts.

"*Mayflower* Fact or *Mayflower* Fiction?" Answer Key

1. Fiction—The *Speedwell* was supposed to sail with the *Mayflower*, but the *Speedwell* sprang too many leaks.
2. Fact
3. Fact
4. Fiction—There was a group of people on the *Mayflower* known as "strangers" who did not follow the religious practices of the Separatist Pilgrims.
5. Fiction—The Pilgrims only wore black-and-white clothing on Sunday or for formal occasions. Most of the time, women wore red, green, brown, blue, violet, or gray dresses. Men dressed in white, beige, black, green, and brown clothes.
6. Fact
7. Fiction—The pilgrims only brought chests and boxes. They had to make their furniture after they landed.
8. Fiction—The *Mayflower*'s destination was the Hudson River (in New York), which was considered Northern Virginia at that time.
9. Fact
10. Fiction—Historians aren't sure what happened to the original *Mayflower.* The ship kept in Plymouth is a replica called the *Mayflower II.*

Note to the teacher: Use with "*Mayflower* Fact or *Mayflower* Fiction?" on page 246.

EXPLORING

Social Studies

From the Ground Up

Investigating culture

Help students understand the ins and outs of culture by having them create an imaginary one. To begin, guide each small group of students to choose a site in a state, region, or country where a tributary enters a major river. Next, have the group establish the details about its invented society by completing a copy of the outline on page 249. When each group finishes its outline, provide access to construction paper and craft materials and have each student create a facsimile of a different important object the people would have used. Then have the student write a description of the imaginary culture and explain how his artifact was used. Finally, set aside time for the students in each group to share their artifacts and describe their imaginary culture. James B. Livingston, Minneapolis, MN

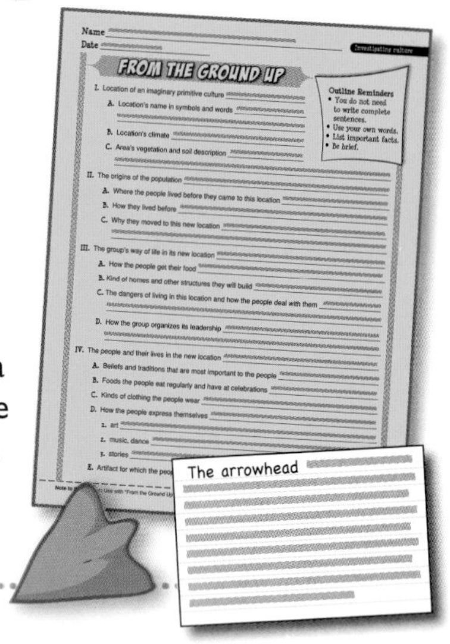

Where Am I?

Map skills

Review map skills with this anytime whole-class game. Display a wall map of the United States or have students open their textbooks to a map of the United States. Next, secretly pick a state. Then let each student ask a "yes" or "no" question to guess the secret state. Continue playing until each student has a turn or the state is identified. Then pick a new state and play again as time allows.

Use this game to reinforce state concepts too! Just pick a county, city, or physical feature and have students refer to a map of the state.

To Whom It May Concern

American Revolution, writing a persuasive letter

Here's an activity that helps students really connect with history. Review with students the British actions that enraged colonists and eventually led to the Revolutionary War. Then have each child choose the act that, for her, seems most offensive. Next, guide the student to imagine that she is an angry colonist who writes a letter of protest to the British Parliament or King George. In her letter, she describes the law and then explains how it is unfair. When a student is ready to write her final draft, have her tape a feather to her pen or pencil and then write her letter in her best handwriting. After students finish their letters, have parent volunteers bring in tea and cookies for students to enjoy as they read their letters aloud. Kelly Shock, Clinton Valley Elementary, Mt. Clemens, MI

Dear King George,
The laws Parliament and you have put in place are intolerable!

The Proclamation of 1763
The Revenue Act of 1764 (The Sugar Act)
The Quartering Act
The Stamp Act
The Townshend Acts
The Tea Act
The Intolerable Acts

Name ____________________

Date ____________________

FROM THE GROUND UP

Outline Reminders
- You do not need to write complete sentences.
- Use your own words.
- List important facts.
- Be brief.

I. Location of an imaginary primitive culture

A. Location's name in symbols and words ____________________

B. Location's climate ____________________

C. Area's vegetation and soil description ____________________

II. The origins of the population

A. Where the people lived before they came to this location ____________________

B. How they lived before ____________________

C. Why they moved to this new location ____________________

III. The group's way of life in its new location

A. How the people get their food ____________________

B. Kind of homes and other structures they will build ____________________

C. The dangers of living in this location and how the people deal with them ____________________

D. How the group organizes its leadership ____________________

IV. The people and their lives in the new location

A. Beliefs and traditions that are most important to the people ____________________

B. Foods the people eat regularly and have at celebrations ____________________

C. Kinds of clothing the people wear ____________________

D. How the people express themselves ____________________

1. art ____________________
2. music, dance ____________________

Note to the teacher: Use with "From the Ground Up" on page 248.

EXPLORING Social Studies

Map It Out

Geography, map skills

To set up this independent center, copy and cut apart the natural feature cards on page 251 and make a class supply of the map on page 252. Also provide colored pencils, a folder for students' work, and a physical map of the United States. A child takes a blank map. Then she takes a card and finds its natural feature on the physical map. Next, the student draws and labels the feature on her map. She takes additional cards as time allows and then tucks her work in the folder so she can return to the center and continue adding features to her map. **Cathy Ogg, Happy Valley Elementary, Johnson City, TN**

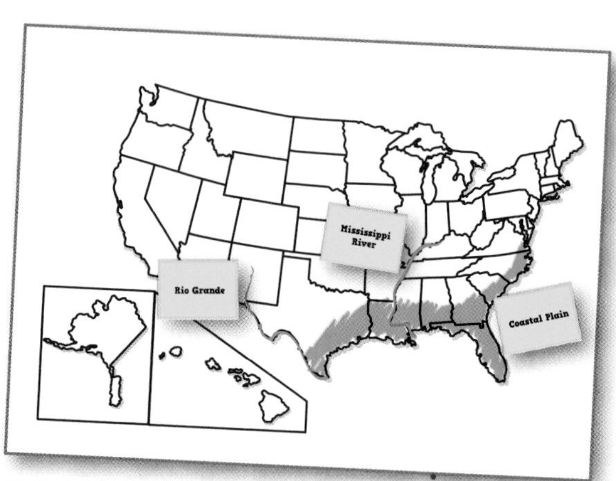

Key Players

History

Want to help students remember which historic figures are important and why? Here's a super solution. After covering a chapter that includes several key players, have each child draw a caricature of each person on the unlined side of an index card. Then have him flip the card and explain why the person is important. Next, have each student tape his cards together, edge to edge, and accordion-fold the cards to make a tidy stack that turns into a fantastic study tool! **Teresa Vilfer-Snyder, Fredericktown Intermediate, Fredericktown, OH**

Just Desserts

State agriculture

For this activity, have students research agriculture and food manufacturing in your state. Then challenge each child to nominate a recipe to become your state's official dessert. Tell students that the main ingredient in each dessert recipe must be a food that is grown in your state. For a fun follow-up, choose five of the dessert recipes and have each small group of students prepare one of the desserts. Then let students sample the desserts and pick a winner.

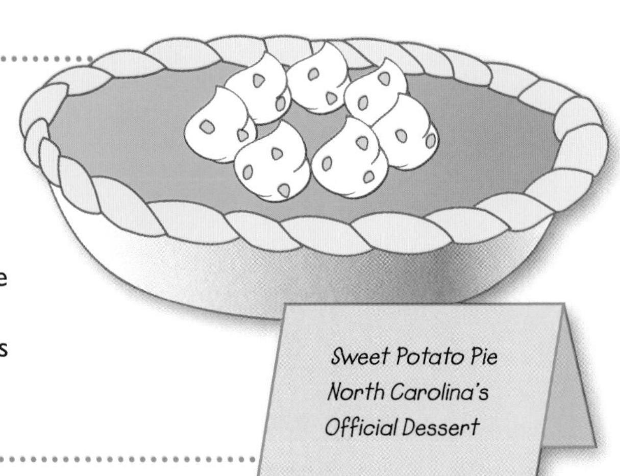

Natural Feature Cards

Use with "Map It Out" on page 250.

Alaska Range TEC44059	Aleutian Islands TEC44059	Appalachian Mountains TEC44059	Arkansas River TEC44059	Cape Cod TEC44059
Cascade Mountains TEC44059	Central Plains TEC44059	Chesapeake Bay Coast Range TEC44059	Coastal Plain TEC44059	Colorado River TEC44059
Cumberland Gap TEC44059	Death Valley TEC44059	Florida Keys TEC44059	Galveston Bay TEC44059	Grand Canyon TEC44059
Great Basin TEC44059	Great Salt Lake TEC44059	Hudson River TEC44059	Illinois River TEC44059	Lake Champlain TEC44059
Lake Erie TEC44059	Lake Huron TEC44059	Lake Michigan TEC44059	Lake Ontario TEC44059	Lake Superior TEC44059
Mauna Kea TEC44059	Mississippi River TEC44059	Mississippi Delta TEC44059	Missouri River TEC44059	Mojave Desert TEC44059
Mt. McKinley TEC44059	Mt. Rainier TEC44059	Mt. St. Helens TEC44059	Niagara Falls TEC44059	Ohio River TEC44059
Pecos River TEC44059	Piedmont TEC44059	Platte River TEC44059	Potomac River TEC44059	Rio Grande TEC44059
Rocky Mountains TEC44059	St. Lawrence River TEC44059	Sierra Nevada Range TEC44059	Snake River TEC44059	Sonoran Desert TEC44059

United States Map

Use with “Map It Out” on page 250.

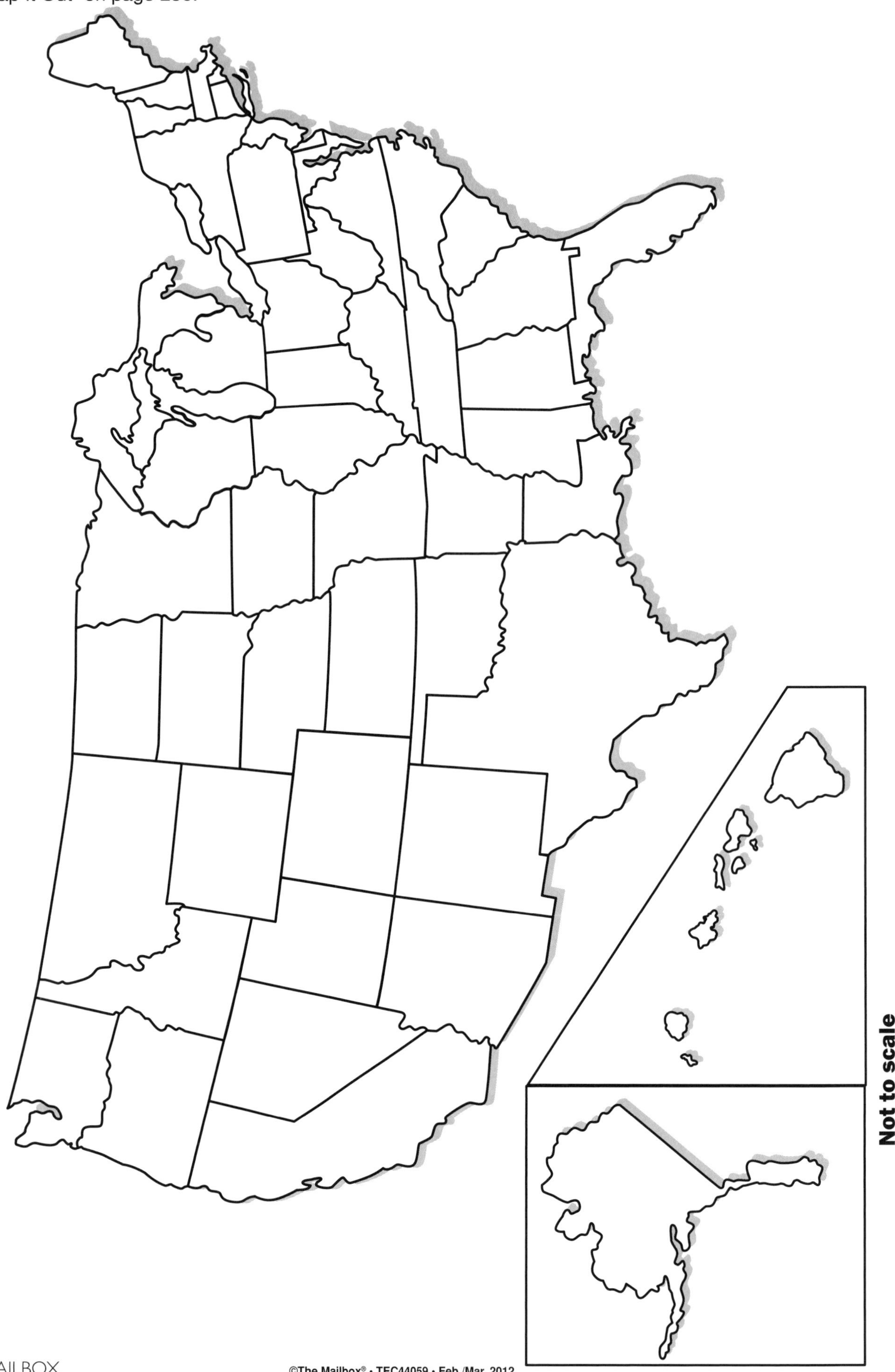

Our Civic Duties

Citizenship

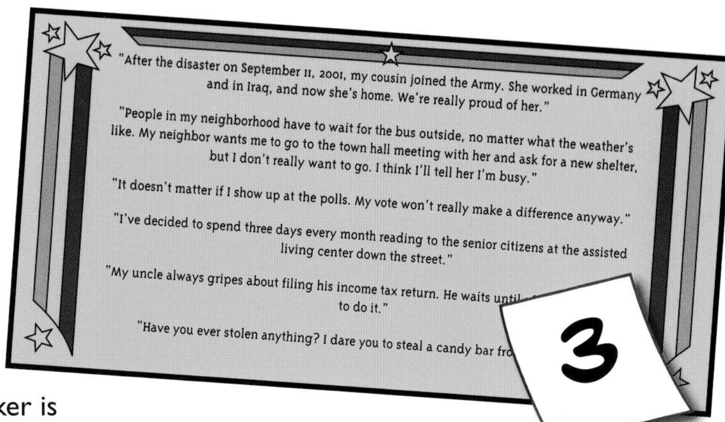

"After the disaster on September 11, 2001, my cousin joined the Army. She worked in Germany and in Iraq, and now she's home. We're really proud of her."

"People in my neighborhood have to wait for the bus outside, no matter what the weather's like. My neighbor wants me to go to the town hall meeting with her and ask for a new shelter, but I don't really want to go. I think I'll tell her I'm busy."

"It doesn't matter if I show up at the polls. My vote won't really make a difference anyway."

"I've decided to spend three days every month reading to the senior citizens at the assisted living center down the street."

"My uncle always gripes about filing his income tax return. He waits until [illegible] to do it."

"Have you ever stolen anything? I dare you to steal a candy bar fro[illegible]

For this idea, cut apart the civic duty quotes and citizenship cards from a copy of page 254. Then have each student cut a sheet of paper into six pieces and number them 1–6. Next, display a numbered list of citizenship duties, such as the one shown, and read aloud one of the quotes. Guide students to decide whether the speaker is showing good citizenship, decide which duty is at issue, and hold up the matching number card. Repeat with the remaining quotes. Then have each pair of students take a citizenship card and create a one-minute dialogue between two citizens as guided on the card. When students are ready, have each duo present its dialogue. After each presentation, have students hold up the number card that identifies the civic duty. **LaVone Novotny, Liberty Elementary, Caledonia, OH**

Duties of Citizenship

1. Pay taxes.
2. Defend your country.
3. Obey the country's laws.
4. Vote in elections.
5. Try to help other people.
6. Learn about public problems.

Cell Phones From the Past

History

After students study an important event, find out what they know about the people involved with this hip project! Have each child choose an important figure from the event and imagine what his or her cell phone might have revealed. Have each child draw the cell phone that might best suit the person and then draw the phone's screen shape four times. In the screens, the child shows who the person's contacts might have been, two text message conversations, and a log of the phone calls he or she missed. For a fun display, post students' work on a board titled "Historic Callers." **Libby Arnold, Little Hocking School, Little Hocking, OH**

Contacts

Text Messages

Text Messages

Missed

tip Challenge your early finishers to draw additional screens that show which apps the historic figure might have had!

Civic Duty Quotes and Citizenship Cards

Use with "Our Civic Duties" on page 253.

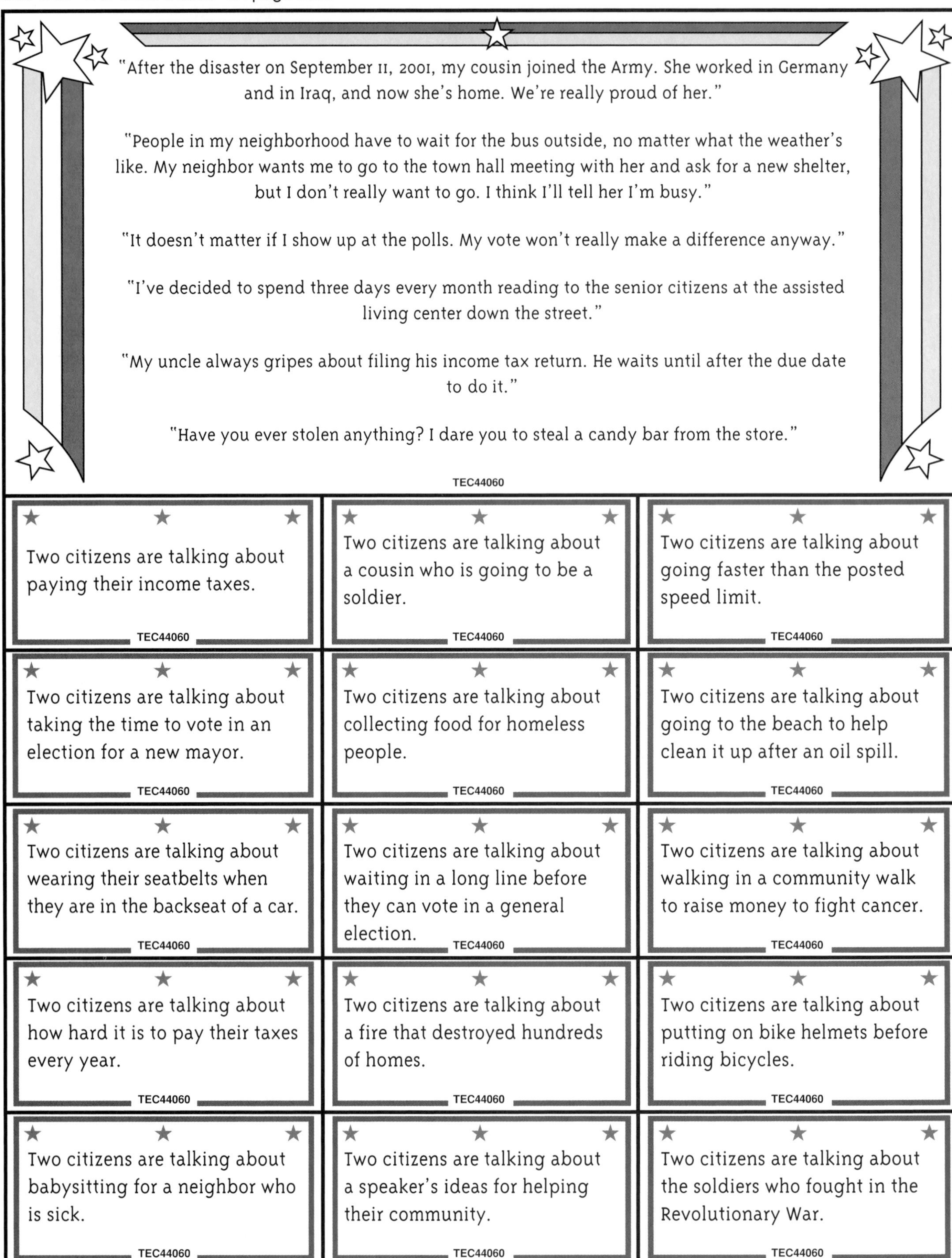

"After the disaster on September 11, 2001, my cousin joined the Army. She worked in Germany and in Iraq, and now she's home. We're really proud of her."

"People in my neighborhood have to wait for the bus outside, no matter what the weather's like. My neighbor wants me to go to the town hall meeting with her and ask for a new shelter, but I don't really want to go. I think I'll tell her I'm busy."

"It doesn't matter if I show up at the polls. My vote won't really make a difference anyway."

"I've decided to spend three days every month reading to the senior citizens at the assisted living center down the street."

"My uncle always gripes about filing his income tax return. He waits until after the due date to do it."

"Have you ever stolen anything? I dare you to steal a candy bar from the store."

TEC44060

Two citizens are talking about paying their income taxes.

TEC44060

Two citizens are talking about a cousin who is going to be a soldier.

TEC44060

Two citizens are talking about going faster than the posted speed limit.

TEC44060

Two citizens are talking about taking the time to vote in an election for a new mayor.

TEC44060

Two citizens are talking about collecting food for homeless people.

TEC44060

Two citizens are talking about going to the beach to help clean it up after an oil spill.

TEC44060

Two citizens are talking about wearing their seatbelts when they are in the backseat of a car.

TEC44060

Two citizens are talking about waiting in a long line before they can vote in a general election.

TEC44060

Two citizens are talking about walking in a community walk to raise money to fight cancer.

TEC44060

Two citizens are talking about how hard it is to pay their taxes every year.

TEC44060

Two citizens are talking about a fire that destroyed hundreds of homes.

TEC44060

Two citizens are talking about putting on bike helmets before riding bicycles.

TEC44060

Two citizens are talking about babysitting for a neighbor who is sick.

TEC44060

Two citizens are talking about a speaker's ideas for helping their community.

TEC44060

Two citizens are talking about the soldiers who fought in the Revolutionary War.

TEC44060

EXPLORING Social Studies

What's Your Position?

Map skills

Whether your class is studying one specific state or all 50, here's an independent activity that's sure to "peak" some interest. Place at a center a supply of paper and a state, country, or world map that is marked with grid lines. A student chooses ten locations, such as cities, unique landforms, or historic landmarks. For each location, the child records the map coordinates. Next, he writes a clue about the location. Then he flips his paper and writes an answer key on the back of his paper, listing each location's name and coordinates. When students finish, post their work along with the appropriate maps at a center for an independent skill-building center that's self-checking! **LaVone Novotny, Liberty Elementary, Caledonia, OH**

Map Coordinates	Clue
H, 2	capital city
G, 2	site of the first sit-in to protest segregation
J, 2	first town of North Carolina
F, 3	site where the first gold nugget was found in the US
L, 2	site of the first successful airplane flight

Dear General Washington,
Thank you for defending the rights of the American colonists. Because of your courage and strong leadership, your army crossed the Delaware River and defeated the British. The American Revolution helped our country gain its freedom. It's too bad that you didn't live long enough to see how much your work changed our country. You are a hero to me!
Sincerely,
Quinton

Let Freedom Ring

Historic figures, research

To get this patriotic idea started, guide students to brainstorm a list of people who played important roles in securing the country's freedom. Then have each child choose and research a different person. Next, have the student draft a letter to the person describing the difference he made in the country's history. If desired, have each student write the final copy of her letter on a Liberty Bell–shaped piece of construction paper and add it to a display titled "Let Freedom Ring!"

Land "Feet-ures"

Geography vocabulary

Here's a partner game sure to keep your students thinking. Give each pair of students a copy of page 256 and a die. Then guide the partners to follow the directions to play the game and review important landform terms. **Jennifer Otter, Oak Ridge, NC**

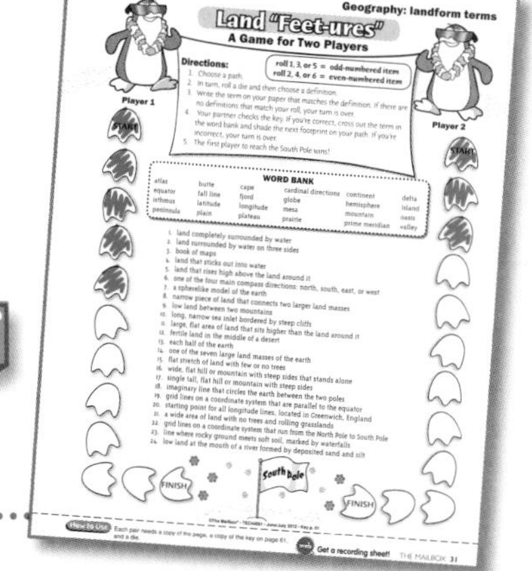
Geography: landform terms
Land "Feet-ures"
A Game for Two Players

Land "Feet-ures"

A Game for Two Players

Directions:

roll 1, 3, or 5 = odd-numbered item
roll 2, 4, or 6 = even-numbered item

1. Choose a path.
2. In turn, roll a die and then choose a definition.
3. Write the term on your paper that matches the definition. If there are no terms that match your definition, your turn is over.
4. Your partner checks the key. If you're correct, cross out the term in the word bank and shade the next footprint on your path. If you're incorrect, your turn is over.
5. The first player to reach the South Pole wins!

Player 1

START

Player 2

START

WORD BANK

atlas	butte	cape	cardinal directions	continent	delta
equator	fall line	fjord	globe	hemisphere	island
isthmus	latitude	longitude	mesa	mountain	oasis
peninsula	plain	plateau	prairie	prime meridian	valley

1. land completely surrounded by water
2. land surrounded by water on three sides
3. book of maps
4. land that sticks out into water
5. land that rises high above the land around it
6. one of the four main compass directions: north, south, east, or west
7. a spherelike model of the earth
8. narrow piece of land that connects two larger land masses
9. low land between two mountains
10. long, narrow sea inlet bordered by steep cliffs
11. large, flat area of land that sits higher than the land around it
12. fertile land in the middle of a desert
13. each half of the earth
14. one of the seven large land masses of the earth
15. flat stretch of land with few or no trees
16. wide, flat hill or mountain with steep sides that stands alone
17. single tall, flat hill or mountain with steep sides
18. imaginary line that circles the earth between the two poles
19. grid lines on a coordinate system that are parallel to the equator
20. starting point for all longitude lines, located in Greenwich, England
21. a wide area of land with no trees and rolling grasslands
22. grid lines on a coordinate system that run from the North Pole to South Pole
23. line where rocky ground meets soft soil, marked by waterfalls
24. low land at the mouth of a river formed by deposited sand and silt

FINISH

FINISH

Note to the teacher: Use with "Land 'Feet-ures'" on page 255.

GEOGRAPHY PUZZLERS

SOCIAL STUDIES

PUZZLER 1

Which of the following world cities are located in the Tropics (between the Tropic of Cancer and the Tropic of Capricorn)?

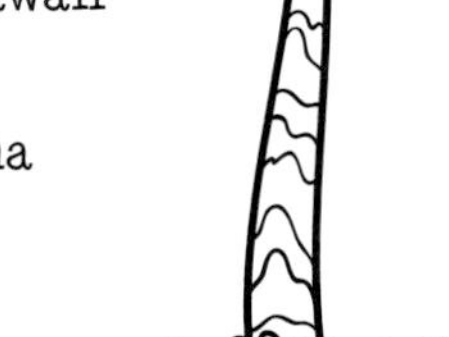

A. Darwin, Australia
B. Miami, Florida
C. Santiago, Chile
D. Honolulu, Hawaii
E. Cairo, Egypt
F. Beijing, China

TEC44058

PUZZLER 2

In which cities and states would you find the following man-made landmarks?

A. **Gateway Arch**
B. **Faneuil Hall Marketplace**
C. **United Nations Headquarters**
D. **Independence Hall**
E. **US Naval Academy**

TEC44058

PUZZLER 3

The *mouth* of a river is the place where a river flows into a larger body of water. Into which body of water does each of the following rivers flow?

A. Nile River
B. Murray River
C. Amazon River
D. Ganges River
E. Seine River

TEC44058

PUZZLER 4

In which directions would you travel if you flew from Chicago to each of the following cities?

A. San Francisco
B. Washington, DC
C. New Orleans
D. Seattle

TEC44058

PUZZLER 5

Many US state capitals are named for famous people. List five state capitals that were named for people.

TEC44058

PUZZLER 6

A. I am the largest lake in the western United States. No fish live in my waters. No rivers or streams flow away from me. What am I?

B. I am about one-fifth the size of the rest of the United States. I have the fourth smallest population. I am home to the highest mountain in North America. What am I?

TEC44058

PUZZLER 7

Over time, names of places can change. Match each old name (A–D) with its new name or names.

A. British Honduras
B. Burma
C. Rhodesia
D. British East Africa

Myanmar

Belize

Kenya

Zambia and Zimbabwe

TEC44058

PUZZLER 8

What do the following European cities have in common?

A. Barcelona
B. Marseille
C. Rotterdam

TEC44058

How to use: Display this page or give each student a copy of the page (or one card at a time) to work on during free time.

Social Studies Activity Cards

Use as center or free-time activities.

Culture

A Cultural Site

Plan a website that advertises three different art forms from your state, such as music, dance, literature, theater, painting, or sculpture. Show the homepage and a separate page for each art form.

TEC44060

History

All About the Details

Write ten or more trivia questions (and their answers) about your state's history. Write each question on an index card. Then add a picture clue and write the answer. Use the cards to quiz classmates on your state's history.

TEC44060

Landforms

Sticking to It

Create three bumper stickers that advertise three of the most unusual or interesting landforms in your state.

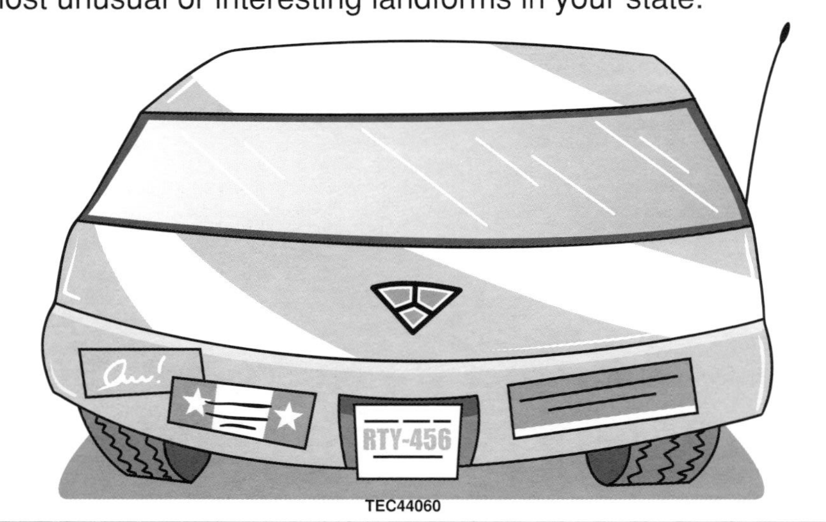

TEC44060

Population

Charting the Changes

Make a chart that shows the current population of the five largest cities in your state. Make two more charts that show the populations of those same cities at least ten and twenty years ago.

TEC44060

World Geography Activity Cards

Use as center or free-time activities.

Location

Where in the World?

Choose a country. Draw its outline. Show where the country's capital is and list the capital's latitude and longitude coordinates. Inside the country's outline, list the countries and landforms that form its border.

TEC44060

Place

A Great Read!

Choose a country. Fold a large sheet of paper in half to create a magazine cover about the country.

- On the front cover, show the country's official name, its size, and its population. Draw a cover illustration that shows one of the country's important customs or traditions.
- Inside the covers, create an advertisement about one of the country's traditional foods.
- On the back cover, create an advertisement about a popular type of recreation in the country.

TEC44060

Movement

On the Road

Choose a country. Choose an important product produced in the country. Create a flowchart that shows the product's creation and transportation to market.

TEC44060

Regions

Mapping It Out!

Choose a country. Draw a map of the country. Using colors and a key, show the country's political regions.

TEC44060

Displays That Do More Than Decorate

DISPLAYS That Do More Than Decorate

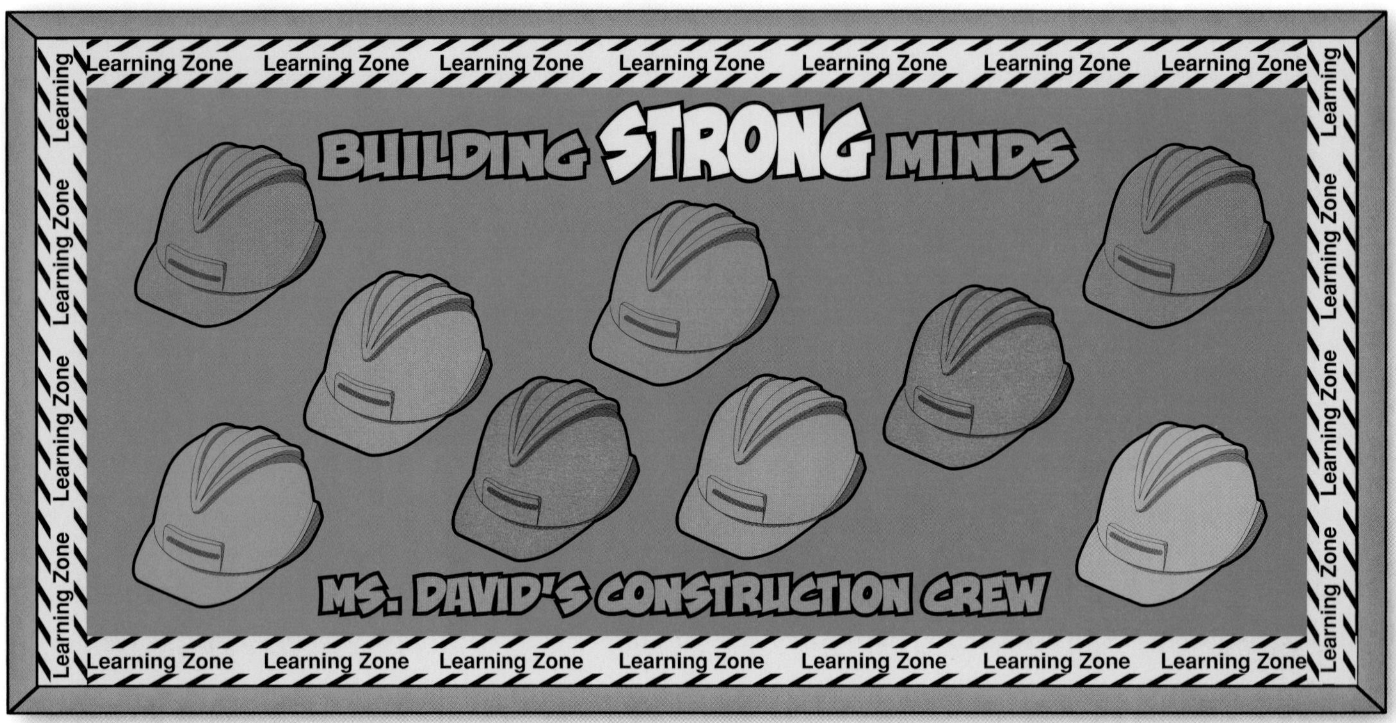

For this back-to-school display, write each student's name on a construction paper hard hat (pattern on page 269). Then post the hard hats on a board decorated as shown. (See page 270 for a border pattern.)
Angel David, Paradise Elementary, Pineville, LA

Yoo-hoo!
Here's What's *NEW!*

Make it easy for students to share their best work. First, give each child a sheet of construction paper and have her draw a border with her name and symbols of her favorite things. Laminate each student's sheet and add to a display decorated as shown. (See page 271 for an owl pattern.) When a child has work she'd like to share, she simply tapes it onto her sheet. **Colleen Dabney, Williamsburg, VA**

DISPLAYS That Do More Than Decorate

No need to bat around a way to post good papers! Here's a quick fall display that does the trick. Have each student create a construction paper bat and post it next to an example of her excellent work. **Colleen Dabney, Williamsburg, VA**

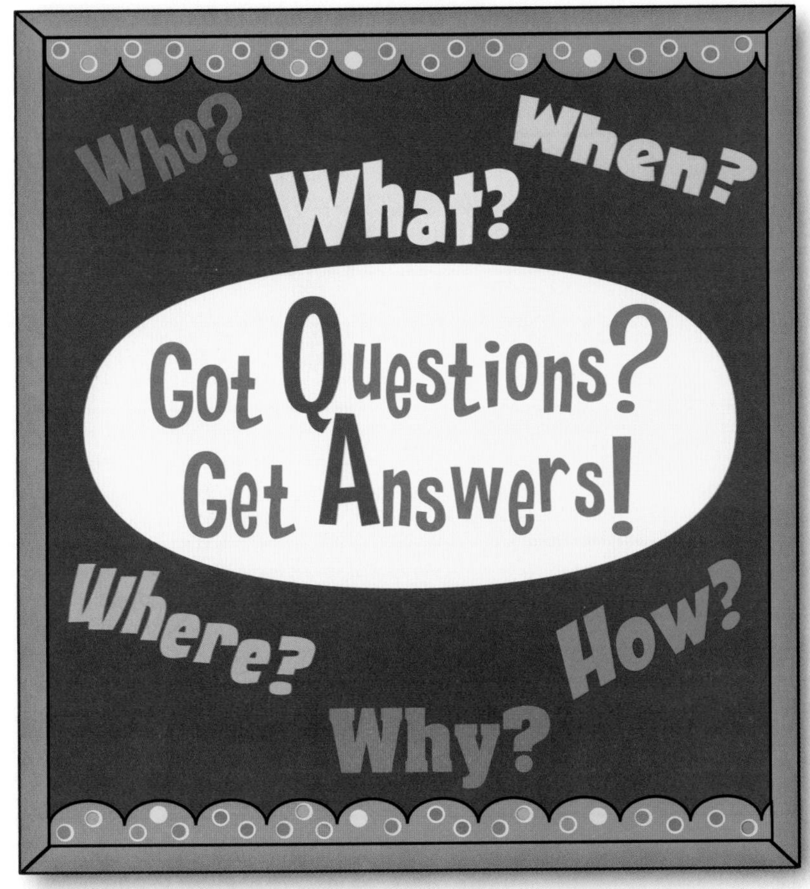

Post this attention-getting display near your classroom library to inspire students to ask questions while they read. **Lucinda Schooler, Jefferson County Christian School, Mingo Junction, OH**

DISPLAYS That Do More Than Decorate

Enlarge the elapsed time problems from the bottom of this page and post them on a board decorated as shown. (A turkey pattern is provided on page 272.) Then have students solve the problems during free time. They're sure to gobble up the practice!
Colleen Dabney, Williamsburg, VA

Elapsed Time Problems

Use with "From Time to Time" on this page.

1.	Aunt Marie gets to the grocery store at 11:15 AM. It takes her one hour and 25 minutes to finish shopping. What time does Aunt Marie leave the store?	**7.**	Uncle Herb starts making his famous stuffing at 7:10 AM on Thursday. Grandma needs the stuffing by 8:30 AM. How long does Uncle Herb have to make the stuffing?
2.	Uncle George helps Aunt Marie put the groceries away. It takes the two of them 25 minutes. They finish at 2:00 PM. What time did they start?	**8.**	Grandma puts the turkey in the oven at 9:00 AM. She takes it out of the oven at 12:45 PM. How long was the turkey in the oven?
3.	Uncle Herb and Aunt Suzy are driving to Grandma's house. They leave Tuesday at 5:15 PM and drive for three hours and 40 minutes. What time do they get to Grandma's?	**9.**	The family sits down to eat at 2:45 PM. They finish eating 50 minutes later. What time is it?
4.	Aunt Suzy makes the pumpkin pies on Wednesday. She puts them in the oven at 3:30 PM. The pies have to bake for one hour and 15 minutes. What time will Aunt Suzy take them out of the oven?	**10.**	Uncle George and Uncle Herb volunteer to wash the dishes. They start at 4:35 PM, and they want to finish before the game starts at 6:10 PM. How long do they have?
5.	Aunt Marie and Uncle George prepare the rolls, mashed potatoes, and yams. They start at 8:00 AM and finish at 1:50 PM. How long did they work?	**11.**	The game starts at 6:10 PM and lasts two hours and five minutes. What time does the game end?
6.	It only takes Aunt Marie and Uncle George 35 minutes to get to Grandma's. They get to Grandma's on Thursday at 10:00 AM. What time did they leave?	**12.**	Uncle Herb falls asleep on the couch at 7:20 PM. He sleeps until 2:10 AM. How long does Uncle Herb sleep on the couch?

DISPLAYS That Do More Than Decorate

For this wintry good-work display, have each student choose a piece of work to post. Next, give her writing paper from page 274 and have her write a paragraph that explains her choice. Then post each student's paragraph next to her work on a board decorated as shown. (See page 273 for a snow leopard pattern.)

Welcome the New Year by guiding each student to make a meaningful resolution. Next, have the child write his pledge on a music bubble and add a brightly colored horn (pattern on page 275). Then post students' work as shown.

DISPLAYS That Do More Than Decorate

Use this playful display to have students identify an author's purpose when they read and also to focus on the purpose when they write! Enlarge the porpoise patterns on page 276 and the beach ball patterns on page 277 and display them on a board decorated as shown. When students are reading, have them name the author's purpose and then have a student put a beach ball cutout next to it. When students are writing, remind them to keep the purpose in mind by putting a beach ball next to the appropriate one. **Colleen Dabney, Williamsburg, VA**

For this good-work display, have each child choose an example of her best work. Then have her explain her choice on a soccer ball cutout (pattern on page 277) and post her work on a board decorated as shown.

DISPLAYS That Do More Than Decorate

Hold students accountable for identifying a story's theme with this rewarding display! After reading a fictional selection, a student describes the story's theme and summarizes the plot on a construction paper rectangle (brick). Then she records the story's title and author's name on the brick and adds it to a display decorated as shown. (Flower patterns are provided on page 278.) When the path is complete, reward students with a session of reading with friends. **adapted from an idea by Sarah Knoles, Cross Timbers Elementary, Edmond, OK**

For this character-building display, cut the flaps off eight envelopes. Then label each envelope with a character trait, staple it to a board, and fill it with colorful star cutouts. When a student sees a classmate showing a positive character trait, have the child write a note on a star about her classmate's actions. Post the stars on the board and watch your students shine when they see they've been caught being good. **Karen Slattery, Marie of the Incarnation School, Bradford, Ontario, Canada**

DISPLAYS That Do More Than Decorate

Have each student pass along some good advice to next year's students by writing an "If…then" statement about a study habit or behavior she knows is important. Next, have the child write her statement on a construction paper basketball. Then post the basketballs on a board decorated as shown. (See page 279 for a backboard and net pattern.) This is a great year-end or back-to-school display! **Colleen Dabney, Williamsburg, VA**

Here's a display that's a great way to review math skills your students learned this year! Have each student choose a math skill and describe it on a peanut cutout (pattern on page 280). Then have him show an example of the skill on an elephant cutout (pattern on page 280). **Ann Fisher, Toledo, OH**

Hard Hat Pattern

Use with "Building Strong Minds" on page 262.

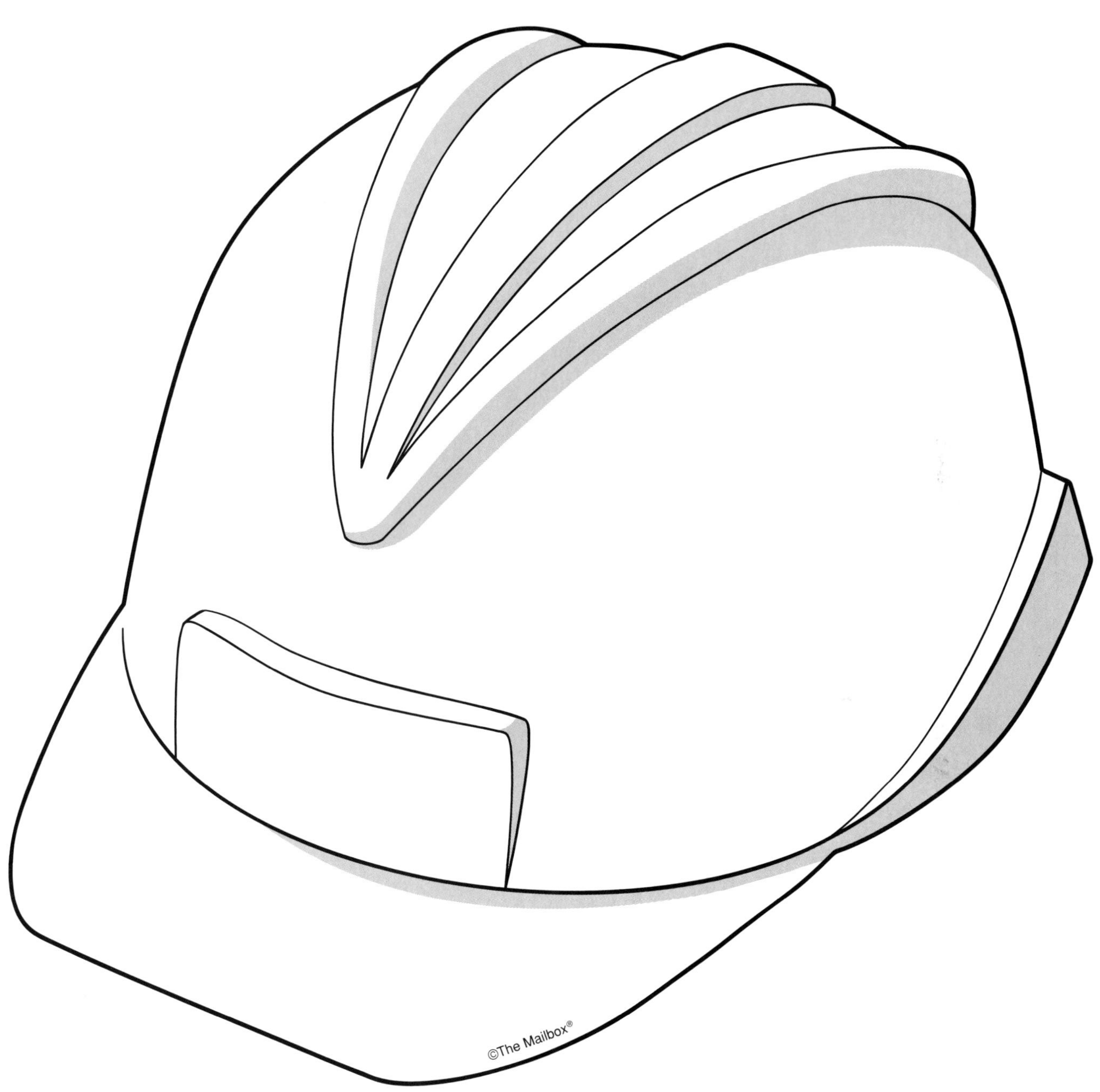

Border Pattern

Use with "Building Strong Minds" on page 262.

Owl Pattern

Use with "Yoo-hoo! Here's What's New!" on page 262.

Turkey Pattern

Use with “From Time To Time” on page 264.

Snow Leopard Pattern

Use with "Look Who's Been Spotted Doing Great Work!" on page 265.

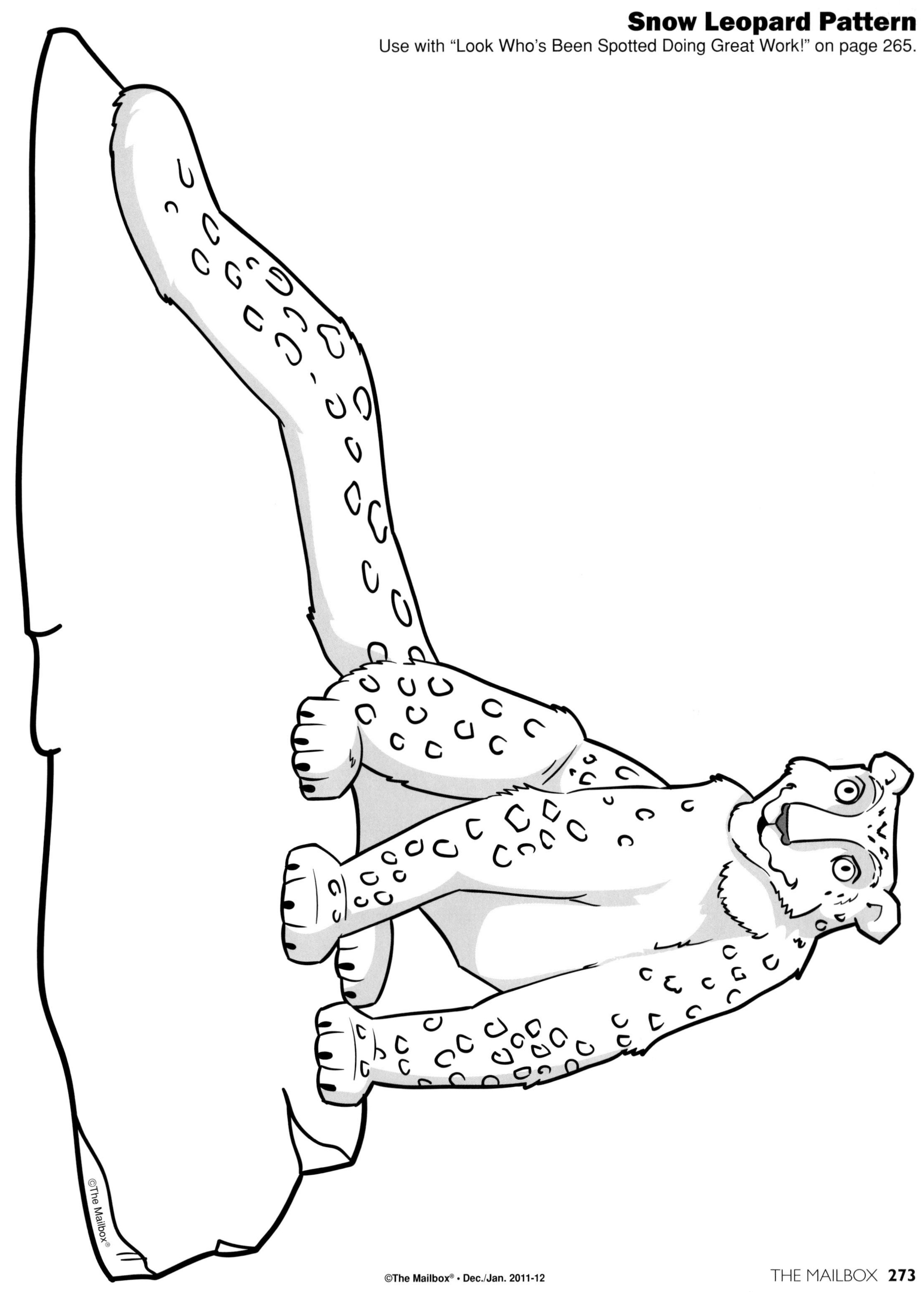

©The Mailbox® • Dec./Jan. 2011–12

Note to the teacher: Use with "Look Who's Been Spotted Doing Great Work!" on page 265.

Horn Patterns

Use with "A Tuneful New Year" on page 265.

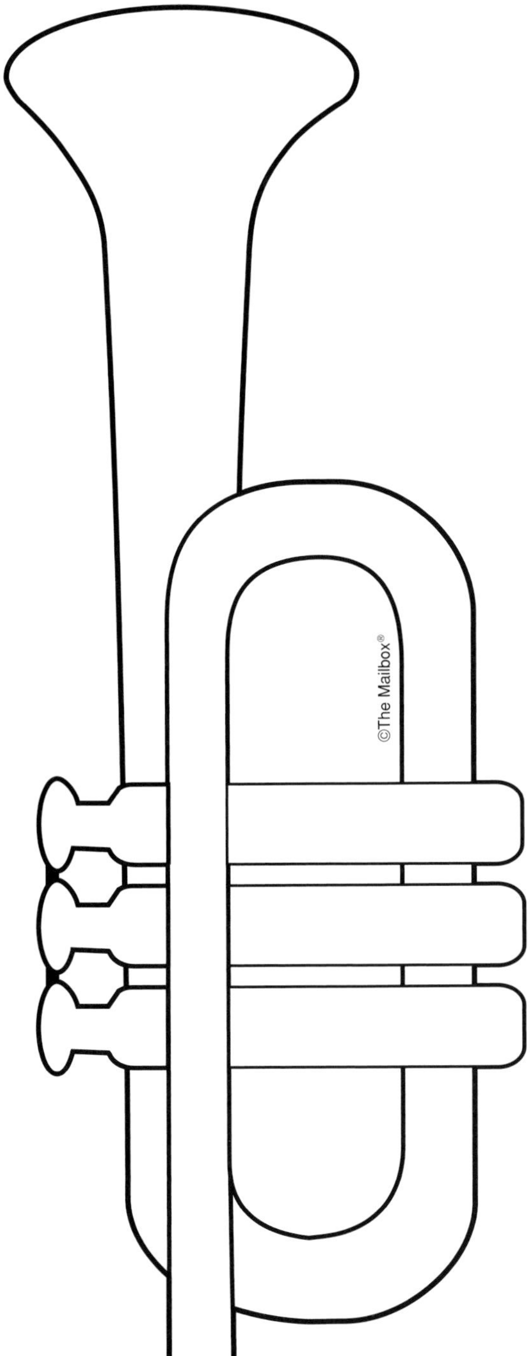

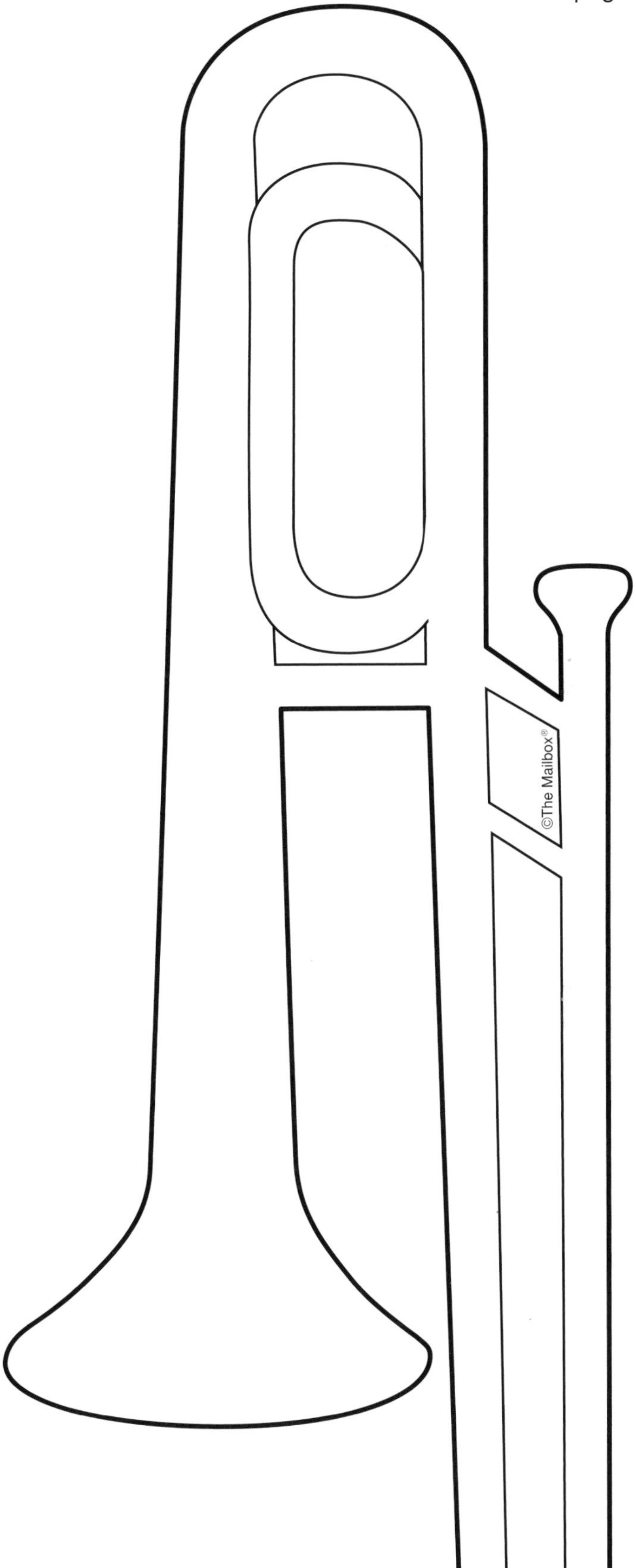

Porpoise Patterns

Use with "Know the 'Porpoise'!" on page 266.

Beach Ball Patterns

Use with "Know The 'Porpoise'!" on page 266.

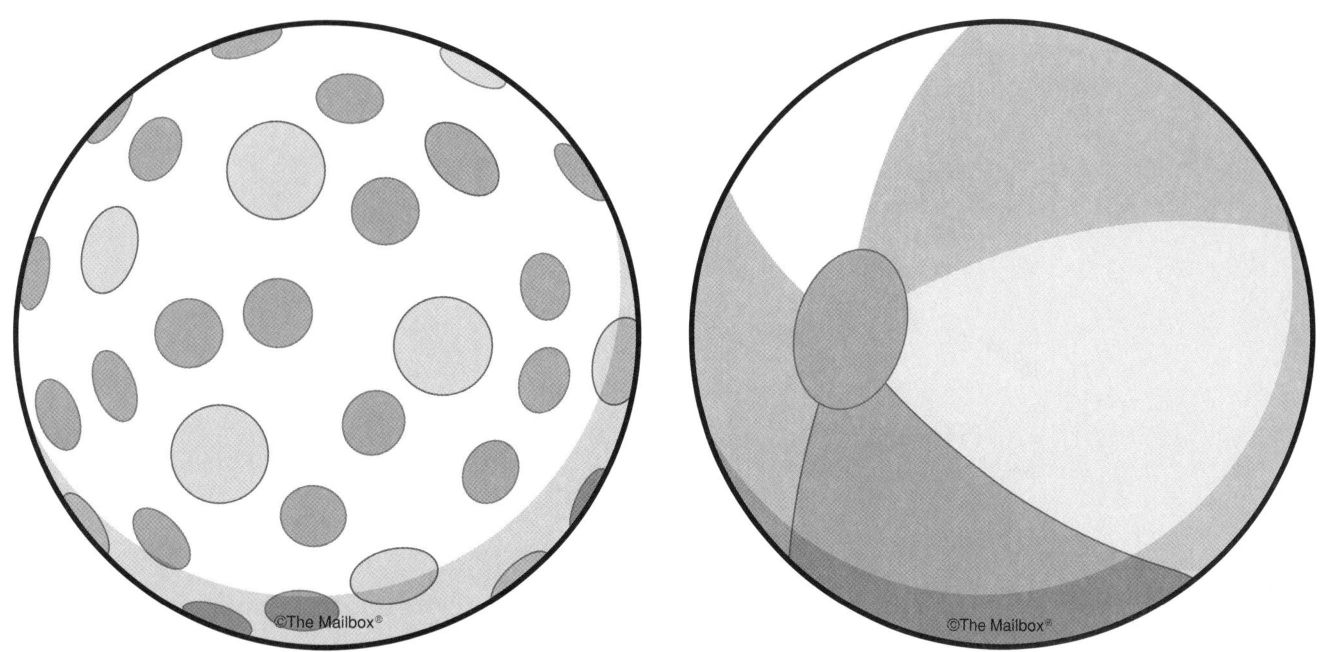

Soccer Ball Pattern

Use with "Learning Scores!" on page 266.

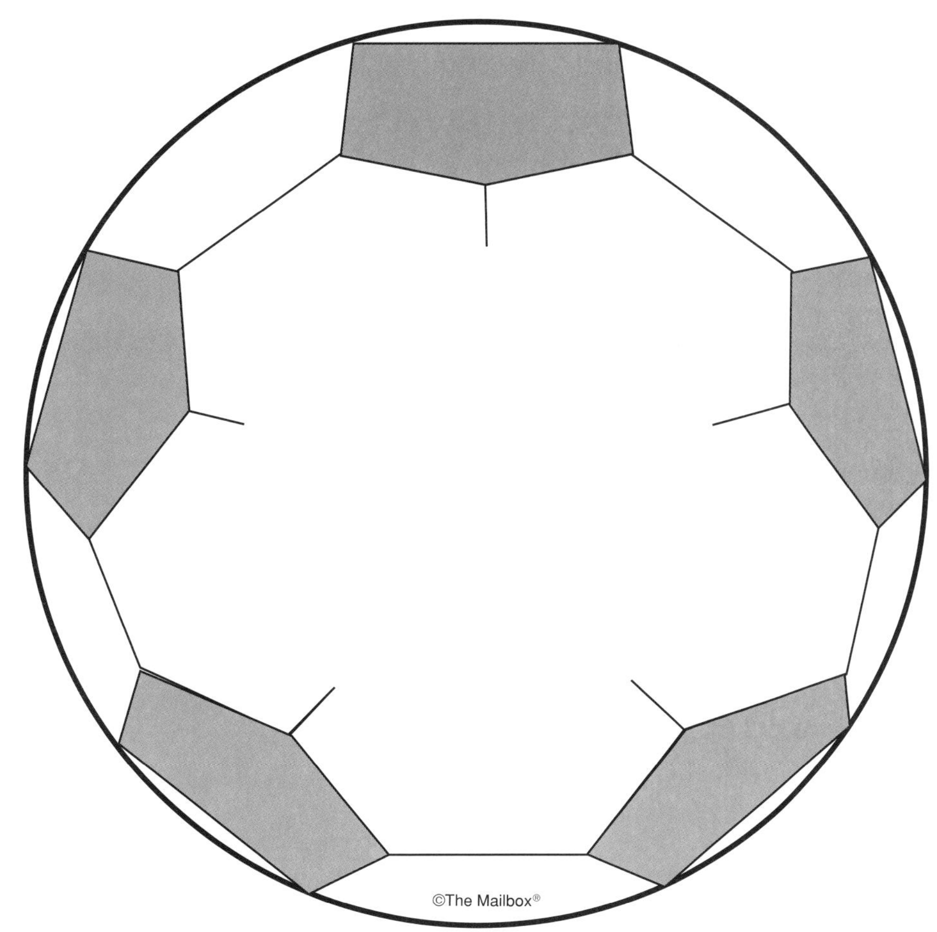

Flower Patterns

Use with "A Literary Path" on page 267.

Use with "A Literary Path" on page 267.

Backboard and Net Pattern

Use with "Winning Points" on page 268.

Elephant and Peanut Patterns

Use with "Math Skills We'll Never Forget..." on page 268.

Problem Solved!

Q&A Problem Solved!

Your Solutions to Classroom Challenges

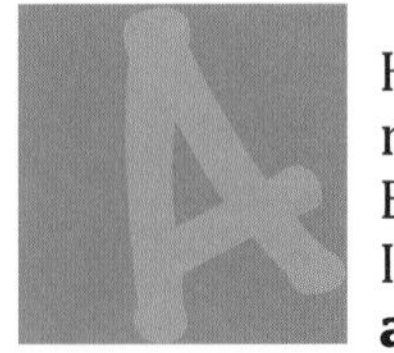

Here's a hint for cutting down on the number of lost homework papers. Each year on my school supply list, I request a **red pocket folder and a green pocket folder** for each student. Students know that anything I have them put in the green folder goes home; anything I have them put in the red folder stays at school.

Clare Delano, Oak View School, Bloomfield, NJ

The ten-minute rule works!
Researchers at Duke University looked at **more than 60 research studies** and found that *ten minutes of homework multiplied by the student's grade level* (fourth graders have 40 minutes of homework, fifth graders have 50 minutes of homework, and so on) is about the right amount to maximize the benefit.

How do you help students *keep up with homework?*

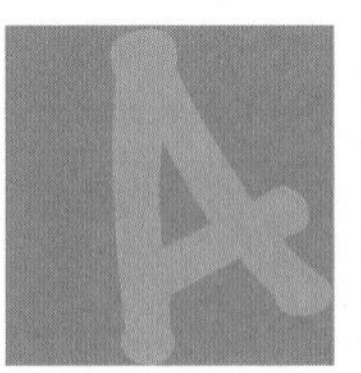

One year I had a **very large class,** and I didn't have time to track down forgotten assignments. I instituted this system: for every ten assignments that every student turned in on time, the class got to do a fun activity. Students took the initiative to remind one another about turning in work! *(Editor's note: It might be fun to create a display to track this. Try making a chart titled "Take Ten!" Then, when the class reaches its goal, give students ten minutes of free time or extra recess!)*

Meggan Tavel, Monroe Elementary, Janesville, WI

I motivate students with something I call **test question stickers**. If a student doesn't have any late assignments during the month, she receives three stickers. (I use the small colored circles sold at office supply stores.) Any time a student doesn't know the answer to a test question, she can place one of her stickers on the question and I count it as correct. It's a great motivator!

David Wolff, Trojan Elementary, Osawatomie, KS

TAKE TEN!	
① Spelling	✓
② Math in Minutes	✓
③ Spin a Story	✓
④	✓

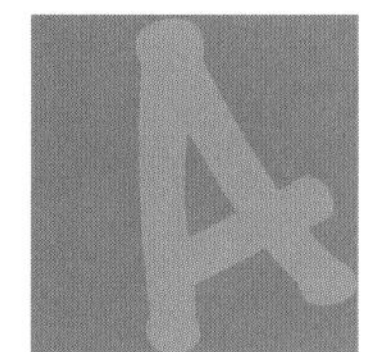

I purchased a small bank. Every time we have a successful "no late homework" week, I allow each student to **put a plastic coin in the bank.** Once we fill the bank, we have a class party to celebrate!

Fran Rivett, Seneca Grade School, Seneca, IL

It's your turn! We're always looking for your tips, ideas, and suggestions. **Go to TheMailbox.com to share!**

Q&A Problem Solved!

Your Solutions to Classroom Challenges

To solve the problem of students wanting to use the noisy pencil sharpener throughout the day, I keep extra pencils in a cup. If a student needs a sharper pencil, he **trades his dull pencil for a sharp one** in the cup. At the end of the day, I have a classroom helper sharpen the pencils in the cup so they're ready for the next day. *Sally McGuire, Greensboro West Elementary, Greensboro, AL*

Research by Robert J. Marzano et al. found that, over a year's time, a single class will have between **980 to 1,800 disruptions!**

How do you *manage classroom disruptions?*

I use a three-card system to **manage student requests** when I'm working with small groups. I have each student write her name on three small, brightly colored index cards. Next, I have each child tape a library pocket to the side of her desk and slip the cards inside. Then, if a student needs to go to the bathroom, sharpen her pencil, or ask me a question, she silently shows me the appropriate card. Without stopping what I'm doing, I nod to say yes or shake my head to say no. If permission is granted, the child leaves the card on her desk while she's away. As soon as she returns, she slips the card into her desk pocket and gets back to work. *Kathryn KinCannon, Cunningham Elementary, Beloit, WI*

yellow card = bathroom pass
blue card = sharpen a pencil
green card = talk to the teacher

To eliminate disruptions in my classroom, I teach my students these simple **silent signals**. A student signals he needs to go to the bathroom with one thumb up. To get a drink, the signal is holding one pinkie up. When a student needs to sharpen his pencil, he simply holds his pencil in the air. I require each student to make eye contact with me while he is signaling. If I wink, he has permission. It doesn't take my students long to learn that, if I am in the middle of instruction, my "winker" won't work! *Jacqueline Hills, Concord Community Schools, Concord, MI*

I made a **Frequently Asked Questions** (FAQ) board to keep from wasting time giving the same old answer to the same old question. For most questions, a class rule covers the answer. So the answer I post is a reminder of the class rule. For other questions that come up again and again, I have listed the most common answer. Now, if a student asks me one of the same old questions, I simply point to the board. (Substitute teachers love this!) *Melissa Shuey, Finksburg, MD*

Ms. Shuey's FAQ
Can I sharpen my pencil?
Can I go to the bathroom?
Can I get a drink of water?
What should I do when I finish my work?
Can I get something out of my backpack/locker?
Can we start getting ready to go home?

It's your turn! We're always looking for your tips, ideas, and suggestions. **Go to TheMailbox.com to share!**

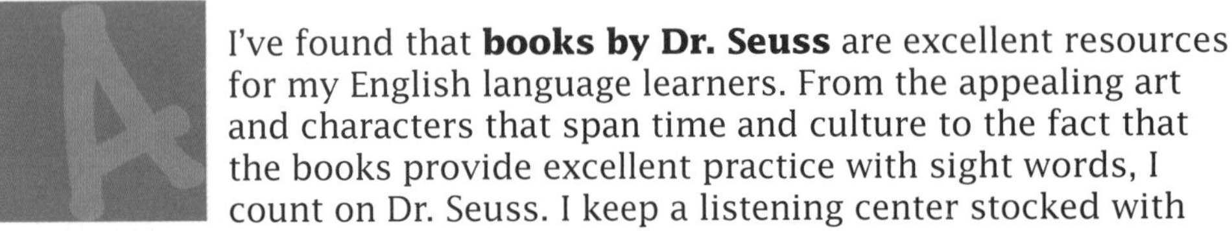

Problem Solved!

Your Solutions to Classroom Challenges

I've found that **books by Dr. Seuss** are excellent resources for my English language learners. From the appealing art and characters that span time and culture to the fact that the books provide excellent practice with sight words, I count on Dr. Seuss. I keep a listening center stocked with Dr. Seuss books and their audio versions. Once my ELLs are comfortable reading a Dr. Seuss book, we use the book to create a readers' theater script that engages all my students. *Dr. Virginia Zeletzki, Delray Beach, FL*

How do you *meet the needs of your English language learners (ELLs)?*

I have a student volunteer accept the role of **advocate for a non-English-speaking student**. As her classmate's advocate, the child supports, looks out for, and encourages her ELL buddy. *Sue Fleischmann, St. Mary's Visitation School, Sussex, WI*

I use sign language to help my ELLs **learn class routines**. I start by giving a hand signal when I announce a routine, such as lining up, turning in homework, or taking restroom breaks. Once the student is comfortable with our routines, I start announcing them without using their hand signs. After each announcement, I pause, giving my English language learner time to process the command. If she's unsure about what to do, I add the sign and repeat the command. Before long, my ELL is confidently keeping up! *Roxanne LaBell Dearman, Charlotte, NC*

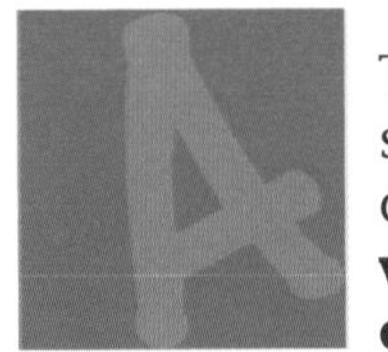

To help build my Spanish-speaking ELLs' vocabularies and confidence, I feature **anchor words that are cognates**—words that sound similar, look similar, and have similar meanings in English and in Spanish. Each time I introduce a cognate or a student recognizes one in his reading, I write the word and its Spanish counterpart on a paper anchor shape. Then I post the anchors on a board titled "Cognates Keep Us Anchored!" *Kim Minafo, Apex, NC*

diamond diamante

tip: Look for French, Italian, and Portuguese cognates too!

Between 1979 and 2008, the number of school-age children who spoke a language other than English at home grew from **3.8 million to 10.9 million.** (US Department of Education)

It's your turn! We're always looking for your tips, ideas, and suggestions. **Go to TheMailbox.com to share!**

Q&A Problem Solved!

Your Solutions to Classroom Challenges

Studies show some students don't actually realize that their efforts directly affect their success. They have to learn that!

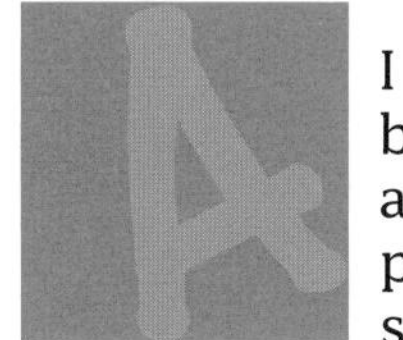

I have a **Wall of Fame** in my classroom. I decorate a bulletin board with a border of spotlights and stars and leave the center blank. When I notice a student putting her best effort into a project, I give her a star sticker. When she earns three star stickers, she becomes a classroom celebrity. She traces her hand on the bulletin board and signs her autograph beneath the tracings. *Amy Satkoski, Orchard Park Elementary, Indianapolis, IN*

How do you *keep your students motivated?*

I use **Classroom Reward Bingo** to motivate my students. I make a bingo grid on a sheet of poster board and laminate it. Next, I label cards with the grid's coordinates, put them in a bag, and post the grid. To reward perseverance, excellent behavior, or good citizenship, I have students write their names on the grid using wipe-off markers. When the grid is full, I randomly draw five cards and announce the coordinates. The students who have written their names in those spaces win homework passes. After handing out the passes, I clear the board and we start a new round. *Jill Zloty, Charles England Intermediate, Lexington, NC*

My answer is in the cards. I buy **inexpensive decks of cards** and give students the cards from one deck to reward and motivate their participation in class and group activities. When I've given away all the cards in one deck, I draw ten cards from another deck, announcing and showing each card as I draw it. Then I award each student holding a matching card a small prize. *Amy Bruening, Sacred Heart School, Yankton, SD*

I give students **Learning Medals of Honor**. I write words of encouragement on construction paper medals and keep a supply of them handy. I give the medals to students who are working hard, encouraging each other, following directions, and making other positive choices. Students can save their medals or turn them in for bonus points on homework assignments. *Colleen Dabney, Williamsburg, VA*

It's your turn! We're always looking for your tips, ideas, and suggestions. **Go to TheMailbox.com to share!**

Q&A Problem Solved!

Your Solutions to Classroom Challenges

I put a hanging file folder for each student in a small desktop file box and keep the box near my desk. When a student is absent, I put the day's assignments, announcements, or other paperwork on her desk throughout the day. Then, at the end of the day, I clip everything together, add the date, and **put the packet in the child's folder**. When the student returns to school, she knows right where to gather her makeup work.

Georgia Boethin, Humbolt Elementary, Canyon City, OR

How do you *help students who've been absent keep up with their makeup work?*

I designate several responsible students as scribes. When a child is absent, I give a scribe a sheet of **reusable carbon paper** and a blank sheet of paper. Throughout the day, anytime the child takes notes or records an assignment, she slips the carbon paper between her page and the blank sheet. As my scribe writes, she automatically makes a copy for her absent classmate!

Michelle Bayless, Fredericksburg, VA

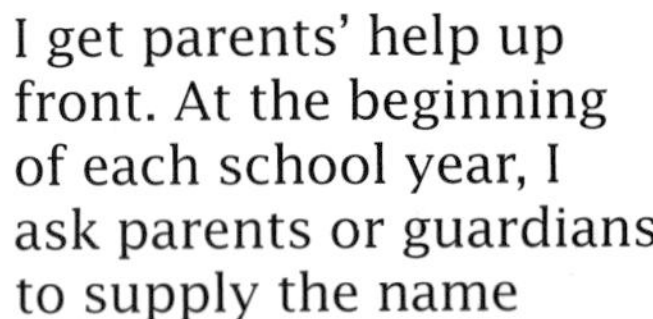

I get parents' help up front. At the beginning of each school year, I ask parents or guardians to supply the name of **another student in our school** with whom I could send makeup work home. Getting makeup work home quickly helps absent students keep up, and parents really appreciate not having to scramble to figure out how to get the work when their children are sick.

Jill Burrows, Halifax Elementary, Halifax, PA

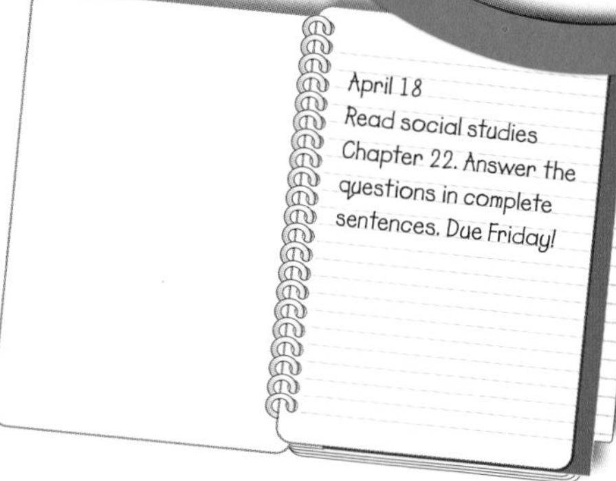

*Statistics show that, on average, **10% of K–12 students nationwide** are considered chronically absent—they miss about one of every ten days of school.*

I motivate students to complete all their makeup work (and regular homework too!) with this simple tip. I **pick a mystery problem or question** on every assignment. If the student completes a mystery problem, he earns a small treat or a few extra points. Since the child doesn't know which item I've picked, he's more likely to attempt all of them!

Rebecca Juneau, Highland Elementary, Lake Stevens, WA

It's your turn! We're always looking for your tips, ideas, and suggestions. **Go to themailbox.com to share!**

Our Readers Write

Our Readers WRITE...

(and EMAIL and BLOG and TWEET and POST)

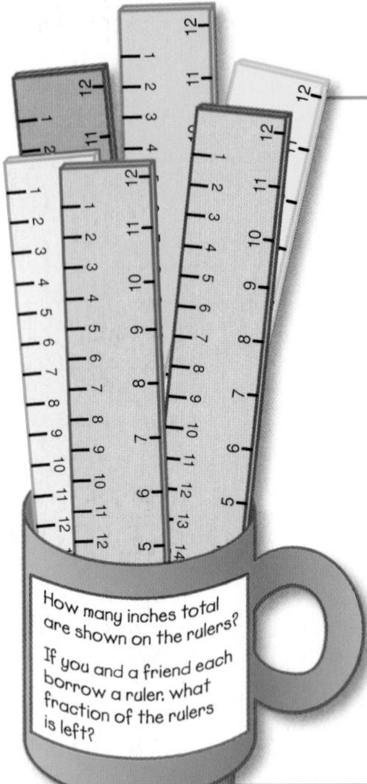

Math Walk

At the beginning of the year, I weave math practice into a tour of the classroom. In advance, I label spots in the room with math-related tasks and questions. Then I send small groups of students from location to location. Each child carries a notebook for recording his responses. My students become familiar with the room, and I get a peek at their math skills! *Trisha Koch, Batesville Intermediate, Batesville, IN*

"I LOVE your magazine. I have been using it in my classroom since 1990."—*Cajsa Howland Sheen via Facebook*

"Great teaching ideas! My students love them all!"—*Jennifer Marcinkus Chumbley via Facebook*

Hands Free

Trying to keep students' attention when manipulatives are within reach can be tricky, so I use these fun directions. I teach my students that when I say "roller coaster," they are to put anything that is in their hands on their desks. Then they raise their hands in the air as if they are riding a roller coaster. When I see all hands in the air, I say "straps" and have students cross their arms as though they're strapped in their seats. It works great every time! *Shelie Collins, First Baptist Christian Academy, Pasadena, TX*

EMAIL REMINDERS

I make it a priority to get a frequently accessed email address from each student's parent or guardian. Then I enter the email addresses into a distribution list on my computer, making sure to include the school year in the group's name. I email the group a few days before a test or project due date, putting the reminder in the subject line. I list the chapters, assignment particulars, extra credit options, and links in the email. I can quickly keep parents in the loop, and my students are much more prepared! ***Sheri Switzer, Northridge Middle, Crawfordsville, IN***

"Thank you for the wonderful ideas that you provide every month! I look forward to my new edition like it's Christmas morning!"—*Rolanda Staley, Aiken, SC, via The Mailbox® Blog*

Our Readers WRITE...
(and EMAIL and BLOG and TWEET and POST)

"I have subscribed to *The Mailbox*® since 2000. I love it and use it all the time!"—*Linda M. Huttman via Facebook*

WORLD WONDERS

I use this transition activity to improve my students' global perspectives! I keep a world map posted that shows the time zone divisions. When students are lining up or waiting to leave for the day, I pose questions about different time zones that require students to locate and compare cities and countries around the world. It's a simple way to make every minute count!
Marie E. Cecchini, West Dundee, IL

If it's 6:00 PM in London, what time is it in San Francisco?

"*The Mailbox* has the best of everything. We teachers could not do without you!"—*Darlene Taig, Westland, MI, via The Mailbox® Blog*

It's Official!

I make badges to help students remember their cooperative group roles! First, I make a class set of cooperative group job cards, listing a role on one side and its description on the back. Then I buy badge holders and place a job card in each one. When it's time for a science investigation or literature circle, I give each student in a group a different badge. Every child knows his job and can easily see the roles of the rest of his group. *Deb Martin, Starside Elementary, DeSoto, KS*

Use the same color card for each job. It will make the cards easier to sort, and just a glance will tell you who is performing which job.

In the Box

My students have no trouble rounding numbers or decimals when they use these simple steps!

1. Look at the number. Find the place to which you need to round. Draw a box around the digit in that place.
2. Study the number to the right of the box. If that number is four or less, the number in the box will not change. If that number is five or greater, the number in the box will be rounded up.
3. Rewrite the number, keeping the numbers to the left of the box the same. Change the number in the box if it needs to be rounded up. Otherwise, leave it the same. Then convert each digit to the right of the box to a zero. *Judy Kaegi, Hardin County Elementary, Elizabethtown, IL*

123.456
123.460

Our Readers WRITE...

(and EMAIL and BLOG and TWEET and POST)

PARTNERING UP

With just a little prep, my parent volunteers become reading helpers for my students and me! When the volunteer arrives in my room, I give her a reading selection and a copy of a simple form like the one shown. I introduce the volunteer to a student and ask her to take notes as the student reads aloud. Not only does my student get some one-to-one reading time, but I can use the volunteer's notes, along with my own observations, to keep track of the student's skills. Everybody wins! ***Nicole Weber, Edna Ferber Elementary, Appleton, WI***

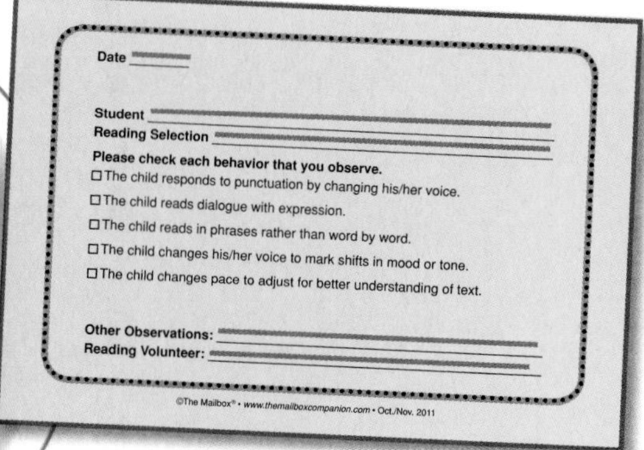

Date _____

Student _____

Reading Selection _____

Please check each behavior that you observe.

- ☐ The child responds to punctuation by changing his/her voice.
- ☐ The child reads dialogue with expression.
- ☐ The child reads in phrases rather than word by word.
- ☐ The child changes his/her voice to mark shifts in mood or tone.
- ☐ The child changes pace to adjust for better understanding of text.

Other Observations: _____

Reading Volunteer: _____

©The Mailbox® • www.themailboxcompanion.com • Oct./Nov. 2011

"I love *The Mailbox*!!! I have been a subscriber for nine years!"—*Diana Oldham via Facebook*

Who, What, Where?

To help build my students' questioning skills, I save one-page flyers that end up in my yard, on my mailbox, in my mailbox, or in the newspaper. (Some of them even come in plastic resealable bags that protect the paper!) I number the flyers and put them at a center. Then I have each child pick a flyer, study it, and write at least five questions based on the information on the page. Once every student has rotated through the center, I staple students' questions to the flyers. Then I have each child pick a different flyer and answer his classmates' questions. Cynthia Woodard, Fayetteville, GA

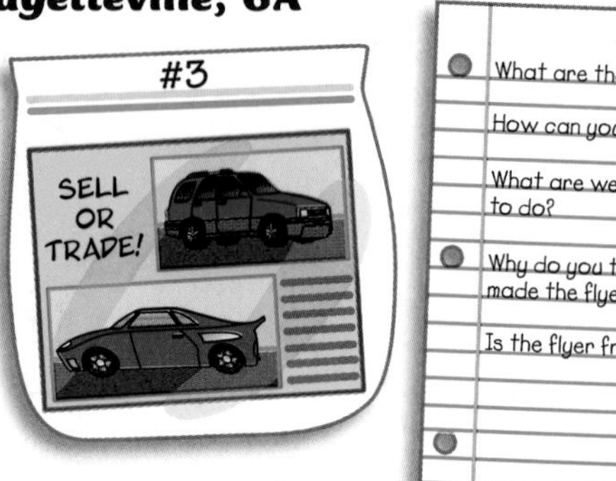

The MAILBOX BLOG

"I am so thankful for *The Mailbox* and all the teachers who share their ideas."—*Ruth Zabelin, Kingsville, TX, via The Mailbox Blog*

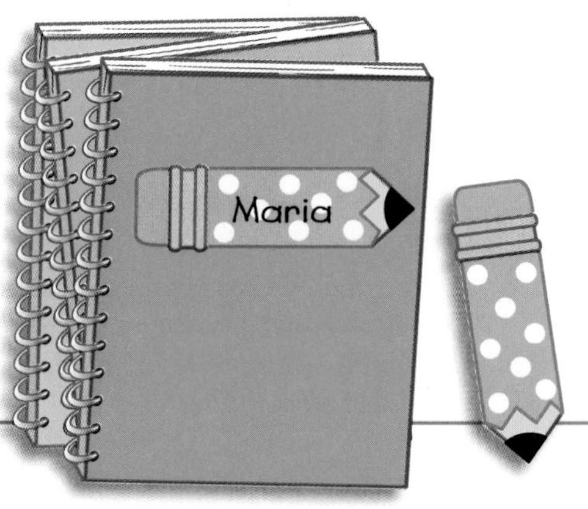

Purposeful Patterns

Here's a tip that serves double duty—it helps me organize students' journals into easy-to-review groups and gives each journal a decorative touch. I buy colorful scrapbook paper in six different patterns. Next, I make six die-cut shapes out of each pattern. I keep one of each patterned cutout. Then I have each student choose a cutout, write her name on it, and glue it to the front of her journal. When I'm ready to review journals, I tape a cutout to the board and the students with the matching pattern know it's their turn to pass me their journals. *Kim Pankey, Euper Lane Elementary, Fort Smith, AR*

Our Readers WRITE...

(and EMAIL and BLOG and TWEET and POST)

"I love *The Mailbox* magazine. It has enhanced my classrooms since the 1980s."—*Lisa Parks Reed via Facebook*

Where? There!

My students had a hard time knowing when to use *their, there,* and *they're* in their writing. So I taught them two tricks that have made a big difference! First, I taught them to substitute *they are* for the mystery word and then reread the sentence. If the substitution makes sense, the right word is *they're*. Then I taught each student that if she wants to use the place word, she should make sure her spelling of *there* includes the word *here*. Simple and effective! **Samantha Call, Father Anglim Academy, Fort Myers, FL**

They're is they are.

8.04

8.14

8.4

DO THE DECIMAL SHUFFLE

When my students get a little antsy, I have them practice ordering decimals! First, I have each child take an index card on which I've written a decimal. I have students hold their cards without looking at them. Then I turn on fun, upbeat music and have students cha-cha around the room. After a moment or two, I turn off the music and challenge students to arrange themselves in order as quickly as possible. If we have time for another round, I collect and shuffle the cards. Then I hand out the cards again and turn the music back on. We keep a class record of our times. My students love the challenge of trying to beat their best time. ***Brooke Beverly, Dudley Elementary, Dudley, MA***

A Tuneful Reminder

To help my students remember the difference between prime and composite numbers, I wrote this fun song. *Lisa Geraci, Eden Elementary, Eden, NY*

Digital Ditty

(sung to the tune of "Frère Jacques")

I'm a prime number. I'm a prime number.
Yes, I am. Yes, I am.
I only have two factors—yes, just two factors,
One and me, one and me.

I'm composite. I'm composite.
Yes, I am. Yes, I am.
I have more than two factors, more than two factors,
More than two, more than two.

"Thank you for the ideas I have gotten from *The Mailbox* magazine over the years. My fellow teachers think I am so smart—even when I tell them my idea is from *The Mailbox*."—*Linda Jones, Austin, TX, via The Mailbox Blog*

Our Readers WRITE...

(and EMAIL and BLOG and TWEET and POST)

A COZY READ

To encourage my students to talk about books, I turn my classroom into a makeshift coffeehouse every Friday. I give each child a cup of hot chocolate to sip during uninterrupted silent reading time. Then students gather together to share summaries of their books or to update the group about exciting plot events. The relaxed atmosphere helps students feel comfortable talking about their books and helps us end the week on a positive note. ***Annmarie Andersen, Gretchen Reeder Elementary, Omaha, NE***

"*The Mailbox* is an excellent resource for my teaching plans. Thank you for helping me find great ideas to implement in my lessons each and every week."—*Cathy Jo McCall via Facebook*

$\frac{1}{3}$ $\frac{1}{3}$ $\frac{1}{3}$

$\frac{1}{4}$ $\frac{1}{4}$ $\frac{1}{4}$ $\frac{1}{4}$

$\frac{1}{5}$ $\frac{1}{5}$ $\frac{1}{5}$ $\frac{1}{5}$ $\frac{1}{5}$

Quick Comparison

To keep my students' fraction concepts sharp, I give each pair of students a sentence strip. Then I assign each duo a different number from 1 to 12 and guide the partners to fold their strip into that many equal sections. Next, I have the students trace each fold line and label each section with its fraction. We display the strips in a column and, voila! Students have instant fraction references. *Becky Fuentes, Highland Elementary, Lake Stevens, WA*

On the Ball

Sometimes my students have trouble dragging interactive elements across our interactive whiteboard. To solve this problem, I give the child working at the whiteboard a tennis ball. The ball helps the student apply just the right amount of pressure as he touches the onscreen element and successfully drags it with the ball. *Nicholas Sveum, Edgerton Community Elementary, Edgerton, WI*

"I totally love *The Mailbox* website and magazines!"—*Karen Lesmerises, Allenstown, NH, via The Mailbox Blog*

Our Readers WRITE...

(and EMAIL and BLOG and TWEET and POST)

"I love the various types of activities in *The Mailbox* magazine. It's really a pleasure to have it!"—*Rola Abou Dargham via Facebook*

Dewey's Decimals

I combine library skills with math skills and introduce my students to interesting nonfiction materials during one session in our school library. Beforehand, I set aside a stack of assorted nonfiction books for each small group. Then we discuss the Dewey decimal classification system. Next, I have each group take a stack of books and arrange the books by their classification numbers. When the group's books are in the proper order, I guide the students to return the books to their shelves. Students get practice ordering decimals, they learn how to find nonfiction resources, and they're introduced to some great new book titles! ***Cathy Pate, Unicoi County Intermediate, Erwin, TN***

"Tri" This!

When my students need help remembering the attributes of an equilateral triangle, we sing this song. To further reinforce its meaning, I give each child three cotton swabs and have her use them to form an equilateral triangle. ***Debbie Ashworth, Foust Elementary, Greensboro, NC***

Equilateral Triangle

(sung to the tune of "Three Blind Mice")

Three straight lines,
Three straight lines
Make a triangle,
Make a triangle!
The sides connect at the vertices.
When angles measure 60 degrees
And lengths all show equality,
It's equilateral,
Equilateral.

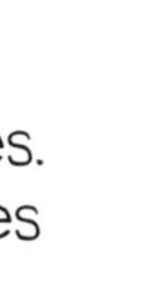

CHANGE OF PLANS

For days when bad weather or illness keeps a large number of students away from school, I have the students who do come create board games. Each small group of students makes up a themed gameboard that includes a path and writes question cards that review facts and skills from every subject. After the games are all done, the students play and evaluate each other's games. What a great review for everyone! ***Kerri-Lynn Hickman, Coloniale Estates School, Beaumont, Alberta, Canada***

This is a great idea for keeping students busy during recess when bad weather or cold temperatures keep them indoors.

I have made many games and activities from ideas in *The Mailbox*. I love this magazine!"—*Cindy MacDonald, Raynham, MA, via The Mailbox Blog*

Our Readers WRITE...

(and EMAIL and BLOG and TWEET and POST)

Time Will Tell

I replaced my classroom clock with a clock that has roman numerals instead of the digits 1 through 12. My students practice reading roman numerals all year, and they love doing it! ***Loida Estella Howard, Moss Point Upper Elementary, Moss Point, MS***

It's 11:30—lunchtime!

KEEP 'EM THINKING!

Do you have a few early finishers you need to challenge? I did! So I collected 25 single-serving cereal boxes. Next, I cut construction paper pieces to cover the fronts of the boxes and wrote a large letter on each one. I taped each letter onto a cereal box and arranged the boxes in a 5 x 5 grid to resemble a Boggle game. Every Monday morning, I rearrange the boxes and switch out a few of the letters to create a new puzzle. Then I give students until Friday to find words of three or more letters within the grid. I award homework bonus points for students' discoveries. A three-letter word earns one point. A four-letter word earns two points and so on. ***Jennifer Defeo, Silver Run School, Millville, NJ***

whale + 3
sea + 1
hare + 2
where + 3
share + 3
were + 2

tip: Clean, plastic single-serving cereal bowls work great too, and they stack together for storage.

"I love the new layout of *The Mailbox* magazine. It's easy to find what you need, and the latest tweets and messages from Facebook get published. I can't wait to use it!"—*Nicole DeVincenzo via Facebook*

Divide and Conquer!

To ramp up students' interest in my division center, I created a division bracket using scrap pieces of PVC pipe and a 90 degree elbow fitting. I cut 4- and 12-inch lengths of pipe and then slid each section into the elbow as shown. Next, I put a deck of cards without the tens and face cards at the center. When a student visits the center, he draws five cards, putting four cards inside the bracket and one outside to form a division problem. Then he solves the problem on his own paper and returns the cards to the bottom of the stack. As time allows, the student draws five more cards and creates a new problem. ***Idy Stemaly, Ruth Hoppin Elementary, Three Rivers, MI***

"Thanks so much for striving to make learning fun!"—*Sarah Chestnut via The Mailbox Blog*

Our Readers WRITE...

(and EMAIL and BLOG and TWEET and POST)

"I love this magazine. I have used it most of my 28 years of teaching and will continue to use it until I retire! Thank you for all the wonderful 'tools' you have given me over the years!"—*Lisa Reed via The Mailbox Blog*

...from TheMailbox blog

A Reason to Write

I capitalized on the abundance of items in our school Lost and Found to give my students real-world practice writing descriptions. Each student picked an item and wrote a vivid description of it. Then students used their descriptions to create eye-catching posters that we put up around the school in hopes of reuniting students with their lost items. *Nancy Simpson, London, Ontario, Canada*

Found

Are you missing a fuzzy orange sweater? This sweater has

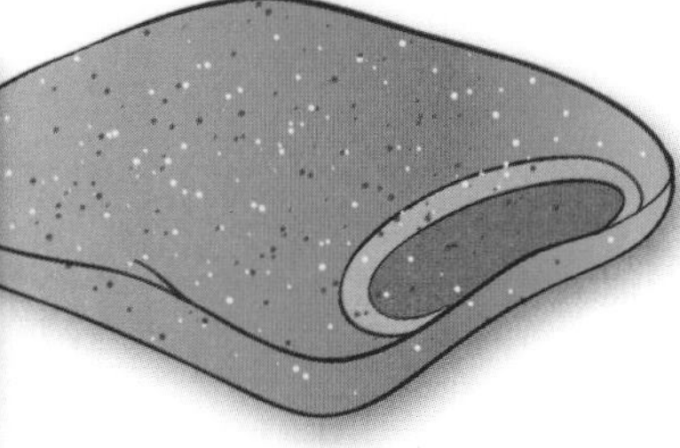

Top-Notch Practice

I use toy spinning tops to give my students practice measuring time and gathering and analyzing data. (The tops are sold as party favors in the party supplies section of a local discount store.) I give each pair of students a top and a stopwatch and have them take turns spinning the top. When one partner spins, the other partner times the duration of the spin and records the time in seconds. After each partner spins the top three times, the partners draw a bar graph to display their data. Next, the partners find the range, mean, median, and mode of their spinning times. Finally, each twosome shares its results and we create a bar graph of the class's results.
Debbie Berris, Poinciana Day School, West Palm Beach, FL

Read and Read Again

I've found a great (and simple) way to boost my students' reading comprehension and engagement during novel studies. As students read each chapter in a novel, they complete journaling, comprehension, and vocabulary activities. When students finish a chapter's activities, I read the chapter aloud and have students follow along in their books. This creates excellent opportunities for discussion, clarification, pronunciation corrections, identifying figurative language, and celebrations of an author's style. To top it off, my students love it! ***Debbie Berris, Poinciana Day School, West Palm Beach, FL***

"Thank you, *Mailbox.* I have subscribed to this magazine for more than a decade, and I love how it has continued to evolve with the changes in education."
—Theresa Clevenstine via The Mailbox Blog

Our Readers WRITE...

(and EMAIL and BLOG and TWEET and POST)

Revise-o-Rama

To give my students authentic practice revising, I've built a file of student writing. I just cover students' names, copy the pages, and organize them by writing genre, trait, and skill. For example, I had a group of students who tended to rush through their conclusions. So I shared with my students a folder of previous students' work that had poor endings. They were quick to notice the inadequate endings, which made it easier to recognize the weaknesses in their own writing. Every year, I add new writing samples to the file, so now I have several examples for any writing lesson! **Becky Fuentes, Highland Elementary, Lake Stevens, WA**

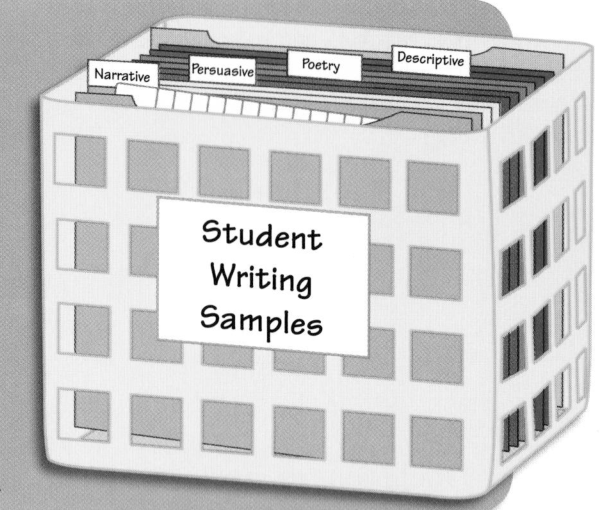

"My favorite magazine!"—*Julie Viano via Facebook*

"I really love reading all the tips and ideas from my fellow teachers. *The Mailbox* magazines are great!"—*Linda Stoffan, Rio Rancho, NM, via The Mailbox Blog*

Brain Booster Booklets

I use index card booklets that make keeping track of daily warm-ups a cinch. Each Monday, I give each student six index cards stapled together. On the top card, the student records his name and the date. After I post a warm-up, the students take out their booklets and do the work on the next available index card. My students keep their booklets during the week. The corrected booklets make handy study guides for students, and I collect them periodically to track students' progress and as work samples for parent conferences. ***Shayla Palin, Cedar Creek Middle School, Youngsville, NC***

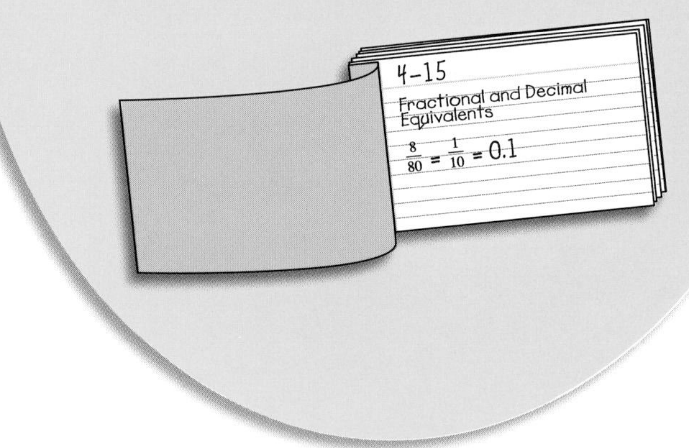

Rainy Day Scientists

When rainy days keep my students inside for recess, we use the extra time for science! I keep easy-to-do science activities and experiments together with any necessary materials in resealable plastic bags. Then I hand them out, and students work with partners to complete the activities. I get to squeeze in a little more science time, and my students look forward to indoor recesses! *Missy Goldenberg, Overland Park, KS*

Our Readers WRITE...

(and EMAIL and BLOG and TWEET and POST)

...from The Mailbox Blog

Poetry Pick-Me-Ups

Every day I set aside a short period of time for my students to read or compose poetry. We find poems that are quick and fun to read. I make it a point to let my young poets share their work with the class. Then I save my students' poems throughout the year and combine them in a class anthology that becomes a treasured part of my class library! ***Jill Exe, Harold Kavelook School, Kaktovik, AK***

"I love *The Mailbox*. The activities are so colorful and creative."—*Nancy C. Allen, Glen Allen, VA*

Color by Number

Transforming coloring pages into math worksheets is a snap! I just download and print a coloring page. Before making copies, I program the page with math problems and create a color code. I like to pick colors you wouldn't normally associate with the image on the page, so my students are surprised when they finish. **Alana Haider, Trailside Elementary, Anchorage, AK**

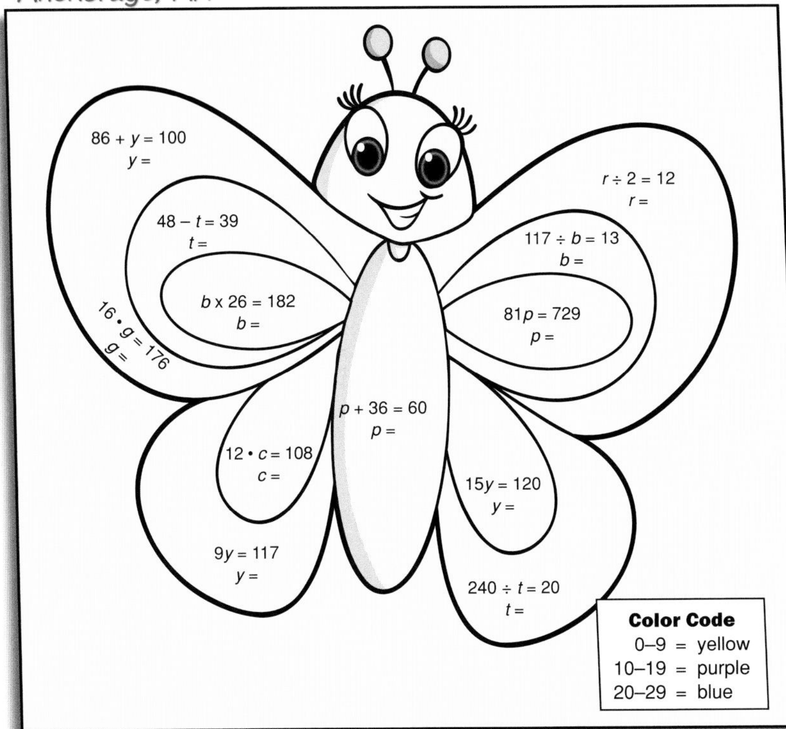

BREAK DANCE

My students know that every Wednesday at 11:00 we take a five-minute break for musical movement! The fun lies in the surprise of my music choice. I play all sorts of music, from swing to rock and roll to classical to music from foreign lands. My students are invited to get up and move to the music or just stay in their seats and enjoy the musical break. We follow up with a quick discussion about the music. Not only is the break energizing, it's a great way for me to bring cultural diversity into the classroom and evoke dialogue that might not otherwise take place. ***Barbara Samuels, Riverview School, Denville, NJ***

"Love *The Mailbox*. It's been a big part of my classroom for many years!"—*Lynn McMinds Harrell via Facebook*

Our Readers WRITE...

(and EMAIL and BLOG and TWEET and POST)

Goin' Round in Circles

To review parts of a circle, we play an upper-grades game based on Duck, Duck, Goose. To play, the leader walks around the circle two times, saying "circumference" each time. Then the leader taps a student (the runner) and calls, "Go circumference," "Go radius," or "Go diameter." Then the runner runs around the outside of the circle and returns to her spot for circumference, races to the center of the circle for radius, or runs straight across the center of the circle for diameter. When the runner reaches her destination, the sitting students repeat the part's name. Then the leader and the runner switch places, and the game continues. After a little running around, my students remember the parts of a circle! ***Deeann Schertz, Riggs Elementary, Gilbert, AZ***

"*The Mailbox* has been a main staple in my life since I started teaching full time in '97. I don't know what I would have done without it as I started my career and was looking for any and all ideas—from classroom management to open house." *Stacey Kavalak St. Peter via Facebook*

Come Clean

I use the acronym SOAP to help my students look for and **identify figurative language**. Whenever we study an author's writing style, I ask my students whether the author used any SOAP. Then we scour the passage for examples. It's an easy way to help my students remember forms of figurative language! *Maria Bickel, Myerstown, PA*

S = similes
O = onomatopoeia
A = alliteration
P = personification

A SWEET BUNCH

At the end of the year, I make lollipop bouquets for my students. I simply take apart a floral lei, stick a lollipop in the center hole of each silk flower, and slide the flower to the base of the lollipop. Once I have four lollipop blooms, I wrap floral tape around the lollipop sticks underneath the flowers. Then I attach a personalized note to the bouquet with curling ribbon. My students get a kick out of these sweet surprises! ***Lisa Cullen, Parkview Elementary, Rosemount, MN***

"*My*MAILBOX and *The Mailbox* magazine get extra gold stars for always being great."—*Heather Check via The Mailbox Blog*

Special Features

WHAT CAN YOU DO WITH A MINUTE OR TWO?

Use these activities to make every minute count!

Make It a Math Moment

Think of two numbers. Quickly calculate and then post the numbers' sum, difference, and product. Next, challenge students to guess your original numbers, guiding each child to explain the method behind his guess. Congratulate the successful guesser and play again as time allows.

$x + y = 20$
$y - x = 6$
$xy = 91$

x equals seven and *y* equals thirteen.

Get Them to Listen

Write a series of simple tasks on separate index cards. When you have a few minutes, display the cards and have a student volunteer draw three or more cards. Read each card aloud. Then have the child try to perform the tasks in order. If he remembers all the instructions, he gets to read the cards for the next student. If he forgets a task, classmates supply the missing direction, and another student takes a turn.

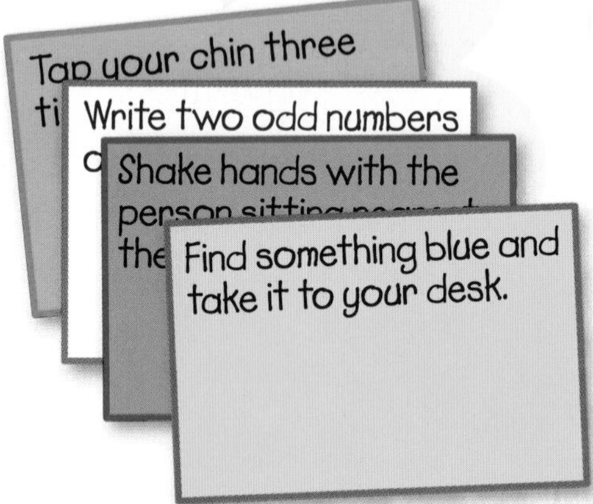

Issue a Sentence Challenge

Write four letters on the board. Then challenge each student to write as many different sentences as she can using words that begin with those letters in that order. For example, write *D, S, P,* and *R* and share a sentence of your own, such as "Dad saves purple rocks." As time allows, have students share their sentences.

Rev Up Reading Motors

Choose several books from your class library. Next, use a sticky note to mark an exciting or interesting passage in each book. Then place the books in a basket near your desk. The next time your class is ready and waiting for a specials teacher, assembly, or bell, dramatically read aloud a book's marked selection. Then put the book back in the basket and get ready for a chorus of "May I read that book?"

Review On-the-Spot

Have each student write on an index card two questions about a current unit of study, including the answers in parentheses. Next, have the child rate each question's value at two or three points. Then collect students' cards and keep them handy. When you have a few extra minutes, draw a card and read a question aloud. If a student volunteer answers correctly, award the class the noted number of points. Keep track of the class's points for an ongoing game students will love.

A Class Act

5 Timely Tips and Ideas for Putting Character Education Into Practice!

Encourage Each Other.

Make Mottoes

For this idea, share several mottoes, such as the Boy Scouts' Be Prepared, or the Coast Guard's *Semper Paratus*, which means "always ready." Next, introduce character traits one at a time and guide students to create a memorable motto for each one. Then post the mottoes near your classroom's main door to provide daily reminders. ***Debbie Ashworth, Julius I. Foust Elementary, Greensboro, NC***

Start With a Song

Choose three to five upbeat songs that have positive messages and combine them on a tape, CD, or MP3 player. Each morning, just before students enter the room, turn on the songs so that they play quietly as students come in, put their things away, and get started on the morning's work. The music will start each day on a positive note, and it naturally discourages chatter! ***Kim Minafo, Apex, NC***

Do a Demo!

Want students to be more thoughtful and careful in the things they say to and about each other? Try this simple demonstration. Squeeze a big blob of toothpaste onto a toothbrush and then tell students you've made a mistake and want to get the extra toothpaste back in the tube. *(As you try, the toothpaste tube gets messy.)* When you are unable to get the toothpaste back into the tube, guide students to think of the toothpaste as a rumor someone spread about someone else or as mean words someone accidentally said about someone else. Then point out that once any of us says something, it's very hard to take it back and there is often a mess afterward. ***Neda Issa, Aqsa School, Bridgeview, IL***

Create a Thought-Provoking Display

Decorate a bulletin board with oversize sticky notes made from construction paper and glued to the board. On each note, list an important character trait. Then, at the beginning of each week, give each student a sticky note and guide him to set a personal goal using one of the traits, write it on the note, and stick his note on the board. At the end of the week, have each student retrieve his note, assess his progress, and write about it on the note's flip side. Have students keep their notes inside their journals for occasional review and reflection. ***Melissa Bodnar, Zephyr Elementary, Whitehall, PA***

End on a Positive Note

Make dismissal count by wrapping up each school day with compliments. At first, model giving and accepting compliments. Next, encourage students to notice a fellow student's exemplary behavior. Then set aside five to ten minutes near the end of the day, and have students share compliments about each other. ***Marie E. Cecchini, West Dundee, IL***

tip: Guide students to jot quick notes anytime they spot a classmate's compliment-worthy actions. Then, when it's time for the end-of-the-day compliments, they'll be ready to share!

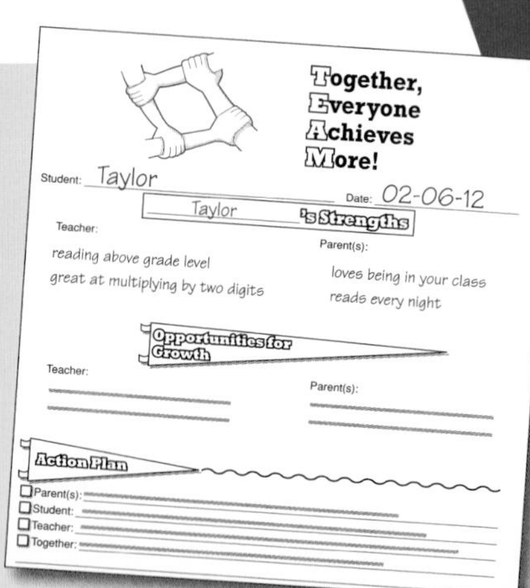
Together, Everyone Achieves More!

Student: Taylor Date: 02-06-12

Taylor 's Strengths

Teacher:
reading above grade level
great at multiplying by two digits

Parent(s):
loves being in your class
reads every night

Opportunities for Growth

Teacher:

Parent(s):

Action Plan

☐ Parent(s):
☐ Student:
☐ Teacher:
☐ Together:

1 There's No *I* in Team!

Think of each conference as a team meeting, and set the tone for positive collaboration. To prepare, fill out the top of a copy of page 303 for each child. During each conference, share your notes and record parents' concerns, hopes, and ideas on the page. Then work with parents to create a plan that includes actions for the student, his parents, and you. After the meeting, send a copy of the form home and keep the original for follow-up as needed. **Kelly Smith, Cranberry Township, PA**

I'm proud to be on your team!
Ms. Newsom told us that you are great at two-digit multiplication. Way to go, Taylor! Love, Mom and Dad

©The Mailbox® • TEC44059 • Feb./Mar. 2012

2 On a Positive Note

When it's time to wrap up the conference, just cut off the conference form's bottom section. Hand it to the student's parent and ask her to write a quick note to her child. Then fold the message for privacy and tape it to the student's desk to give the child a surprise greeting when he sits down at his desk. **Leigh Newsom, Cedar Road Elementary, Chesapeake, VA**

3 Hang On to It!

Here's a simple tip for making sure you have examples of student work to share with parents. Stock a file cabinet drawer with a hanging file for each student. When you spot a work sample that will be useful to share with a child's parents, set it aside. Quickly summarize your thoughts on a sticky note and put the note on the page or pages. Then slip each sample into the student's folder. When conference time rolls around, just pull out each child's folder, and you're ready to share! **Krystle Short Jones, Charlotte, NC**

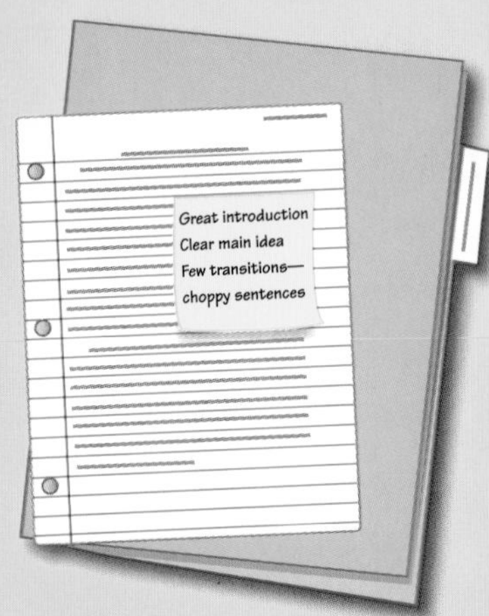

4 Prime-Time Viewing

Treat your parents to a behind-the-scenes look at their children. Make a digital slide show from photos and/or video clips of students at work or giving presentations. Then set up the slide show on a computer or TV in the hall so parents can watch their children and your class while they wait for their conference. If desired, set up the slide show in your classroom instead. Then start each conference with a clip of the student being discussed. Parents will be happy to see their children in action, and you have a minute to focus on that student and collect your thoughts. **C. J. Gray, Melrose Elementary, Wooster, OH, and Darlene Parks, Open Door Christian School, Troy, VA**

Together, Everyone Achieves More!

Student: ______________________ Date: ______________

______________'s Strengths

Teacher:

Parent(s):

Opportunities for Growth

Teacher:

Parent(s):

Action Plan

- ☐ Parent(s): ______________________
- ☐ Student: ______________________
- ☐ Teacher: ______________________
- ☐ Together: ______________________

I'm proud to be on your team!

Note to the teacher: Use the top form with "There's No *I* in Team!" on page 302. Use the note at the bottom with "On a Positive Note" on page 302.

FUN "4" ALL

Get your review questions ready—these simple-to-play games work with any subject!

1 TO THE TOP!

For this game, display a copy of the gameboard from page 305 and choose game markers to use with the paths. (Depending on your display surface, use magnets or pushpins or shade the spaces using different-colored markers.) Then divide students into two teams and designate each team's side of the mountain. When a student correctly answers a review question, move his team's marker along its path. The first team to reach the summit wins! **Kim Minafo, Apex, NC**

2 FOR FIVE MORE POINTS...

Don't let the name fool you—this game isn't just for math. Divide students into four teams and pose a question to a player from one team. If the child answers correctly, award her team five points; then ask the next team a question. If the student answers incorrectly, a student from another team can try to answer the question. If that student answers correctly, give his team 10 points. If that student is not correct, keep asking the question, adding five points to the total each time until the question is answered correctly. Repeat as time allows and award the team with the most points a small treat. **Julie Kaiser, Pine View Elementary, New Albany, IN**

3 IN ORBIT

Challenge each student to be your classroom's most-traveled astronaut with this variation of Around the World. Name one student the astronaut and have him stand next to another child's desk. Then read a review question to the student pair. If the astronaut is the first to answer correctly, he moves to the next student's desk. If the astronaut answers incorrectly or the other child gives the correct answer first, the seated student becomes the astronaut, and the former astronaut takes the new astronaut's seat. If neither student can answer the question, set it aside to review at the end of the game; then pose a new question. Keep playing as time and review material allow. **Ross Princiotto, Greenville, OH**

4 ACROSS, DOWN, OR DIAGONAL

This twist on tic-tac-toe, similar to a Hollywood Squares game, really gets students thinking! Have nine student volunteers, the game celebrities, sit in three rows of three, like a tic-tac-toe grid. Have each celebrity draw a large X on one side of a sheet of paper and draw a large O on the other side. Then divide the remaining students into two teams—the Xs and the Os.

To play, a player from team X names a student celebrity and both students listen as you read aloud a question. The celebrity responds with a real answer or made-up response. Then the player decides whether he agrees with the celebrity. If he agrees and the celebrity is correct, the player wins the space for his team. The celebrity holds up her paper, showing the X. If the player agrees and the answer was not correct, the other team wins the space. The celebrity holds up her paper showing the O. If the player disagrees with the celebrity's answer, he gives the answer he thinks is correct. If the player is correct, he wins the space for his team. If the player's response is incorrect, the other team wins the space. Keep playing until one team wins three spaces in a row or until the game comes to a draw. **Beth Walsh, McMurray Elementary, McMurray, PA**

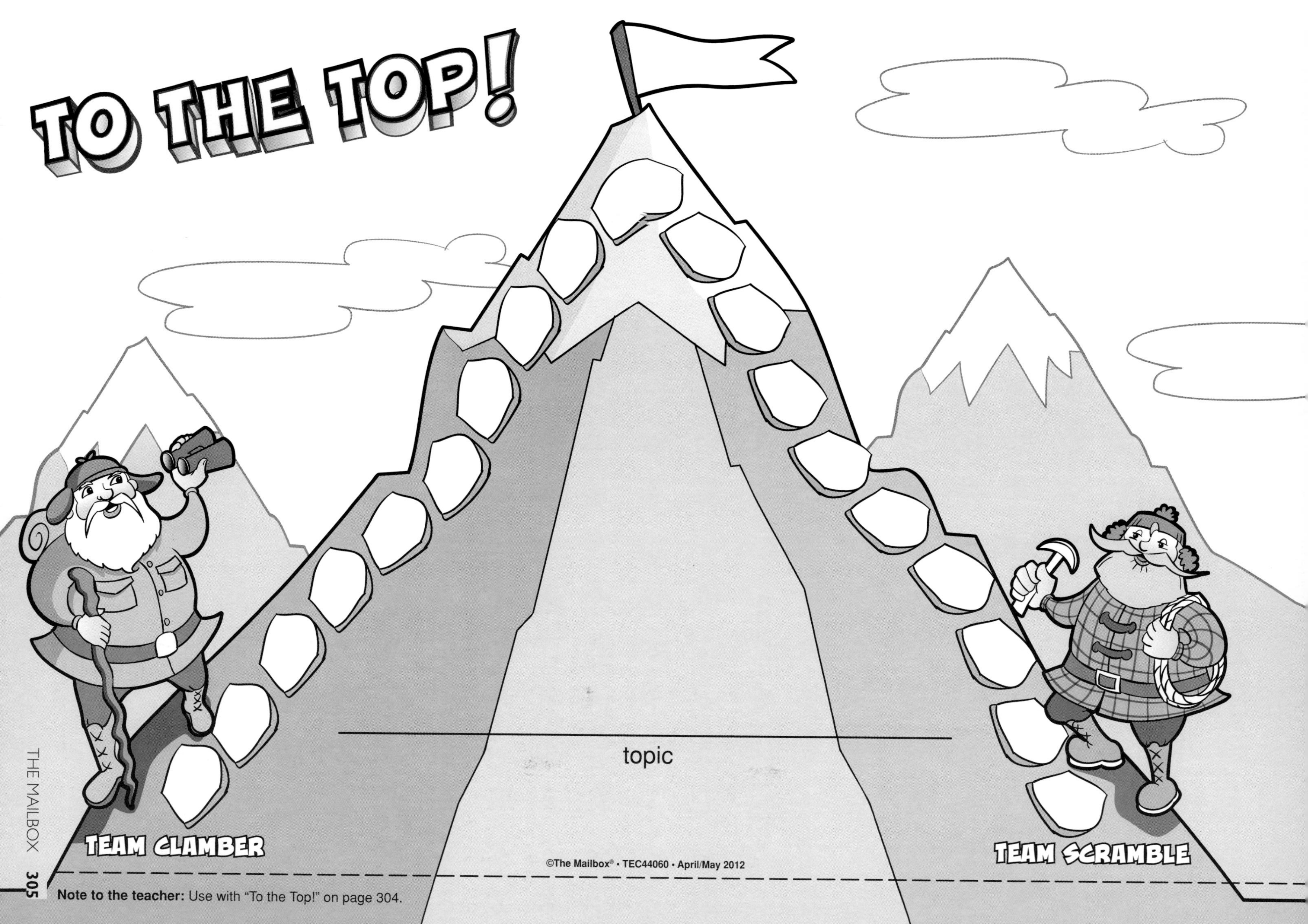

Note to the teacher: Use with "To the Top!" on page 304.

Finding the "Write" Words

35 Ready-to-Use Report Card Comments

Work Quality

The overall quality of __'s work

exceeds grade-level expectations
reflects focus and effort
reflects creativity
shows improvement
meets grade-level expectations
reflects his/her attention to creativity over skill
meets grade-level expectations in the following areas: ____
shows improvement but falls short of grade-level expectations
does not reflect focus and effort
reflects his/her struggle with ____
does not meet grade-level expectations
does not meet grade-level expectations in the following areas: ____

Positive Progress

I am pleased with ____'s

improved attitude
commitment to maintaining a passing grade average
increased class participation
efforts to complete and turn in his/her class work/homework/____
improvements in using his/her time wisely

I appreciate the way(s) __

follows directions
completes his/her work
contributes to class discussions
follows school and class rules
works independently
demonstrates self-control
participates in class activities
pays attention in class

Room for Improvement

Looking ahead, I believe ____'s school success will benefit from him/her

attending school regularly
improving his/her work habits
working on his/her ____ skills
consistently listening to and following directions
paying attention in class
being prepared and bringing necessary supplies to class
completing and turning in assignments
following all classroom rules
respecting the needs of fellow students
improving his/her self-control

Positive Descriptors

agreeable
astute
attentive
brilliant
careful
clever
confident
conscientious
considerate
cooperative
diligent
eager
encouraging
enjoyable
entertaining
enthusiastic
fantastic
friendly
good-humored
hardworking
helpful
imaginative
lovely
magnificent
mighty
neat
outstanding
pleasant
polite
practically perfect
precise
respectful
responsible
sharing
superior
thoughtful
well-adjusted
well-liked
witty
wonderful

Answer Keys

Page 8

Fraction written as words: one-fourth, two-thirds, seven-eighths, three-fourths, one-half

Number word from twenty-one to ninety-nine: thirty-five, fifty-nine, eighty-two, forty-seven, sixty-three

Compound word that begins with "self": self-employed, self-esteem, self-taught, self-control, self-respect

Two- or three-word family member name: sister-in-law, mother-in-law, father-in-law, brother-in-law, great-aunt

Capital letter joined with a noun: U-turn, G-rated, T-shirt, U-boat, V-neck

Adjective of two or more words that is used before a noun: one-way street, bottom-feeding fish, happy-go-lucky children, old-fashioned jeans, left-handed student

Page 11

children's	frogs'	teeth's
babies'	sheep's	oranges'
monsters'	pirates'	robots'
pickles'	sharks'	geese's
mice's	spiders'	monkeys'
castles'	laptops'	dragons'
dinosaurs'	deer's	people's
bugs'	feet's	pizzas'
cacti's or cactuses'	dice's	elves'
hippopotamuses'	men's	women's
flies'	gnomes'	songs'
movies'	singers'	bicycles'

Page 33

1. worried, worrying
2. stirred, stirring
3. delayed, delaying
4. guarded, guarding
5. gained, gaining
6. trapped, trapping
7. squealed, squealing
8. questioned, questioning
9. quoted, quoting
10. studied, studying
11. tried, trying
12. crammed, cramming
13. sprawled, sprawling
14. merged, merging
15. learned, learning
16. skated, skating

Bonus: worry, stir, trap, quote, study, try, cram, merge, skate

Page 34

I.
1. uneasy or unsettled
2. restful
3. prepared or set
4. unreliable
5. compulsory or mandatory
6. optional
7. recalls
8. unrealistic
9. down-to-earth or practical
10. bogus
11. opposed
12. distant or outlying
13. tense
14. free

II. Answers will vary.

Bonus: Answers will vary.

Page 35

1. tougher
2. biggest
3. younger; youngest
4. strongest; stronger
5. shorter
6. tallest; taller
7. tallest
8. stronger; strongest
9. bigger; biggest
10. oldest
11. older
12. bigger; biggest
13. heaviest; heavier
14. lightest
15. smaller
16. strongest; stronger
17. wildest
18. littlest
19. largest; larger
20. strongest; stronger

Bonus: comparative—1, 4, 5, 6, 11, 13, 15, 16, 19, 20; superlative—2, 3, 7, 8, 9, 10, 12, 14, 17, 18

Page 36

1. solvent, noun and adjective
2. defendant, noun and adjective
3. student, noun
4. hesitant, adjective
5. defiant, adjective
6. insistent, adjective
7. servant, noun
8. contestant, noun
9. propellant, noun and adjective
10. superintendent, noun
11. lubricant, noun and adjective
12. pleasant, adjective
13. repellent, noun and adjective
14. observant, noun and adjective
15. radiant, noun and adjective

Page 36 (continued)

16. The superintendent (N) was hesitant (A) to correct the observant (A) student (N).
17. The game show contestant (N) was insistent (A) that the words *happy* and *content* were similar but not the same.
18. In court, the defendant (N) was defiant (A).
19. Jane's pleasant (A) face was radiant (A) when she was told she would no longer be a servant (N).
20. Joe reported that water is a solvent (N) and oil is a lubricant (N).

Bonus: To add the suffix *-ent* or *-ant* to a word that ends in e, drop the final e and then add the suffix.

Page 37

Part 1

1. When Ben spent the day on a lobster boat, he learned a lot.
2. The boat's owners, Lola and Lou, have been working on boats since they were young.
3. Lola sets out lobster traps, or pots, one day, and she comes back in a day or two.
4. Each trap is connected to a colorful buoy so it will be easy to find.
5. Ben helps Lola and Lou look for and then pull up their pots.
6. Ben realizes the traps were baited with dead fish, and they are smelly!
7. Wearing gloves helps Ben keep the stinky smell off his hands.
8. If there are two or more lobsters in a trap, they might fight.
9. The first thing Lola does after she pulls a lobster out of a pot, is put a strong rubber band around both of its claws.
10. "How do you keep from getting pinched?" Ben asks Lola.

Part 2

11. Lola laughs as __she__ pulls a small lobster out of a trap.
12. As Lola tosses the lobster back, __she__ says, "__I__ get a lot of practice, and __I__ always wear gloves!"
13. Ben watches Lou pull up the next trap, and __he__'s amazed by the size of the lobster inside.
14. Lou pulls the enormous lobster out of the pot; __it__'s madly waving __its__ claws.
15. Even though Lola helps Lou, __they__ struggle to get bands around the lobster's giant claws.
16. Lola and Lou put fresh bait in __their__ traps and set __them__ out before __they__ head back to shore.

Page 39

1. It was a windy Saturday, and my dad was planning to work most of the day. (green)
2. Consequently, it was my job to keep my little sister, Lillie, and myself busy all day. (red)
3. We had two movies, a new video game, and lots of microwave popcorn. (yellow)
4. There was plenty to do, so I wasn't worried about staying out of Dad's hair. (green)
5. All of a sudden, we heard an ear-splitting crash. (red)
6. Lillie screamed, and we both ran to the window. (green)
7. As we watched, the gigantic oak tree in our yard crashed to the ground. (red)
8. The mailbox, our fence, and a power line collapsed under the fallen tree. (yellow)
9. As the TV screen faded to black, Lillie squealed, "What are we going to do now?" (purple)
10. I realized we couldn't play video games, watch TV, or even pop any microwave popcorn! (yellow)
11. I moaned and said, "This could turn into a long day, Lillie." (blue)
12. Just then, Dad came into the room carrying a big box. (red)
13. He set the box down and announced, "This box is the answer to your problems!" (purple)
14. "What is it, Dad?" we asked. (blue)
15. "These are old family photos," he replied. (purple)
16. For the rest of the day, Lillie and I went through the box of pictures. (red)
17. As we looked at pictures, we got curious about our aunts, uncles, grandparents, and great-grandparents. (yellow)
18. When the power came on, we made microwave popcorn and ate it while Dad took a break and told stories to go with the pictures. (red)

Bonus: Answers will vary.

Page 40

Part 1:

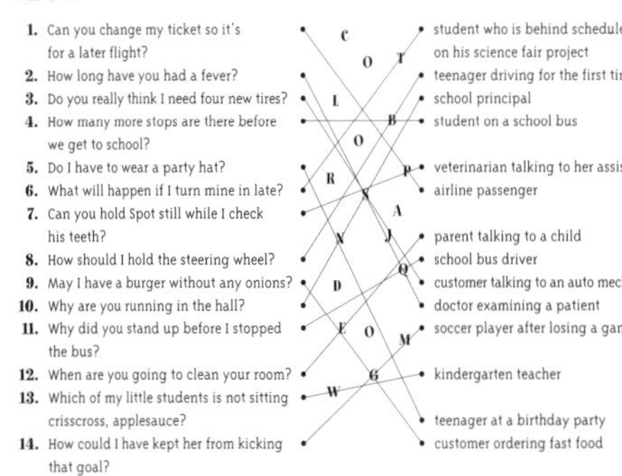

1. Can you change my ticket so it's for a later flight?
2. How long have you had a fever?
3. Do you really think I need four new tires?
4. How many more stops are there before we get to school?
5. Do I have to wear a party hat?
6. What will happen if I turn mine in late?
7. Can you hold Spot still while I check his teeth?
8. How should I hold the steering wheel?
9. May I have a burger without any onions?
10. Why are you running in the hall?
11. Why did you stand up before I stopped the bus?
12. When are you going to clean your room?
13. Which of my little students is not sitting crisscross, applesauce?
14. How could I have kept her from kicking that goal?

- student who is behind schedule on his science fair project
- teenager driving for the first time
- school principal
- student on a school bus
- veterinarian talking to her assistant
- airline passenger
- parent talking to a child
- school bus driver
- customer talking to an auto mechanic
- doctor examining a patient
- soccer player after losing a game
- kindergarten teacher
- teenager at a birthday party
- customer ordering fast food

Part 2: 15, 16; Answers will vary.

"COLOR-ADO"

Bonus: Answers will vary.

Page 41

A.

It was the friday morning, the day of the schoolplay. Emma said she couldnt eat breakfast because she was too nervus about being on stage. Emmas Mother told her over and over that she'd be fine

"But, mom," Emma whined "I'm really nervous. What if I for get my lines?" "I think You'll be fine, Emma" her mom said. "You're al ways making me laugh with your silly jokes, and riddles. You'll probly get on stage and absolutely love it."

The school day whized by, until it was time for the Play. Ms. Ellaneous, the school Principal, welcomd the audience, and thanked everyone for comeing. Then the lights dimmed and Ms. Ellaneous steped off the stage.

Every one waited for the curtains to open but they stayed shut. Ms Pelling, the music teacher, pulled hard on the ropes. nothing happened. So she pulled harder. All of a sudden, she lost her balance and lurched forward, falling through the velvet Curtain onto the stage. Ms. Pelling stepped back, groan groaned, and brushed her self off. Then he quickly smiled, bowed and dashed backstage.

"Emma" she called, Would you please go out their and tell a few of your best jokes? While you do that, I'll figure out how to get these certains open!

B. Endings will vary.

Bonus: Stories will vary.

Page 42

1. ATM
2. OH
3. mfg.
4. temp.
5. etc.
6. mph
7. CIA
8. Sr.
9. TN
10. dept.
11. e.g.
12. tbsp.
13. hr.
14. ICU
15. RSVP
16. oz.
17. VFW
18. NASA
19. CEO
20. bldg.

TO GET HIS TEETH CROWNED!

Bonus: FDA, Food and Drug Administration; govt., government; EPA, Environmental Protection Agency; PIN, personal identification number; natl., national

Page 43

Feathers by sentences 2, 4, 5, 8, 9, 10, and 11 should be shaded.

2. They have studied all kinds of bird calls. Some calls sound the same.
4. Bill looks for big birds, and he is often the first person to spot one.
5. Bill watches several birds fly by. He thinks one is a bald eagle.
8. This tiny bird only weighs about one-tenth of an ounce. It's about as big as a walnut shell.
9. Bill dreams of spotting the world's biggest bird. He wants to see an African ostrich in the wild.
10. This ostrich can weigh 345 pounds. That's gigantic compared to a bee hummingbird.
11. Bridget spots two robins and a swallow, and the bird Bill thought was an eagle is a crow.

Bonus: Answers will vary.

Page 44
Part 1: Sentences 1, 3, 5, 6, and 8 are correct.

Part 2:

1	Flash (known for his clever racing tactics) is ready for the race.
2	Flash's crew follows its prerace checklist: checking the fuel tank, checking each tire's pressure, and checking the engine's status.
3	By 8:00 Flash's car is set to race.
4	Flash (a speedy starter) gets a quick lead.
5	Flash figures he has just three things to think about: his car's speed, track conditions, and the other racers.
6	Zelda (a daring young driver) passes Flash to take the lead.
7	Flash's pit crew (one of the best in racing) completes the last pit stop in record time.
8	Flash (confident he can win) has already won four races this season!
9	Flash's car (the number two) is running well.
10	Flash closes in on Zelda (the leader) for 12 laps.

Bonus:

2	At 6:00 AM, Zelda and her crew start getting ready.
4	Zelda's car (built for speed) is gassed up and ready to go.
7	Max (the race's grand marshal) waves the green flag to start the race.
9	At the first pit stop, three crew members do everything on their lists: fill the fuel tank, check the tire pressures, and clean the windshields.
10	Zelda (tired after 428 laps) moves too far right and scrapes the wall.

Page 45
1. believe
2. neighborhood
4. preschool
5. announcement
6. crowded
8. neither
9. handkerchief
10. frowning
11. allowance
12. kangaroo
14. cauliflower
17. mountain
18. powder
20. crackdown
22. ceiling
24. drought
25. height
26. ground
28. overlook
29. retrieve

Bonus: *ei*: ceiling, height, neighborhood, neither; *ie*: achieve, believe, handkerchief, masterpiece, niece, retrieve; *oo*: balloon, kangaroo, overlook, preschool, shook; *ou*: announcement, compound, discount, drought, ground, mountain; *ow*: allowance, cauliflower, cowardly, crackdown, crowded, frowning, however, powder, prowling

Page 48
Answers for 1 and 3–5 will vary.
2. THE FIRST STEP IS THE HARDEST.
6. Answers will vary. bomb, climb, crumb, dumb, limb, numb, plumb, thumb, tomb; bomber, climber, debt, dumber, doubt, plumber
7. minute, miracle, mirror, misdeed
8. Answers will vary. binoculars, clothes, jeans, pants, police, scissors, shorts, tongs

Page 49
Answers for 2, 5, and 7 will vary.
1. hole, whole
   heal, heel, he'll
   loan, lone
   whoa, woe
3. bread, drab, bad, ad, a, at, rat, tear, water
4. We were up a creek without a paddle.
6. although, dough; enough, tough
8. A. darkness
   B. kindness
   C. truthfulness
   D. friendliness
   E. sameness

Page 50
Answers for 1, 4, 6, and 8 will vary.
2. A. giant or elephant
   B. distant
   C. instant
   D. infant
   E. assistant
3.

M	O	S	T
O	N	C	E
S	C	A	R
T	E	R	M

5. A. hot, cot
   B. sea, pea
   C. talk, walk
   D. cold, gold
7. A. Louisiana, LA
   B. Indiana, IN
   C. Pennsylvania, PA
   D. Hawaii, HI
   E. Oregon, OR
8. Possible answers include *jaded, jazzy, jerky, jolly, juicy, jumbo, jumpy,* and *junky.*

Page 51
Answers for 3, 6, and 7 will vary.
1. all, allegiance; which, with
2.

b	l	i	n	d
i		d		r
t	h	e	s	e
e		a		a
s	a	l	a	d

or

b	i	t	e	s
l		h		a
i	d	e	a	l
n		s		a
d	r	e	a	d

Students' diagrams will vary.
4. A. There are 12 numbers on the face of a clock.
   B. There are 11 players on a soccer team.
   C. There are three wheels on a tricycle.
5. A. beard – r = bead – e = bad – b = ad – d = a
   B. dinner – n = diner – r = dine – e = din – d = in – n = I
   C. paint – i = pant – t = pan – p = an – n = a
8. A. hare chair
   B. slim limb
   C. big wig
   D. loud crowd

Page 52
1.

S	T	A	R
H			A
O			S
W	I	T	H

2. inventor, beginning, discouraged, eighth, attempt, making, process, purifying, elements, failed
3. Answers will vary.
4. Answers will vary but may include the following: cantaloupe, carrots, cheese, cheese crackers, gelatin, oranges, orange soda, sherbet, sweet potatoes, and yams.
5. toadstool
6. A. Atlanta, Georgia B. Juneau, Alaska C. Frankfort, Kentucky D. Providence, Rhode Island
7. Answers will vary but may include the following: *bends, beds; broad, brad; costs, cots; found, fond; hunts, huts; lefts, lets; limes, lies; pound, pond; punts, puts;* and *rasps, raps.*
8. sad, glum; edgy, nervous; leap, spring; change, revise

Page 53
1. eight, five, four, nine, one, seven, six, ten, three, two; eighty, fifty, forty, ninety, one hundred, seventy, sixty, ten, thirty, twenty; eight, eighty, fifty, five, forty, four, nine, ninety, one, one hundred, seven, seventy, six, sixty, ten, thirty, three, twenty, two
2. Possible synonyms for *small* include *puny, tiny, short, slight, little,* and *trivial.* Possible synonyms for *huge* include *mega, super, giant, cosmic, monster, massive,* and *whopping.*
3. strength, birthplace, eighths

4, 5. Answers will vary.

6. A. stale B. tales C. steal D. least
7.

s	m	p	a	s
p	e	a	c	h
y	n	t	e	e

8. A. red, white, blue
   B. first, second, third
   C. peas, corn, carrots

Page 54
"Your Move"
1. Taylor is going to the Chicago Chess Championship.
2. She started playing chess in second grade.
3. no errors
4. She is scheduled to play Josh Wagner, a Canadian player.
5. Taylor's coach, Abby McQueen, believes Taylor will win the championship.

"Make It Vivid!"
Order will vary.
Sight: crinkled, fuzzy, fluffy, murky, colorless, shimmering
Touch: crunchy, gooey, gritty, slimy, spongy, dry, burning
Hearing: crackle, gurgle, hiss, pop, slosh
Smell: burning, musty, pungent, salty, smoky, sour
Taste: bitter, peppery, salty, sour, tart, tasteless

"In Other Words"
1. Mrs. Lane flits like a butterfly
2. Anthony jogs as slow as a snail
3. braces are as colorful as a rainbow
4. Alexis feels like a sardine
5. backpack is as heavy as a ton of bricks
6. yellow tie is as bright as the sun

Page 56
"Raining Cats and Dogs"
Answers will vary.
1. The school bus's tires are being exaggerated.
2. The length of time standing in line is being exaggerated.
3. The writer's appetite is being exaggerated.
4. The age of the writer's bike is being exaggerated.
5. The amount of money Derek has is being exaggerated.

"Comfortable?"
dependable: can be depended on
edible: fit for eating
flexible: can be bent without damage
horrible: liable to cause horror
impossible: cannot be done
laughable: liable to be laughed at
likable: liable to be liked
predictable: can be predicted
renewable: can be renewed
responsible: can be blamed for
sensible: liable to have good sense
terrible: liable to cause terror
uncomfortable: not able to find comfort
visible: can be seen
washable: can be washed
workable: can be used

Page 57
"Ancient Origins"
Explanations will vary.
Sentences 1, 3, and 5 are incorrect.

Page 58
"Of Capitol Importance"

Washington, DC, is the United States capital. This unique city is not part of any of the country's 50 states. When it was time to choose a permanent location for the nation's government, the members of Congress had a hard time agreeing on a site. Northerners didn't want the capital to be in the South. Southerners didn't want it to be in the North. Congress passed the Residence Act of 1790, which gave President Washington the power to choose the spot. He chose land north of the Potomac River that belonged to Maryland and land south of the Potomac River that belonged to Virginia. Both states turned their land over to the federal government. Then the city was named for the president, and the area around it was called the District of Columbia, abbreviated as DC.

"Pick of the Bunch!"
Answers will vary.

Word	Synonyms	Antonym
cold	arctic, chilly, freezing	blazing
clean	antiseptic, spick-and-span, spotless	filthy
sad	blue, down, glum	cheerful
bright	brilliant, dazzling, shiny	dull
pretty	darling, delightful, pleasing	unpleasant
ask	query, question, quiz	answer

"Up Close and Personal"
1. An adult grizzly bear may be 6 to 8 feet tall. An adult male bear may weigh 600 pounds; an adult female bear may weigh 400 pounds.
2. Students should list five of the following: fish, berries, grasses, leaves, insects, roots, and land animals.
3. They sleep in dens.
4. Answers will vary but may include that people have destroyed a lot of grizzly bears' habitats by clearing land.

Want ads will vary.

Page 120
Numbers from least to greatest:

0.01	$\frac{1}{8} = 0.125$	$\frac{1}{3} \approx \frac{33}{100} = 0.33$	$\frac{2}{3} \approx 0.67$
0.02	0.15	$\frac{3}{8}$	$\frac{7}{10}$
$\frac{3}{100}$	$\frac{1}{6}$	$\frac{2}{5} = 0.4$	$\frac{3}{4} = 0.75$
0.05	$\frac{1}{5} = 0.2$	0.48	$\frac{4}{5} = 0.8$
$\frac{7}{100}$	0.22	$\frac{1}{2} = 0.5$	$\frac{5}{6}$
0.08	$\frac{23}{100}$	$\frac{3}{5} = 0.6$	$\frac{7}{8} = 0.875$
0.09	$\frac{1}{4} = 0.25$	$\frac{5}{8} = 0.625$	$\frac{9}{10} = 0.9$
$\frac{1}{10}$	$\frac{3}{10} = 0.3$	0.65	$\frac{99}{100} = 0.99$

Page 123
Answers will vary.

1. 2. 3.

4. 5. 6.

7. 8.

9.

10.

Page 129

1. $p = 28$
2. $g = 13$
3. $e = 42$
4. $l = 31$
5. $m = 18$
6. $j = 11$
7. $a = 27$
8. $h = 23$
9. $d = 17$
10. $n = 31$
11. $c = 19$
12. $b = 36$
13. $o = 22$
14. $k = 45$
15. $f = 21$
16. $i = 12$

a 27	b 36	c 19	d 17
e 42	f 21	g 13	h 23
i 12	j 11	k 45	l 31
m 18	n 31	o 22	p 28

The sum of each row and column is 99.

Bonus: yes; Explanations will vary.

Page 130

A. 3,480; 3,500; 3,000
B. 6,550; 6,600; 7,000
C. 1,900; 1,900; 2,000
D. 860; 900; 1,000
E. 12,600, 12,600; 13,000
F. 35,170; 35,200; 35,000
G. 54; 53.8; 53.81
H. 50; 49.7; 49.68
I. 24; 24.5; 24.46
J. 17; 17.0; 16.96
K. 803; 802.9; 802.92
L. 8; 7.9; 7.90

Bonus: 4.057; 15.281; 2.640; 6.210; 3.710; 29.915

Page 131

1. is perpendicular to
2. is parallel to
3. is perpendicular to
4. intersects
5. intersects
6. is parallel to
7. intersects
8. is perpendicular to
9. is parallel to
10. is perpendicular to
11. obtuse
12. right
13. acute
14. obtuse
15. acute
16. right
17. square
18. triangle
19. parallelogram
20. rectangle
21. trapezoid
22. rhombus

Bonus: Answers will vary.

Page 132

COUPONS										
Store	A	B	C	D	E	F	G	H	I	Total Savings
Little's Vittles	0.50	1.00	0.55	0.75	0.80	0.45	2.00	0.60	0.25	6.90
Edie's Edibles	1.00	1.00	1.10	0.75	0.80	0.90	2.00	1.20	0.50	7.20
Chloe's Culinary Corner	1.50	1.00	1.65	0.75	0.80	1.35	2.00	1.80	0.75	6.95

Page 133

Part 1: 12° = T
16° = B
25° = P
30° = F
42° = E
48° = U
55° = A
60° = I
65° = O
90° = N
105° = G
108° = M
130° = W
160° = Z
175° = D

Part 2:

1. Angles P, B, and F are ~~obtuse~~ acute angles.
2. Angle N is a ~~straight~~ right angle.
3. Angles G and Z are ~~acute~~ obtuse angles.
4. Angles M, G, W, and Z are ~~right~~ obtuse angles.
5. Angle I is one degree ~~smaller~~ larger than angle O.
6. Angle T is the ~~largest~~ smallest angle.
7. Together, angles A and I would form an ~~acute~~ obtuse angle.
8. ~~Obtuse~~ Acute angles F and T would both fit inside a right angle.

Bonus: Acute angles: A, P, U, T, F, O, I, E, B
Right angle: N
Obtuse angles: M, G, W, Z, D

Page 134

A. $3^{11}/_{12}$
B. 7
C. $8^{2}/_{15}$
D. $5^{13}/_{40}$
E. $14^{2}/_{3}$
F. $5^{3}/_{4}$
G. $3^{1}/_{4}$
H. $5^{17}/_{24}$
I. $3^{13}/_{20}$
J. $8^{5}/_{8}$
K. $2^{1}/_{4}$
L. $3^{4}/_{9}$
M. $1^{5}/_{8}$
N. $4^{7}/_{10}$
O. $10^{1}/_{2}$

Bonus: Answers will vary.

Page 135

A. 76
T. 86
N. 68
I. 24
G. 29
W. 3,657
S. 2,747
O. 5,292
U. 4,032
E. 4,232
L. 32
P. 25,345

IT WAS NOT "PEELING" WELL!

Bonus:
A. 76 x 7 = 532
N. 68 x 4 = 272
G. 29 x 3 = 87
T. 86 x 8 = 688
I. 24 x 4 = 96
L. 32 x 74 = 2,368

Page 136

1. 13
2. 9
3. 189
4. 45
5. 11
6. 34
7. 3
8. 99
9. 67
10. 4
11. 90
12. 8
13. 82
14. 86
15. 53
16. 36
17. 17
18. 6
19. 50
20. 7

THEY ALL GREW SQUARE ROOTS!

Bonus: $x + 17 = 56, x = 39$
$56 \div x = 8, x = 7$

Page 137

1. 13 hours, 30 minutes
2. 40 minutes
3. 1 hour, 35 minutes
4. 18 hours, 35 minutes
5. 19 hours
6. about 13 hours
7. about 12 hours
8. 2 hours, 55 minutes
9. 12 hours, 5 minutes
10. 6 hours, 5 minutes
11. 11 hours, 55 minutes
12. about 11:00 AM; Explanations will vary.

Bonus: about 3:00 AM

Page 138

1. 53.4
2. 90.74
3. 12.48
4. 49.28
5. 17.748
6. 0.234
7. 0.048
8. 1.134
9. 2.43
10. 74.86
11. 63.054
12. 4.092
13. 18.648
14. 4.65
15. 3231.41
16. 1645.2
17. 0.174
18. 47.212

Bonus: The decimal point is in the wrong place. The product should be 20.115.

Page 139

1. 2
2. 6
3. 3
4. 32
5. 4
6. 16
7. 128
8. 28
9. 1
10. 48
11. 8
12. 80
13. 11
14. 40
15. 24
16. 12

JUST CALL ME THE HOTTER OTTER!

Bonus: A. $6^{1}/_{4}$
B. 192
C. $8^{3}/_{4}$

Page 140

1. $^{7}/_{20}$
2. $^{6}/_{25}$
3. $^{9}/_{20}$
4. $^{1}/_{8}$
5. $^{1}/_{2}$
6. $^{27}/_{50}$
7. $^{5}/_{12}$
8. $^{7}/_{25}$
9. $^{5}/_{16}$
10. $^{1}/_{4}$
11. $^{7}/_{16}$
12. $^{3}/_{8}$
13. $2^{1}/_{4}$
14. 9
15. $2^{2}/_{3}$
16. $13^{1}/_{8}$
17. $^{3}/_{5}$
18. $^{9}/_{16}$
19. 6
20. $1^{3}/_{4}$

Why did the temperature in the stadium rise after the ball game?

Bonus: The product will be less than the whole number factor. Examples will vary.

Page 141

1. I♡Games, NEWGMR, NBR1, QuickDraw, and GamePrincSS.
2. NBR1 has a higher ratio; She wins more of the games she plays.
3. yes; He will be ranked eighth.
4. I♡Games 5. RDY2PLAY 6. Rocky
7. yes; She will be ranked second.
8. QuickDraw, I♡Games, and Rocky
9. 216 games 10. $^{102}/_{216}$ or $^{17}/_{36}$

Player	Rank	Games Won	Games Lost	Number of Games Played	Ratio of Games Won to Games Played
I♡GAMES	1	15	10	25	$\frac{15}{25}$ or $\frac{3}{5}$
NEWGMR	2	12	9	21	$\frac{12}{21}$ or $\frac{4}{7}$
NBR1	3	10	8	18	$\frac{10}{18}$ or $\frac{5}{9}$
QUICKDRAW	4	17	15	32	$\frac{17}{32}$
GAMEPRINCSS	5	9	8	17	$\frac{9}{17}$
JOYFUL1	6	9	9	18	$\frac{9}{18}$ or $\frac{1}{2}$
TOPDOG	7	10	11	21	$\frac{10}{21}$
RDY2PLAY	8	5	10	15	$\frac{5}{15}$ or $\frac{1}{3}$
GAMEKING	9	7	15	22	$\frac{7}{22}$
ROCKY	10	8	19	27	$\frac{8}{27}$

Bonus: NBR1 and QuickDraw will be tied for third, so GamePrincSS will be fourth and Joyful1 will be fifth.

Page 142

Part 1: Quadrant I: U, O, F
Quadrant II: E, D, M
Quadrant III: I, Z, A
Quadrant IV: S, L, T

Part 2: A. (–1, –1) D. (–4, 3) E. (–8, 2) F. (9, 1) I. (–8, –4) L. (5, –2) M. (–3, 1) O. (1, 1) S. (2, –1) T. (3, –7) U. (1, 7) Z. (–5, –8)

Part 3: I'M ALL FIZZLED OUT!

Bonus: Points and coordinates will vary.

Page 143

Answers for 7 and 9 will vary.

1. fraction: a way to show parts of a whole or parts of a set
numerator: the number that tells how many equal parts a fraction describes
denominator: the number that tells into how many equal parts a whole has been divided
2. A. $^{1}/_{3}$ of a pie
B. $^{1}/_{4}$ of a candy bar
C. $^{1}/_{2}$ of a window
D. $^{5}/_{6}$ of a carton of eggs
3. A.
B.
C.

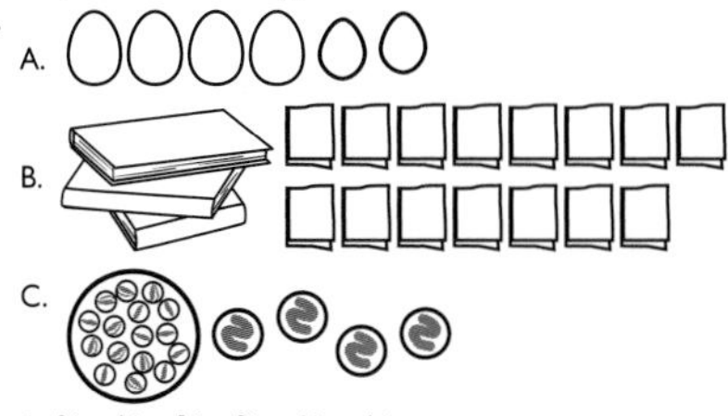

4. A. $^{2}/_{3} > ^{1}/_{2} < ^{5}/_{7} > ^{3}/_{8} > ^{4}/_{16} = ^{1}/_{4}$
B. $^{1}/_{3} < ^{1}/_{2} > ^{2}/_{5} < ^{2}/_{3} > ^{1}/_{3} = ^{2}/_{6}$
5.

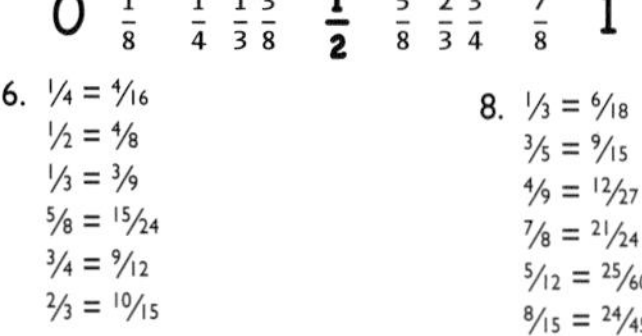

6. $^{1}/_{4} = ^{4}/_{16}$
$^{1}/_{2} = ^{4}/_{8}$
$^{1}/_{3} = ^{3}/_{9}$
$^{5}/_{8} = ^{15}/_{24}$
$^{3}/_{4} = ^{9}/_{12}$
$^{2}/_{3} = ^{10}/_{15}$
8. $^{1}/_{3} = ^{6}/_{18}$
$^{3}/_{5} = ^{9}/_{15}$
$^{4}/_{9} = ^{12}/_{27}$
$^{7}/_{8} = ^{21}/_{24}$
$^{5}/_{12} = ^{25}/_{60}$
$^{8}/_{15} = ^{24}/_{45}$

Page 144

1. The pattern is the Fibonacci sequence: each number is the sum of the two previous numbers.
2. The shaded section moves clockwise in each step.
3. A. 19, 23, 27, 31 B. 70, 85, 100, 115
C. 39, 36, 33, 30 D. 10, 12, 13, 15
4. A.
B.
C.
D.

5.

45	19	64
31	89	120
63	9	72
47	16	63
55	29	84

6. The last number in each row is the sum of the first two numbers in that row.

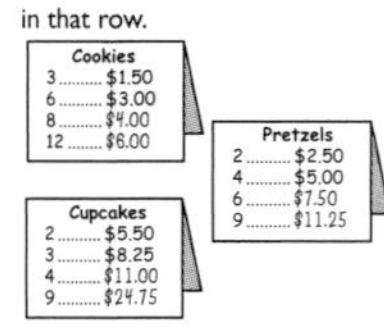

7.

Bags	Tokens	Tickets
1	3	6
2	6	12
3	9	18
4	12	24
5	15	30

8. Answers will vary.
9.

Page 145

Answers will vary for 1, 3, 5, 8, and 9.

2. acute angle: angle that is less than 90°
angle: figure formed by two rays with a common endpoint
obtuse angle: angle that is greater than 90° and less than 180°
ray: part of a line that has one endpoint and continues on in the other direction
right angle: angle that measures exactly 90°
vertex: point where two rays meet
4.

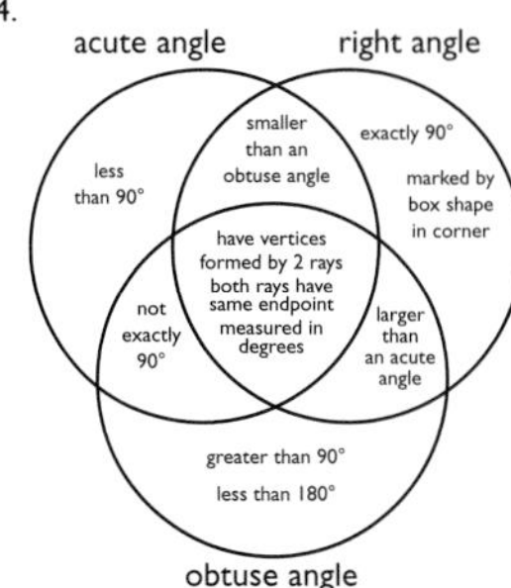

6. Angles will vary. The angles around each vertex should total 360°.
7. central angle: angle whose vertex is the center of a circle
congruent angles: two angles that have the same measurement
degree: unit of measure used for angles
protractor: tool used to measure and draw angles
reflex angle: angle that is greater than 180° and less than 360°
straight angle: angle that measures exactly 180°

Page 146
Level A
1. 14
2. 8,573,261; 1,480,752; 500,837,650; 623,578,913
3. parallel: I, N, E, M
   perpendicular: L, I, E, T
   both: I, E
   neither: S, G
4. 1:05 PM
5. Alecia
6. 0–8

Level B
1. A. $n = \frac{5}{8}$
   B. $n = \frac{1}{4}$
   C. $n = 3$
2. $4.50
3. 68 minutes
4. acute, right and obtuse
5. 18 outfits
6. 24 students; Eight students brought sack lunches.

Page 147
Level A
1. He didn't change the fractions to have common denominators; he added the denominators.
2. helmet = $36.00, gloves = $23.00, light = $9.00, backpack = $16.00, bell = $6.00; yes
3. 10 days
4. length of a plastic fork, 14 cm
   height of a door, 2.5 m
   depth of your math book, 4 cm
   liquid in a paper cup, 100 mL
5. A. 117, 146, 175
   B. 43, 26, 9
   C. 1,680; 15,120; 151,200
6. Both have an equal chance of occurring.

Level B
1. $\frac{1}{4} > 0.213$
   $\frac{2}{5} < 0.407$
   $\frac{1}{8} = 0.125$
   0.407 is the greatest overall.
2. The quotient for 714 ÷ 16 is larger.
3. Each guppy is $3.50.
4. the chicken pen
5. $2n - 3 = 9$ or $2(n - 3) = 9$; $n = 6$
6. The mean is highest.

Page 148
Level A
1. 1, 2; 5, 6; 0, 1
2. $n = 10$
3. no
4. $\frac{1}{10}$, or 1 out of 10
5. B has the larger sum.
6. 18.75 centimeters

Level B
1. $3.14
2. B has more possible solutions.
3. You can draw one line segment and two rays.
4. 8 + 7 + 3 = 18; (8 – 7) + 3 = 4; 8 + (7 x 3) = 29
5. Chef Jackie turns the ovens off at 9:05 AM.
6. The numbers 4 and 2 and either the 3 or 17 are wrong.

Page 149
Level A
1. $n = 60$
2. Students should name three of the following: 6 units x 8 units, 12 units x 4 units, 16 units x 3 units, 2 units x 24 units, or 1 unit x 48 units.
3. odd numbers less than ten
4. no
5. A. cylinder B. cube or rectangular prism C. cone
6. five

Level B
1. 163
2. Eight had candy, four had stickers, two had coupons for free doughnuts.
3. B
4. Add 9. The tenth number will be 132. The 16th number will be 186.
5. Angles A and B are congruent, and angles D and E are congruent.
6. Answers will vary.

Page 150

Level A	Level B
1. Problem B	1. 10.0816
2. three $20 bills	2. <
3. about 33 meters	3. 11:45 AM
4. 98	4. B and D
5. 18	5. A

Page 151
Level A
Answers for 2 and 6 will vary.
1. A. 148, 163, 178: Add 15.
   B. 100; 1,000; 10,000: Multiply by ten.
   C. 25, 5, 1: Divide by five.
3. no; The cones will cost $11.16.
4. yes
5. $29.93

Level B
1. no 2. 82.5 pounds 3. one variable
4. Estimates will vary; penny = 2.5 g, dime = 2.268 g, quarter = 5.67 g, half dollar = 11.34 g
5. 24
6. no; Her fractions add up to more than one whole.

Page 152
1. 200 bricks
2. 252
3. 5
4. Answers will vary.
5. DCCCLXV, DCCCLXIX, MXXII, MCMV
6. Apples cost $0.05 more per pound than kumquats.
7. A and C
8. 10:15

Page 153
1. A. Maine ($93.00)
   B. Iowa ($60.00)
2. sometimes true; 2 + 3 = 5, 11 + 3 = 14
3. squirrel, elephant, kangaroo, giraffe
4. D is largest (28), C is smallest (20)
5. A. 60 yards
   B. 65 yards
6. 570 minutes
7. A. $2\frac{1}{2}$ feet, 1 yard, 38 inches
   B. 1,750 yards; 1 mile; 5,290 feet
   C. 400 millimeters, 3 meters, 378 centimeters
8. Each sum is a palindrome. 725 does not fit the pattern. To fit the pattern, the sum of the first and third numbers must be less than 10 and the middle digit must be less than 5.

Page 154
1. highest: $84 \times 76 = 6{,}384$ lowest: $48 \times 67 = 3{,}216$
2. 24; The arrow can appear in four different directions on each of six sides.
3. 324 tiles
4. $7\frac{1}{2}$ inches
5. Answers will vary but may include the following:

quadrilateral — four-sided polygon
quadrant — any of four equal parts
quadruple — verb to make four times as many
adjective
quad means four parts, noun

6. 121
7. 17
8. two ways; four quarters, four dimes, and 2 nickels or five quarters and five nickels

Page 155
1. Some possible answers are (3 + 2) – 4 = 1, (2 x 3) – 4 = 2, 2 + (4 – 3) = 3, and 4 ÷ (3 – 2) = 4.
2. Answers will vary.

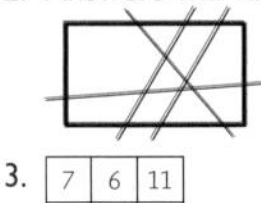

3.

7	6	11
12	8	4
5	10	9

4.

5. 9 knots
6. 1, 6, 18; 4, 9, 12; 3, 4, 18
7. 1
8. 47 in 2012, 46 in 2013

Page 156
1. p = 72 inches, or 6 feet; a = 324 square inches, or $2\frac{1}{4}$ square feet
2. 840
3. Answers will vary but a possible solution is 3; then the puzzle will have one 1, two 2s, three 3s, four 4s, and five 5s.
4. For shape A, 22 faces would and 8 would not be painted; for shape B, 20 faces would and 10 faces would not be painted.
5. 18 bananas
6. 95 (1, 5, 19, 95) and 10 (1, 2, 5, 10)
7. Answers will vary, but a possible solution is

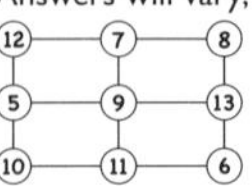

8. A. 1 out of 4, or $\frac{1}{4}$ B. 1 out of 2, or $\frac{1}{2}$ C. 0

Page 157
1. $10.45
2. 153, 157, 159, 351, 357, 359, 751, 753, 759, 951, 953, 957; You can't write any more three-digit numbers that have all these qualities.
3. three
4. Answers with descending digits: A. 654; B. 54,321; E. 7,654
   Answers with like digits: C. 333, D. 555, F. 444
5. ten
6. A. 100, 89, 77, 64, <u>50</u>, 35, <u>19</u>; Subtract 11, subtract 12, subtract 13, and so on.
   B. 1, 4, 9, 16, 25, 36, <u>49</u>; Add 3, add 5, add 7, and so on.
   C. 10, 20, 40, 70, <u>110</u>, 160, <u>220</u>; Add 10, add 20, add 30, and so on.
7. 4,617,908,352
8. B. 222,222 C. 37,037 D. 12 E. 37,037 F. 999,999

Page 158
"Going Places"
1. 1,000,010
2. 1,070,010
3. 1,070,019
4. 1,073,019
5. 1,573,019
6. 1,573,819
7. 2,573,819

Order will vary.
1. Change the 1 in the tens place to a 9.
2. Change the 9 in the ones place to a 1.
3. Change the 5 in the hundred thousands place to a 0.
4. Change the 8 in the hundreds place to a 4.
5. Change the 2 in the millions place to a 3.

"Just Nutty"
A. $n = 157$
B. $n = 369$
C. $n = 281$
D. $n = 143$
E. $n = 121$
F. $n = 1{,}312$

121; 143; 157; 281; 369; 1,312

Page 159
"Flea Market Finds"

Paperback Books
5 books for $2.50
10 books for $5.00
15 books for $7.50
18 books for $9.00
20 books for $10.00

Classic Rock CDs
2 CDs for $5.50
3 CDs for $8.25
4 CDs for $11.00
5 CDs for $13.75

Teeny Tiny Stuffed Animals
5 for $3.00
7 for $4.20
9 for $5.40
10 for $6.00
12 for $7.20

"'Weight' a Minute!"
A. 2.894 kg
B. 15.422 kg
C. 124.003 kg
D. 0.563 kg
E. 109.604 kg
F. 18.947 kg
G. 0.955 kg
H. 15.247 kg
I. 14.004 kg
J. 99.999 kg
K. 1.045 kg
L. 0.068 kg
M. 20.075 kg
N. 0.789 kg
O. 11.834 kg
There are 272.388 kg in the column with A–G.
There are 163.061 kg in the column with H–O.
Altogether, there are about 435.449 kg.

"Chair Share"
Diagrams will vary but should show nine blue chairs, 12 red chairs, nine brown chairs, and six yellow chairs. Four chairs should be circled.

Page 161
"Cryptographers Welcome"

Code

ə = 0	□ = 5
△ = 1	± = 6
# = 2	◇ = 7
₸ = 3	> = 8
✱ = 4	⍝ = 9

1. 0 + 0 = 0
2. 5 + 5 = 10
3. 5 x 3 = 15
4. 5 + 3 = 8
5. 5 – 4 = 1
6. 3 x 2 = 6
7. 9 – 8 = 1
8. 4 + 3 = 7

"Evenly Divided"
Has a vertical line of symmetry: A, H, I, M, O, T, U, V, W, X, Y
Has a horizontal line of symmetry: B, C, D, E, H, I, K, O, X
Has two lines of symmetry: H, I, O, X
Does not have a line of symmetry: F, G, J, L, N, P, Q, R, S, Z

Page 162
"A Caterpillar Conference"
Caitlyn should leave at 6:26.
Carter should leave at 6:32.
Clover and Candace should leave at 6:23.
Calvin should leave at 6:18.

"Keep Going!"
A. Add three; 87
B. Add four and then subtract one; 26
C. Double each number; 1,024
D. Each number is the sum of the two previous numbers; 89
E. Multiply by one, then two, then three, and so on; 1,814,400

Page 163
"Hot on the Trail"
0.407 + 0.599 = 1.006
2.511 + 0.498 = 3.009
1.167 x 6 = 7.002
Each answer has zeros in the tenths and hundredths places.

"At the Races"
A. $5\frac{4}{5}$ B. $13\frac{1}{3}$ C. $6\frac{12}{13}$ D. $128\frac{4}{7}$ E. $97\frac{5}{8}$

"Getting Warmer!"
1. 5°C 2. 30°C 3. 35°C 4. 20°C 5. 25°C

Page 166
Answers for 1 and 9 will vary.
2. $17\frac{1}{2}$ miles, $52\frac{1}{2}$ miles
3. 324 cranberries; 648 cranberries
4. $4,754.20; $4,862.25
5. 42 quarts of water, 21 gallons of water
6. 2 hours and 45 minutes, 33 hours
7. 737 reindeer; 1,474 antlers
8. 33 feet, ten days
10. five cookies, 90 cookies
11. 12 turkeys, 14 pies
12. 252 dishes and glasses, 336 pieces of silverware

Page 175
Cranberry Sauce for Eight
$\frac{2}{3}$ cup sugar
$\frac{2}{3}$ cup water
$3\frac{1}{2}$ cups cranberries
$\frac{1}{2}$ teaspoon ground cinnamon

Cranberry Sauce for Twelve
1 cup sugar
1 cup water
$5\frac{1}{4}$ cups cranberries
$\frac{3}{4}$ teaspoon ground cinnamon

Stuffing for Eight
$\frac{1}{2}$ cup butter
$\frac{1}{2}$ cup chopped onion
$\frac{2}{3}$ cup chopped celery
6 cups dry bread cubes
$\frac{1}{2}$ cup chicken broth
1 teaspoon ground sage
$1\frac{1}{2}$ teaspoons celery salt
$\frac{1}{2}$ teaspoon ground black pepper

Stuffing for Twelve
$\frac{3}{4}$ cup butter
$\frac{3}{4}$ cup chopped onion
1 cup chopped celery
9 cups dry bread cubes
$\frac{3}{4}$ cup chicken broth
$1\frac{1}{2}$ teaspoons ground sage
$2\frac{1}{4}$ teaspoons celery salt
$\frac{3}{4}$ teaspoon ground black pepper

Pumpkin Pie for Eight
$\frac{2}{3}$ cup milk
1 cup canned pumpkin
1 small package instant vanilla pudding mix
$\frac{1}{4}$ teaspoon cloves
$\frac{1}{4}$ teaspoon nutmeg
$\frac{1}{2}$ teaspoon ground cinnamon
1 cup frozen whipped topping
8 mini graham cracker crusts

Pumpkin Pie for Twelve
1 cup milk
$1\frac{1}{2}$ cups canned pumpkin
$1\frac{1}{2}$ small packages instant vanilla pudding mix
$\frac{3}{8}$ teaspoon cloves
$\frac{3}{8}$ teaspoon nutmeg
$\frac{3}{4}$ teaspoon ground cinnamon
$1\frac{1}{2}$ cups frozen whipped topping
12 mini graham cracker crusts

Page 178
$\frac{3}{100} = 0.03$ $\frac{9}{100} = 0.09$ $\frac{1}{8} = 0.125$ $\frac{1}{5} = 0.2$ $\frac{1}{4} = 0.25$
$\frac{6}{20} = 0.3$ $\frac{3}{10} = 0.3$ $\frac{2}{5} = 0.4$ $\frac{1}{2} = 0.50$ $\frac{18}{30} = 0.6$
$\frac{7}{10} = 0.7$ $\frac{3}{4} = 0.75$ $\frac{4}{5} = 0.8$ $\frac{9}{10} = 0.9$ $\frac{3}{3} = 1$
$\frac{13}{10} = 1.3$ $1\frac{1}{2} = 1.5$ $\frac{3}{5} = 0.6$

Page 179
1. 60,000
2. 28 units
3. obtuse
4. $\frac{1}{2}$
5. radius
6. <
7. 369
8. $m = 7$
9. 9,603
10. 28,000
11. 80,000 + 3,000 + 10 + $\frac{3}{100}$
12. $1\frac{1}{4}$
13. 4
14. 141
15. 90°
16. 64 square units
17. $\frac{2}{3}$
18. 4
19. $x = 56$
20. 7,076
21. $7\frac{2}{3}$
22. 388
23. 29
24. 10
25. 2 hours, 35 minutes

Page 190
A. $1\frac{5}{8}$ inches, crescent butterfly
B. $1\frac{1}{16}$ inches, common bumblebee
C. 18 centimeters, walkingstick
D. 1.5 centimeters, black carpenter ant
E. $3\frac{7}{8}$ inches, widow skimmer
F. 5.9 centimeters, broad-winged katydid
G. 12.6 centimeters, Goliath beetle
H. $\frac{1}{2}$ inch, gallnipper mosquito

Page 191
A.
1. It is
2. We are
3. We have
4. do not
5. Here is
6. one is
7. You will
8. there is
9. cannot
10. You are
11. I have
12. Who is

B.
13. she's
14. You're
15. I've
16. shouldn't
17. mustn't
18. Who's
19. What's
20. isn't
21. I'd
22. wouldn't

Bonus: must not, there have, should not have, will not, would not have

Page 192
A. 90
B. 45
C. 45
D. one sibling
E. 5
F. 25
G. 20
H. 20
I. basketball
J. 25
K. girls who prefer running, 5
L. 7
M. 3
N. boys with two or more pets

Bonus: Answers will vary.

Page 193

1

Input	Output
6	30
9	45
18	90
4	12
Rule: Multiply by 5.	

2

Input	Output
60	10
36	6
72	12
12	2
Rule: ÷ 6	

3

Input	Output
44	57
92	105
12	25
38	51
Rule: + 13	

4

Input	Output
64	55
81	72
43	34
59	50
Rule: – 9	

5

Input	Output
45	15
12	4
63	21
27	9
Rule: ÷ 3	

6

Input	Output
6	21
17	32
25	40
32	47
Rule: + 15	

7

Input	Output
9	81
3	27
12	108
8	72
Rule: x 9	

8

Input	Output
84	21
56	14
16	4
36	9
Rule: ÷ 4	

9

Input	Output
71	63
28	20
39	31
14	6
Rule: – 8	

10

Input	Output
100	75
62	37
59	34
47	22
Rule: – 25	

11

Input	Output
18	34
36	52
25	41
51	67
Rule: + 16	

12

Input	Output
5	35
3	21
12	84
9	63
Rule: x 7	

Page 194
A. independent
B. impossible
C. ineffective
D. disorder
E. disinterested
F. illicit
G. imperfect
H. disagreed
I. discord
J. disliked
K. inalienable
L. inequality
M. illegal
N. disobey
O. immigrate

1. H
2. A
3. E
4. L
5. N
6. G
7. B
8. K
9. F or M
10. F or M
11. J
12. C
13. I
14. D
15. O

Bonus: Answers will vary.

Page 195
1. fact
2. opinion; Vampire bats are the worst kinds of bats.
3. fact
4. opinion; Vampire bats probably have the world's sharpest teeth.
5. opinion; Even a vampire bat's scientific name, *Desmodus rotundus*, is scary.
6. fact
7. fact
8. opinion; The most interesting fact about vampire bats is that they don't live in North America.
9. opinion; It's silly to be afraid of vampire bats because they are only about three inches long.
10. fact
11. opinion; You would never want to run into a vampire bat.
12. fact
13. opinion; The most awful thing about vampire bats is that they drink human blood.
14. fact
15. fact
16. opinion; Tigers may be scary but vampire bats are creepy.

Bonus: Paragraphs will vary.

Page 196
Answers will vary.
1. one string cheese finger and five cups of punch
2. one hot dog mummy, one cookie, and one cup of punch
3. one hot dog mummy, six cookies, and one cup of punch
4. four hot dog mummies and two cups of punch
5. four hot dog mummies, two string cheese fingers, and one cookie
6. three string cheese fingers, seven cookies, and one cup of punch
7. ten string cheese fingers, two cookies, and six cups of punch
8. four hot dog mummies, four string cheese fingers, five cookies, and two cups of punch

Bonus: Answers will vary: three hot dog mummies, 12 string cheese fingers, six cookies, and seven cups of punch.

Page 197
1. On Veterans Day
2. in the United States Armed Forces
3. to veterans
4. with parades
5. During those parades, inside fancy cars
6. along the route
7. about soldiers' sacrifices
8. by soldiers' graves
9. at Arlington National Cemetery
10. across the Potomac River, from Washington, DC
11. upon the Tomb, of the Unknowns
12. for veterans, throughout the country

13–15. Answers will vary.

Bonus: Sentences will vary.

Page 198
1. 2,400
2. 3,915
3. 854
4. 1,593
5. 4,277
6. 17,227
7. 27,404
8. 18,815
9. 13,978
10. 39,368
11. 34,804
12. 117,450
13. 129,888
14. 190,957

The turkey on the right will receive a pardon.

Bonus: Answers will vary.

Page 199
1. went
2. began
3. woke
4. felt
5. drove, slept
6. got, risen
7. took
8. set, slid
9. found
10. cut, brought
11. sat
12. drank
13. stood, fell
14. froze
15. flew
16. knew, caught
17. saw
18. kept
19. ate
20. told
21. left
22. said

Bonus: chose, forgot, read, shrunk, strode, swung

Page 200

A. 1. > 2. > 3. < 4. =
5. < 6. > 7. > 8. =
9. < 10. < 11. > 12. =

B. 13. < 14. > 15. = 16. >
17. = 18. > 19. > 20. <
21. = 22. > 23. < 24. <

C.

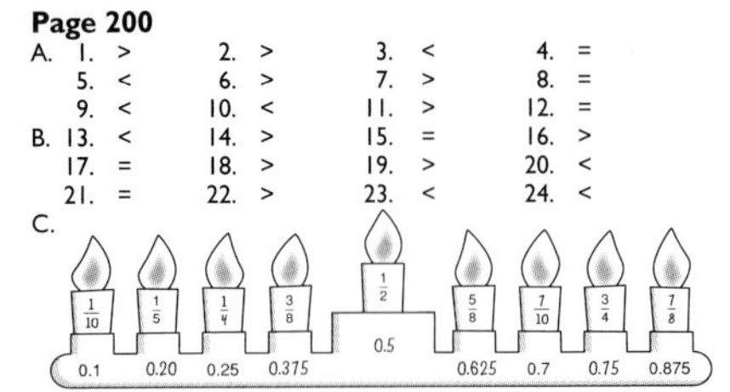

Page 201

Across
A. 11
C. 16
D. 5,280
E. 257
G. 14
H. 21
J. 236
L. 78
N. 7,040
P. 35
Q. 264

Down
A. 1,584
B. 12
C. 102
F. 72
G. 197
I. 17
J. 24
K. 303
M. 864
O. 22

	A 1	B 1		C 1	6			
	D 5	2	8	0				
	8			E 2	5	F 7		
G 1	4					H 2	I 1	
9		J 2	K 3	6			L 7	M 8
N 7	0	4	0			O 2		6
			P 3	5		Q 2	6	4

Bonus: 10,560

Page 202

Sentences will vary.

Tenth Annual Martin Luther King Day Parade

1. The parade will start at City Park and end at Lincoln School.
3. Fire trucks from three stations and police cars are scheduled to join the parade.
5. Our mayor will be the parade's grand marshal and dedicate the new Martin Luther King Library after the parade.
8. Two local high school bands and the jazz band from City University will march in the parade.
10. In honor of Martin Luther King Day, our city will host a parade and offer special events.

Fast Facts About Martin Luther King Jr.

2. Millions of Americans and people in other countries supported Martin Luther King Jr.'s nonviolent campaign.
4. Over 200,000 American people joined the March on Washington in 1963 and listened to Dr. King speak.
6. Martin Luther King Jr. was an important civil rights leader who gave dynamic speeches.
7. Martin Luther King Jr. and other civil rights leaders organized the March on Washington.
9. As part of the March, Martin Luther King Jr. gave his "I Have a Dream" speech and shared his hope that all Americans could be treated equally.

Bonus: Articles will vary.

Page 203

1. important
2. would
3. Southern
4. dance
5. familiar
6. drummers
7. developed
8. instead
9. making
10. known
11. popular
12. famous
13. singer
14. would
15. jazz
16. many

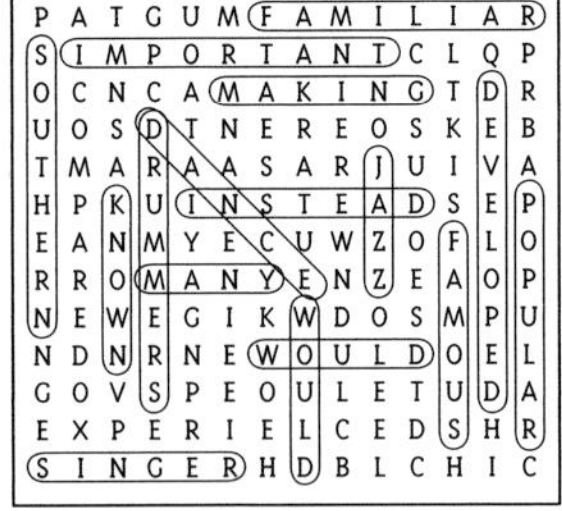

Bonus: Answers will vary.

Page 204

K: $\frac{4}{12} + \frac{6}{12} = \frac{5}{6}$
E: $\frac{5}{6} - \frac{1}{6} = \frac{2}{3}$
H: $\frac{10}{15} - \frac{5}{15} = \frac{1}{3}$

A: $\frac{4}{9} + \frac{3}{9} = \frac{7}{9}$
P: $\frac{9}{18} + \frac{7}{18} = \frac{8}{9}$
D: $\frac{6}{10} + \frac{3}{10} = \frac{9}{10}$

G: $\frac{1}{7} + \frac{5}{7} = \frac{6}{7}$
S: $\frac{4}{12} - \frac{2}{12} = \frac{1}{6}$
C: $\frac{6}{8} - \frac{2}{8} = \frac{1}{2}$

O: $\frac{6}{11} - \frac{1}{11} = \frac{5}{11}$
N: $\frac{5}{6} + \frac{3}{6} = 1\frac{1}{3}$
W: $\frac{7}{9} - \frac{2}{9} = \frac{5}{9}$

T: $\frac{9}{10} - \frac{2}{10} = \frac{7}{10}$
T: $\frac{5}{8} + \frac{7}{8} = \frac{1}{2}$
M: $\frac{5}{7} - \frac{1}{7} = \frac{4}{7}$

C: $\frac{8}{15} + \frac{7}{15} = 1$
L: $\frac{7}{14} + \frac{6}{14} = \frac{13}{14}$
I: $\frac{14}{18} - \frac{6}{18} = \frac{4}{9}$

STICK WITH ME, AND WE'LL GO PLACES!

Bonus: Answers will vary.

Page 205

1. blue
2. blue
3. red
4. blue
5. red
6. blue
7. red
8. blue
9. red
10. blue
11. red
12. red
13. blue
14. red
15. blue

Bonus: Answers will vary.

Page 206

1. 70°
2. 30°
3. 15°
4. 40°
5. 20°
6. 90°
7. 35°
8. 60°
9. 130°
10. 115°
11. 155°
12. 110°
13. 90°
14. 15°
15. 75°
16. 40°
17. 30°
18. 50°
19. 40°
20. 20°
21. 110°
22. 130°
23. 90°
24. 120°

Bonus: 360°

Page 207

A. 109
B. 254
C. 21
D. 95
E. 48
F. 26
G. 147
H. 29
I. 516
J. 145
K. 12
L. 203
M. 86
N. 15
O. 23
P. 87

Bonus: 442 ÷ 13 = 34

Page 208

1. After the rain, the earth breathes a sigh of relief.
2. The fresh spring air lures the gardener outside.
3. Dewdrops wink from each blade of grass.
4. The blades of the gardener's tiller grab chunks of the moist soil.
5. Seeds jump out of the packets, eager to be planted.
6. The freshly dug rows of soil swallow the seeds.
7. Trees dance merrily in the spring breeze.
8. Between each row, weeds beg to be pulled.
9. The soil crowds around the weeds' roots, refusing to let go.
10. At the end of the day, the gardener's back groans from the hard work.

Answers for 11–15 will vary.

Bonus: Answers will vary.

Page 209

1. 1 out of 3, or ⅓
2. 1 out of 3, or ⅓
3. 3 out of 3, or certain
4. 2 out of 3, or ⅔
5. second race
6. third race
7. 1 out of 3, or ⅓
8. Don isn't in that race.
9. six
10. first or second race
11. 1 out of 3, or ⅓
12. 1 out of 2, or ½

Bonus: No, all the ducks have the same probability of winning.

Page 210

A. 6 $ft.^3$
B. 20 m^3
E. 24 $in.^3$
G. 135 cm^3
I. 16 $in.^3$
O. 27 $ft.^3$
P. 168 m^3
R. 126 $ft.^3$
S. 48 $in.^3$
X. 343 cm^3
Y. 100 $in.^3$
Z. 81 $ft.^3$

Never recycle A GREASY PIZZA BOX.

Bonus: Since all sides of a square are equal, the length and width of the box are each 6 feet. The height of the box is 8 feet. The volume of the box is 6 x 6 x 8, which is 288 cubic feet.

Page 211

1. cattleships and bruisers—battleships and cruisers
2. chipping flannels—flipping channels
3. trailing sip—sailing trip
4. dishing with my fad—fishing with my dad
5. fig bish—big fish
6. bo sig—so big
7. dig bay—big day
8. may ny same—say my name
9. hot nook lappy—not look happy
10. race furn ted—face turn red
11. pool druddle—drool puddle
12. doring snisturbs—snoring disturbs
13. vummer sacation—summer vacation
14. lood gesson—good lesson
15. mad banners—bad manners
16. sang a hign—hang a sign

Bonus: Sentences will vary.

Page 212

A. $4\frac{1}{12}$
B. $5\frac{8}{9}$
C. $1\frac{4}{5}$
D. $\frac{7}{20}$
E. $4\frac{1}{12}$
F. $12\frac{9}{35}$
G. $5\frac{2}{3}$
H. $\frac{2}{3}$
I. $2\frac{3}{4}$
J. $5\frac{1}{9}$
K. $3\frac{10}{21}$
L. $1\frac{4}{15}$
M. $8\frac{2}{5}$
N. $\frac{5}{12}$
O. $9\frac{3}{16}$
P. $2\frac{2}{9}$
Q. $1\frac{1}{14}$
R. $8\frac{3}{5}$

Bonus: $5\frac{6}{8} - 3\frac{4}{9} = 2\frac{11}{36}$ $2\frac{11}{36} + 3\frac{4}{9} = 5\frac{3}{4}$

Page 213

Explanations will vary.

1. I
2. E
3. A
4. H
5. D
6. B
7. G
8. J
9. C
10. K
11. F
12. L

Bonus: Answers will vary.

Page 214

1. 2 hot dogs
2. seventh inning
3. 21 large tubs
4. 158 cups
5. $2.50
6. fifth inning
7. about 83 ice cream cones
8. 87 juice boxes

Bonus: Answers will vary.

Page 215

1. 32
2. 2,000
3. 16
4. 16
5. 1
6. 16
7. ¼
8. 1¼
9. 1⅔
10. 45
11. ½
12. 3,600
13. 2,640
14. 12
15. 54
16. 28⅛

She heard IT WAS MADE FROM CONCENTRATE!

Bonus: 8 ounces = 1 cup
2 pints = 1 quart
16 ounces = 1 pound
2,000 pounds = 1 ton
5,280 feet = 1 mile

Page 241

Answers for 1 and 6–9 will vary.

2. Each tropical storm gets a name that helps scientists keep track of its unique behaviors. The World Meteorological Organization issues four alphabetical lists of names that include both men's and women's names that are popular in countries where hurricanes tend to hit. The first storm of the year gets a name that begins with *A*. The second storm gets a name that begins with *B*, and so on. Certain letters are not used.
3. Texas, Oklahoma, Kansas, Nebraska, and Iowa
4. cold front: leading edge of a cold air mass

   dry line: boundary that separates moist and dry air masses

   occluded front: slow-moving front that forms when a cold air mass overtakes a warm air mass and wedges itself under the warm air mass, causing heavy rain that is followed by steady light rain or snow

   squall line: line of active thunderstorms

   stationary front: front between warm and cold air masses that moves very slowly or not at all

   low-pressure system: area where the pressure is lower than the surrounding area, can cause high winds and warm air **L**

   high-pressure system: area where the pressure is higher than the surrounding area, can result in clear skies and calm weather **H**

   warm front: leading edge of a warm air mass

5. The first signs may be light rain followed by heavier rain and then rain mixed with hail. The hailstones may grow large. When the hail stops, a funnel-shaped cloud may form and descend until it touches the ground. If it's too dry for rain and the funnel cloud, the first sign may be dust swirling just above the ground.

Page 256

1. island
2. peninsula
3. atlas
4. cape
5. mountain
6. cardinal direction
7. globe
8. isthmus
9. valley
10. fjord
11. plateau
12. oasis
13. hemisphere
14. continent
15. plain
16. mesa
17. butte
18. equator
19. latitude
20. prime meridian
21. prairie
22. longitude
23. fall line
24. delta

Page 257

1. A. Darwin, Australia
   D. Honolulu, Hawaii
2. A. St. Louis, Missouri
   B. Boston, Massachusetts
   C. New York City, New York
   D. Philadelphia, Pennsylvania
   E. Annapolis, Maryland
3. A. Mediterranean Sea
   B. Encounter Bay
   C. Atlantic Ocean
   D. Bay of Bengal
   E. English Channel
4. A. southwest
   B. southeast
   C. south
   D. northwest
5. Answers will vary.
6. A. Great Salt Lake
   B. Alaska
7. A. Belize
   B. Myanmar
   C. Zambia and Zimbabwe
   D. Kenya
8. They are the second-largest cities in their countries. The only city larger in each country is the country's capital.

Page 264

1. 12:40 PM
2. 1:35 PM
3. 8:55 PM
4. 4:45 PM
5. five hours and 50 minutes
6. 9:25 AM
7. one hour and 20 minutes
8. three hours and 45 minutes
9. 3:35 PM
10. one hour and 35 minutes
11. 8:15 PM
12. six hours and 50 minutes

INDEX